WOMEN AND DEMONS

Cult Healing in Islamic Egypt

BY

GERDA SENGERS

BRILL
LEIDEN · BOSTON
2003

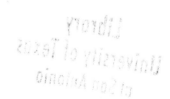

This book is printed on acid-free paper.

This book was translated by Dr. D.E. Orton with financial support
from the Netherlands Organization for Scientific Research (NWO).
© Copyright 2000 (Dutch edition) – Het Spinhuis, Amsterdam, The Netherlands

Library of Congress Cataloging-in-Publication Data

Sengers, Gerda.
  Women and demons : cult healing in Islamic Egypt / by Gerda Sengers.
    p.cm.-- (International studies in sociology and social anthropology ;
ISSN 0074-8684 ; v. 86)
  Includes bibliographical references (p.) and index.
  ISBN 9004127712
  1. Spiritual healing—Egypt. 2. Healing—Religious aspects—Islam. 3.
Zār—Egypt. 4. Women—Egypt—Cairo—Social conditions. I. Title.
II. Series

BF1275.F3 S463   2002
297.3'9--dc21   2002028201

Die Deutsche Bibliothek - CIP-Einheitsaufnahme

Gerda Sengers: Women and Demons : Cult Healing in Islamic Egypt – Leiden ;
Boston : Brill, 2003.
  (International Studies in Sociology and Social Anthropology ; Vol. 86)
  ISBN 90-04-12771-2

ISSN 0074-8684
ISBN 90 04 12771 2

© Copyright 2003 by Koninklijke Brill NV, Leiden, The Netherlands

PRINTED IN THE NETHERLANDS

WOMEN AND DEMONS

INTERNATIONAL STUDIES
IN
SOCIOLOGY AND SOCIAL ANTHROPOLOGY

VOLUME LXXXVI

CONTENTS

PREFACE

At the beginning of this book I want to thank the various people who have contributed over the years to its coming into being. These are in the first place those who helped with my research in Egypt — the many women I was privileged to associate with for shorter and longer periods of time and who were willing to answer my many questions. I am particularly grateful to *umm* Mustafa, Hanan who accepted me so hospitably into her house, the *zar* leader Zahra, the *tambura* player Hassan, and *sheikh* Fathi. I was always able to drop by any of them and ask for clarification about what I had seen and heard. I am also grateful to the Koran healers who allowed me to be present during their work, and the many other people in Egypt who helped me, directly or indirectly, with this project. In the second place I would like to thank my thesis supervisor Prof. Dr. W.M.J. van Binsbergen, who led me through the various stages of the writing of a doctoral thesis and continued to support and encourage me to find my way through my material.

I received creative and intellectual support from Nellie Duursma, Eelkje Verelst, Thera Rasing and Berend van der Woude, who were willing to read my work and comment on it. I thank Ben van den Camp for his help with the preparation of the published edition of this dissertation, and David Orton for the beautiful translation of the Dutch text. Klaas I would like to thank because he always believes in me and Carol Anne in Cairo because I was often allowed to "come round" at her home. Many friends not separately mentioned by name here are also thanked for listening again and again throughout the years to my "demon stories".

Gerda Sengers
Amsterdam, July 2002

TRANSCRIPTION AND PRONUNCIATION OF THE ARABIC SCRIPT

For the transcription and pronunciation of Arabic words and names I have tried to keep to as simple and clear a system as possible. I make a distinction between colloquial Egyptian Arabic and modern standard literary Arabic. Words that occur in conversations with my conversation partners are written in accordance with colloquial language and for titles of books and personal names I follow the conventional transcription of modern standard Arabic. Generally I follow El-Said Badawi and Martin Hinds, *A Dictionary of Egyptian Arabic* (1986) and Hans Wehr, *A Dictionary of Modern Written Arabic* (1980). I make no distinction between long and short vowels (*a, i, u*), nor between the various consonants that can be grouped under *d, h, s* and *t*. I make an exception for such words as *dhikr*, where the *dh* sounds like a soft *z*, and *hadith*, where the *t* sounds like a soft *s*, which I render as *th* and for words with a *sh* sound (as in *sheikh*). The *y* is pronounced as in "yet", but at the end of a word it sounds like the *y* in "pony". The Arabic letter *hamza* is given as ' and the *'ayn* as ', and the *ghain*, which has a gently rolling sound, is written as *gh*. The letter *jim*, written as *j* in the transcription of modern standard Arabic (as in *jinn*), sounds like the *j* in "jug" but in colloquial Egyptian it is pronounced as a soft *k* and I write it as *g* (as in *gann* = demon). The hard *ch* sound (as in Scottish "loch") is given as *kh*. Often in colloquial speech the *q* sound is not pronounced and in such cases I render it with an apostrophe, e.g. *'arina* instead of *qarina* as in modern standard Arabic. I first give the Arabic plural (e.g. *sheikh-shuyukh*) and thereafter the English plural form, as in *sheikhs*. When I take over Arabic words or names from the literature, I use the transcription applied there. Translations from Arabic books are mine. This is also the case for conversations I have conducted with the conversation partners in Egyptian Arabic.

CHAPTER ONE

LIVING AND WORKING IN CAIRO

Hanan and her children live in a small two-room flat in one of the numerous deprived areas of Cairo. She is thirty years old and her first child was a long time in coming, much too long by Egyptian standards. She had almost given up hope of ever becoming a mother when things finally worked out after all and she became pregnant. The second child followed the first in short order, and so now she is busy with her homemaking. Too busy, I think, when I look at her. She is thin in her long colourful skirt, and with her hair drawn straight back under a scarf her face looks pale and tired. But Hanan is happy in her home and with her children. Her husband Ashraf works as a *bawwab* (porter/odd-job-man) in an apartment block somewhere in a more well-to-do part of the city. Both of them come from the countryside and like so many others have sought their fortune in Cairo where there is more and better-paid work than in their village. She lived for four years with Ashraf in a small two-by-two metre room under the staircase in the foyer of the apartment block he works in. It was only six months ago that she came here to live. Ashraf found this flat via acquaintances in his own village, who have family in this area. They have borrowed six thousand Egyptian pounds (about £ 1000 sterling/US$ 1500) from his employer to pay the *khili-ww* (deposit). The six thousand pounds is being paid off in monthly instalments of fifty pounds (the employer is not charging interest on the loan). The monthly rent of forty-five pounds is additional to this, plus fifteen pounds for electricity and two pounds fifty for water. Hanan does not know how much Ashraf earns. He gives her twenty pounds a week for *masarif* (household expenses) and regularly brings in yoghurt for his little daughter. He has expenses of his own, since he lives together with his brother, who is also a porter, in the room under the stairs in the apartment block where he works. He has to provide his own food. On account of his work, which requires his presence at night too, he comes home only once or twice a week.

It is clear that the family belongs to the poor class, but Hanan will not take a penny from me. I am her "sister" and a guest, and I "lighten the house" (*minawwara al-beet* — an expression intended to make the guest feel welcome). The two little rooms in the flat are each no bigger than two metres by three. In addition there is a toilet, and Hanan told me proudly that it is not a *baladi* toilet (a "hole in the ground") but an *afrangi* toilet (a western/European toilet), and just next to the toilet is the *bahraya*, a separate room about one meter square in which there is a sink with a tap. This is the "kitchen", in which Hanan prepares the meals on a primus stove. The kitchen tap and the "western toilet" are an illusion, since there is no running water. Hanan can only pump water up from downstairs for one hour a day, by means of an electric pump. The water is collected in pots, pans and jugs and whatever is to hand. The kitchenette is full of them. This water is also used to flush the toilet. Besides the kitchen area there are two beds and a stool in the flat and on the walls hang pictures of the Great Mosque in Mecca and pious texts from the Koran.

Loud recitations from the Koran emanating from the neighbour's transistor radio and street noises penetrate the room from the open doors of a small balcony. This balcony (like all the others in the street) is full of laundry hung up to dry. Sometimes I think Hanan is occupied full-time with washing the children's clothes. She sits on her haunches in the meter-square kitchen, heats up water on the primus stove, wrings and rinses ... In the meantime her daughter runs in and out of the neighbours' flat. But Hanan keeps an eye on her, at the same time conversing loudly through the open front door with her women neighbours on all the floors. Her newborn son is lying on Hanan's bed in one of the rooms. He lies on a cloth to prevent the urine and faeces from seeping through — Pampers are not used here. There is no money for such things. A rag between the legs, pants on top, and Bob's your uncle. This accounts for the mountains of washing every day, because Hanan is proud that she is clean and that her children look clean. She has to interrupt the washing at regular intervals to give her baby son the breast when he wakes up, which he announces with loud wailing. Neighbours walk in and out to visit Hanan and to take a look at me, the *agnabiyya* (foreigner). Hanan is proud that I am staying with her. It means she gets extra attention and gains additional respect from her neighbours. After all, not everyone has a foreign friend. As I drink cup after cup of very sweet tea I explain where I come from and that I have come to live with Hanan in order to conduct a *baht igtima'i* (sociological research) and that I want to talk with women about their lives, their customs and their traditions. I am treated most cordially. Everyone invites me to tea, to visit their house, to come for dinner or to stay overnight. It is as if I have suddenly gained a large family. In the evenings we all sit together drinking more tea and talking about ourselves or the neighbourhood.

The homes and living conditions of my Muslim friends, like Hanan, are not much different from those of my Coptic friends.[1] They all want me to come and stay with them. This is not possible, of course, and so I have arranged to visit every day and then sleep at one or the other's home (and this is what happened). I have to work cautiously. Caution in the sense that I do not offend anyone. There is a certain social distance between Christians and Muslims. Everyone likes to stay on their own territory, especially since fundamentalist Muslims have caused considerable unrest in this neighbourhood in the recent past. Members of the *al-jama'a al-islamiyya* (a militant splinter group of the Muslim brotherhood, which was set up in Egypt in 1928) have burnt down Coptic churches and shops on a number of occasions.

I do not always find it easy to stay with Hanan. This has to do, above all, with the family's poverty and the inadequate sanitary facilities. The narrow streets are scattered with rubbish, among which dogs, cats, goats, sheep and chickens scavenge for something edible. Chickens, ducks or rabbits are kept on the little balconies alongside the washing. This does not make things more pleasant, since the animals' excrement is hardly ever cleaned up. With all these small animals the neighbourhood has the look and feel of a village. Often there are large puddles of muddy water in the street. Someone has tipped away the washing water from their balcony, a shopkeeper has decided to deal with the dust by spraying water, or the drains have broken down for the umpteenth time and flooded the street (this neighbourhood does have sewerage and piped water, but not all the houses are connected). Cars and horse-and-carts wend their way through the narrowest of streets. Mopeds disseminate their stink and their noise. Each household seems to have its own favourite radio station and everywhere the televisions are switched on. In the street children play, women do their shopping or sit next to each other chatting on their doorsteps. There are little shops everywhere — grocers, greengrocers, fruit-sellers, chicken-sellers and bakeries. Butchers hang out their wares bare and bloody on the street, and sometimes they wrap the slaughtered meat in white cloths to protect it from the swarms of flies.

---

[1] Ninety percent of Egyptians are (Sunni) Muslims and ten percent are Christians (primarily Egyptian orthodox Copts).

At the corner of the street stands the coffee house where men seem to while away the whole day. I ignore the men and the growing lads as much as possible. The women I greet return my greeting in a friendly way. After a few days I am such a familiar sight that I am regularly invited to come and sit and have tea with them.

After a few days I also go and visit a few women who are said to be, or to have been, *malbusa* (possessed by *jinn*/demons). My intention is to gain a picture of the significance of this possession by demons and how women particularly from the lower groups of society deal with this. So I talk to them about being "touched" or "clothed" by *jinn* (demons) or *asyad* (*zar* masters/demons) and about two of the many healing practices that are occupied with the spirit world: the *zar* ceremony and Koran healing.

Research

In my study of anthropology I have already occupied myself with research into views of the supernatural causes of sickness. In 1994 the subjects of spirit-possession and Koran healing suddenly became hot topics in the Egyptian press. A number of people who were "afflicted by demons" had committed a murder and many others let it be publicly known that they were occupied with exorcism. It seemed as if a veritable plague of demons had broken out. This state of affairs troubled me and I wondered how it was possible that in a world city like Cairo there could be such a revival of the traditional belief in demons and the practices associated with it. I decided to go more deeply into the subject and that same year began to read on the subject of demons and Koran healing in as many Egyptian daily and weekly newspapers as possible: *al-Akhbar, al-Ahram, al-Arabi, al-Liwa' al-Islami, al-Ahali, Akhbar al-Hawadith, al-Musawwar, Ruz al-Yusuf, Akhir Sa'a, al Muslimun, 'Aqidati* and *al-Kawakib*. A number of Koran healers published books in which they explain their view of demons, possession, the causes of sickness and so on. I studied a number of these works, comparing them with my own experience in practice.

Observation and personal conversations

These can be divided into two groups. First, those conducted through attendance at sessions of Koran healing and *zar* ceremonies and conversations with Koran healers, *zar* leaders and various "experts" in the field of demonology. And second, from visiting and speaking with women I met at the healing sessions. Through making friends with a woman who went to Koran healing sessions, I came into contact with a Koran healer who permitted me to sit in on his healing sessions. After that I had no problems worth mentioning in coming into contact with other healers. Most of them I tracked down through the newspaper articles that gave their names. After I had made it known that I wanted to conduct research into their work, they generally permitted me to be present during the treatment of the patients and they were keen to talk to me about their work, considering it important that I was going to write about the miracles of the Koran. The only condition they required of me was that I should wear "Islamic" dress (see below, p. 198). I had no problem with this and it meant that I was scarcely distinguishable from the other women.

As a result of the great interest in spiritual healing that was coming to light in the press, there were sometimes accounts of another method of being healed of demons, namely the *zar* ceremony, which was generally depicted as corrupting and un-Islamic. I decided to attend these meetings (*hadra*) regularly too. A *hadra* is a gathering for possessed women who have undergone the private rituals necessary to identify the demons and who now come to "speak" with their demon on a weekly basis. Here I danced with women to the rhythm of music that has a more (black) African than Arab feel to it, and observed their behaviour. No special clothing was required for these occasions, but I wore long skirts and a scarf. At first it was difficult to get into contact with *zar* leaders — the women who carry out the whole private exorcism ritual — who had no objection to my being present. Negative experiences with the press meant that they preferred to keep a low profile as far as possible. So in the beginning I only attended the *hadra*, but at a later stage I was lucky enough to make the acquaintance of a very well-known *kudya* (*zar* leader), who first took me hospitably into her house and then allowed me to accompany her to the healing meetings.

While attending Koran healing and *zar* in various districts of Cairo, I was able to do observations of women (and of men, in a few cases). After the ceremonies were over I was permitted to drop by some of them at home to talk about their experiences. Besides this, I was able to have deeper personal conversations with fifty women from roughly the same neighbourhood, about their life and their "possession". I met some of them during the observations, and I made the acquaintance of some in the neighbourhood I was temporarily living in. I would probably never have been able to talk so intimately with women without their help. *Umm* Mustafa in particular did a great deal to help familiarize me with the neighbourhood and vice versa. My conversations with these women constitute a significant part of this book.

Attending Koran healing and *zar* ceremonies, as well as tracking down the time and venue of the sessions, is a time-consuming business. The former sessions are mostly during the daytime and last for several hours, while the latter begin late in the evening and last the whole night, sometimes a number of successive nights. The visits and conversations with the women also take up a lot of time. It is not possible to get straight down to business. I had to show a good deal of patience, especially if the person in question was not at home for the umpteenth time, had forgotten our appointment, or was simply too busy with other worries. When I finally lived in the *baladi* district with Hanan, things went better and I was generally able to move smoothly on from one thing to another.

This study is limited to women. As a foreign woman I was able to talk freely with men in the environment of the household, but I could not follow them to work, the coffee houses or the mosques. Men have their own problems and they too can suffer from symptoms that are determined to be the result of demon possession. With very few exceptions healers did not allow me to be present at the healing rituals of their male clients.

Reflexivity

In order to carry out the fieldwork one needs to have knowledge of the local language and of the general rules and norms of behaviour. In connection with my studies in Arab languages and cultures and then in anthropology I have been coming to Egypt for fourteen years. Right from the beginning I have had a good deal of contact with women from the lower classes of society.

It was not difficult for me as a foreign woman to get into contact with women. It was, however, sometimes difficult to get them to tell me about painful events. The anthropologist has to build up trust, be patient and be able to gauge when an informant has got into the swing of telling of her own life and can be "pushed through" to that part of her life in which possession occurred. I think the fact that I am a foreigner has been more of an advantage than a disadvantage in this regard. For example, they did not have the worry that I might talk to their neighbours about their intimate experiences. I always told them right at the beginning what the aim of my conversations was, namely that I wanted to investigate what possession is and how it can happen. The women's stories build up a perspective on their own life and it emerges in what context they use terms about demons and illnesses.

The perspective of *baladi* women is smilingly dismissed by better-educated and more well-to-do Egyptians as irrelevant. Many have no notion of what *baladi* society is like either. People laugh about the superstition of these "undeveloped people". I have considered this "superstition" with the question: what is possession? What is being said by this? What are *labs*, *lams* and *mass*? What does it mean when a woman is convinced that a being from an invisible world has invaded her body and is making her sick or prompting her to behave in a socially unacceptable way? What does possession have to do with the female body? Is a reference to an invasive spirit a strategic explanation and mitigation of "strange behaviour" or is there more to it than that? What does society have to do with it? Is this an expression of collective self-suggestion, or is it linked with other aspects? I have tried to find an answer to these questions by letting the women talk for themselves and by describing my own findings against a theoretical background.

Working method

My premise is primarily to stay as close as possible to my participants' world of experience. It is an approach with a great preference for interpretation of communicative events, by which the specific points of the beliefs system I am studying are brought to the fore. Such theoreticians as Van Binsbergen (1999) and Fabian (1985) also view ethnography as a research method that produces unique insights.

> Participation, for the anthropologist, is not only a source of primary information from observations and conversations, and not only a means (by awakening trust and showing humility) of lowering the hurdles to communication. Participation has, above all, a unique validation function: precisely as someone learning a language produces linguistic utterances, presents them to native speakers for assessment and

improvement, and thus tests and increases his own language skills, in
the same way participation provides practical feedback on the implicit
and explicit insights that were obtained earlier in the same fieldwork
(Van Binsbergen 1999: 23).

Anthropologists should study religion 'ethnographically', i.e. in and
through instances of action/interaction describable as (communicative)
events. The point of this is that these events are not just to be taken as
occasions producing 'data' or information; it is its event-character that
distinguishes ethnography from other types of research.
    Specifically, systems of beliefs (signs, symbols, myths, doctrines, etc.)
and ritually organized sequences of acts or activities are to be studied
as they are actualized in (or mediated by) events which, as social
events, occur in a physical setting, in real time, and in the presence of
actors; they involve a choice of modes, channels, and codes of communication (Fabian 1985: 145-146).

It is my conviction that fieldwork demands an empathetic approach
and "absorption" in the world that is studied and interpreted. As an
ethnographer I tried to sense the social and emotional experiences of
the participants in my research and to feel with them. This was never
one hundred percent possible, however, since the cultural differences
are so great. During the fieldwork I was always in search of a balance
between "being like them" and being different, between involvement
and letting go: releasing myself from my own culture and world of
experience and becoming involved in the society I was studying. To
the best of my ability I tried to be a guest and a friend and sometimes
a 'daughter'. I tried to get to know from the inside the cultural orien-
tations of the women I associated with. So during the healing sessions
I attended I tried as far as possible to join in with them and if, just like
them, I closed my eyes and let the Koran texts or the *zar* music have
its effect on me, my mood changed. But I do not believe in demons in
the same way they do, and as far as I am aware I was not possessed
and thus I never became exactly like them. There is nothing contra-
dictory or undesirable about this, since though empathy is a requirement for the ethnographer, it is just as important to maintain distance, instrumentality and a critical regard for the other person. I
entered the field quite deliberately "empty-handed"; that is to say, as
far as possible I initially left out of consideration preconceived ideas
and knowledge that I might or might not have been able to take over
from earlier research. This is not completely possible either, since this
knowledge had already (pre-)formed me and thus did indeed play a
part in my interaction with "the other". I learned by practical experi-

ence to respect the thinking of the women I was working with, no matter how far they diverged from my own. I let them have their say to the extent that I did because in my opinion this is the best way to get to know the other culture. Their stories occupy an important place in this study, since the essence of their existence in all its facets was opened up in their words and gestures and I was able to penetrate through to their feelings.

I let women talk about their lives and I listened to their conversation among themselves. Sometimes I was able to record the stories told to me on a cassette recorder and sometimes I had to remember them until I could write them down somewhere else, later. When I was in their homes I joined in with "everyday life", and during the Koran healing sessions and *zar* ceremonies, as far as possible I joined in with the "special events", the prayers and/or dancing. I made a selection from all their stories and surrounded them with a good amount of data taken from literature in order to place it in the context of Egyptian society. The aim of this is to represent and interpret these women's world of experience as precisely as possible.[2] This research strategy is supplemented by bibliographic research into religious views of demons and the causes of sickness (Arab and western sources). It also meant gathering information on Islam in Egypt and on historical connections with belief in demons in other cultures, the pre-Islamic period, present-day formal Islam and the popular Egyptian variant. I also gave attention to the mutual links between magicians, sorcerers and exorcists and between forms of spiritual healing and magic and "prophetic medicine".

Many new non-scholarly publications have appeared on the market in Cairo on witchcraft, magic, "touching" and "clothing" by demons. I read a large number of these pamphlets and deal in this book with the authors' ideas. Some of the pamphlets place emphasis

---

[2] This could be called empirical research. While collecting the data I also ordered and analysed it. Actions in one phase led to new actions in another phase. In each phase I had to decide which data I should continue to collect, and where and from whom I should look for it. By collecting information from various points of view (triangulation) knowledge and practices in relation to possession and healing were elucidated. This way of working has a number of points of contact with the research model of symbolic interactionism as elaborated by Glaser and Strauss (1991) and Wester (1987). To deepen my insight into the many aspects of anthropological fieldwork I studied among other works Hammersley & Atkinson 1983, Peacock 1986 and Burgess 1991. For an overview of discussion on the ways in which anthropologists can use life stories, see Langness 1965 and Langness & Frank 1985.

on healing through the Koran, others are intended to give instruction in "white" magic and how "black" magic can be prevented. In the first category it is considered a minimal requirement that one knows the Koran well in order to conduct healing, and in the second category the emphasis is on prescriptions and "recipes" for preparing amulets and how one can find healing with the aid of potions and such like. Common to both methods is that they constantly refer to "authorities" such as the Prophet Suleiman (King Solomon, who according to the Koran learned magic from angels), Ibn Qayyim al-Jawziyya (theologian, legal advisor, healer and champion of "prophetic medicine": see also E12, vol. III, pp. 821-822) as well as the Koran and *hadith* (traditions and sayings of the Prophet).

In the Egyptian press much has been written, and is still being written, about traditional healing. There are journalists who are genuinely interested in it, but most articles have a markedly sensationalistic undertone or are written from the point of view of a clear abhorrence of these practices. *Zar* in particular is depicted as a devilish, wild dance that exhausts body and spirit.

Cairo

The population of Cairo is estimated to be sixteen million. It is not the biggest city in the world, but certainly one of the most overpopulated. Forty-seven percent of the Egyptian population lived in city areas (primarily Cairo and Alexandria) around 1990. By 2000 it was expected that this would have risen to sixty percent (World Bank report 1992: 1). Overpopulation has all kinds of side-effects, such as air and water pollution, noise, stress, housing shortages, insufficient public transport and inadequate state amenities. But Cairo's slum areas are different from slum areas in many other large cities. Those in Cairo are ugly, smell bad and there are conflicts. On the streets, however, there is markedly little violence and even at night one can feel reasonably safe there. Innumerable migrants from the countryside have settled in this sort of district in the hope of constructing a new existence. Alongside them are families who have already lived in the city for several generations. Most people live in a family environment. The streets are full of children, but there are no "street-children". The population is poor or very poor, but there is a feeling of solidarity and in times of financial crisis family and neighbours try to help each other out.

Accommodation was already one of the biggest problems in Egypt before Gamal Abdel Nasser (1952-1970) came to power. In the urban areas lived the mass of educated and uneducated workers, in unsuitable housing and in slum areas. Rich Egyptians and foreigners lived in splendid villas along the Nile and in the better residential areas. The Nasser regime began subsidized housing construction in Cairo and Alexandria. However, the policy proved inadequate because it could not keep up with the steep rise in the population. The housing situation deteriorated fast in the period 1960-1975 when the population increased by ten million, while housing construction was unable to meet as much as a quarter of the demand. In 1970 the population density in some areas of the city was three times as high as in the slum areas of other poor countries. Fifty percent of Cairo's homes consisted of one-room flats in which on average a family of five people lived. Forty percent of the available housing was dilapidated and on the point of collapse. On the flat roofs of the already existing houses half a million shacks had been added for homeless people, and 80,000 people inhabited the tombs of the deceased in Cairo's cemeteries (without running water, electricity, gas or sanitary facilities). During the Sadat period (1970-1981) and his *infitah* ("open-door policy", in full: *al-infitah al-iqtisadi*, that is: economic liberalization, which began in 1974), the situation deteriorated considerably. Restraints on rent charges were lifted, which led to a steep rise in living costs. Only the construction of luxury residential areas was stimulated. The poor living conditions for the lower classes and the poor increased apace. In 1984 one in three people was living in unfit accommodation. A government initiative instituted a study which showed that more than two and a half million homes needed to be built in the next twenty years to be able to deal with the crisis. Another study indicated almost twice this figure for the year 2000. Housing is being built, but only few of the homes are *masakin sha'biyya* (subsidized homes). The houses in the districts that have been built are so poorly maintained that after just a few years they are hovels. The rooms are small and lack modern conveniences. The streets are so narrow that you can literally see into the home of the neighbour opposite you. Paving stones are generally lacking, which means dust blows about. Since there is no drainage and no refuse collection service, a pungent stench fills the air. In these districts there is often no public transport of any description, so that inhabitants have to rely on private transport which is dearer than public transport.

In 1993 it was established that Cairo has more than one hundred slum areas that can be said to have urgent problems with sewerage, drinking water provision and electricity. The government once again announced a programme for this. A report by the *al-Ahram Strategic Studies Center* (1996) reveals that none of the goals that were set has been attained. The programme announced was largely a result of the conviction of the Ministry for Internal Affairs that militant Islamic groups were operating from these slum areas (the *al-Ahram Strategic Studies Center* report indicates that thirty-one percent of persons occupied with activities directed against the state come from Imbaba, fourteen percent from al-Sahel and twenty-four percent from Bulaq al-Dakrur — all three of these being large slum areas in Cairo). With extensive security measures the Ministry did succeed in driving the *al-Jama'a al-Islamiyya* out of these areas, but was unable to realize further plans.

The social hierarchy in Cairo is reflected in the settlement pattern. The elite live in the villa districts of Zamalek, Garden City, Ma'adi or Misr al-Jadida (literally: New Cairo). The upper middle class (captains of industry, managers, doctors, lawyers) live in the modern, spaciously designed areas with high apartment blocks (Muhandiseen, Dokki). The industrial working class, lower officials, small businessmen and less educated workers live in the transitional areas between the luxury districts and the traditional districts, or in the new suburbs with less luxury but still modern districts. The rest of the population (the greater part) live in the well-established population areas in older parts of the city (Misr al-Qadima, literally: Old Cairo, Bulaq and the districts around the *al-Ashar* mosque), or in areas of government housing that have recently risen from the ground. The poorest of the poor live in self-constructed little houses on roofs or in a number of "dead cities" where they have built shelters between the tombs of the deceased.

In the first two districts mentioned there is busy modern life and the shops are filled with western consumer goods, in the lower middle-class districts the shops are more "Egyptian" in character and in the fourth category, the people's districts, there are only small shops with exclusively Egyptian goods.

From the point of view of ideas and lifestyle the present-day elite and the upper middle class are oriented towards the west and maintain a distance from the lower middle class, the working class and "the people". They protect their lives, luxury and higher status by means of their own "clubs" and by sending their children to expensive (western-oriented) private schools and universities. For the middle and lower middle classes, the western lifestyle has long been a means of climbing the social ladder and of at the same time distancing oneself from the lower classes. Under the influence of religious fundamentalism, in the last few decades many have turned away from a western lifestyle and have begun to live in a more "Egyptian" ("Islamic") way. If financially possible, the middle class also like to send their children to "foreign" schools (French, English, German or Italian in orientation). "Western" schools and consumer goods lie completely beyond the reach of the lower middle and working classes.

During the Nasser government there was a clear strategy based on making basic health services accessible to the whole population. When the Nasser regime came to power, there were scarcely any medical facilities in the country areas, where seventy-five percent of the population lived. In the city areas (Cairo and Alexandria) the amenities were inadequate. Hospitals were understaffed and standards of hygiene were poor. In the period up to 1964 the number of medical centres in rural areas increased, as well as attention to preventative health care.[3] During the Sadat period, however, there came an end to this policy and national health care became largely dependent on foreign aid. The part of the population that did well out of Sadat's "open-door policy" (the rich and "nouveaux riches") did not have to suffer from this deterioration in the health service since many doctors and medical specialists built new, western-equipped private clinics and hospitals in the big cities, specially for them. Under the Mubarak regime too, the privileged classes are in no way deprived.

---

[3] In 1952 there was a military coup by the Free Officers. Quite soon after this Gamal Abdel Nasser became their leader and head of state. The new regime had ambitious plans in the area of improving national health. In 1953 the Public Council for Public Welfare Services was set up. The first five-year plan aimed at an extension of the health units in rural areas that had been initiated by the previous government in 1942 and 1946, after a number of disastrous malaria and cholera epidemics. Each unit was to consist from now on of a health centre, a school and an agricultural and service centre. Medical students and doctors were obliged to work there for a number of years. The Nasser regime recorded great successes in the area of national health, but gradually failed to meet its targets. For the poor classes in the Egyptian population such sicknesses as fevers, malaria, cholera, tuberculosis, syphilis and bilharzia remained great enemies. The same applies to extreme poverty, malnutrition and illiteracy. For an overview of the situation with regard to Egyptian national health from the Middle Ages to the twentieth century see: Dols 1984, 1992, Ammar 1954 and Gallagher 1993.

So one can still say there is a twofold division in the health service: private care for the wealthy and a government system, "stripped" by insufficient finance and planning, for the less well-off (Korayem 1996: 46-50). The quality of many government services has improved to some extent in recent years with financial support from abroad. Eighty-six percent of the population now have access to clean drinking water and fifty-four percent have access to sanitary facilities (but by no means always with running water and connection to the sewers).

Life in a people's district

The district in which I conducted a large part of my research is known as a "typical people's district" of Cairo, where many poor people live, but not the very poorest. Egyptians call this sort of district *sha'biyya* or *baladiyya* (see also Abu-Lughod 1971). Both terms have divergent meanings in various contexts. Although this means that they are scarcely translatable, I will attempt below to clarify what is meant by them.

Up to the twentieth century the population of Cairo's older districts was rather homogeneous. From time immemorial the traditional urban class lived here, the *awlad al-balad* (lit. children of the land, often used as an expression for those who adhere to traditional values). Successive waves of migrants later flooded these areas with inhabitants who came from other parts of Egypt. "Old" slum areas were extended with legally or illegally built "new" slum areas and nowadays in older and newer districts one finds *sa'idis* (Egyptians from the south), *bahrawis* (Egyptians from the north, the Delta), original oasis dwellers and dyed-in-the-wool Cairoans living side-by-side. In these districts there is a veritable cacophony of noise twenty-four hours a day. In the daytime it is children playing in the street, sellers commending their wares and the many radios and televisions turned up to full volume. In the evenings and at night the sounds die down a little but in this compact society one can then hear the joyful noise of wedding celebrations, the crying and wailing of mourners or the bickering of arguments. Everyone is touched by the lives of his or her neighbours.

In *baladi* districts there is no economic homogeneity, (very) poor people and richer people live next to each other. This is because Egyptians are often strongly attached emotionally to the place they were born and/or brought up in. If they have become better off they prefer not to move to another area since they would then have to leave their family, friends and acquaintances behind.

The coexistence of these various groups with their various ways of life runs quite smoothly in general, although from time to time a certain social aloofness is noticeable which sometimes can lead to conflicts. Two factors are of great importance in this regard. First, the enormous overpopulation in these districts which leads to tensions, and second, the downward trend in the economic standard of living of part of the population, which makes life more difficult and with fewer prospects. But the Egyptian *baladi* population has *damm khafif* ("light blood": a sense of humour), it enjoys a good laugh and has *karama* (friendliness, hospitality), so that people do not treat each other in a destructive way and life in poverty remains livable.

In particular women who have to make ends meet from day to day do not have it easy. While men can find some sort of relaxation and recuperation in the coffee houses, this is not granted to women. Problems sometimes mount up until the point where something has to give. This can come to expression in "strange" behaviour, which is referred to by their environment and themselves as "possession". The women I spoke to come from the lower income classes, are Muslims and live in *baladi* districts. This does not mean that the same views of possession do not predominate among Coptic women. I know from experience that there are many points of agreement, but it would require a separate study of Coptic culture to give an adequate description of their religious customs and practices. The term "lower class" is used in this study in a general sense for people who find it extremely difficult to keep their heads above water from an economic point of view.

Sha'bi and baladi

According to *A Dictionary of Egyptian Arabic* (El-Said Badawi & Martin Hinds 1986), the adjectives *sha'bi* (feminine form: *sha'biyya*) and *baladi* (feminine form: *baladiyya*) both mean "popular" and "traditional". *Sha'bi* refers to a great diversity of practices regarded as indigenous. Westernized Egyptians used the word *sha'bi*, for instance, to distinguish themselves and their way of life from those of the popular masses. *Sha'bi* also indicates a collective identity, a sort of authenticity or genuineness. *Sha'bi* people believe that they represent the values and convictions of "real" Egyptians.

Baladi has a more ethnic meaning and refers to land or nation, but also to village or town. The term is associated with people from the peasant class and from the rural areas "who have maintained the values and traditions". In an urban context it is used to indicate a particular category of people and their habitat. There is always a strong association with a particular lifestyle and the practices connected with it. Al-Messiri (1978) has written about the historical background of the meaning of the word *baladi* in an engaging study. She says that although the *fellahin* (peasants and farmers), who constitute the largest section of the Egyptian population, would be justified in identifying themselves as *awlad al-balad* (children of the land), the term is primarily used by the Muslim Cairo population, which thereby distinguishes itself from the peasants, the Copts (orthodox Christians) and westernized Egyptians (see also Lane 1895). Al-Messiri tells us, further, that two broad contexts are recognized in which the terms *ibn al-balad* and *bint al-balad* are used (namely son and daughter of Cairo, the place of birth). The terms can be used to refer to features and norms of behaviour and in order to indicate a specific group of Egyptians. In various situations and/or periods, variations are possible. Currently these expressions usually indicate persons who indulge in certain behaviour and practices that are primarily associated with the lower economic groups. What determines this is by whom, when, and in what context the word is applied. *Baladi* has a double meaning: the word is used both for something of inferior value and also for something that is felt to be superior. It indicates the type of particular districts and categories of inhabitants, it refers to economic status, it distinguishes Egyptians from non-Egyptians and what is traditional Egyptian from modern Egyptian. In addition to the terms *sha'bi* and *baladi*, the term *afrangi* (Frank, European, western) is used to make a cultural and economic distinction between the traditional but poor lower class in the popular districts and the richer westernized class in the neighbourhoods that have expensive apartment blocks and villas. Notions associated with this are that *baladiyyin* (plural) regard themselves as authentic, reliable, just and religious. They stand with both feet on the ground, know the popular traditions well, speak the local dialect, are generous and hospitable and have *damm khafif* (light blood). They generally dress traditionally in a *gallabiyya*, a long, ankle-length loose shirt for men, while women wear a long black loosely hanging dress and a transparent black headscarf. *Afrangis* are not supposed to possess the noble characteristics of the *baladiyyin*. The *afrangis* in turn regard *baladiyyin* as common, sly, superstitious and backward.

The life of the baladiyyat

Egyptian "popular women" who live in the poorer districts are consistently called *baladiyya* (plural: *baladiyyat*). Although this does not mean that every woman who calls herself *baladiyya* has an economically marginal position, the adjective *ghalbana* (poor, needy) is automatically linked with *baladi(yya)*.

It is not possible to give a universal, cross-cultural definition of poverty, since poverty is difficult to quantify. In the first place it describes the structural impossibility of satisfying normal needs and in the second place that the needs are culture-related and time-related. The *baladi* class of Cairo cannot, for instance, be compared with the poor population of some other city in India. Their accommodation is often inadequate, there is not enough money, but few people go hungry at night. Egyptians like to eat a lot, and meat is an indispensable part of their diet. I discovered that among many, *tabikh* (cooked food with meat or chicken sauce) is eaten at the most once a week. Most people make their meal with beans, eggs, cheese, vegetables and a great deal of bread, and they feel that this is poverty. Since the experience of poverty is in large part culture-related, it seems to me better here, and in Chapter 7, to describe the conditions in which the women in my research live.

Wikan (1980) writes that the category of "poor" comes from interaction and is a personal perception. People must regard their own living situation as poor and have this confirmed by others. If there is no class with which one can compare oneself then one's own situation cannot be experienced as poor. If I maintain the subjective experience of social inequality as emphasized by Wikan then I have to conclude that *baladi* people in Cairo unfortunately have every occasion to feel inequality and poverty. Every day they set off for work in the bursting buses of public transport or in the many small privately operated "minibuses". They spend hours in the traffic and then have all the time in the world to observe their rich brothers and sisters in their luxury cars, while they themselves try to overcome their tiredness and maintain their balance in the bus. On their return from work *baladi*

men and women are confronted with accommodation where basic
necessities such as gas, running water and sanitary facilities are lacking or minimal.

The experience of poverty has more dimensions to it than just
social perception. During my research I noted that the experience of
poverty also has to do with the perception of physical unease or of
fear of not having the means to pay for the doctor or for medicine if a
child is seriously ill. Arguments are very frequently about material
things: a spouse who brings in too little money or spends too much of
his wages in the coffee house, a loan that is not being repaid, not
keeping to contributions in costs, the exchange of gifts, and so on.
Money matters run like a scarlet thread through all other problems
(Early 1993; Singerman 1996; Wikan 1980, 1996).

The *baladi* class can measure itself against the lives of the rich in
other ways than those mentioned above too. The many soaps and
other programmes on television show the interiors of the expensive
flats and villas. In the same television series people from their own
milieu are often caricatured. Television and newspapers show such
events as a mass wedding party organized by Susan Mubarak in the
hockey stadium (among others, *al-Ahram* and *The Middle East Times*, 15
September 1996) for 1200 couples from the poor class who had to
keep postponing their weddings because of lack of funds and who
have now had all their costs paid by the government. *Baladiyyin* know
that the middle and rich classes celebrate their weddings with much
glamour and fuss in expensive western hotels, while their own marriage parties are celebrated in their own street with a glass of Coca
Cola and a few sweets.

For *baladiyyin* a higher education does not automatically mean a
good standard of living and often it is very difficult to escape the influence of one's origins and milieu. This applies in particular to young
women with a higher education who have to continue to live with
their family in their own neighbourhood. For this they sometimes
have to pay a high price in social terms — on one hand because they
do not want their colleagues at work to know where they live and on
the other hand because in their own environment they can identify
only with few women with a higher education. The same applies of
course to young men, but they have greater freedom of movement.
There is a great deal of dissatisfaction among young people in *baladi*
districts because despite their efforts to make progress socially they
have to stay below the material wellbeing of the other classes. So it is

no wonder that some *baladi* areas are known for their militant Islamic movements (Joffé 1996).

Generally people manage, but the struggle to survive is associated with a good deal of jealousy (Early 1993; Wikan 1980, 1996). People envy one another for material and non-material things (Inhorn 1994, 1996; Sengers 1994). One accuses the other of begrudging him luck in business, or in general. One's own material situation is constantly compared with that of others and there is a great deal of rivalry. It is said that people have *wisheen* (two faces), the good, friendly side which praises and compliments the other person on some business success or on a new pair of shoes, and the other side which leads to the evil eye being cast, out of jealousy, which has the effect of turning one's luck. It is very common for the "evil eye" to be blamed for all possible adversity.

One way of distinguishing oneself from others is by means of material things or by morality. In the streets everyone is kept under observation and other people's business is discussed and criticized. Recognition is attained when a woman is praised by her friends or neighbours for her moral behaviour. *Kalam an-nas*, gossip, is a dangerous weapon and in many cases serves less to show up the supposed imperfections of the other person than to put one's own qualities in a better light. In addition, gossip is an indirect form of social control, since every girl or woman is afraid of what others say about her which might mean her losing her good name. The claim to be maintaining moral values is also used by *baladiyyat* to set themselves off against the higher classes, who in their eyes may be rich but are also immoral (al-Messiri 1978). The self-image is that they themselves possess high moral values, great capabilities and a range of social skills. This provides a certain degree of comfort and self-justification (Wikan 1980, 1996).

The *baladi* value system implies mutual help. Precisely because people are heavily dependent on each other, people are ready to help one another out in difficult times. Korayem (1996) and Singerman (1996) write in this connection that the *baladi* class, which makes up the largest part of the Egyptian population, is vital and inventive and disposes of an extensive informal network for the protection of its own interests. These informal institutions play an important part in the advancement of one's economic interests, arbitrate in mutual disputes, and are guarantors for basic needs such as food, work, education and reproduction.

Vitality and inventiveness are qualities that are certainly to be found among *baladi* women, who have learned to help themselves. Spouses are largely concerned with the daily concerns of the household — the government does not make particularly great efforts to improve the living situation, and the bureaucracy is difficult to approach. A *baladiyya* has to look after her own interests.[4]

Practices associated with Islam

In this study I talk about "popular Islam". This is a cultural category, not a theological one. The term popular Islam is described in various ways in the literature. Over against the official Islamic doctrine stand ideas and practices of the broader strata of the population which frequently deviate from the formal rules. In formal Islam the concern is supposed to be with pure faith and orthodoxy. In popular or local Islam it is a matter of regional variations, the way in which the broad masses understand Islam. Here we have to do with the veneration of saints, mystical brotherhoods, specific forms of piety and practices, superstition and heresy.[5]

Gellner (1972: 308-309) discusses the relationship between popular Islamic customs and orthodox Islam in the Atlas mountains of Morocco. He links Sufism and folk mysticism (veneration of saints, pilgrimages) with the urban populations and calls it an alternative to the Islam of the *'ulama* (Islamic scribes) who are the norm-setters within the community of believers. In rural parts of Morocco the *'ulama* play a limited role and the local *sheikh* (a function transferred from father to son or from teacher to pupil) is the authority in religious matters.

The rural parts of Egypt can certainly not be viewed in isolation from the big cities of Cairo and Alexandria. In the first place these cities are populated with migrants from the country, and secondly through the increasing popularization of Islam via television, radio

---

[4] On living conditions among Cairo's poor see: Rugh 1979; Korayem 1996; Singerman & Hoodfar 1996; Shoukry 1994; Wikan 1980, 1996. On Islamic fundamentalism in Egypt see: Guenena 1996; Ibrahim 1980; Joffé 1995; Sullivan & Abed-Kotob 1999.

[5] Any form of religious thinking, "official", "popular", or "superstition" is a socio-cultural construction. See: Van Binsbergen 1981; Brandt 1994; Buitelaar 1993; Crapanzano 1973; Ende & Steinbach 1996; Koningsveld 1988; Jansen 1985; Mernissi 1975, 1977; Rabinow 1977; Waardenburg 1979; Westermarck 1926.

and through a flourishing market in religious books and cassettes, the ideas of formal Islam, as propounded by the *'ulama*, are disseminated throughout the whole land. The Islamists, or fundamentalists, too, make every effort to disseminate their version of Islam. In the third place, folk customs in Egypt are not always linked to Sufism or Islam. The *zar*, for instance, has little to do with Islam or Sufism, though it does contain Islamic elements. The same applies to the "seven-day festival", the *subu'a*, on the birth of a child (Sengers 1994) and for the spring festival *shamm an-nisim*, which is popular throughout Egypt.

Many authors who take the Middle East or North Africa as their area of study apply the term popular or folk Islam to non-canonical Islam. I do this myself, with the proviso that popular Islam is a typical western expression which is not generally used in the Islamic world itself. Here people prefer to speak of *'adat* and *taqalid* (customs and traditions) and of *bid'a* and *kufr* (renewal/apostasy and unbelief/godlessness: Wehr 1980). No value judgment is attached to the first two concepts, but there is to the latter two. They contain a direct condemnation of certain phenomena. The texts of the Islamic scholarly tradition may serve as a point of reference in a description of popular Islamic behaviour and thinking. In daily life there is an interaction between text and practice and it is exciting to see how different popular customs are being integrated within orthodoxy and how they are also legitimated by it.

Popular Islam draws both from orthodox and from local practices and traditions. This does not mean that everyone adheres to popular Islam or practises it in the same way, or that people do not keep to the rules prescribed by orthodox Islam. Religion and practice are, as I have already said, in many cases dynamic interactions of orthodox, textual tradition and local practices (cf. Buitelaar 1985, 1993). The *'ulama* reject certain festivals and customs, such as popular festivals (*mulid*), that are held each year in honour of a saint, the visiting of tombs of the saints and the *dhikr*, a mystical sufi ritual in which there is dancing and the "beautiful names" of Allah are repeated incessantly. Despite the formal rejection the population carries right on with its customs and festivals and most of them would be amazed to hear that they are not acting in accordance with Islam.

The *zar*, the exorcism ritual I discuss in this book, is more rigorously classed as an abhorrent popular practice than the former, since it is supposed to be "something devilish".[6] Things are quite different with

---

[6] Faruq abdel-Mahid in *al-Ahram*, 26 September 1994.

'ilag bil-qur'an (Koran healing), which will also be discussed, because it
claims to be "genuinely" Islamic and is based on recitation of the
Koran, which can hardly be abhorrent. One comes across both apol-
ogists for it and others who dismiss it.[7]

It is often supposed that women have no knowledge of and no
share in the official Islamic regulations and that their faith life is situated completely outside official Islam. When such statements are
made the attention is directed to sex-specific religious practices (such
as visiting graves of the saints, but also attendance of the *zar*). But this
is not to say that the faith and practice of women can simply be
stamped as essentially "unorthodox" by comparison with the faith
and practice of the "orthodox" male world. The women in my
research regard themselves as "good Muslims" and broadly keep
Islamic regulations. I found that their "unorthodox" convictions are
often shared by men (even if sometimes they do not like to admit it
openly). It is certainly the case that many popular religious practices
are regarded by better-educated Egyptians as manifestations of back-
wardness and underdevelopment. An exception to this would perhaps
be the *dhikr* of the *Naqshbandi* sufi order, which is attended precisely by
many better-educated people.

A significant element of Islamic popular belief is that alongside the
existence of natural causes of illness it is also assumed that there are
supernatural causes too which cannot be remedied by biomedical
health care (Crapanzano 1973). Such illnesses need a different
approach and in various Islamic countries one can also find, on a
grand scale, spiritual healers such as magicians, sorcerers, dream-
interpreters, amulet-writers and therapies such as visiting saints'
graves.[8]

Possession

My account is concerned with possession as experienced by a section
of the population that belongs more or less to the same social class. It
should not be regarded as an attempt to lay bare the present-day
Egyptian way of life. *Mass* or *lams* ("touching") and *labs* ("clothing")

---

[7] For instance in *al-Liwa al-Islami*, 29 September 1994. Sheikh Shara'rawi, a well-
known and popular TV theologian, was fiercely criticized in *Akhir Sa'a*, 2 September
1994, because he had confessed to exorcising demons on a regular basis.

[8] Bakker 1993, Van Binsbergen 1985, Donaldson 1938, Doutté 1980/1967, Lambek 1993, Masse 1938, Westermarck 1926.

are words used by the women and the healers to express a spiritual or physical condition which in anthropological literature is described as "possession". The possession generally relates to an individual behaving as if he or she has temporarily lost control over his/her own behaviour, in which state deliberate actions are transformed into involuntary actions, the indwelling spirits direct the individual's actions, and the person concerned is afterwards no longer aware that he or she has performed particular acts (Shekar 1989).

Anthropologists, psychiatrists and others have often explained demon-possession as, among other things, (1) a dramatic way of expressing repressed conflicts or desires, in which actions are induced by the possessing spirit and not by the individual him/herself; (2) as an alarm signal to communicate with others and gain their attention through the adoption of a sick person's role; or (3) as a form of culturally sanctioned behaviour that enables people to adjust to social situations (Ward 1989).

In Egypt *jinn* and *asyad* (demons) are held responsible for "touching" and "clothing" (possession). *Jinn* are powers that form part of the same cosmic order as God, angels and saints, and since they are mentioned in the Koran, they constitute part of the faith system. *Asyad* are not mentioned in the Koran. These "demon masters" derive partly from other cultures and in the opinion of many Egyptians they are non-Islamic.

The women I am writing about have physical or psychological problems which, according to the (male or female) healers they consult, have a spiritual cause, i.e. are caused by demons who have entered the body through "openings". This invasion can be the result of magic, the evil eye or of the emotional or religious weakness of the person in question. In order to restore the person to health these demons must be humoured also in a spiritual way or be driven out. This occurs through the *zar* leader, who helps the sick person to engage in conversation with the possessing spirit by means of music and dance, in order to make "friends" with the spirit, or by the Koran healer, who drives out the evil spirits through recitation of the Holy Scripture. In the first case, then, it is a matter of *pacification* of the demons and in the second of *exorcism*.

The healing practice of the *zar* has the goal of pacifying the demons. This occurs in the course of extensive ceremonies which may last several days and to some extent resemble healing rituals in sub-Saharan Africa. The evil that has overcome the possessed person is

not her own fault: the fault always lies with the demon that has
entered her body. Outsiders view the *zar* as un-Islamic and unacceptable. Women are aware of this criticism, but continue with the ceremonies. They are able to justify this resoluteness to themselves by
pointing out that they fulfil their formal Islamic duties.

Koran healers appeal to the Holy Book in order to drive spirits out
of the body for ever. They say that particular verses of the Koran
have a special power and light, known only to initiates such as them.
Despite the misgivings of many that they are using the Koran for
their own ends, their number has increased greatly in recent years,
both in the cities and rural areas. They often have large numbers of
patients and ask considerable sums of money for their services. The
physical and spiritual problems of the possessed person are explained
by them as their "own fault", since the person in question is not
focused on Allah and thus has fallen into a state of apostasy, allowing
the demons to strike. Women have a special susceptibility for this
since their rational powers are weaker than men's and they are more
emotional. They are, moreover, impure for a number of days each
month, which makes them specially attractive to the *jinn*.

Music plays an important role in the *zar*, since there is a "sign" in
the music through which the spirit can manifest itself. For the Koran
healer the recitation is the "instrument" to call up the possessing spirit. The recitation must take place in accordance with particular rules
of rhythm, tone and pitch and a good recital sounds like music to the
believer. In both forms of healing, the "music" is loud and enters into
the body through "openings", prompting a particular state of mind
that may be described as trance.

In *zar* healing and Koran healing one finds trance, catharsis, abreaction and manipulation of the evil into a situation of wholeness. The
women are expected to join a "cult group", i.e. in both cases they are
to adjust their lifestyle. From now on they will come together regularly in the *zar* group to dance before their demons, or they will be stimulated by the Koran healer to lead a stricter Islamic life, involving the
wearing of the veil, submission and subordination to the man.

The Koran moves people to orient themselves to the transcendent
world and divine providence. In daily life this does not always work,
however, and a strict application of the regulations of the Holy Book
turns out not to be feasible. This cleavage is noticeable in both of the
healing practices I shall be describing. In *zar*, the leader interacts with
all the demon masters and can manipulate them. Koran healers

therefore accuse *zar* leaders of acting in an "impermissible way" (i.e. in a way rejected by Allah) because they consort with spirits and acknowledge their power. This is forbidden, they say, since God alone has power. But they are guilty of the same thing, since these apparently fundamentalistically-minded Koran healers do the same as what happens in *zar*: they acknowledge the power of the *jinn* and interact with them. But they are open to less criticism than the *zar* leaders, since what they do has an Islamic aura about it.

The structure of this book

In Chapter 2 a description is given of local cosmology: the way in which the world of experience is structured in relation to "supernatural reality". I deal with the historical connections between belief in demons from other cultures, the pre-Islamic period and present-day formal Islam, and the Egyptian popular variant. I discuss the connection between contemporary forms of spiritual healing, magic and the so-called "prophetic medicine" that came into being centuries ago.

In Chapter 3 we go into anthropological approaches to possession and healing. Afterwards I discuss the work of a number of researchers who have studied *zar* rituals in Islamic Sudan and Egypt. This is in order to indicate how my quest developed for a satisfactory way in which to interpret my own insights and perceptions.

In Chapters 4 and 5 I describe in turn and in detail the rituals of *zar* and Koran healing, how *zar* leaders and Koran healers deal with possession and healing and how they construct their "authority".

Chapter 6 deals with possession as a central element in local cosmology. I also look at *zar* and Koran healing in relation to sufi brotherhoods and graves of the saints.

Chapter 7 gives a kaleidoscopic picture of Egyptian society. The personal story and the sociographic context stand in central position. I let women speak for themselves. On the basis of experiences in their own life it emerges how and when women use the terms reserved for demons and illness.

Chapter 8 is a concluding look in which I briefly consider once again the method, the subject and the sequence of the book.

CHAPTER TWO

LOCAL COSMOLOGY

Most Egyptians have Islam as their religion. Allah and his prophet Mohammed have a central place in their lives. Five times a day this is reinforced in the call to prayer, as "There is no God but God and his prophet is Mohammed" echoes from the minarets. God is the only God and polytheism (*shirk*) is strictly forbidden. God's omnipotence is seen in his ability to create. Natural phenomena are "signs" of God (*ayat*) and these are ordered in such a way that they contribute to the continued existence and maturity of human life. The human will is completely subordinate to the will of God, so that humans cannot even want or do anything without God willing it. The teaching of the Koran, however, does lay individual responsibility upon people for their deeds, for which they will be judged at the Last Judgment. Life itself and everything that is good in life comes from God. He has power over everything. In everyday language, people confirm this in an almost rhetorical way, for whether one is inquiring into someone's health or asking how things are going in business or asking whether someone has enjoyed their meal, invariably one hears *al-hamdu-lillah*, "God be praised", before the answer comes. When enquiring whether the train has arrived on time, or asking if it is possible to make an appointment at a particular time one almost automatically hears *in-sha'-allah* ("God willing") first, and the answer only after that. To the outsider such expressions often seem hackneyed and lacking in conviction. But it is true for most Egyptians that God is the power behind all events, even if they are caused by people.

Aspects of contemporary cosmology

Learning about Islam in present-day Egypt

The holy book of Islam is the Koran. For Muslims the Koran contains the divine revelations in written form. It is the absolute and only book essential for gaining knowledge about Islam. The Koran is written in Arabic and all translations into other languages are regarded by believers as merely commentary on the original and as secular books. The meaning of the word koran, or in Arabic *al-Qur'an*, is originally "what is to be recited". Recitation of the Koran verses out loud (performed in an elevated, sing-song tone) is held in high regard by Muslims. In the traditional system of Islamic instruction, the art of recitation (*qira'a* and *tajwid*) holds a significant place alongside semantic interpretation (*tafsir*) (Nelson 1985).

The most important religious institute in Egypt is the *al-Azhar* in Cairo. This mosque is also a university for Islamic studies. It was established in the tenth century and to the present day enjoys great religious authority in the sunni-Islamic world. For centuries young men have been coming here to develop their competence in the Arabic language, Islamic theology, exegesis and *hadith* (traditional literature: everything the Prophet did or said about the sayings or deeds of others was noted down already in his lifetime and studied by later Islamic scholars) and *shari'a* (Islamic law). When they have gained a more or less advanced knowledge of the Koran and memorized it, they can find a job as *imam* (leader of prayer in the mosque) or schoolteacher. Others pursue their studies until they attain the *ijaza* (a "diploma" permitting them to teach students). These people are called *'ulama* (scholars). *'Ulama* (plural of *'alim*) means "persons with a great formal knowledge of Islam", knowledge based on the Koran, *hadith* and Islamic law.

The *'ulama* are often portrayed as traditionally orthodox: sufism (*al-tasawwuf*), which arose in Iraq in the eighth century, would be its ideological opposite. In sufism the aim is to reach spiritual union with God by means of certain rituals. There is great respect for the inner convictions of the individual. Right from the beginnings of the *turuq* (plural of *tariqa*, sufi order), within the Islamic orthodox world there has been a great deal of criticism of their version of Islam, and they are tolerated or persecuted depending on the political authorities of the day. In the twelfth and thirteenth centuries in particular, the sufi orders nonetheless grew quickly in size and number. Respected sufi *sheikhs* gathered followers around themselves, instructing them in their specific doctrine. It was also said of many *sheikhs* that they possessed mystical powers and knowledge given to them by God on account of their piety. With these powers (*baraka*) they were able to perform miracles. The veneration of saints (*'ibada li-l-wali*), which is vigorously rejected both by orthodoxy and by fundamentalist religious groups because God alone may be venerated, is closely linked with sufism. Despite criticism from "reformists" like ibn Taymiyya († 1328) and many others after him, sufism and belief in saints have continued to

exist, appealing as they do more to the people and meeting their religious feelings better than the abstract doctrines of orthodoxy. In
Egypt too, each saint has his own *mulid* (the annual birthday festival of
a saint) and sufi orders like the *Rafa'iyya*, *Qadiriyya*, *Ahmadiyya* and
Burhamiyya have a large following both in the cities and in the
villages.[1]

The orthodox attach great importance to knowledge (*'ilm*) of Islam
gained from (sacred) books, but sufism gives preference to mystical
intuition and experience (*ma'rifa*). These are obtained through the
dhikr (the repeated uttering of the sacred divine names and of specific
sufi formulas) and the performance of rituals in the course of music
and dancing. A second difference is formed by the fact that the *'ulama*
consists of persons who have gained religious knowledge through formal study and that the sufi *sheikhs* can be both highly educated people
and illiterates who have gained their knowledge of Islam primarily
through the oral teaching of their masters. Since no specific knowledge is required for participation in the *dhikr*, the sufi orders have
been very important for learning about Islam in the lower social classes. "Ordinary" people without much school education gain their
knowledge of Islam orally too. They try to learn some chapters from
the Koran by heart and to recite them in their daily prayers. Their

---

[1] The person who established the first "brotherhood" and who was at the root of the
massive spread of sufism is Abdel Qadir al-Jilani (1077-1166). Al-Jilani is the author
of a number of books that have become very well known, such as *The Secret of Secrets*
(*Sir al-asrar*) and *The Revelation of the Hidden* (*Futuh al-Ghaib*). His most important work,
however, was the establishment of a mystical brotherhood (sufi order) called "way" or
"path" (*tariqa/turuq*). His example was followed by other *sheikhs*, the best-known of
whom are Ahmad al-Rifa'i (the *Rifa'yya* order), Abu-l-Hasan al-Shadhili (the *Shadhili*
order), Mawlana Jalal ad-Din Rumi (the *Mevlavi* order) and Baha ad-Din Naqshband
(the *Naqshbandi* order). The founders of such sufi orders were considered to have *baraka* (grace of God) at their disposal, which they could pass on to their followers. During
their meetings the members (*muridun*) of an order endeavour to experience direct contact with God. They do this by reading out mystical texts and by music (*sama'*),
singing (*ghina'*), dance (*raqs*) and evocation of the holy names of God (*dhikr*). Sufis legitimate their rituals by reference to sura *al-'Imran* (3): 191 "Those who remember
Allah, standing and sitting and lying on their sides and thinking about the creation of
the heavens and the earth" and sura *al-Ahzab* (33): 41 "O you who believe, remember
Allah, remembering frequently (*dhikr*)". Sufis are tolerated by orthodox Muslims and
criticized by fundamentalists. They are accused of being interested only in *'alam al-
ghaib* (the transcendental world) and *'ilm al-ghaib* (occult knowledge), of rejecting the
physical world and of not keeping the Islamic laws. The sufi ritual is regarded with
more respect than *zar*, since it is based on the Koran. In the eyes of some Egyptians
the *dhikr* is thus a sort of "middle way" (Catherine 1997; Gilsenan 1973; Haeri 1990;
Kovalenko 1981; Nicholson 1907/1979; Ohtsuka 1990).

dependency on other, better-educated people is an additional problem since there is a great difference in grammar and pronunciation
between everyday colloquial language (al-'ammiya) and the Arabic of
the Koran (al-fus'ha).

From the days of Muhammed Ali (1805) stricter control was generally exercised over members of the 'ulama and the sufi orders. Secular
institutions for higher education were set up in the European style
and in 1908 the first Egyptian university followed, which was a private facility. Through the establishment of non-religious institutions
the state was able to break the monopoly of the al-Azhar in the field of
education. Intellectuals with a secular education would in future dis-
place the traditionally educated 'ulama. From this point one can speak
of a conflict between traditional Muslim authorities and "modernists". A new intellectual class emerged (called afandi [effendi]; see al-
Messiri 1978), with a marked preference for a western lifestyle and
ideology. Paradoxically enough, at more or less the same time a
group came into being that called itself the Muslim brotherhood,
under the leadership of the idealist Hassan al-Banna (1928). Their
goal was to breathe new life into Islam and to bring Egypt back from
a western secular ideology to a "true" Islamic ideology. It is also paradoxical that the leaders of this early "fundamentalist" group were not
students at the al-Azhar but precisely from the modern western-oriented schools and institutions. Members of later fundamentalist and
more militant groups which emerged in Egypt in the seventies and
eighties gained their education largely in modern secular institutes of
higher education (Ibrahim 1980). Persons who followed a traditional
education at the al-Azhar previously adopted a generally critical
stance vis-à-vis fundamentalistically inspired movements. From the
eighties and the early nineties the al-Azhar has been regarded by
many as a notable source of inspiration behind conservative forms of
Islam (Leemhuis, personal communication).

The question is how "fundamentalist" students with an education
at a secular institution extended and deepened their knowledge of
Islam. Ohtsuka (1990) assumes that their modern academic knowledge enabled them to see their Islamic faith convictions in a broader
perspective. Their studies conducted independently of the al-Azhar
produced new interpretations, which then led to new political and
religious movements which are currently referred to as "Islamic fundamentalism".

Not only did "fundamentalist Islam" with a militant activist programme in political matters engage the interest of secularly educated young people, but sufism too re-emerged (Gilsenan 1973). In contemporary Egypt there is a great deal of interest in *dhikr*, rituals and in a contemplative view of everyday life. Some of these new sufis are more critical than they used to be of "popular" manifestations of saint-veneration, but they are milder than orthodox and fundamentalist Muslims who reject totally all acts that derive from popular faith. The traditionally educated intellectuals from the *al-Azhar*, the orthodox *'ulama*, are also subjected to criticism — on the part of secular modernists, religious fundamentalists *and* sufis. Ordinary people who gained their knowledge of Islam through oral teaching from their sufi *sheikh*, have in the meantime received considerable help. Religious programmes on radio and television, besides the many cassettes with Koran recitations and sermons by popular media-*sheikhs*, are available for sale everywhere. There is a choice of orthodox, fundamentalist or sufi-oriented Koran interpretations.

Transactions between supernatural beings and Muslims

Islam is a monotheistic religion and this means that the faithful acknowledge only one God, Allah, whose will is to be obeyed without question. The Koran tells us that believers will receive their reward (*thawab* or *ajr*) for good deeds and devout behaviour, in the hereafter or in this world (*al-Nisa'* [4]: 134; *al-Isra* [17]: 19-20; *Luqman* [31]: 17; *al-Qari'a* [101]: 6-9). In everyday practice, however, one finds that Muslims "negotiate" with God to influence his preparedness to give blessings and beg for good gifts, or to turn away his anger. To this end one should give him non-material gifts such as the performance of daily prayers, fasting during the holy month of Ramadan or making the pilgrimage to Mecca. It is equally customary to offer material presents (in the form of sacrifices). So one may speak of "direct exchange": the believer gives to God and receives something special in return, either in this world or in the hereafter (Ohtsuka 1990). Believers are also encouraged to engage in "indirect exchange". Forms of this are the giving of alms, such as the compulsory *zaka*, religious donations (*waqf*) of possessions to hospitals or mosques, or, as is very common at religious festivals, the giving of money or food to the poor. In this type of exchange the believer gives something to his fellow, God sees this and regards it as a good deed, and a reward follows later.

"Negotiations" are conducted not only with God but also with other supernatural beings. This applies in the first place to relations with the Muslim saints (*awliya'*). The custom among the people is to visit the graves of saints (*ziyara*) to ask for mediation in gaining blessings so that an illness is alleviated or disappears, infertility is remedied, blindness is healed or prosperity in material things is the result (Blackman 1927; Early 1993; Leeder 1973; see also Van Binsbergen 1985). As mentioned above, visits to the graves of the saints are condemned by the orthodox as well as fundamentalists, and in some cases also by a few contemporary sufi leaders. The most important point in this regard is the question: who is asking what of whom, and who is giving what to whom? In popular belief it is assumed that saints can perform miracles (*karamat*) since they have been granted special powers (*baraka*) by God. The grave or tomb visitor thus prays to the saint and his or her wish is then (one hopes) fulfilled. But precisely prayer to the saint and the request for the saint's *baraka* is seen by religiously schooled people such as the orthodox and fundamentalists as counter to the confession of the unity of God (*tawhid*), and is suggestive of polytheism. A request for blessing or the fulfilment of a petition may only be made to Allah, and only Allah is able, if he is willing, to honour that petition. For some there is a mitigation of the accusation of "polytheism". According to them, though the petitioner prays to the saint, this is done in the expectation that the saint will in turn use his special position in relation to God to set aside more power for the petition of the visitor. Here too, then, one can speak of "indirect exchange".

Finally, there can be "negotiations" with Satan and demons. The existence of *al-shaytan* (the devil) and *jinn* (demons) with their leader *Iblis* is acknowledged in the Koran. Although interaction with humans (*al-Ahqaf* [46], *Muhammad* [47] and especially *al-Jinn* [72]) is mentioned, this is strongly discouraged. For most Egyptians, devils and demons are part of their religious conviction. The *jinn* are lackeys of the devil, whose purpose is to bring calamity to humans, and it is better to stay well away from them. There are, however, people who actively seek out the *jinn* and negotiate with them. They can manipulate them into doing good or bad things. These are magicians/sorcerers who use the *jinn* in order to practise magic (*sihr* or *'amal*). The sorcerer who wants to use the *jinn* makes a contract with him and he must therefore do all kinds of things for the devil that really should be done only for God, such as fasting and sacrifices. Sorcerers also use the Koran in an impure way and commit immorality (see Moham-

mad Mahmud abd-Allah, Cairo, n.d.).[2] By negotiating with the
demons or entering into an agreement with the devil, one commits
one of the worst sins since one gives God a rival (*shirk*): power is attributed to the devil and demons, while only God has power.

Magic has played an important role in Islamic countries throughout the centuries and in contemporary Egypt there is still fascination
with magic, even if it does not have the same significance and power
for everyone. But one can frequently listen to stories of people who
have suffered damage from sorcerers and in the newspapers criminal
acts are commonly explained as being supposedly inspired by devils
and demons.

Influences

Notions of demons from other cultures have been of influence on
notions of the Koranic *jinn* but are particularly noticeable in popular
religion.

Babylonian and Assyrian influences

Assyro-Babylonian demons are generally malevolent beings. Good
spirits are half human, half animal and are generally guardian spirits
in origin. They are used by the magician to oppose the evil spirits.
This view has been adopted by Islam, and good spirits are also used
against the evil spirits.

The use of Islamic magic in talking of seven *jinn* kings comes from
Babylon, where many demons were also known by personal names.
The Babylonian demons, like the *jinn*, are without form, but they can
assume the appearance of bulls, panthers, snakes, scorpions and

---

[2] The request for advocacy (*shafaʿa*) is given a negative answer in the Koran (*Hud*
[11]: 48) but not completely ruled out, if it occurs with permission from God (*al-
Baqara* [2]: 255; *al-Zumar* [39]: 44). In the course of time Mohammed was considered
to be in a position to ask clemency for sinners on the Day of Judgment. Later it was
considered possible that angels, prophets, martyrs and devout people could ask for
clemency (*Marjam* [19]: 87; *al-Zukhruf* [43]: 86; see also Wensink in EI2, vol. IX,
1976/7: 177-178). Belief in advocacy later extended to pious acts or a confession of
faith. Martyrs can ask for clemency in the name of their family and friends, and children in the name of their parents. In prose and poetry throughout the Islamic world
people sing about how Mohammed leads his people into Paradise on account of his
shafaʿa (Schimmel in EI2, vol. IX, 1995/6, 177-179; Lane 1895: 246-249).

birds. Their favourite food is blood and they like to settle on desolate places from which they put fear into people. In the Babylonian case it is often the female demons that are the most evil. They cause fever, illnesses, madness, hatred, jealousy and so on. The most important of these demons are: *Lamastu*, the childbirth demon who, according to Zbinden (1953) and Winkler (1931) is the precursor of the *qarina* in Islamic popular religion, and *Lilu, Lilitu* and *Ardat Lili*, the demons of the night, who attack men (in Morocco their name apparently changed to the single demon '*Aisha Qandisha*; Westermarck 1926, Vol. 1: 392). The demons are supremely powerful and can even bring about an eclipse of the moon. This idea has not been adopted by Islam, in which there is no moon cult.[3] The storm spirits, on the other hand, were indeed adopted. It was possible to protect oneself against all this evil. Zbinden writes (1953:107) that the Koran says that magic was invented in Babylon (sura *al-Baqara* [2]: 102). The Babylonian magicians use fire and smoke to drive out the demons and despite the fact that according to Islam the *jinn* were created out of fire, some Islamic magicians do the same. The Babylonians also used number mysticism which was taken over into Islamic magic by way of the Kabbala (a "system" or "method" of Jewish mystical devotion with certain magical elements). This also applies to the use of exorcism formulas, metal and silver charms, amulets, talismans and incense (see also Budge 1961; Fahd 1971; Leibovici 1971; Paret 1958).

Ancient Egyptian influences

According to Zbinden (1953) the influence of ancient Egyptian demonology is clearly in evidence in popular religion. The ancient Egyptians believed, for instance, that everything that was bad and malevolent came from the spirits of the dead, who lived below the surface of the earth. Spirits of the dead are unknown both among the Arabic heathen (*al-jahiliyya*) and in the Koran (though there are references to the *ham* or *sada'*, a sort of spirit of the dead who appears as an owl on the grave of a murdered person and calls for revenge; cf.

---

[3] Perhaps the lunar calendar year in Islam, in which the new month is determined by means of viewing the new moon, may be a residue of something like this. In Egyptian popular religion there is mention of *mushahara*, a "bewitching" which is caused by the transgression of taboos before the new moon appears (Inhorn 1994; Sengers 1994).

Fahd, EI, vol. VIII, 1994/5: 706), but they are included among the *ginnis*[4] of Egyptian popular religion, who also live below ground (these are the *'afarit*, who, principally in Upper Egypt, are the spirits of deceased persons; see el-Sayed el-Aswad 1987). According to another view, the *qarin* and the *qarina* are doubles of humans. This is said to go back to the *Ka* of the ancient Egyptians. Zbinden writes that the Babylonians knew a demon of childbirth, who could be the precursor of the *qarina* from Islamic popular religion, but in view of the fact that the ancient Egyptians were also familiar with such a demon, it is more probable that the Egyptian *qarina* developed independently of her Babylonian colleague after the ancient Egyptian model. This runs counter to the view of Winkler, who claims there is no evidence of such a demon in ancient Egyptian culture (1931: 169-175). I shall return to this specific demon since it is very important in popular belief. The view that the most malevolent demons are red in colour, as in the case of the "red king" (*al-Ahmar*) in popular belief, is also of ancient Egyptian origin. Red was the colour of Seth (Osiris's evil brother) and so this is the colour of evil. In Egyptian popular religion there is a strong connection between magicians, saints and *ginnis*. The magician and the saint are supposed to be in contact with the "brothers and sisters under the ground" (demons) whom they can call up and make useful to humans (magic/sorcery is also mentioned in the Koran).[5] It is striking that these useful spirits have personal names and are explicitly not called *jinn*. This means, according to Zbinden (1953: 111-117), that ancient magical powers have continued to exist under cover of belief in the *ginni*. Like the Babylonians, the ancient Egyptians believed that illnesses are caused by demons invading the human body. By using exorcism texts they made them leave the body again. This still occurs in almost the same way in, among other

---

[4] (a) Wellhausen (1927: 185) notes that the spirit of a deceased person comes back as a bird (an owl). The spirits of the dead are also supposed to appear as *jinn* in graveyard and lonely places (*ibid*. 189).

(b) There is no difference between *jinn* and *ginni*. It is simply a matter of nomenclature and transcription. In the case of Egypt, one speaks of *jinn* in classical Arabic texts and of *gann* and *ginn* in the Egyptian vernacular. In all cases it is a collective noun, a singular form indicating an unspecified number.

[5] Sura *al-A'raf* (7): 116 "He said: Cast. So when they cast, they deceived the people's eyes and frightened them, and they produced a mighty enchantment." Sura *Ta-Ha* (20): 66 "He said: Nay! cast down. Then lo! Their cords and their rods — it was imaged to him on account of their magic as if they were running" (translation M.H. Shakir).

things, the *zar* ceremony and Koran healing. Even the custom of dissolving magical formulas (or Koran texts) in water and drinking them in order to bring about healing, was applied by the ancient Egyptians. The same is true of animal and harvest sacrifices (see also Meeks 1971).

Jewish influences

Zbinden (1953: 126-130) believes that Jewish legends and superstition had an important influence on Islamic notions of demons and magic. In accordance with Jewish doctrine, demons are "intermediary beings". They have wings and are supposed to look like angels. Like humans, they eat and drink and engage in sexual intercourse. One finds the same understanding of demons in Islam. The Jewish demons are ruled by twelve kings, the most important of whom is Sammael. They are the produce of the relationship between Adam and Lilit (she is the Jewish "man-seducer" and "childbirth demon"), assume the appearance of animals and reptiles (including snakes) and live in trees, wells and so on. The idea of associating demons with calamity is originally a Jewish one. The view that demons have a predilection for impure places and that one should therefore observe all kinds of purification regulations so that they do not invade the body, is of Jewish origin. Belief in the anti-demonic effect of words from the Holy Scriptures also comes from Judaism, along with the myth of the special powers of Solomon and the use of the "seals of Solomon" in driving out demons. This applies also to light, water, salt and iron, in which there is latent power, according to the kabbalists, to drive out demons (see also Caquot 1971; Trachtenberg 1939).

Jinn and other non-human beings

In pre-Islamic Arabia (which believers call *al-jahiliyya*, since the Revelations had not yet been given) all sorts of *jinn* (demons) were known, both good and bad. Among their most dominant characteristics was the fact that they were invisible and without shape and appeared especially at night. They preferred to spend their time in dirty or deserted places and could cover great distances at high speed. They were regarded as the instigators of all kinds of sickness. The *jinn* of the Koran often seem to have retained the same characteristics they had before Islam. Eichler (1928: 30-39) writes that the Prophet knew three categories of *jinn*. In the first place he distinguishes the demons from ancient Arabian heathen religion which cause fear and calamity, mostly in the guise of snakes. In the second place he mentions the jinn who as "intermediary beings" (between God and humans) are a sort of confidant in heaven and are venerated by humans; according to sura *al-Jinn* (72): 11, 14, they can convert to Islam. These *jinn* can fly as far as the lowest heaven, where they listen in on conversations. A watcher of the angels, however, keeps these *jinn* at a suitable distance so that their power is limited (*al-Jinn* [72]: 1, 8, 9) (see also Chelhod 1964: 72-84). In the third place there are the *jinn* who are "Doppelgänger" of humans.

Zbinden writes (1953:87) that the Koran knows of not three but four categories of *jinn*, namely demons of heaven, protection, nature and possession. It is the demons of possession that correspond to the ancient Arabian belief in demons. In his view this is also the case with the demons that possess supernatural powers and who are mentioned as special *jinn* in the myth of Solomon (*Saba'* [34] and *Sad* [38]). According to Zbinden it is very likely that Mohammed tried to strip the *jinn* in the Arabian heathen tradition of their demonic character by setting them on the same level as humans (see also Wellhausen 1927: 157).

The jinn of the Prophet

That *jinn* were a reality to the Prophet is evident from sura "The Jinn" (*Surat al-Jinn* [72]), which dates from the second Meccan period. In many other suras in the Koran too, one encounters notices of the existence of *jinn*. Like humans, the *jinn* are created, though not out of clay like humans, but of fire (*al-Hijr* [15]: 26, 27). As created beings, like humans they have to give an account of their doings on the Day of Judgment and may be condemned to remain in hell (*Hud* [11]: 119). Like humans the *jinn* must serve God (*al-Dhariyat* [51]: 56) and they can also enter Paradise and enjoy all the wonderful things that are there. There are not only believing *jinn* (*jinn mu'minun*) but also unbelieving (*jinn kafirun*). It is possible for unbelieving *jinn* to be converted and the Revelation is meant for them too (*al-Jinn* [72]: 1,2). *Iblis*, who is said in the Koran (*al-Baqara* [2]: 34) to be a fallen angel, is the leader of all unbelieving and malevolent spirits. He tries to incite people into apostasy from the faith and to other evil things (*Sad* [38]: 82).

Alongside the *jinn*, *al-Shaytan* is also spoken of. This is the personal name of the Devil. Such scholars as Eichler (1928: 41-42) and Zbinden (1953: 88) are of the opinion that the devil in the Koran is influenced by ideas current in Arabian paganism and by Hebrew ideas of Satan (see also Otto 1923). The Koran also apparently makes a distinction between *shaytan* (plural *shayatin*) and *al-Shaytan*. The former are malevolent spirits and the opposite of angels (*mala'ika*) and the second is the Devil. Bell and Watt (1970: 155) call both the *Shaytan* and *Iblis* "The Devil". Tritton (EI, vol. IV, 1934: 307-308) notes there is no clarity regarding the *Shaytan* as the Devil, the *shaytan* (*shayatin*) as malevolent helpers of the Devil and other *jinn*. Rippin says (EI2, 1995/6, vol. IX, 406-408) that the personal name *Shaytan* should be distinguished from the plural form *shayatin*, which is used in reference to devils who "can belong both to the human race and to the *jinn*" (*al-An'am* [6]: 112).

The Koran also mentions the *'afarit*, who are a kind of malevolent demon with their own characteristics, but are only mentioned once in the Koran as "demon of the *jinn*" (*al-Naml* [27]: 39) and the *marid*, called a "stubborn satan" (*al-Hajj* [22]: 3). Winkler (1934: 7) and Padwick (1923: 423) are of the opinion that this name relates not to one demon but to a group of demons. In addition there are the *taghut*, who are mentioned as a sort of "false deities" in the Koran in *al-Nisa'* [4]: 51, but referred to in [4]: 76 as "the satan's lackeys". Finally there is the *qarin*, a demon who is the "fellow" of a human.

The qarin: a separate category of jinn

I return to the *qarin* at this point since they play a very important role in popular religion. The *qarin* is mentioned in the Koran (*al-Nisa* [4]: 42; *al-Saffat* [37]: 49-54; *Fussilat* [41]: 24-25). He is the "fellow" who belongs with every human, but he is not clearly described. In the *hadith* (the traditional literature) there is talk of two "fellows", one of the *jinn* (*qarin min al-jinn*) and one of the angels (*qarin min al-mala'ika*) (see e.g. the exegete Muslim † 875 in: al-Suyuti 1989: 97). Among Koran commentators opinion is divided over these beings. For some it is a companion and for others the devil. Winkler (1931:58-64) thinks that the word *qarin* has a neutral meaning, in the sense that each person has a "companion", but according to *al-Zukhruf* (43): 35 only the devil has an evil fellow. In present-day Egypt *qarin* sometimes means an evil spirit and sometimes a guardian spirit. People also say

that humans have an evil spirit on their left shoulder and an angel on
their right shoulder; both are personal "companions" (see also D.B.
Macdonald in EI2, vol. IV, 1978, 643 and T. Fahd in EI2, vol. IX,
1995/6, 407).

Jinn *in popular Egyptian religion*

I am aware that "formal" religion constitutes only one aspect of Islam
and that caution is required in the use of the term "popular Islam",
which of course, by definition, is not the same in all Islamic countries.
Local traditions and customs in each country have exercised considerable influence on interpretation of formal doctrine. I must be care-
ful, moreover, not to draw a fixed picture of religious ideals and ritual
practices. Not all Egyptians share the same worldview with regard to
devils and demons.

   In popular belief the place of the *jinn* and their activities is much
clearer than in formal religion. In Egypt they are called *ginni* (feminine form: *ginniyya*). They are held responsible for all the evil that can
overcome humans and animals, but women and children in particular are the targets of these malevolent beings (see also Merschen 1982:
24). They are invisible but can assume various shapes (snakes, scorpions, birds, dogs, cats and sometimes human figures) and they utter
strange noises. In houses they like to stay under the foundations and
under doorsteps, and in toilets and bathrooms. But they also like to
live next to wells, rivers, caves and potholes, graves, ruins, crossroads
and at lonely places. Although they mainly stay underground, they
are in fact fire spirits. So they are also to be found by fire. In Egyptian
popular belief there are many stories of *ginnis* and they are
euphemistically called *as-sukkan taht al-'ard, al-ikhwat taht al-'ard* or *al-
tahtaniyyin* ("the dwellers underground", "our brothers and sisters
underground" or the "subterrestrials"). Since the *ginnis* live under the
surface of the earth, it is good to ask them for permission or pardon
(*dastur*) if one accidentally stamps on the ground or digs in the earth. It
is forbidden to pour hot water through the toilet or drain in the
evening or at night since the *ginnis* may be disturbed by this and may
take revenge. If one wants to build a new house or make use of a
house that has stood empty for some time, it is better first to sacrifice
a chicken or a sheep, for one can never know whether a *ginni* is living
here and will have to be pacified first. Farmers sacrifice a small por-
tion of the harvest in order to curry favour with the *ginnis*.

According to the many books available all over Cairo which deal with "being touched" and "possession" by demons (see bibliography), *jinn* and *shayatin* are two names for one and the same being and all demons belong to the family of Iblis (see Mohammed Mahmoud abd-Allah, Cairo, n.d.).

Besides *ginnis* (a collective name) or *tahtaniyyin*, of all known demons the following are most frequently mentioned in present-day Egypt: the *Shaytan* (the Devil) and the *shayatin*, demonic beings which help Satan in his diabolical works (their leader is Iblis) and the *'afrit* (plural *'afarit*), who is extremely malevolent and is known in Upper Egypt in particular as a spirit of the dead. The *qarina* is alternately malevolent and benevolent and is also called *ukht* (sister). When a human being is born, simultaneously a *qarin(a)* is born, that is, a *doppelgänger* who resembles the person he or she belongs to in every respect. Even nowadays *doppelgänger* constitute a specific category of *ginnis* that must certainly be taken into account.

A demon already known before Islam is the Ghul (fem. Ghula). This demon is not mentioned in the Koran, but is seems that the Prophet was *au fait* with the fact that his contemporaries believed in its existence. Characteristic of this demon is that it lives in the wilderness, changes appearance frequently and suddenly turns up in order to lead travellers astray. He generally assumes the form of an animal or a snake. In Egypt one no longer hears the Ghul mentioned much these days, but it is still used as a sort of bogey-man for small children (Lane 1895: 236; Macdonald in EI, vol. II, 1971, 1078-9; Padwick 1923: 421-4).

Finally there are also the *zar* demons. *Zar* embraces both the pantheon of the separate demons, the ceremony, and the sickness phenomen. These demons have no basis in the Koran. The *zar* ceremony is known in Egypt only from around 1870 onwards (Kriss & Kriss-Heinrich, 1962, vol. II: 142). *Zar* demons, especially among women, are responsible for mental afflictions and possession.

Relations between humans and jinn

Questions and remarks about relations between human beings and demons are primarily concerned to ask whether *jinn* can "dwell" in a person and make him or her sick. Is a marriage possible between a human being and a *jinn*? I myself have been told stories a number of times about marriages between humans and demons and I have seen that these stories are taken very seriously (Leemhuis 1993; Sengers 1994).

Jinn or *ginnis* are part of the religious conviction. This does not mean that every Egyptian believes that *jinn* can make someone sick or that sexual relations with them do in fact occur. What it does indicate is that the boundary between what is orthodox and what is popular belief is porous, as is also evident from the conversations I conducted with *umm* Mohammed,[6] a forty-seven-year-old woman who is illiterate and lives in one of Cairo's people's districts, and with *sheikh* Fathi, a man with a better than average knowledge of the Koran who says he heals sick people by applying his knowledge of the Koran. In both cases the conversations were concerned with the *jinn/ginnis*, and the question of where they live and what they do. Translations and commentary of my own are placed in parentheses.

Umm Mohammed:

> A man and a woman both have a *qarina*, and she lives below ground. She gets jealous if a woman is beautiful and then she kills her. That is what happened with my daughter, too. My daughter saw her *qarina*. He appeared three times in the night and stood facing her. He looked like a human being, but it was not human. He was an angel, he was white and he was wearing a white *gallabiyya* (a sort of long tunic also worn outdoors). Three times he said to my daughter *ana muslim w-awahhid bi-llah* (I am a Muslim and believe in God). My daughter was not sick at all, but after a week she was dead. This sort of thing happens to beautiful women, women who are pregnant or with women standing in front of a mirror.[7] This is really what happened to my daughter! The *qarina* is *zayyi as-shaytan*, *zayyi al-'afrit*, *zayyi al-ginn* (just like the devil, the *'afrit*, the *jinn*)! If the woman's *qarina* is bad, then she dies." In another conversation she says that the *qarina* is the same as "the sister underground". This sister punishes her if she does something wrong. "The *qarina* is a *ginn*, and so at night you must not hit, knock or stamp on anything or she will get angry. And it is not allowed to pour hot water down the WC without apologizing in advance or saying *'an iznukum ikhwati* (pardon me, my brothers and sisters)." I gradually discover that she makes a small distinction between the *qarina* and the "sister". "The *qarina* is *min 'andi rabbina* (from our Lord) and sits in your body and the 'sister' belongs in the world of the *ginnis*. But she does not necessarily only do bad things. Children do not have a *qarina*,

---

[6] *Umm* means mother of the eldest son, called Mohammed. In the Islamic world the custom is to name the mother or father after the eldest child.

[7] This sort of notion is also found in other cultures; see e.g. Becker 1995: 55.

but a 'sister' who protects them. Only adults have a *qarina*. It is only when children get older, cry a lot or are sick that they get one too. The sister protects them against evil from others, but if the mother is bad for her child then she takes revenge by killing the child.

Sheikh Fathi:

That *jinn* live underground is not written in the Koran. Jinn means 'that which cannot be seen' and that is the reason Allah gave them this name. No one knows where they live, but this is said in Egypt and so *ginnis* are also called *sufliyyin* or *tahtaniyyin* (low/common spirits, subterrestrials). In bathrooms and latrines live a sort of *ginni*, that is the *shayatin* (devils/demons). That is why when we go to the bathroom or WC we have to say *bismillah* (in the name of God) or *a'uzu mil-khubs wa-l-khabayis* (God protect me against all impurification), and this is how Allah protects us against evil from these demons. It is also *sunna*[8] that a man keeps his body covered when he makes love with his wife. Then the devil can't see him and slip into the woman through the vagina. To be on the safe side it is better to say a verse from the Koran, so that if a child should result, it will be protected against the devil. Before meals you must say *bismillah* too, or before you go into a house. You do this in case a *shaytan* (devil, singular of *shayatin*) is present, for then you are protected by God. It says in the Koran that there are *jinn* who are believers (i.e. Muslim). Believing *jinn* are brothers in the faith, but that is all. We are not allowed to call them *ukht* or *akh*, even if they are Muslim *jinn*. Only fellow human beings who are believers can be called this. We must not come into contact with them either, because they are created differently from humans. Sometimes there is a *ginni* who has power over a man or a woman and wants to make love with him or her. There are also people who say that they are married to a *ginni*. I think this is not possible because they are made of fire and humans are made of clay. The *qarin* is from the Koran, and no *qarina* is mentioned there. The *qarin* incites people against God. This is the only *qarin* there is. This *qarin*, or *qarina*, if people want to call it that, cannot cause any sicknesses! The belief that *ginnis* can make people sick comes from the far distant past, long before there was a religion, when people did consort with *ginnis*. It is wrong to believe that *ginnis* have this power, but unfortunately there are still many people who do so! A person who believes knows better. He knows that everything comes from Allah and not from these beings."

---

[8] The word *sunna* is a term from Islamic legislation. In the beginning of Islam it meant "custom of community behaviour". Later tradition-scholars were of the opinion that *sunna* may apply only to "the customs of the Prophet", in the form of a prayer or a prohibition, or through his example alone. Through the influence of the legal scholar as-Shafi'i († 820 in Egypt) this concept became dominant.

Many Egyptians believe that demons are lackeys of the devil, whose intention it is to make people sick or cause something bad to happen to them. The *jinn* of popular belief are shaped according to orthodox Islamic notions, but in popular religion they have gained attributes that point to influences from other and older cultures. Formal religion supports belief in demons since this has its basis in the Koran, but dismisses the deviant acts of the popular demons, which are regarded as superstition. My experience is that stories about demons are very common.

Magic

After the Islamic conquests the Arabians came into contact with views of the supernatural and magical practices from other peoples. These were mixed with Koranic and Arabian understandings. It can also be assumed that after the coming of Islam, "paganism" did not suddenly disappear on the Arabian peninsula (this did not happen in other cultures either: cf. Giordano 1983). Many variations in views of the supernatural seem to have existed side by side, but eventually they gain a predominantly Arabian/Islamic colouring.

Magic has played an important role with regard to sickness and healing in Islamic countries through the centuries, and it still does. In some social circles in Egypt people are still afraid of *'amal* and *sihr* (magic/sorcery). It is not my intention to go into Arabian magic in great detail, but since magic, like the *jinn*, is held responsible for sickness and accident, and since the *jinn* themselves are supposed to be the helpers of the magicians both in the causation and healing of sickness and accident, I will consider here views of contemporary magic, as experienced by the women I spoke with.

The literature on magic in the Graeco-Roman, Coptic, Ancient Egyptian and Mesopotamian world displays great continuity (see Van Binsbergen & Wiggermann 1997). One of the most important books in the field of magic written by an Islamic scholar is *Shams al-ma'arif al-kubra* by al-Buni (died 622/1225). This work formed the basis for many other writings on magic and also for the preparation of magical amulets and talismans (charms credited with sacred power). Besides this work by al-Buni a great number of books are known which deal with magic and Islamic/Arabian sorcerers and scholars by means of a series of documents and borrowings. Western orientalists and doctors educated in the west have also consulted magical books.[9] Manuals for the preparation of amulets and talismans and the practice of magic are available in the streets everywhere.

Discussions of magic

There have always been discussions among Islamic scholars on the permissibility or otherwise of magic. The point of departure for the discussion was of course the Koran. The striking thing about this is in the first place that the Koran adopts an ambivalent position towards *jinn* since they are not totally bad or good. Secondly, it was the angels Harut and Marut who instructed Solomon in magic in Babel (*al-Baqara* [2]: 102). At various points the Koran speaks of sorcerers and magic and there is never any account of a prohibition of them. Thus the prophet Moses, for instance, is regarded as a sorcerer (*al-A'raf* [7]: 109; *Yunus* [10]: 76; *Ta-Ha* [20]: 63, 71; *al-Shu'ara'* [26]: 34; *Ghafir* [40]: 24 and *al-Dhariyat* [51]: 39). Even Mohammed is accused several times (*Yunus* [10]: 2; *Sad* [38]: 4; *al-Dhariyat* [51]: 52) of being a *sahir* (sorcerer).[10] The Koran verses 113 and 114, furthermore (called the *mu'awwidhatan* verses), are used precisely as a measure against magic. One *hadith* says that these verses were revealed specially by Allah when the Prophet himself was sick because he had been put under a spell by the Jewish man Labid ibn A'asam. Through reciting these verses he was healed. That is how they come to be used and worked into amulets and talismans to the present day. Besides the Koran verses mentioned above, the following verses are also effective measures against magic: *al Fatiha* (the opening sura of the Koran) and the

---

[9] The genre of religious-magical literature includes manuals with detailed instructions for the prevention and healing of all kinds of dangers and evils caused by magic or the evil eye. Among these are the works of Abu Hamid Mohammed b. Muhammed al-Ghazali at-Tusi (died 1111 AD), Muhammed b. Muhammed b. Muhammed ibn al-Hajj al-Fasi al-'Abdari al-Qayrawani at-Tilimisani (died 1336 AD), Shihab ad-Din Ahmad b. Ahmad b. al-Latif ash-Sharji az-Zabidi al-Hanafi (died 1488 AD) and Jalal ad-Din 'abd al-Rahman as-Suyuti (died 1505). Western scholars (among others): Canaan 1914, 1929; Donaldson 1938; Doutté 1908; Kriss & Kriss-Heinrich 1960; Lane 1895; Masse 1938; Winkler 1930, 1931.

[10] On Moses: sura *al-A'raf* (7): 109 "The chiefs of Firon's people said: most surely this is an enchanter possessed of knowledge." On the Prophet: sura *Yunus* (10): 2 "What! is it a wonder to the people that We revealed to a man from among themselves, saying: Warn the people and give good news to those who believe that theirs is a footing of firmness with their Lord. The unbelievers say: This is most surely a manifest enchanter."

al-Shifa' verses (Koran verses which speak of healing: *al-Tawba* [9]: 14; *al-Nahl* [16]: 69; *Yunus* [10]: 57; *al-Shu'ara* [26]: 80; *al-Isra'* [17]: 82; *Fussilat* [41]: 44).

According to Ibn Khaldun (1332-1406), historian, sociologist and philosopher, no rational person can doubt the existence of sorcery and its influence, since it is referred to in the Koran. Some people, he claims, are able, with or without external help, to bring about special effects. He divides magicians/sorcerers and their actions into: people who are able to exercise power over other people with their mind/intellect, people who use astrology and know different techniques for preparing talismans and people who are able to call up all kinds of spiritual apparitions and visions by making use of the imagination of others. Prophets can exercise influence on worldly affairs with the help of God, divine powers and angels. Sorcerers, who have specific psychic powers at their disposal, do this with the aid of Satan; by means of devilish powers they are able to perceive "hidden things". In all magical activities we find different sorts of veneration, submission and humility. In magic/sorcery it is a matter of dedication and veneration that are not directed to God. Sorcery is therefore a sign of unbelief. The question whether sorcery is real or imagined relates only to confusion regarding the sorts of sorcery as mentioned above. Magic is prohibited by religious laws because it can cause damage to individuals. Ibn Khaldun makes a distinction between miracle and magic. A miracle is brought about by a pure soul, like the Prophet. Magic is the work of a bad person and the result is bad. The paradoxical thing is that he rejects all magic/sorcery because it can damage other people and does not have trust in Allah as his premise, but that this does not apply to "white magic", although it is better avoided. He also rejected fortune-telling, geomanticism, the preparation of talismans and magic squares (a form of letter magic), and occupation with *jinn* or activities designed to get into contact with the "hidden things" or the Unseen. The latter does not apply to rituals performed by Muslim mystics (sufis). Their only goal is to get closer to God. By performing particular rituals and through secret knowledge some can gain control over the "hidden things", but this is not their ultimate goal. If they were to seek mystical knowledge for the sake of that knowledge, this would be equivalent to polytheism. Some theologians condemn the sufi movements for fear that the miracles of saints might be confused with the miracles of the prophets (see further: Macdonald 1965: 109-118, 130-133, *Enzyklopädie des Islams*, IV, 1954,

438-47; EI2, vol. IX, 567-571; *Handwörterbuch des Islam*, 1941, 697-698, and the *Muqaddimah* in the Rosenthal translation 1967).[11] Discussions of *jinn* and magic are carried out in the present-day Islamic world too. Not everyone of course believes in magic in the same way and developed people in particular often have some ambivalence towards it. People do believe in the existence of supernatural powers because this is mentioned in religious texts, but the message and the significance of it in contemporary reality are less important to them than to less well-educated people. It is an important criterion in the practice of magic that "white" magic is permitted, but "black" magic is forbidden. The practicians of "white" magic say they are God's instruments and that they act in his name. The second group claims to have subjected the *jinn* by concluding a contract with them. Although magic and sorcery are spoken of in the Koran, these practices are certainly not encouraged by formal religion.[12]

---

[11] Wali ad-Din Abu Zaid 'Abd ar-Rahman b. Muhammad *Ibn Khaldun* al-Hadrami al-Ishbili born in Tunis, 1332, died in Cairo 1406. Letter magic is the use of Arabic letters and numerals, the "ninety-nine beautiful names of God" and Koran verses in the preparation of amulets. Geomanticism is fortune-telling with sand figures. According to Ibn Khaldun all the occult sciences are nonsense and a person can only get into contact with the Higher from his own spirit. Macdonald writes that because of his rationalism Ibn Khaldun occupies an exceptional position among his contemporaries (1965: 109-118, 130-133; see also *Enzyklopädie des Islams*, IV, 1934, 438-47.

[12] Some magical practices Muslims occupy themselves with are viewed as typical of "popular Islam". These would be influences that have crept into Islam through mystical customs from pre-Islamic Arabia and/or through peoples who converted to the new religion but remained partly attached to the old customs and beliefs. Doubtless this is true up to a point, but it is incorrect to assume that orthodox Islam is supposed to be "magic-free". Magic is not encouraged by formal religion, but it is acknowledged. The *al-Azhar*, university/mosque, the highest religious institution in Egypt, where Islamic orthodoxy is watched over, has published a book: *Bayan lil-Nas* ("Guideline for people", 1989), in which positions adopted by formal religion are explained in lay terms. The most varied religious matters are included, among them also *jinn*, magic and other occult matters. The *fatwa* (formal juridical proclamation) with regard to sorcery/magic (*sihr*), maintains the position that one can conclude from Koran verses that magic is a historical fact. Sorcery/magic is mentioned sixty times in the Koran with varying nuances in meaning "from the bizarre and unusual to the attracting of attention and the occasioning of astonishment" (1989: 236-149). In a conversation I conducted in June 1996 with Dr. Abdul Aziz Ezat Abdul Jalil, member of the Fatwa commission of the *al-Azhar*, he confirmed that the practice of magic is prohibited. But it is primarily the intention that determines whether magic is good or bad. The conviction must be that God alone has knowledge of what is hidden and that only his will counts.

Magicians, sorcerers and exorcists

Dols (1992), Doutté (1908), Kriss and Kriss-Heinrich (1960), De Jong (1984) and Zwemer (1920), among others, describe how magic has played an important role in middle-eastern society since antiquity. Thus de Jong (1984: 492) writes that magical ideas are a component of religion. Magic also often formed a threat (and this seems still to be the case) for established religion since in part it is "fishing in the same pool". But non-Islamic sources are also demonstrable. A good deal of knowledge for instance has been handed down from ancient Egypt and Babylon, from Christian and Jewish-kabbalistic sources.

Magic, Dols writes, is not necessarily bad in itself, although this is often assumed to be the case. In the middle ages "good" Islamic magic was even a recognized way of helping someone to get over an affliction or illness, and medicine itself (*tibb*) was often viewed as a form of counter-magic (1992:262-263). Therapeutic magic is sanctioned by various *hadiths*. There are six important collections of these, of which that by al-Bukhari and Muslim enjoys the greatest authority († 870 and 875 AD respectively). After the Koran, which forms the basis of the Islamic theological system, the *hadiths* gradually came to be accepted as the second authority in the realm of theoretical and practical detail in Islam. For Moslims the *hadiths* are guidelines for life. Moslims have deduced from the Koran and the *hadith* that, as long as there is no question of polytheism, i.e. as long as healing is carried out in the name of Allah (and not in the name, for instance, of a particular *jinn* or another spirit), the use of magic is permitted.

Over against "good" (white) magic stands "bad" (black) magic. By white magic we mean all activities that have as their goal to bring a person advantage, success and good luck, without anyone being harmed in the process. By black magic we mean all magical activities that have as their goal to bring a person disadvantage, failure and bad luck. This is of course a division used by people who believe in magic. But the reasoning behind whether magic is white or black depends on one's own point of view. What one person practises and calls "good" magic is often seen by the other person (the victim) as "bad" magic. This sounds cryptic, but in illustration I offer the following stories told me by *umm* Sabah and *umm* Rabi'a.[13]

---

[13] White magic is used on the following occasions, among others: evoking a strong love, causing sexual excitement, attracting customers, gaining wealth, agreeing to a

Umm Sabah:

> When I was just married, there was a woman who was madly in love
> with my husband. She gave him food and clothes and then he stayed
> with her. When he came back from her, he hit me and so I was always
> tired and sick and kept bleeding. I went to a doctor. I had to pay two
> pounds for this and then buy medicines as well, but it didn't help. A
> neighbour told me that I should go to a *sheikh* (magic specialist) because
> my husband's other woman was not good and had had "writing" done.
> What is that, "writing"?, I ask her. 'That is to cast a spell for someone.
> That is what the woman had done to make me sick so that my husband
> goes to her. If you know that that has happened, you have to go to
> someone who can make you better again. Well, the *sheikh* took a white
> plate and laid seven kinds of ears of grain and seeds in it (seven is an
> important number in magic and is also used for the seven *jinn* kings)
> and poured a glass of water over them. I had to eat up the grains one
> by one; a grain of corn and a sip of water, a grain and a sip of water …
> and he said that I should come back in three days. I didn't do that
> because the bleeding had stopped.' When you were better, did you
> ever go back to him? Yes, a few years later I went again for my little
> boy, because his *ukht* (the "sister underground") was making him very
> restless. He is a beautiful child and a woman neighbour was jealous.
> She just kept saying that he was such a beautiful child and so nice and
> chubby and white, but in the meantime she cast the evil eye on him,
> which made his "sister underground" jealous of him. When he lay
> sleeping on my lap he kept making those strange jumps in the air with
> his body (convulsions? epilepsy? anxiety dreams?). His "sister" did it.
> Then I went with him to the same *sheikh*. He "read" for him seven
> times and stroked his head seven times. Then he spat in his face so that
> the bad spirit would leave him (the saliva of a holy man or a healer is
> often seen as having healing properties). He also made an amulet for
> him which I had to place under his clothes, and *al-hamdu li-llah* (God be
> praised) the boy was fine after that.

Umm Rabi'a, a neighbour of *umm* Sabah, has come in. She comes
from Aswan, but has lived in Cairo for the past twenty years. When I
tell her that I want to know something about *'amal* (magic), and
whether she "believes in it", she nods and says:

> A woman who is cross with her husband, or if her husband has another
> woman and she wants it to be over and she knows where a *sheikh* or a
> *sheikha* lives, then she goes there for help. What else can she do? The

---

marriage, obtaining fertility, making gold, solving a theft, finding lost objects. For
malevolent ends, black magic is used among other things for: hatred, impotence,
sterility, causing serious illnesses, causing madness, divorce, cursing, the prevention of
a marriage (see the sorcery books of al-Tukhi in the bibliography).

sheikh says to her: go and get an *atar* from him (a personal item used in magic) and I will see to it that everything is sorted out. *Khalas!* (All over!) He does ask a lot of money, but it helps, because the woman disappears out of his life." Both women call this white magic, because it is for a good cause. But there are all sorts of black magic, such as for instance: "*'amal bis-sufli* (magic with the aid of lower/common demons), but this is forbidden because you are doing something bad to someone this way." But does it work? "O yes, if you want to have it done, you generally go to a priest or a Christian *sheikh*, since they are the best at this sort of magic. They have *suflis*, demons that are used to work magic with. Women who have this done are Muslims, yes, but they are not good women. I have heard of a woman who went to one of these priests. He needed an *atar* and for this she had to sit on the ground with her legs apart. Then he himself took a bit of her husband's semen out of her vagina and he used this to write an amulet with. *Da ghalat!* (That is wrong!) That sort of magic can't ever be undone again either. So you do that if you are really mad at someone." I ask if there are other sorts of magic and she tells me: "there is *'amal bis-samak* (magic with the fish). The fish used for this is called *armut* (a sort of wolf-fish) and it must still be alive when it is "written" on, because it is then thrown back into the water to do its dirty work. This *'amal* can't be "undone" either. Another way to do it is to have *'amal bis-shagara* (magic with the tree) done. A married woman who loves another man a lot, for instance, and wants to get rid of her own husband, she has something like this done. The *sheikh* writes something on a piece of paper, which she immediately has to hang up in a tree out of sight. The wind makes the branch of the tree wave to and fro and everything she likes comes to her and her own husband goes crazy. There are also women who have *'amal bil-karahiyya* (magic with hate) done. This happens if the woman notices that her husband has gone off her or hits her a lot. This sort of magic is done to make him change. On the other hand, *'amal bil-hubb* (magic with love) is meant to make someone love you. For instance, a woman who loves a man who is already married, goes to a *sheikh* to have an amulet made in order to pull the man away from his wife. If you want to have *'amal* done, then you need to know for sure where a *sheikh* lives who does this. Since all this has to happen in secret, you ask your neighbour or someone else … until someone tells you they know one. It is forbidden." Later she admits, with some embarrassment, that she herself once had "writing" done.[14]

---

[14] Every Sunday morning Muslim and Christian women stream into a well-known church in old Cairo to consult a priest that works there about magic.

The giving of an *atar* is giving something private. What is claimed here is not only exceptionally private, but also in all respects specially impure and a gross transgression of the norms which mark relationships between women and men who are taboo to them. Perhaps it is also an expression of a desire to have power over the spouse through something entirely beyond his control that can be used against him.

Rabi'a says that a woman who has a priest "write" is not a good woman, since he only does black magic. This seems like a rationalisation to me — in the first place because she goes to a non-Muslim for magic, and then indeed for "bad" magic, and secondly because she knows that magic is morally objectionable and she is appealing to a forbidden cosmological category. Magic with demons is forbidden (even if it is carried out by a Muslim sorcerer), not only because it does something bad to someone, but also because, even if demons might be good for you, which is conceivable in the world of magic, still interaction with them is forbidden.

I have often encountered such stories as Rabi'a's about the priest who took semen out of a woman's vagina, and it is impossible to control them. Everything that has to do with the female body and/or sexuality is a charged topic in Egypt. A person or an action can very quickly be judged to be "shameful". Personally I find it difficult to believe such a story as Rabi'a's and I think that in her rationalisation she is letting herself be carried away by her imagination. I have often been surprised by the uninhibitedness with which women (and men) are able to talk about sexuality, as if chastity did not stand in the way. This applies to Egypt, but also to other Islamic countries: on one hand striking reticence and on the other an apparently naïve lack of inhibition in the way in which people sometimes talk about it. The two women's stories above also show how little grasp people have of the mechanisms of supernatural causality that they presume to be operative. The best they can do is to try to defend themselves from calamity with magic.

To protect themselves against magic, many Muslims use different sorts of protective and therapeutic methods, in which the use of amulets plays an important role. In times past the most varied sorts of amulets (*higab*) were used, a sort of metal box (*bait ma'din*) with little fish, bells, eyes and so on dangling from it, made of material or claws and written amulets sewn into little leather bags (*bait higab*), often worn around the neck or worn under the armpits, sewn into material. These days the amulets are generally worn around the neck and are equipped with religious inscriptions to which magical powers are ascribed (Sengers 1994). The application of amulets originally came from ancient oriental or Jewish-Christian customs and only later became part of Islamic culture (Budge 1961). The Islamic character of the amulet inscriptions is manifest in the *du'a*. A *du'a* is a standard formula (petition) for calling upon God or the Prophet for protection in time of fear. Well-known *du'as* that are used prophylactically are *astaghfar Allah* (I seek my refuge in God), *hasha-llah* (God protect) and *ma sha-llah* (exclamation against the evil eye). People are convinced that human happiness is at the mercy of the almighty power of God. One may turn only to him for protection because he alone possesses power.

The permitted way and the prohibited way according to Islam

Dols (1992: 272) writes that the historian Hajji Khalifa (seventeenth century) made a distinction between exorcism (*'aza'im*) and sorcery or sympathetic magic (*ruqya*). *Aza'im* is supposed to be derived from the word *al-'azm*, which means steadfastness/resolve. Hans Wehr's dictionary of modern written Arabic notes that the root of *'azama* means "to decide", "to invite" and "to enchant". So it would be a command with a clear intent that is binding on the other person. When an exorcist (*mu'azzim*) says *'azamtu 'alayka* (I order you) to a *jinn*, then he compels the *jinn* to obedience, subordination and submissiveness. *Ruqya's* are magic spells, but in the case of Koran healing they are extended recitations of special verses from the Koran which offer protection against *jinn*, *'afarit*, sorcery/magic or the evil eye.

The same distinction is still made, but the dividing line between sorcerer and exorcist (demon-expeller) is not sharply drawn. Why is one a sorcerer and the other an exorcist, while in both cases it is a matter of conjuration? The difference lies in the personal relationship with the demons. A magician/sorcerer (*as-sahir*) I had a conversation with (and others confirmed this) told me that he has power over the *jinn* and the other spirits (*arwah*) because he made a contract with them. He said he could call up the demons and use them whenever he wanted. Demons are the lackeys and servants of the magician/sorcerer. They help him in the practice of his work (magic). Nothing is more abhorrent than this, writes the "demon expert" Mohammed Mahmoud abd al-Allah, mentioned above, because the devils, demons and spirits take pleasure precisely in doing what God has forbidden. And it is also said of sorcerers that since they consort with demons, they themselves are bad and oppose the will of God. Sorcerers apparently do not say their prayers, do not fast, slaughter animals in a prohibited way, and so on.

Exorcists/Koran healers (*al-mu'azzimin/mu'aligin*) on the other hand say that they have power over *jinn* and other spirits, not because of their personal relationship with the *jinn*, but because Allah has given them the power on account of their piety. They claim to keep to the holy laws and they know the Koran by heart. The exorcist/Koran healer heals by calling upon God's name and by reciting his words, which are written in the Holy Koran. The Koran healer therefore calls himself an "instrument" of Allah's power (personal communication, Abu Salim 1996 Cairo). The Koran healer always begins with calling upon God and after that orders the *jinn* to leave the body of the possessed person. This is indeed what happened in all the healing sessions I attended.

The most important criterion is whether magic is carried out in the name of *asyad/jinn* (demons) or in the name of God. From this point of view the magician/sorcerer (and thus also the *zar* leader) heals in a "not-permitted way" (*al tariqa al-madhmuma*) and the Koran healer in a "permitted way" (*al tariqa al-mahmuda*). The Koran healer enjoys a certain degree of respect or at least is tolerated because he practises magic in the name of God. The sorcerer, Koran healer and *zar* leader are specialized in healing the same sicknesses, which are caused by supernatural beings.

Aspects of Islamic methods of healing

The Koran, jinn, possession and healing

Belief in demon possession (and therefore madness/mental illness) is mentioned in the Koran, in suras *al-An'am* (6): 71; *al-Mu'minun* (23): 25; *Saba'* (34): 8, 46 and elsewhere.[15] Mohammed is not, however, named as an exorcist/expeller of demons. Nor is he said to be as a healer of the sick or someone with supernatural powers. Stories and

---

[15] Mohammed's opponents accused him of being possessed (*majnun*) by *jinn* and that the revelation could be nothing other than *sihr* (sorcery/magic). His supporters emphasized on the other hand that the Revelation had been given through the angel Gabriel and that they had nothing to do with demons because they would not be able to convey divine messages. The Koran also says that the *jinn* that had heard Mohammed reciting the Koran became believers as a result (*al-Ahqaf* [46]: 29-32 and *al-Jinn* [72]: 1). The term *majnun* had a double meaning. It could refer both to possession that was the work of bad jinn, and also to a special state of mind instilled by God, in the sense of a supernatural wisdom or gift: someone with insight or knowledge that passed ordinary people by, or someone who was mentally ill. Nowadays *majnun* is more often used in the sense of mad/crazy than in the sense of being possessed or of being in a special state of mind. But today too, the context in which someone is called *majnun* is of importance in evaluating the right meaning.

traditions about the Prophet in connection with exorcism and healing came into being only later.[16] The presentation of *jinn* in the Koran in relation to illnesses is unclear. "Healing" (*shifa'*) is mentioned six times: twice in the sense that the Koran itself is healing, twice with a more or less spiritual meaning, once in a reference to honey "in which there is healing for humans", and once in a reference to the God of Abraham who heals the believer when he is sick. These Koran verses are still used today in prayers for healing and in "magic formulas".[17]

Despite the fact that the Prophet is not mentioned as a healer, many indications in the field of medicine are ascribed to him, which were not only included in traditional collections (*hadith*) but which also formed the basis for many pseudo-medical texts. In the Middle Ages in particular the concept of *jinn* and magic was elaborated in relation to illness. Many manuals were written with references to the Prophet ("what did Mohammed do in such a case"). Commentary is given and pointers are given as to how to prepare amulets and talismans. The books of *Ibn al-Qayyim*, *As-Suyuti*, *Ash-Shafi'i* and *Al-Azraq* belong to this genre.[18] All four have written about *tibb an-nabi* (literally: "medicine of the Prophet", also called *tibb nabawi*. Following other scholars, from now on I shall call this "prophetic medicine"). It is primarily the first of those mentioned, Ibn al-Qayyim (born in Damascus in 1292, died in 1350), who is repeatedly quoted today (by *al-Azhar* scholars too) when it is a matter of *mass*, *lams* and *labs* (respectively "touching" and "possession" by demons). This Hanbalitic theologian, legal advisor

---

[16] According to Dols (1992: 9-10, 115), Muslims are the "heirs" of a rich Christian and Jewish tradition in the area of spiritual healing and exorcism. From the Middle Ages onwards Muslims began to regard the Prophet as a person with miraculous powers. There then followed holy men who by virtue of their special position with God could bring healing and perform miracles (see also Elgood 1962; Kriss & Kriss-Heinrich 1960: 6-10; they call the veneration of saints "a creation of popular religion").

[17] Respectively: suras *al-Isra'* (17): 82 and *Fussilat* (41): 44; *al Tauba* (9): 14 and *Yunus* (10): 57; *al-Nahl* (16): 69; *al-Shu'ara'* (26): 80.

[18] Shams ad-Din Abu Bakr Muhammad b. Abi Bakr Az-Zar'i *Ibn Qayyim* al-Jawziyya (Hanbalitic theologian and juridical advisor and student of the famous scholar Ibn Taymiyya); Abu al-Fadl 'Abd ar-Rahman b. Abi Bakr b. Muhammad Jalal ad-Din *as-Suyuti* al-Khudayri ash-Shafi'i (born in Cairo to parents of Persian origin): Abu 'Abd Allah Muhammad b. Ahmad Shams ad-Din ad-Dahabi at-Turkomani al-Fariqi *ash-Shafi'i* (*hadith* scholar who studied in Cairo but worked in his birthplace, Damascus); Ibrahim b. 'Abd ar-Rahman b. Abi Bakr *al-Azraqi* (student of al-Sanawbari and al-Kirmani). Elgood (1962: 40-50) gives an overview of the literature concerning prophetic medicine.

and doctor was of the opinion that most illnesses that afflict humans are caused by *jinn* and that Koran verses are more important in the healing of sickness than (secular) medical principles. He found the suras *al-Falaq* (113), *al-Nas* (114), the *Fatiha* (the Opening sura) and the *Ayat al-Kursi* (the Throne verse *al-Baqara* [2]: 255) very important. He also advises having the sick person drink water in which these verses have been "washed" (dissolved) for healing. In addition he notes formulas that promote healing and protection, such as: "I seek my refuge in the sight of the mighty God", "I seek my refuge in his perfect words, which no pious person and no sinner can pass by", and "I seek refuge, away from the evil that he has created." The book written by ibn al-Qayyim (*At-tibb an-nabawi*) is a textbook example of "prophetic medicine". I shall first describe the origin of this kind of medicine and then discuss this doctor's ideas.

The development of medicine in Islam

Three developments have been important in the Islamic world in reference to medicine: Arabian-Islamic medicine, prophetic medicine and sufism. Before the coming of Islam many illnesses were ascribed to supernatural causes. Their treatment occurred largely through the conjuration of the evil forces and the use of honey and medications based on herbs. After the coming of Islam, Koran and *hadith* became important in the treatment of illness.

Under the Umayyads (an Islamic dynasty that emerged in 660 in Damascus), medicine was primarily in the hands of Jewish and Christian practitioners. It was a secular, medical-empirical science in which the body stood in central position in relation to its surroundings. Two things were important in this regard. The first, the maintenance of balance in the body and in the universe (*tawhid*): by nature, the human being exists in a state of balance, harmony, health and happiness. He or she must strive to sustain this state. The second is the originally Greek theory of elements. This is a cosmological doctrine in which energy plays a very important role. The starting-points are fire, water, air and earth, with the corresponding attributes: heat, cold, moisture and dryness. The universe is constructed from these elements and in the body too these fluids can be recognized. The work of the Greek doctor Galen (131-200), which is based on the theory of elements, was very well known. This doctor/scholar can be called the founder of medicine of the humours (Arabic: *tibb al-mizaj*). According to Galen the human body consists of a combination of four body-fluids: black and yellow bile, mucous and blood, each with its own inherent qualities which need to be in balance with each other. When there is a good balance between these body-fluids a person enjoys optimum health and when the balance is disturbed illness ensues. In the diagnosis of illnesses an examination is made to see whether the *mizaj* (temperament, physical disposition, state of mind, energy tracks) is sufficiently in balance. If this is not the case, or if one of the qualities of heat, cold, moisture and dryness dominates, then illness may be the consequence. In order to maintain a state of good health one must take care to achieve a balanced relationship between spiritual, mental, emotional and social factors. A proper pattern of diet, rest and relaxation and ecological factors also exercise great influence.[19]

In Arab-Islamic medicine, the following illnesses are distinguished: first, functional illnesses that manifest themselves through disturbances in the *mizaj*, and structural illnesses in the organs (stomach, liver, kidneys, bones etc.). Second, psychological illnesses (anxiety, hysteria, paranoia) and disturbance of consciousness and mental functions (e.g. schizophrenia, madness, mental illness). Strong emotions such as joy, sorrow, fear, anger etc. were also acknowledged to have influence on the body. Third, illnesses with a "spiritual" background caused by supernatural forces, expressing themselves in disturbances of various mental and physical functions.

For the treatment of functional and structural illnesses a restoration of the balance in the *mizaj* was sought, honey and herb-based medicines were used, and surgical operations such as bloodletting, the compressing of bloodvessels, burning and cupping (preheated glass bulbs were placed on the body in order to "draw out" the illness).

For the treatment of psychological and psychiatric problems, a "shock therapy" was known, which awakened intense reactions of shock. Besides this, herbs were used (and, in some cases, wine) to calm the spirit, as well as prayer and recitation of the Koran.

So-called "prophetic medicine" (*tibb nabawi*) built upon guidelines from the Koran and traditions of the Prophet Mohammed.

In the Koran, sura *al-Isra'* (17): 82, we read "And We reveal of the Quran that which is a healing and a mercy to the believers." From this sacred text it is clear that God is the first and most important

---

[19] The medical insights of Galen were extremely influential in Egypt from the Middle Ages onwards; see Dols 1984.

source of all physical and mental health; doctors, medicines and domestic remedies come only after that. As I have already pointed out, in the Koran itself little is said about healing or medicines. According to Dols (1992: 243-246) the *hadiths* contain more tangible material on the subject. These are generally accepted traditions of the doings of the Prophet, which exercise a great deal of influence on the life of Muslims. He claims that prophetic medicine consists largely of a collection of *hadiths* which relate not so much to what the Prophet used to do with regard to illness, but to later Muslim lawyers' views on health and illness. These people applied Galen's foundations in their own commentaries on the *hadiths*. The goal in this was to give Muslims values and a code of behaviour in relation to their physical wellbeing as well as rules for daily life that were based on the example, the life and the sayings of the Prophet. The emphasis lay in general on the maintenance of health by means of a regulated life, a moderate diet and the avoidance of sources of sickness and injury. Besides the fact that prophetic medicine expressed a number of theological views in a simple way, which had an influence on the thinking and behaviour of pious Muslims, indigenous practices and (religious) views also come into their own. According to Dols prophetic medicine consists of three elements: popular medicines from the Arabian Bedouin, Galenian views about humoral pathology, temperament and characteristics, and the overarching principle of divine causation.

In the approach to illness two currents may be distinguished. First, the current which distinguishes "natural" causes of illness. Reference is made here to advice and exhortations of the Prophet to use honey and herbs (which were created by Allah) in medical treatment. Second, the current which pointed to "supernatural" causes of illness, such as magic, the evil eye and the actions of malevolent *jinn*. In this current a distinction is made between the treatment of physical illnesses and that of illnesses that have to do with the mind. "Illnesses of the mind" in turn are separated into spiritual illnesses caused by magic and malevolent jinn (fear, nostalgia, insomnia, a feeling of suffocating, palpitations, dizziness, haziness, speech disorders, absent-mindedness, spastic movements, cramps, hallucinations, etc.) and psychiatric (soul) illnesses (disturbance of consciousness and of mental functions). For the treatment of spiritual illness the use of a religious therapy was advised (amulets, conjurations, prayers and the recitation of the Koran). Under the influence of sufism, gradually the veneration of saints and healing through prayer were added. Psychiatric illnesses needed to be treated with therapeutic herbs, rest, prayers and a great trust in God.

In sufism emphasis is placed on esoteric aspects. The concern is with inner experience and a striving to come to a state of union with God. Popular forms of sufism are occupied with the "undoing" of magic. In the *dhikr* (the singing repetition of the pure beautiful names), alternating with Koran recitations and the singing of *anashid* (songs), believers reach a state of *hal* (ecstasy). Through the *baraka* (healing power: the opposite of the evil power and mischief of *bas*) of the protecting saint, who is also the founder of the order, a sick person can recover from his ailments.

Gradually a conflict emerged between the principles of scientific medicine and those of religion. This came about, Dols writes, both through a denial of natural cause and effect and through the fact that professional medicine was practised primarily by non-Muslims and had strong ties to Greek philosophy. Proponents of prophetic medicine regarded this science as "divinely revealed" and the secular empirical direction as inferior because it was not based on the Koran or *hadith*. Since God is the ultimate creator of everything, including medicines, theologian, sufi and doctor could often find common ground. The guidelines taken from the Koran and the *hadith* ultimately gained precedence above secular medicine. Prophetic medicine became an integral part of Islam and a speciality of Koran teachers; the secular direction was driven into the universities and hospitals. Both medical traditions have never operated in complete independence of each other, but have always overlapped. Both know a written tradition, which made possible an exchange and adoption of knowledge (Abdus Sattar 1980, 1982; Dols n.d., 1992; Hoffer 1994, 1995; Shadid & Van Koningsveld 1983).

Illness and healing through the eyes of Ibn al-Qayyim

I am giving more detailed attention to the views of ibn al-Qayyim than to those of his contemporaries because the premises and treatment methods of modern present-day Koran healers, which I discuss in Chapter 5, are based on them. The most famous books by this doctor/theologian/lawyer are *Shifa' al-'ali fi l-qada'wa l-hikma wa t-ta'lil* ("The healing of the sick: on [God's] disposition, wisdom and justice"), *Ad-da' wa-dawa'* ("Sickness and healing"), *Tibb al-qulub* ("Medicine of the hearts") and *at-Tibb an-nabawi'* ("Prophetic medicine").

The last-named book is still used as a reference work and for guidelines, although in practice these days Koran healers lay greater
emphasis on the causation of illness by *jinn* (though through transgression of the divine commandments) than through divine causation.
God is, however, the "Great Healer" (see also Laoust 1971). For a
discussion of the premises of ibn al-Qayyim I studied an edition of his
book *At-tibb an-nabawi*, published in Cairo in 1926.[20] A few pages from
this in translation from the Arabic follow in summary form:

> Magic is described by ibn al-Qayyim as a mixture of influences of bad
> spirits and a reaction to this by nature. The best remedy for magic is
> the word of God. So he recommends calling upon God, the recitation
> of Koran verses and the saying of prayers as a counter attack against
> the magic spells of bad spirits. The more often this is done the more
> effective the treatment. Ibn al-Qayim compares this procedure with
> two armies entering the field of battle. Both want to win the day, but in
> the end it is the stronger (the good spirit) that wins over the weaker
> (bad spirit). So, if the heart of a person is full of love for God and of
> trust in him, worships him and calls upon him in prayer, then he will
> win the battles against evil. Trust in God and calling on him can be
> regarded as preventative measures to protect the pious person against
> magic formulas. Magicians, says ibn al-Qayyim, know very well that
> their magic formulas will hit weak, atheistic and sensual souls. It is
> therefore primarily women, young people, the illiterate and Bedouin
> who are affected by them. The magic spells also affect people who
> have inadequate knowledge of their religion, insufficient confidence in
> God, or who do not believe in the Almighty One. Magic also affects
> those who do not protect themselves by *al-wird* (that is private recita-
> tion — besides the five prescribed and compulsory prayers — of par-
> ticular parts of the Koran, at specific times of the day and night), or
> who are unprotected because they do not use the prayers and *at-ta'wiz-*
> *at* of the Prophet (petitions calling for God's help). Magic affects weak
> and easily influenced hearts that have a tendency to *as-suffliyat*
> (low/common spirits or low/bad acts). Ibn al-Qayyim notes a special
> prayer (1926: 136), recommended by the Prophet, who said that when
> a Muslim is suffering from an illness or when he hears of the complaint
> of another Muslim he must be encouraged to say: "O God in heaven,
> your name is holy and your commandments in heaven and on earth.
> Since your grace is victorious in heaven, give us your grace on earth
> too. Forgive us our faults and sins. Thou art benevolent and gracious.
> Give us your divine grace and heal us from this sickness, *bi idhn Allah*
> (with God's will)."

In the treatment and healing of illness ibn al-Qayyim looks at

---

[20] See also *Kitab at-tibb an-nabawi*, Aleppo 1334, published in Cairo in 1927.

Koran verses and *hadiths*, which are more important for him than medical principles. The use of medicines must above all be in accordance
with the divine law.

Ibn al-Qayyim is an "advocate" of exorcism par excellence, since he
saw with his own eyes how well it works. His premise is that bad *jinn*
can make people sick since they do not enjoy protection through lack
of true belief. *Jinn* can gain great influence over a person, which can
drive him to madness. The only appropriate treatment against it is a
spiritual one in the form of exorcism: one must let the good spirits fight
against the evil ones.

Since the sick person is "possessed", in the treatment the spiritual
state of the patient and the healer must be paramount. The sick person
must possess a great deal of trust in God and the healer needs to have a
pure heart, which equips him to heal the sick simply by saying "go out
of him" or "in the name of God". Sometimes the healer/exorcist
speaks with *jinn* himself, who then tells him who he is and why he has
entered into the person. If the *jinn* is recalcitrant and refuses to leave
the body, it is recommended that he be driven out by beating.

In Egypt the existence of demons is acknowledged by the dominant
Islamic ideology, but interaction with these beings is condemned. Elements of belief and practices that are not an official part of orthodoxy
are ascribed to local traditions from pre-Islamic times and dismissed
as heresy and unbelief. But in everyday practice the popular views of
supernatural beings are very varied and extensive. In dealing with the
work of modern professional commercial Koran healers we may say
that their views on sickness and healing connect with principles from
prophetic medicine and with those of ibn al-Qayyim.

CHAPTER THREE

ANTHROPOLOGICAL APPROACHES TO POSSESSION AND HEALING

Possession is a universal phenomenon, which takes different forms in different cultural contexts and is variously interpreted. My research is oriented specifically to Egypt and in the first chapter I explained how people in this culture speak of "touching" and "clothing". By this a mental or physical condition is meant which is paraphrased in anthropological literature as "possession". I showed that in most cases of possession the person concerned is an individual who behaves in a way different from the usual. The explanation for this is that spirits have invaded the person's body and are directing his or her actions. In much ethnographic work it is noticeable that women have to do with possession more frequently than men. In anthropological studies, explanations for this generally refer to the individual and socially unfavourable position of women in society, their economic dependency and political powerlessness, cultural customs and views of women, and the psychological reactions of women to all this. Invariably these studies come to the conclusion that in particular for women in socially subordinate positions, possession forms a "therapeutic escape valve". I investigated how possession is interpreted in Egypt. I looked into two healing methods for demonic possession, namely: the *zar* cult and a modern contemporary form of Koran healing called *'ilaj bil-qur'an*. I aim to show grounds for the symbolic constructions that go together with possession and healing and to make its "strangeness" less strange. By way of introduction to the subject I shall now discuss the insights of a number of scholars who have studied possession and healing. The purpose of this is to show in what direction a large section of research into possession and healing has moved.

Research into possession

In particular the *functionalist* approach by the anthropologist *Lewis* (1971) has long been used as a plumb-line for the study of possession, mediumship and trance in various cultures.[1] Taking a social line of

approach, Lewis assumes that possession has a function for the affected person and for the society. He distinguishes two sorts of possession.
First: *central* possession, which has a social function, because it maintains the official morality, religious traditions and the power of the
establishment. This sort of possession is regarded as ritual possession,
which is voluntary and temporary. It occurs in the context of religious
ceremonies and is ascribed to the power of sympathetic spirits. Second: *peripheral* possession, which is not supported by a moral code and
is typically experienced by people on the margins of society. This sort
of possession is often experienced as involuntary and unwelcome.
Lewis says of this that it is a "culturally bound mechanism" that has
as its function to cope with personal suffering, neurosis, emotional
stress and conflict. Lewis's approach analyzes the categories to which
individuals belong that are affected by this and the circumstances in
which it occurs. The cause of the great spread of the possession syndrome among women he ascribes to their weak social position and
their subjection to men. Possession can be regarded as resistance to
this subjection. It is only when a woman has conquered a position
that offers more security and safety that the condition of possession
disappears. Viewed in this way, possession is a spiritual interpretation
of women's problems: it explains illness and is an indirect way of gaining the rights one desires. The dynamic process can, moreover, be
"profitable" in the sense of gaining escape from an unpleasant situation, fantasized wish-fulfilment, reduction of guilt feeling, shifting of
responsibility and manipulation of others. To a certain extent possession thus helps to protect and defend the interests of the socially
weaker.

Many other researchers have followed Lewis's lead and have
attempted to add to his ideas. This applies to *Ward* (1989), who studies behaviour and experience as they occur in different cultures from
the perspective of the transcultural psychologist, and compares them
with each other. She talks of *ritual possession* which is voluntary,
reversible and of short duration and is supported and encouraged by
particular cultural views. It is occasioned in the course of ritual ceremonies and has no connection with cultural notions regarding illness.

---

[1] The functionalist approach goes back to the French sociologist Émile Durkheim
(1858-1917). A "functionalist" premise creates a particular interpretation of the social
reality in which the emphasis lies on social structure, the institutional order and the
tensions and antitheses within (Baal 1971: 109-125).

Over against this stands *peripheral possession*, which is involuntary and can be of long duration. This sort of possession is evaluated negatively in the culture and in general is brought about by stress to which the individual is subjected. There is a pathological reaction, i.e. physical and mental illnesses, for which the possessed person seeks support and healing. Like Lewis, Ward is of the opinion that possession is ideal for coping with a crisis. By concentrating the attention of the individual and his or her surroundings on the possession and the somatic problems, the primary cause, the emotional conflict, is largely left out of consideration. Possession reduces the guilt feeling because the guilt is projected on to the invading demon and it gives the opportunity to manipulate others in order to gain more attention and affection for oneself. The "cure" consists in purifying the body of the evil powers (exorcism). Exorcism and psychotherapy, according to Ward, have many things in common because in both methods the effectiveness rests in large part on the placebo effect. The therapeutic results are influenced by social and psychological factors and processes, such as attention, perception, belief, expectation and motivation.[2]

The anthropologist *Shekar* (1989), similarly, claims to extend Lewis's classification and speaks of: *complete possession, partial possession* and *histrionic possession* (deliberate theatrical display of emotions in order to achieve a particular goal or effect). He gives three explanations for the phenomenon of possession and the psychopathology that goes with it. First, the "dissociation theory" in which possession is explained as the reliving of repressed conflicts and desires which swamp the ego of the individual, which produces dissociation.[3] Unusual actions (such as scolding one's mother in law, for instance) are thought to be occasioned by the possessing element (the demon) and not by the individual. One can speak of primary gain through the alleviation of intrapsychological tension and secondary gain in the form of attention and sympathy. Second, the "communication theory", in which possession is regarded as an alarm signal in order to communicate with others. In an effort to attract the care and attention of others, the possessed person takes on himself or herself the

---

[2] This is not in agreement with the thinking of psychotherapists. The aim of exorcism is expulsion; the aim of therapeutic treatment is change. In present research into the effectiveness of psychotherapy it seems that this method of treatment does indeed have an effect. There are discussions about what precisely are the variables that bring this about.

[3] Shekar uses the term "dissociation" in a different way than in psychopathology.

"sick person's role". In such cases there are generally psychological factors already at work. Third, the "sociocultural theory", in which possession is a culturally sanctioned and institutionalized phenomenon. One thinks for instance of such phenomena as voodoo ceremonies in Haiti, where children are acquainted with possession from an early age and grow up in the expectation that they will themselves have something to do with it. In my view Ward and Shekar are indeed adding a number of other names, but in fact in the main they support Lewis's approach.

Of the researchers who oppose Lewis's approach completely or in part, I would mention *Lambek* (1981, 1989, 1993). This researcher himself claims to proceed from a cultural perspective, since this gives him more analytical room. He criticizes Lewis because he orients himself too much by social conflicts and psychological causes and functions. He disagrees with Lewis's view that the behaviour of possessed women can be understood as a "resistance to the established order". According to him, it probably has more to do with reconciliation with the social facts. By objectifying the immoral qualities of the demons, one can even speak of legitimation and continuation of the social order. Nor does he agree with Lewis's description of trance and possession independently of each other. Both are the product of underlying social relations and cannot be divorced from them. Nor may trance be viewed as a more or less direct manifestation of illness with possession as the social label. It is indeed the case that in many cases trance is linked with sickness, but sickness is not the only thing that can be expressed in trance. Moreover, not all sick people within the same society go into trance and not all people in trance are in a pathological condition. Possession, according to Lambek, stands for a whole range of social complexes, of which trance is simply a part.

Obeyesekere (1977) is occupied with psychocultural exegesis. This is a psychoanalytical orientation in which the personal and psychological experiences of the possessed person and the social-cultural world in which he or she lives are linked together.[4] He thinks that in possession the conditions are culturally structured. This applies to the ecstatic attack, the situation in which this occurs, the visions which the patient experiences and the exorcism that follows. They have a standard form

---

[4] Psychocultural exegesis aims to make understandable the sociocultural context in which possession occurs as well as the way in which personal experience of possession is expressed within a series of standardized cultural meanings.

and a coherent meaning, which are interpretable for society. Obeyesekere looks into the way in which that standard ritual is related to the
patient and how the exorcist and the patient use the ritual to deal with
a specific case of possession. Although the form of ecstatic experience
can be publicly interpreted, this does not apply to the experience itself.
Possession is an absolutely personal experience not shared by the
group. Possession is therefore radically different from psychotic
expression or fantasy because they are "ego-alien" and "culture-alien",
that is, they have no ties to the cultural reality. Possession is indeed an
ego-alien experience, but not a culture-alien one.[5] A successful exorcism (the "cure") leads to the harmonization of an originally traumatic
experience with both ego and culture. Possession does not have rebellion in view, as Lewis says, but precisely integration.

Pattison (1977) works with a psychosocial interpretation. He too
does not agree with Lewis's approach to possession. He does not
mean to say that possession could not be a "defensive-adaptive psychological manoeuvre", but it is not taken to be so from the point of
view of culture. According to Pattison, demon-possession is merely a
subtype of the many concepts in which people and demons are taken
up and there is a connection with specific socio-cultural environments. Possession that suddenly breaks out on a grand scale goes
together, in his view, with social situations. An oppressive social structure, a loss of confidence in the functionality of social institutions and
an apparent incapacity to deal with the "evils" of the social structure
can lead to large groups of people succumbing to possession at the
same time. He rejects Freud's classic psychological formulation that
demons are repressed desires, because this reduces possession to individual neurosis. His view is that western psychiatrists should enter
into cooperative relationships with indigenous healers. Each one can
stay on his own terrain, but refer when necessary. There may be cases
of syncretism, in which indigenous healers are employed by psychiatric medicine. There would then be cases of functional fusion
between two worlds that have no logical links with each other and the
possibility arises of looking at possession from both a western psycho-
dynamic perspective and from the cultural perspective of the indigenous healer and the patients.

---

[5] The psychotic person takes his or her actions for granted, but the social environment does not. The actions of the possessed person move outside his or her control,
but the social environment "recognizes" the situation.

Commentary

My attention is directed especially to what Lewis (1971) calls *peripheral* possession, namely involuntary possession caused by demons. According to this scholar this type of possession comprises a culture-bound mechanism that makes it possible to cope with trauma and neurosis. In my opinion such a term as "functionality" of possession is not entirely satisfactory. I was struck time and again in my observations by the intense physical experience of music and dance or of the Koran recitation, and the "liberation" that followed. Possession is not just a "demon story"; it is a statement about the patient and her social surroundings that cannot be dismissed as an "emotional safety-valve". The questions that continued to occupy me were: what is being expressed by possession, what do the rituals do for the possessed person, and what brings about "healing"? In the work of Devisch (1985), who studied healing cults in Zaïre, I find a number of points of connection. This researcher's attention is focused on physical experience, group, cosmos and society. By unraveling the means and processes in the healing practices he comes to the conclusion that the ritual drama goes past verbal discourse and conceptual representation. This connects with my view that "touching" and "clothing" (possession) and experience during the rituals of *zar* and Koran healing are a combination of symbolism, drama and therapy: all three aspects require research.

In order to indicate how my further research developed to interpret and describe perceptions in a satisfactory way, I shall now discuss a number of investigations carried out specifically into the *zar* cult in Sudan and Egypt. The insights from these studies offer me only in part an explanation for the phenomena of possession and leave a number of things unexplained. Through discussion and commentary on the studies the reader will, however, gain a better view of the many facets of demon-possession and the significance of the *zar* ritual.

Zar *research*

Research into zar ceremonies in Sudan

Lewis studied the *zar* in Sudan (1986). He writes that *zar* is in origin more an urban than a rural phenomenon, and is practised more by rich than by poor women. This was originally the case in Egypt too, but nowadays it attracts more poor women than rich.

In Sudan the *zar* is closely related to the meetings of mystical sufi movements attended by men (see also Böhringer-Thärigen 1996). The meetings begin and end with praises to the Prophet. Many Islamic saints occur in the pantheon. This too is similar to what happens in Egypt and although music and dance in the *dhikr* (ritual dance of the sufi's) differ in style and tempo, the state of ecstasy attained by men (and women) invites comparison with the *zar*. But despite the fact that sufi meetings in contemporary Egypt are not popular with the orthodox and fundamentalists, they are not as strictly condemned as the *zar* meetings, which are supposed to be attended only by "retarded and superstitious women" who have made a pact with the devil. Concerning *zar* rituals Lewis says that they are often described as "exorcism", but that this is in fact an inappropriate term since the treatment often involves periodically repeated rituals and actually belongs with specialized cults. He therefore prefers to speak of "conversion". I myself make a distinction between the rituals of the *zar*, which I call "pacification", precisely on account of the periodically repetitive character of the spirits, and the rituals of Koran healing, which I call "exorcism", because the goal here is that the demons will never return.

Boddy worked in Sudan, where among other things she studied possession and *zar* rituals (1988, 1989). She takes a psychologically oriented approach and says she wants to avoid describing the phenomenon of possession in a way that is accessible to our (western) culture but not to her research group. By explaining things in "functional" terms she would also pass over too much the role the spirits play in the everyday life of her informants. She herself lays emphasis on the "articulating potential" of possession and has exposed the fact that women deduce signals and messages from their own possession, whereby conventional meanings of gender are challenged and other ideas are developed. She presents three proposals. First, *zar* is not a female subculture, because that would mean that the broader culture is monolithic and structurally excludes women. Second, *zar* is not only just instrumental, for this would ignore the richness and deeper significance of the cult. Third, *zar* is a female answer to the practices and privileges of men that proceed from the ideology of the local form of Islam (1989: 6-10). Through the dramatic evocation of the demons, interhuman conflicts can be reformulated and "negotiations" can take place about them. Through exposing vagueness, by reordering meanings and commentating, *zar* becomes a refuge situated at a distance from the everyday world. In her opinion possession has to do with fundamental questions about the personal I (see also Crapanzano 1973; Nelson 1971). For her research field the decisive factor in possession is the capacity for reproduction. A woman's ability to bear children is the most important thing in her life. Her self-image, her own value and social values rest on it. But women cannot always match up to the ideal woman's role and if no children arrive after the course of time, this leads to tensions which in turn lead to sickness because *jinn* have the chance to invade the body. The woman has become possessed. The "cure" in the *zar* sets communication in motion between her and her spirit, which makes it possible for problems to be discussed. The healing powers are not so much borrowed from the trance experience but rather from the whole context of possession. In the context of the *zar*, possession is regarded as irreversible. If someone acknowledges that they are possessed, this means that she must keep on the right side of the responsible spirit(s) for the rest of her life. This also means that she herself is not considered responsible for the fact that she does not match up to the cultural female ideal, but that the blame for this lies with external factors over which she has no control.

Boddy sees direct points of contact between circumcision and fertility and possession and *zar*-attendance. Böhringer-Thärigen (1996), who also works in Sudan, writes, however, that the *zar* goes further than this. *Zar* is the most important element in Sudanese women's culture and therefore has relevance to all facets of a woman's life.

This is not the case in present-day Egypt. That *jinn* exist is a generally acknowledged fact, but far from everyone believes that these beings can cause illness and even less that one needs to attend a *zar* ceremony in order to be healed of one. In Egypt women are circumcised (this is now forbidden by law: *The Post*, 30 December 1997), but in my experience connections have never been drawn between circumcision, fertility and attendance at the *zar*. Circumcision is indeed connected with the "the nice-and-smoothness of the female sex", in order to maintain a girl's chastity and as a necessary preparation for marriage (Ammar 1954; Assad 1980; Blackman 1927). In Egypt it is equally important for married women that they bear children. Nowadays people generally think of physical causes in relation to infertility and people seek biomedical help. But the actions of human adversaries who "cast the evil eye" and the interference of supernatural beings can also prevent conception (Inhorn 1994; Sengers 1994). If something of this sort is suspected, the help of a traditional healer is called in and one sometimes ends up at the *zar* specialist. However, by contrast with Sudan, the *zar* in Egypt is primarily meant for the healing of psychological problems, which does not exclude the possibility that the problems may have their causes in infertility and/or social situations.

After the private *zar* the woman is admitted to a cult group and she attends the weekly *hadra* (meeting at which possessed people dance with their demon). According to Bourguignon (1973) in such a group women can receive much support and understanding and thus gain a better understanding of themselves and the society around them. These last comments are in line with Turner (1967, 1969, 1974). I shall return to this in the description of my own research strategy.

Taken as a whole, Boddy's work shows that the *zar* provides a standardized and acceptable form of expression for the individual that is under pressure from various forms of stress, in particular stress caused by infertility. Boddy's view is that the *zar* is a legitimate psychotherapy; indeed she goes further, calling it a "potentially insightful reflection".

Cloudsley describes the *zar* in Omdurman, Sudan, as she experienced it a number of times. Demon-possession is regarded here as sickness. Included in this category are depression and infertility, but also organic and psychological disorders. *Zar* is the name of the ceremony that is held to pacify the spirits that have "clothed" a woman. The possessed person herself is regarded as the slave of the demon, who sets requirements and must be obeyed. The spirits who strike without taking account of the moral character of their victims are regarded in Omdurman as amoral and fickle. That is to say that women who are affected by a demon are not responsible for it themselves and do not pay the costs of the ceremony either (the husband or the family pays for it). The responsibility rests entirely with the demons.

This researcher writes that the demons may be called peripheral in more than one way. First, because they do not keep to the moral code of the society. Second, because most come from neighbouring tribes or villages (but in Omdurman there are also European, English and other "foreign" or "outside" spirits. See also Böhringer-Thärigen 1996). Third, because the women themselves also occupy a peripheral position in society.

In Omdurman the *zar* is socially accepted. It is organized by women who can afford it financially. Women who cannot, or who do not get permission for it from their husbands, attend the ceremonies as "spectators". By attending another woman's ceremony they find relief from their depression, their monotonous life and their subordinate position in the family. For many others the *zar* means a party (see also Saunders 1977). They wear their best clothes and adorn themselves with their jewelry. Possessed women sometimes behave like men during the *zar*, and then also wear men's clothing. This suggests, according to Cloudsley, that women envy men and bear a grudge because of their dominance. I myself have never encountered this in a *zar* ceremony, but would not rule it out because the demons may give an order for specific clothing to be worn and that could also be men's clothing.

In the *zar* the emphasis lies on misfortune and illness. Attention is placed on healing, not on the attainment of mystical transcendence. Consciously or unconsciously the *zar* is also used to give prominence to women's interests. Cloudsley says it is an interesting aspect that women use this strategy to reach goals by means of their adversity which they would not be able to attain by another, direct way.

It is striking that after making a sacrifice for someone during the *zar*, the *sheikha* (the female *zar* leader) enters into another relationship with the possessed person; a sort of blood-relationship ensues. These "children of the *sheikha*" are invited to join her when she organizes a *zar* outside their own neighbourhood. In Egypt it happens sometimes that some leaders gather a small group of supporters around them, but I have nowhere gained the impression that there is a connection here with sacrifice for these persons. Cloudsley is, like Nelson (1971) and Al-Khuly (1996), of the opinion that the *zar* offers women a chance to support each other psychologically and to build a broader circle of acquaintances and friends. She suggests that the *zar* may also reflect power structures and bring them about among women, but this was not (yet) confirmed by research. Cloudsley sees connections between the *zar* and sexuality. She believes that through circumcision, limited communication with the husband, concern about fertility, and so on, the pressure on women is very great and forms an obstacle to experiencing satisfying sexual intercourse. For some, the dance in the *zar* would then be a substitute for the normal sexual relationship that is lacking. Possibly these women feel themselves physically seduced, perhaps they even experience an orgasm. I have read stories of a sexual undertone in the *zar* in the work of several researchers (e.g. Kennedy, Al-Khuly and Nelson), but also from opponents (not participants) of the *zar*. In my view insufficient research has been done to be able to make a judgment on this. During my attendance at many sessions I have noticed no sexual excesses. Poor and rich women are afflicted by demons and for many social classes the *zar* is a necessary form of expression. The *zar* is on the one hand socially accepted, but on the other hand not welcomed by devout Muslims and the broader society, who regard it as a pagan ritual in which only women who are ignorant of Islam participate.

Research into zar ceremonies in Egypt

Morsy, who has studied popular illnesses in an Egyptian village, says (1978; 1993) that in Egypt there are two broad etiological categories, "natural" and "supernatural" illnesses (*marad gusmani* and *marad ruhani*). Non-localized pains in particular form a diagnostic indication that distinguishes supernatural illnesses from natural ones. Most illnesses are attributed to the fact that all harm is regulated by the supernatural world. Illnesses arise sometimes through the will of God (*amr Allah*) or as a punishment from God (*zanb Allah*); in most cases, however, through suffering or sorrow (*tar'a*) caused by a sudden shocking experience (Kapferer 1979: 199, who did research into demon-possession in Sri Lanka, also mentions a sudden shocking experience as a frequent trigger for possession). Demon-possession (called *'uzr* here) is also an important cause of sickness. It is occasioned by "supernatural staring" (*nazra ardiyya*) or by "human staring" (*nazra insaniyya*), by contact from beings who live under the earth and which are called *awlad ard*, by the evil eye (*hasad*) or by black magic (*'amal bil-marad*). Sometimes reference is made to "winds" (*aryah*) of supernatural beings that make contact with the individual.

In cases of demon-possession one or more demons has "touched" (*lams/mass*) the individual or has invaded the body and has "clothed" or "occupied" (*labs*) the patient. It is only after the spirits have been pacified (*sulha*) and after measures have been taken to improve the emotional and/or social situation of the patient that the affected person regains his or her health.

In her study, Morsy came to the conclusion that a great variety of ailments, from hair-loss to heart problems, are attributed to negative emotions, such as sadness, fear, quarrelling and anger. Thus, fear makes the body susceptible to serious illnesses, painful experiences "shake" the body, anger and sorrow "heat" the blood and excessive sexual intercourse causes prostate problems. Although '*uzr* occurs among men as well as women, in her research group the sick-person's role is assumed especially by young, recently married women in order to legitimate divergent behaviour and problems with adaptation to their new role in the in-law family, or in order to escape temporarily from this role. The healing rituals in which the victim and other important persons participate, are carried out in the presence of as many family members and friends as possible (a "supporters group" of family and friends is important; see also Boddy 1988; 1989; Kapferer 1979; 1983).

Although Morsy to some extent gives "functionalistic explanations", it is clear that she sees possession primarily as an indication of powerlessness, and she recommends studying *zar* in the framework of role models and expectations. It is not the gender role itself that is the cause of sickness, but the stressful situation that emerges through power differences, which may be related to sex, but also to differences in the positions of for instance two women within the same household (different gradations of power such as between the mother-in-law and the daughter-in-law). It may also be about the powerlessness of a young man in relation to his elder brother or father. It is thus a question of the differential accessibility both of material and of non-material sources of prestige and power.

Much of what she writes is recognizable to me (see Chapter 7 below). But I also see an important point of connection in the female body that has symbolically been "opened" by emotions and/or the transgression of taboos, which have "weakened" it and an important means of access has arisen for the illness-causing *jinn* (I describe this in Chapter 6). This weakening has everything to do with the consequences of unbalanced social relationship, the individual psyche and a state of disharmony with occult powers and the divine (see also: Most van Spijk 1982 a/b).

Fakhouri, who like Morsy describes the *zar* cult in an Egyptian village (1968, 1972), applies a "functionalist" approach, but his research does not produce any new insights. It is certainly interesting that he notes that during the ceremony malevolent spirits do not remain malevolent any longer, but through their wishes being met, they change into protective spirits. Morsy (1978) also calls the aspect protection and suggests that although the demons are the cause of illnesses, their actions are normally interpreted in terms of care for the wellbeing of the persons possessed by them. Neither Morsy nor Fakhoury elaborates this topic further. It happened during my research that a woman told me that the possessing spirit protected her against beating and abuse by her husband (this case is described in Chapter 7 below). The theme, "evil spirit changes into good spirit", or vice versa, reminds me also of the *qarina*, a demon mentioned in the Koran only as "companion" of each human being, but who in popular belief is both a good and an evil spirit and is mentioned by some *zar* leaders in connection with the *zar*. The *qarina* can help restore the balance and set priorities, but also through anger and jealousy it can cause harm and sickness. Sickness is then in fact a "warning" preceding the causing of death. The conversion of "evil to good" can also be found in the pacification of the demon. *Jinn*, a general term for non-specific demons, are also divided up according to characteristics. Good *jinn* are always male and *sufli*, lower (in rank) *jinn*, are both male and female (I never heard this from Muslims, but the Copts do generally call the *jinn sufli*).[6] Fakhouri and Morsy carried out their research in villages where perhaps other and older interpretations are adhered to than in the big city (Cairo) where I did my research.

Kennedy (1967, 1978) examines possession ceremonies among the Nubian section of the Egyptian population. He works with a functionalist/psychotherapeutic perspective that emphasizes the usability of the sick-person's role for women. Among the Nubians, the *zar* is intended to conjure demonic evil powers and to heal emotional disturbances and the physical evils emerging from them. The *zar* rituals certainly have to do with ritual impurity, but not with a moral condemnation (I found such a lack of a moral condemnation in each *zar* at which I was present. This is one of the most striking points of contrast with Koran healing). That is to say that behaviour that diverges from the cultural norms is blamed not on the person in question, but on the possessing spirit. Specific to the ceremony is that emotional factors are reinforced by belief and support from among the group of "spectators" and fellow possessed persons (the importance of group support is confirmed by all the researchers named above). The efficacy of *zar* is largely due, according to Kennedy, to the emotional

---

[6] See Wissa Wassef 1971, *Pratiques rituelles et alimentaires des Coptes*; Viaud 1978, *Magie et coutumes populaires chez les Coptes d'Égypte*.

release. Among the Nubians too, demon-possession occurs mostly among women and offers them a socially sanctioned escape valve and a means of reaching goals. The sick-person's role is an instrument of social control that mediates in inherent conflicts in social life. It is a mechanism for maintaining the prescribed roles. Although the ceremonies reflect important Nubian ritual patterns and symbolism, at the same time they also display agreements with healing rituals elsewhere in the world.

A large proportion of the rituals described by Kennedy coincides with what I observed in the Cairo *zar*. A section of the women at these meetings was often Nubian in origin. *Zar* rituals are partly standardized and can partly be "filled in" as needed. So I am not in a position to judge whether or not by their own cultural input Nubian women act "divergently" in the contemporary *zar* by comparison with other women.

Al-Sendiony has published two articles on traditional therapies and therapists in the present-day Arab world and the cultural specificity of mental illnesses (1974). He refers to the long tradition in the Arab world in the field of healing of mental illnesses and the positive protection against harm.

Since psychotherapists or psychiatrists with "western" training are relatively thin on the ground in the Arab world, the popularity of the traditional healers stands firm, according to him. For a large section of the population they are the first choice when problems arise (I have observed that this state of affairs has changed somewhat in the meantime, but the threshold to psychiatric medical help is still high).

Al-Sendiony is occupied with the integration of traditional methods in western psychiatry and writes that there has long been a view that psychological disorders are rare in traditional Arab cultures and typically a sign of imbalance arising through modernity. He thinks this view is not deserved and claims that it is attributable to the non-recognition of such disorders and to the great tolerance that there is for them. Among different peoples there are different theories on the causation of psychiatric illnesses and the separate traditional therapeutic methods are linked with them. As regards the Arab world, non-human beings (*jinn*) move across the earth and have the power to cause sickness and harm among humans. As a result of various causes they are in a position to possess the person and the goal of the therapy is thus to exorcize (drive out) these beings or pacify them (satisfy them by meeting their demands). Belief in these beings is sanctioned by the

Koran, which mentions the *jinn*. Al-Sendiony calls the (low) status of women as the most important cause of stress, which leads to a culture-bound possession syndrome. He deals briefly with the *zar* ceremony. In my opinion he relies (too) heavily on the work of Nelson (1971) and Okasha (1966). He regards possession and the sick-person's role that goes with it as a means to escape stressful situations and as revenge on the husband in order, by means of the ceremony, to make him pay dearly for the suffering and injustice experienced. This is too reductionistic. Women certainly have the possibility of manipulating by means of the sick-person's role, but I have never gained the impression that this possibility is consciously actively used. In a personal conversation with Mohammed al-Sendiony in 1997 he admits to never having been present at a *zar* ceremony himself. His comments on the participation of women at the *zar* he now himself regards as too limited.

Nelson (1971) argues for seeking subtle messages, meanings, worldview and basic understandings of the "self" hidden in the stories of possession, since the *zar* may not simply be dismissed as therapy or an escape valve.

Because in the *zar* it is almost always male spirits that possess and dominate the women, and set requirements, the rituals symbolize fundamental motifs that play a role in the culture (there are also female spirits which seem, however, to play a less significant role; see also Morsy 1978). As a symbolic act the *zar* expresses basic understandings of the "self" and the surrounding world, including the entirety of man–woman relations. Nothing that happens in the social world remains untouched by occurrences in the supernatural world. Spirits constantly lie in wait to come between the two in human life. On the one hand this expresses the understanding of a vulnerability to powers that come from the outside and are uncontrollable, and emphasizes on the other hand that the person him- or herself is not responsible for what happens. The individual exists in a dangerous world dominated by husband and spirits, both of whom constantly need to be kept happy. In short, the *zar* is a mirror-image of daily life, in which a woman must similarly manipulate, plead and calm. At the same time the possession role is a way for women to express themselves in a manner that would not be accepted in the everyday social structure. Possession is used in order to ventilate complaints and to gain personal recognition in an otherwise uncertain marriage relationship. Nelson wonders in what way the *zar* also reflects tensions from the broader Egyptian social system in which those who find themselves in weak, subordinate positions must continually manipulate powers in order to attain their goals. She does not, however, develop this in greater detail.

Like Nelson, I am of the opinion that there are similarities between events in the spirit world and those in the daily social world. It seems a pity that though she claims that women suffer stress under social and psychological pressure, she nowhere demonstrates how this pressure arises. In my work I find it essential to let these women speak for themselves, so that the reader gains an insight into the conditions that cause the stress. In addition, Nelson notes that cases of possession can be caused by the jealousy of a spirit who is in love with a woman. Women have indeed told me stories of jealous demons and I present these in the last part of this book. In these stories I sensed a desire for another sort of relationship with the husband. Nelson writes that she has no statistical evidence for prostitution under the influence of *zar*, but that this is indeed reported. In the Bori cult of West Africa (the *zar* is often compared with this) prostitution seems indeed to occur (Masquelier 1995), but I have never observed such a thing in any *zar* ceremony I have attended. The culture of West Africa, in which a high degree of sexual freedom exists, is completely different from that of Egypt. Böhringer-Thärigen (1976) writes of the Sudanese *zar* that possessed women in this assume the role of a demon called Prostitute. For the *zar* brides, all of whom have undergone infibulation (the closing up of the vulva), this is a role model with which they identify in order to be able to experience in their imagination sexuality and eroticism which have been taken away from them in daily life. Kennedy (1967; 1978) makes the comment that the dance movements in the *zar* look like copulative movements and clearly have to do with forbidden sexual desires. I find Nelson and Kennedy's remarks too speculative. The *zar* is exposed to a lot of criticism from both orthodox and fundamentalist quarters, so remarks on excesses in the *zar* do not surprise me. There is certainly a sensual atmosphere in the *zar*, caused by the music, the dancing, the incense and so on. But I have also noticed that women keep a close eye on each other and protect each other when through the vigour of the dance and in the headiness of the "conversation" with the possessing spirit too much bare flesh is accidentally shown.

Al-Khuly (1996) places the emphasis in her research primarily on gender relations and on everyday forms of women's resistance in the lower income classes in Cairo. She writes about the way in which women cope with everyday conflicts and negotiating strategies in the private and in the public sphere. Her fieldwork has shown that *zar* is certainly not a marginal and exotic ceremony in which only a limited number of women participate. On the contrary, possession occurs rather often among women in the lower social classes and lies embedded in a system of values, convictions and rituals. By analysis of the stories of women she discovered that possession serves as an important alternative language to express dissatisfaction and protest. She describes a number of causes and symptoms of possession, referring to the research data of the above-mentioned Kennedy, Fakhoury and Nelson. Like Nelson (1971) she is of the opinion that the *zar* rituals cannot be "explained away" as a traditional escape valve or therapy for retarded and oppressed women. But possession is indeed a way of setting requirements and of stepping outside the prescribed role for a time. A possibility arises for negotiating with the husband and at the same time of creating self-awareness. Al-Khuly calls possession a "powerful discourse". It gives women a voice and puts them in a position in a subtle way to express a range of thoughts about their life in general and gender relations in particular. Since non-possessed women are also present at the meetings, according to her, commentary is provided and other ideas are set in motion, through which women become aware of themselves.

Al-Khuly notes a number of recurring "messages" in the field of religion and sexuality that emerged in the course of the interviews she held. First, it struck her that exorcism through Koran recitation is a growing phenomenon, but she has not studied this herself. It is also striking how many women seem to be possessed by Coptic (Christian) spirits. She was not able to find anything about this in the existing literature. These Christian demons have specific "anti-Islamic" requirements, such as going without the veil, wearing short skirts, using alcohol and going into a church. She interprets these demands as an expression of the resistance of women to the rising fundamentalism since this aims to curtail their freedom. Second, in the Islamic world men often judge women in terms of "emotions they cannot control" and "excessive sexual desires". From the stories of possession which al-Khuly heard from the women, it turns out that women themselves speak of their sexual desires in quite different terms.

Like al-Khuly I have noted these things and I also discussed them with her in 1995 and 1996. One hears in the *zar* of Christian demons who make "un-Islamic" demands such as to drink whisky and smoke cigarettes. But the cult of the *zar* makes it possible to meet the demons' demands without feelings of guilt (see also Van Binsbergen 1981). The situation is different with Koran healing. Here women are told that their possession is their own fault because they were lax in their faith, so that they did not keep to their Islamic duties. As a result the demons could come into their body and that is why they are suffering from physical and psychological problems. The healers deliberately talk people into feeling guilty (this also emerges in newspaper interviews with healers). Al-Khuly believes that the possession stories contain a resistance by women to the advance of fundamentalism. I do not believe this. Demon-possession, though potentially powerful and challenging, operates in a framework of dominant structures, and al-Khuly's application of the term "powerful discourse" to possession does not convince me.

Okasha (1966) is a renowned psychiatrist resident in Cairo who in 1966 conducted cultural-psychiatric research into the *zar* cult in the United Arab Republic (Egypt/Syria 1958-1961). For his research he made a selection from a hundred women, forty-three of whom, according to the *zar* leader, could not be relieved of their symptoms and were therefore referred to psychiatric clinics. The remaining women were studied, with their permission. As regards the women's background, he writes that they were aged between twenty and about fifty. Most of them were married, widowed or divorced. The majority had only an elementary school education, no job, and spent all their time at home. Those who did have outside work were reasonably successful in it. The women were given a full psychiatric and physical examination, after which the results were evaluated. All of them were suffering from a more or less serious personality disorder. There were other instances of similar disorders in the families of more than half the women. Their symptoms were ascribed by the persons in question to para-psychological phenomena, for which the *zar* was attended. A small group of women claimed to be only accompanying their friends or saw attendance at the *zar* as a preventative measure against possible illness in the future.

According to Okasha's findings, the effects of the *zar* on the patients' symptoms varied. The *zar* was quite effective in the case of hysterical reactions and mild cases of depression. Patients with a compulsion neurosis, schizophrenia or serious depression and melancholy showed no improvement, but the strain associated with such conditions was indeed alleviated to a certain extent.[7] Relapses were quite common if the patients did not maintain regular attendance at the ceremonies.

The intention in the *zar*, according to Okasha, is that through the music and dancing the participants get into a state of nervous excitement, which leads on to frenzy, exhaustion and finally to collapse, followed by a paradoxical uplifting through which they lose their abnormal patterns and return to healthier patterns. Three preconditions are important here. First, the person concerned must be well prepared by familiarity with cultural traditions and be convinced that the method helps. Second, the healer must be experienced and be able to stimulate the involvement of the group. Third, musical and sensual stimulation must be used to bring the central nervous system into a state of excitement.

He is not entirely negative about the *zar*. He says that although the "therapy" is naïve and primitive and is absolutely not based on scientific grounds, it does make use of generally accepted psychotherapeutic principles, such as calming, persuasion, suggestion, imaging, dream interpretation and abreaction. Participation reduces emotional tension, alleviates particular symptoms and produces social training and hopeful possibilities for expression. The *zar* is thus not completely without effect, according to Okasha, but in what the effectiveness consists, he does not say, nor how relapses occur and why improvement is evidently seen in particular cases. Nor does he draw possible connections between the psychological disorders of the affected people and their social conditions.

Okasha writes that the *zar* has the power to attract in particular emotional and fanatical women from the lower and middle classes. In his description of the *zar* as a "hysterical affair", he misses the fact that possession as understood by the women concerned, and dramatic personality disorder, as that is regarded by modern "western" science, are based on different cultural contexts (see also Pattison 1977). In his view many charlatans and thieves hide among traditional healers, but there are also persons who have the sincere intention of helping their fellow human beings. As long as there are insufficient (western-trained) psychiatrists to help all the patients, there will be room for traditional healers. It is the duty of scientifically trained doctors to

---

[7] In current psychopathology the terms applied by Okasha are no longer used.

know what they do. He himself does not want to encourage the *zar*, but to make an attempt to arrive at a scientific interpretation of how and under what conditions the *zar* produces results. In November 1997 I visited him and was able to have a conversation with him. It surprised him that, contrary to his expectation (and an increase in "western-trained" psychologists and psychiatrists), the *zar* is no less popular than it was, but is still flourishing and even enjoys a similarly flourishing "competitor" in dealing with demons, namely Koran healing.

Commentary

My impression is that most of the researchers mentioned above are heavily influenced by Lewis's views on the "usability" of (peripheral) possession for achieving something on the social level, and by Turner's insights on the chances of persons who find themselves between two social or psychological situations (*rites de passage*). They follow each other's tracks and do not offer innovative ideas. Lewis and Turner do offer concepts suitable for anthropologists in making distinctions in categories of possession and in gaining insight into its (possible) social consequences (the *etic* aspect). On the other hand, the phenomenon as conceptualized and experienced by the person in question and his or her nearest and dearest is not clarified (the *emic* aspect, see also Kapferer 1979: 128-129).[8] All the researchers mentioned lay emphasis on the marginal and subordinate position of women and their psychosomatic reactions to it. For their psychological or physical symptoms they seek a "cure" in which trance behaviour is encouraged and is regarded as the best and only way to speak with the cause of the sickness (the demon) and gain his favour, so that the symptoms (temporarily) disappear. There is always talk of "follow-up conversations" within the context of a cult group. In some cases, alongside the disappearance of the symptoms of the illness, there is also talk of "profit" in the sense of escape from an unpleasant situation, wish-fulfilment, the attainment of more attention and support from the immediate surrounds, insight into one's own problems, self-reflection, greater social skills or the development of a circle of friends. Depending on a specif-

---

[8] In anthropology use is made of *emic* and *etic* distinctions: the first refers to distinctions and meanings as utilized by the studied persons in their own worldview, the second refers to the analytical schemes of outsiders (see also Van Binsbergen 1999).

ic context, according to al-Khuly (1996) possession is also used as a form of "everyday resistance" and as a "language" for expressing dissatisfaction. Boddy (1988; 1989) views possession also as a "female answer" to the practice and privileges of men. For Boddy, al-Khuly and Nelson, moreover, possession is also important for the discovery of one's own "I". For all researchers, possession is "functional" for dealing with opposing values and for bringing up matters that could not be talked about in another way.

As I noted earlier, my opinion is that possession and the "cure" that goes with it can indeed be used for solving conflicts and tensions, but this does not necessarily have to be so (see also Kapferer 1979: 121; 1983: 90). By judging demon-possession as a "functional manoeuvre" on the part of the patient in order to achieve particular goals, her personal suffering is ignored and the significance of the event in relation to the close family and the wider social world is left out of consideration.

I do not agree with researchers who think that possession brings about change in the everyday social consciousness or that greater self-confidence and stronger I-awareness ensue from it. At least, I think it is not proven that this sort of experience extends outside the cult group. Precisely by objectifying the immoral qualities of the demons and shifting the blame, acceptance of subordination is fostered and both the legitimation and continuation of the existing social situation are perpetuated. This insight is not new (see e.g. Gluckman 1952: 21; Finkler 1986: 640), but there is more. None of the authors I have mentioned pays attention to the forces that bring the healing process into motion, nor to the significance of the accessibility of the female body through which, via "bodily orifices" both negative and positive forces can do their work. What is also very important is that the rituals give a feeling of being able to cope: you can put something away in an imaginative microcosm while you are powerless in the macrocosm. This happens because the fantasy feels real. It is precisely these aspects that attracted my attention, among others, and it is these that I shall deal with in the following chapters on the *zar* and Koran healing.

It is important to bear in mind that in Egypt possession is not viewed by those concerned as illness. It is the cause of sickness, people become sick precisely because they are possessed. Dissociation, neurosis, hysteria, depression, personal disorders, and so on, are not appropriate terms to describe the situation with the possessed person. These are terms from western psychology and psychiatry and they can easily lead to a misinterpretation of the psychological and/or behavioural disorders of those who frequent the *zar* or Koran healing. Moreover, this places both healing methods outside the meaningful context. Although some researchers compare the *zar* treatment with western group therapy, the great difference lies precisely in the fact that the aim is not to heal the possessed person or to make the social situation change, but that the individual is offered a means of adapting (anew) to his or her living environment. This applies to Koran healing too. I think possession as a cultural expression of distress can best be described from the experience of the possessed person herself and that a good description must take account both of the *etic* and the *emic* aspects — that is to say, taking account of the cultural interpretation of possession and healing and how this is connected with personal feelings of distress, and taking account of the connections with cosmological, historical, economic and social explanations, as well as interaction with society at large. The emphasis in this study is on ethnography, which will show that possession is a situation that produces a particular sort of behaviour (but not "abnormal" behaviour) for which the person who experiences it is not responsible, and that both healing methods are appropriate.

My own research

My position is that possession is a culture-specific metaphor and is not a spiritual disorder. As a consequence of this, I study the aesthetic details of *zar* and Koran healing and the collective views that exist concerning the two forms of healing. For this I approach the two healing methods from three angles. First as a participant in the rituals (participatory observation). Second, from the point of view of the healer, i.e. I give a view of the healing rituals by way of the healer's accounts. Third, I show the perspective of the research group as has emerged by means of long and frequent conversations with women who have or have not experienced possession. Such an approach has not, to my knowledge, been applied before in research into *zar* and has the advantage that the same material is illuminated from various points of view.[9]

---

[9] Koran healers, *zar* leaders and their "clients" are the "principal players" in this study. Besides these I have spoken with many other people about demon possession: "demon experts", Koran scholars, psychiatrists, Egyptian anthropologists and health workers.

Up to now there has been no research into Koran healing in Egypt. Healing with the Koran has been known for centuries and can be compared with what "healing with the Bible" means for Christians. In recent years, however, this has been commercialized and has mushroomed into an "ecstatic cult". I have paid attention to this. I have spoken with many women and asked them why they attend these sessions. It seems to be a question of the same complaints and ailments as prompt women to go to the *zar*. Through the treatment by the healer they hope to find relief. In my view, much of what has been written about possession and the *zar* applies also to possession and Koran healing. In the analysis of my observations I have been inspired by the insights of three experts in the field of rituals: Van Binsbergen, Turner and Devisch.

Van Binsbergen's research, in Zambia (West Africa), was into non-regionally tied "cults of affliction", i.e. cults in which the personal suffering of the individual is in central position (1981). The term "cult of affliction" comes from Turner. It refers to a religious subsystem characterized by two elements: a cultural interpretation of ailments in terms of extraordinary domination by specific non-human beings and deflection of the evil by the admission of the "victim" into a cult in which the non-human beings are confronted in a special way. The primary ritual forms of the cult consist of rituals of divination (predictions) in order to identify the non-human beings, and an initiation rite in which the dominance of the being concerned is recognized in an empathetic way in the presence of others. The conventional means for this are the playing of drums, singing, hand-clapping, sacrifice, and the wearing of special clothing. When the troubles have disappeared, the person concerned remains a member of the cult group and participates in special sessions intended to bolster relations with the non-human beings and to help other affected persons. Van Binsbergen writes that the leaders (male and female) of such cults are talented and passionate people who can skillfully manipulate symbols as songs and dramatic effects. The "leadership" has generally come upon them after a personal crisis (often a physical or psychological illness) or has been "inherited". Hidden behind their drive may also be financial greed, but leadership qualities and a "vocation" to heal others are indispensable attributes. The leadership often goes together with prestige, power and disposal over a local network of persons who assist at the rituals.

Since the same aspects apply also in *zar* and Koran healing in

Egypt, to judge from my observations, in my research I follow a number of recommendations made by Van Binsbergen for the study of
possession cults. I look into how, when and why people interpret their
own condition (possession) and activities (participation in healing rituals) and with what other phenomena in society their perspectives are
connected. I examine whether and to what extent possession is
learned and/or sanctioned behaviour. In other words, does possession need to be viewed as a voluntary and conscious manifestation of
a role the individual wants to play within his or her social environment, or not? Is it part of the whole process of interaction with which
a person tries to realize his goals in relation to others? I look into the
interpretation of the participants with regard to the type of demons,
but also into their relation to each other and to society. Is it, for
instance, a matter of personal invisible beings of human origin, or of
beings of non-human origin such as God or guardian or earth spirits?
I investigate the religious organization, hierarchies, specialized tasks
of the healers (predictive, healing, political) and important supra-local
extensions, such as social structural principles (recruiting of possessed
people and mediums) and the way in which this happens (a personal
possession crisis and/or a learning period). I pay attention to the
organizational structure (hierarchy, roles between possessed and non-
possessed, assistants, leaders of rituals, and so on) and I comment on
the rewards and the costs in terms of prestige and wealth.

Bookcases-full have been written about *Turner*, and I said above
that some of the researchers I discuss have been heavily influenced by
his insights. Turner elaborated the theories of Van Gennep and made
an important contribution to the development of the theory of *rites de
passage*. I make use of his ideas only for analysis of the rituals in *zar*
and Koran healing. Van Gennep was one of the first anthropologists
to study how people categorize their experiences and ritualize their
behaviour in order to mark boundaries of social space and time. Rites
that are coupled with change of position or social status, such as birth,
marriage, death, first menstruation, circumcision, etc., he called *rites
de passage*. *Rites de passage* are also used to order matters concerned with
the universe and to mark transitions in them. Such transition rituals
follow the same pattern and consist of three phases. In the first phase,
the *separation* or *preliminal* phase (limen = threshold), the individual is
released in a symbolic way from the social group or structure. In the
second phase, the *interstructural* or *liminal* phase, the individual finds
himself in a transition. This situation has a double meaning, because

though the individual is free of the earlier situation, the qualities of
the new status are not yet linked with him or her. In the third phase,
the *postliminal* or *incorporation* phase, this is behind the person. The
transition is a *fait accompli* and the individual is relatively stable with
clear rights and responsibilities towards others. He or she is expected
to behave in accordance with the customs and ethical norms of the
new group or structure (Van Gennep 1909/1960).

Turner was primarily interested in the *interstructural (liminal)* phase.
Persons who find themselves in this situation are, in his terms,
"betwixt and between", because they are between "that which was
and that which is still to come". They must as it were reformulate old
elements into new patterns. The ambiguity of this "in-between phase"
comes to expression in many symbols. Liminal persons can be disguised, dress differently than normal, imitate specific social situations,
and so on. Internal processes are given external form in this way.

A feature of the liminal group is *communitas*. This is a rudimentary
or unstructured community of people, but where there is still a certain sense of belonging and comradeship. The members of the liminal
group interact with each other in a spontaneous way and there is a
basis of equality. In this situation people can get to know each other
better and enter into friendships. The relationship between the new-
comer and the leader of the group is one of subordination and reflects
the process of acquiring knowledge and strength to be able to cope
with the new situation in life. Another feature of liminality is that it
offers the individual the possibility of reflection. The ritual participant
can, as it were, stand alongside his or her everyday reality and examine its social structure and criticize its shortcomings. From this van-
tage-point he or she can create an unlimited amount of new possibilities for him- or herself. Turner places *communitas* in opposition to
structure (he calls this anti-structure), regarding it as the counterpart
to the hierarchical society outside the liminal phases.[10] Against the
background of this theory many aspects of the healing cults I have
studied gain in significance. Through attendance at the *zar* and
Koran healing, boundaries are marked, namely the boundaries
between those who are possessed and those who are not. But boundaries are also crossed: dancing, smoking and drinking, as can occur in
the *zar*. Boundary-crossing is less clear in Koran healing, but women

---

[10] Turner 1967: 93-95; 1969: 109, 127-128, 187; 1974: 13-14, 52-57, 242-243,
269. See also Alexander 1991; Morris 1987; Tennekes 1982.

are stimulated to hit and to push against the walls of the treatment
room, to run around and scream. This is behaviour that would not be
accepted in another situation. The places where *zar* and Koran healing are held also have to do with boundary-crossing, because one
does not come here in normal life. On *communitas* as a feature of the
liminal phase, I have a different opinion from Turner in relation to
zar and Koran healing. An atmosphere of equality does emerge, but it
does not break through the hierarchical relationships between the
women. Differences in status that also play a role in everyday life, still
shine through. I also think that in the liminal phase it is not necessarily the case that there should be reflection, change to another state of
consciousness, status reversal or change of social situation. In the liminality of the *zar* ceremony and in the session of Koran healing a (temporary) change in the physical and mental state of the women does
occur, which allows them to sort things out so that they can cope
again for a while in their daily lives, but at the same time through the
revitalization of the old patterns, the existing structure is emphasized.
Instead of change, then, it is rather a question of the "maintenance"
of existing norms and values (see also Handelman 1990: 52-53).
Change in daily social consciousness and life has evidently been noted
by some of the researchers I have discussed (above). I think this is only
very limited and it is more a question of reintegration into the old situation.

Despite the fact that I think differently from Turner on *communitas*,
I can still use his terms in analyzing the rituals in *zar* and Koran healing.[11] The actions during the ceremonies can be divided into the three
phases that mark a *rite de passage*. The separation phase (preliminal)
begins with the "diagnosis" and the preparations of the *zar* leader or
the "intake" of the Koran healer (although here no clear initiation
takes place). The liminal phase starts during the ceremony itself and
has the aim of bringing the woman into contact with the supernatural
forces that are thought to have entered her body. This phase is
marked in *zar* by clothing, music and expressive aspects. In Koran
healing the treatment centres on listening intently to and repeating
Koran verses. The incorporation phase (post-liminal) begins in the *zar*
after the woman is united in a marriage with the possessing demon

---

[11] See also Kapferer 1979: 128 and 1983: 179, who is of the opinion that healing
rituals agree in structure with *rites de passage* and can be interpreted according to the
ideas of Van Gennep and Turner.

and the sacrificial animals have been slaughtered, to be enjoyed together with the family and guests in a festive meal. After the ceremony she goes home in a "restored" condition and as a member of the cult group she will from now on participate in meetings in order to engage with the demon in dance. In Koran healing, the healer exhorts a stricter Islamic life. If the woman dresses and lives in accordance with the guidelines she receives from the healer, one may also speak of incorporation into a new "cult group", for in Egypt it is not common, as in some Islamic countries, for the majority of women to cover their body (and face) completely (see the section on clothing in Chapter 7). In the chapters on *zar* and Koran healing I shall show how, with the aid of Turner's ideas, I analyze the rituals, but this does not provide me with any tools for penetrating through to lived experience. For this I turn to Devisch.

Devisch did his research in Zaïre (currently People's Republic of Congo) into healing cults, and he provides a critique of the analysis of Turner (1993: 245-254). In his opinion Turner gives too much attention to cognitive understanding and moral inspiration, and too little to the symbolism of the body. Rich and extensive though his analyses of ritual symbols are, Turner fails, in Devisch's view, in noting their logic in a broader context of symbolic subsystems and cosmology. Turner regards life as a "social drama" in which power, control and conflict are expressed. For him, an affliction ritual is a story of the core values of a society. He pays no attention to the physical creativity in rituals, since in his opinion the body is no more than a vehicle for ritual drama: it is open to symbolic creativity, but is not the source of it. In Devisch's view, healing rituals reach further than the story; they are more than the dramatic performance of a script. It may seem to an outside observer as if the healing drama runs according to a hidden script which is developed within a firmly delimited order of time and space, but in reality the ritual drama is not primarily intended as representation or as a means for consideration and identification. The rituals refer to nothing and do not form an indication of something. Nor are they substitutes for other more original ideas or a basic story.

In Devisch's approach, a healing ritual is not a liturgy, nor a theatrical performance, a performed explanation of a world order, or a psychodrama. The initiates and other persons present are not uncommitted spectators with a possibility of maintaining a critical distance, who can compare the "performance" with another performance. Ritual is a practice which draws from vast old and new(er) sources in the body and in society. It is quite separate from other practices and is not a tool for the attainment of social goals. Possibly it is even only at the end of the ritual or after its conclusion that the initiate gains a deeper insight and a more critical view of things.

This does not mean that healing rituals are only a naïve place of refuge standing outside the social and cognitive arenas, a flight from reality or oppression. Devisch argues that to the extent that ritual creativity proceeds from possibilities of body, senses and living environment, and not from a storytelling voice or an interpretative awareness, it is not a quest for oneself. The primary goal of ritual is not to tell of reality but is rather a means of exposure or a product of reality. Healing has just as much to do with the satisfaction of desires, strengths and weaknesses as it does with sociability.

I find the way in which Devisch speaks of healing rituals very stimulating. So in what follows I shall work out some of his ideas on the processes that apply before, during and after the performance of healing rituals. I shall not go into what is specific for healing rituals among the Yaka (his research group), but I shall comment on what is applicable to *zar* and Koran healing.

For Devisch (1993: 255-257) the perspective of the experiencing and self-reflecting person is not in central position, but attention is given to the techniques and methods of healing from the body itself. Healing rituals, he says, take place in a more or less pre-established context in the margins of everyday public life and power relationships. Means, procedures and methods are not discussed during the healing rituals. Their potential for renewal is hidden in the devoted initiation and in the transaction between the patient-newcomer and the healer.

The basic principle in ritual healing is the crossing of boundaries, within and between physical, social and cosmological fields. The ritual drama unfolds a *mise en scène* in time and space, in which metaphorical agreements of the patient's body and the life-threatening dimensions from his or her living world are given and are manipulated. By means of the ritual the patient is freed from his state of "possession". The links with those around him and the outside world are knitted together once more and he is, as it were, reconnected with a meaningful and empowering order.

The ritual healer does not simply work away at the patient's psyche. He carefully chooses symbols that are recognized by all those concerned and acknowledged to be suitable in a desired social configuration. He makes use of a range of aids which Devisch calls "transformative devices" or "embodied skills". That is to say that the healer makes use of rhythm, music, dance, gestures, sensory codes, means for interaction and memory support, dimensions of time and space, dream interpretation, massage, steam baths, embrocations, enemas, scorings in the skin, etc. The ritual drama should thus be viewed as a productive process that has to do with expertise.

In ritual therapy everyone in the immediate vicinity of the patient is involved, i.e. the initiates mentioned above, the family members, friends and acquaintances. The goal is to mobilize effects that lead to catharsis and abreaction. During the ritual the malevolent spirit/demon is identified and given a name. The patient expels (or pacifies) the spirit, by which means the "curse" that rests on him is reversed into a wholesome situation. The sacrifice of an animal, the blood of which is sprinkled over the patient, serves to drive the evil out further. The internal and exclusive relationship that exists with the anonymous spirit/demon is thereby transformed into an external and exclusive relationship with a personified spirit.

During the ritual the patient is simultaneously himself and the embodiment of the spirit/demon. As co-actors they together perform the "drama" that is to lead to the patient's individual readjustment: the resurfacing of stuck or broken relationships with others or of compelling traditional regulations. The "performance" of the healer, patients, family and supporting group works on everyone in an uninhibited atmosphere. It is an interaction of metaphors and paradoxes, of images and senses, a withdrawal into oneself — and a display to the surroundings in a playful form.

Body, feelings and life force can influence each other and closely intertwine with each other and with the world of experience of the patient. It is not the healer, the patient, the supernatural being or the "therapy-managing group" that brings about healing. It is the multi-layered "tissue" in and between body, family, group and living world that does that. By sensing and touching the meaningful interwovenness with the family and the surrounding world, the body is deeply touched, strengthened and reconstituted.

Ritual healing has to be understood at the sensory level since manifestations of fear, panic, care and persecution are evoked, things which are impossible to formulate in words, and which during a process that displays correspondences with *rites de passage* are transformed into positive feelings. During the rites the body abandons itself in an all-embracing rhythm to the multiplicity of feelings. The rite is a dream about health and an incarnation of values that by means of metaphors passes language by and evokes attachment instead of a distance-creating self-consciousness. Ritual healing makes use of the human body as an important gathering place of cultural traditions, values and forces. The healer, the patient and the other participants open themselves up to this spontaneously. If the ceremony works, this is because the symbols are creative tools of a special structure. So much, then, for our discussion of the most important literature on possession and how it is interpreted.

CHAPTER FOUR

THE *ZAR*

In the *zar* ceremony a possessed woman is called *milammisa* (from *lamm* — touch), *malbusa* (from *labisa* — clothe) or *ma'zura* (from *'azara* — excuse). *Milammisa* and *malbusa* refer to the fact that she is "clothed" or "dressed" by supernatural beings called *asyad* (masters) *arwah* (spirits) or *'afarit* (demons); *ma'zura* has to do with the fact that she is "excused" because her (deviant) behaviour is the result of demonic intervention.[1] In Egypt, *zar* is an activity in which principally women participate. It displays few points of connection with formal Islam. The belief system and its rituals were probably introduced around 1870 in Egypt among women of the middle class and gradually spread over the rest of the population, where they were adopted into already existing convictions and conventions (Littmann 1950; Kriss & Kriss-Heinrich 1962). The Egyptian *zar* can be classed as a possession cult, a phenomenon found all over the world. A great number of the rituals performed are similar to rituals in (sub-Saharan) African cults, but also to possession cults elsewhere in the world. We also see connections with the *bori* cult of the Hausa in West Africa and the *hadra* (the "trance dance") in Morocco, which is performed in the context of saint-veneration and sufi brotherhoods.[2]

Little is known of the origins of the Egyptian *zar* demon(s). Above I mentioned Littman, Kriss and Kriss-Heinrich, who have researched the *zar*. These authors discussed the ceremony as orientalists rather than as anthropologists, but since they give an accurate description of the rituals as conducted more than fifty and thirty years ago (respectively), their work is interesting as comparative material. Littmann based his study on two Arabic manuscripts, from 1911 and 1930, which talk of the expulsion of demons during a *zar* ritual. His opinion is that the *zar* comes from Ethiopia and originally had to do with the cult of a pagan god who, after the population converted to Christianity, was relegated to the status of demon (1950: 47). Regarding the *zar*

---

[1] See also Blackman 1927; Lane 1895; Leeder 1973; Morsy 1993.
[2] Beattie & Middleton 1969; Bakker 1993; Van Binsbergen 1981; Boddy 1988; 1989; Chandra Shekar 1989; Cloudsley 1983; Crapanzano 1973; 1977; Kramer 1993; Lambek 1993; Lewis 1986; Masquelier 1995; Obeyesekere 1977; Stoller 1989.

in Egypt, he says that there were two sorts that existed side by side —
the Upper Egyptian, which is the more common, and the Sudanese
zar, but he does not indicate what the differences between the two are
(1950: 2). The work of Kriss and Kriss-Heinrich is based on the personal experience of Kriss, who had a ceremony organized for himself
in Egypt. They speak of one *zar* in Egypt, and of two sorts in Sudan:
the *zar bori*, which runs parallel to the West Africa *bori*, in which only
women participate, and the *zar tambura*, which runs parallel to the
Ethiopian *zar*, in which both men and women participate. The two
variants differ in organization, but display agreements in their
demonology, although that of the *bori* is more elaborate than that of
the Egyptian *zar*. They also think that the cult came to Egypt from
Ethiopia. *En route* the *zar* would have picked up some (Sudanese) *bori*
elements, but have undergone further development in Egypt, from
which a separate demonology emerged (1962: 182-183). Böhringer-
Thärigen (1996), mentioned above, whose research in Sudan is much
more recent than that of the authors mentioned, writes that the organization of the *zar tambura* is a male affair. The leader of the ceremony
(*sanjak*) possesses great physical strength, which allows him to dominate the spirits. He adjures the dark and dangerous world of the spirits who cause very serious illnesses. The women who attend these ceremonies generally come from the south of Sudan and are often former slaves (1996: 75). I have observed that in present-day Egyptian
zar there may be differences in the sequence and the extent of the rituals, but that there is no question of there being two sorts of *zar*. The
reasons for organizing a ceremony seem to differ between Sudan and
Egypt. According to Boddy, in Sudan the emphasis lies on fertility
problems (1986; 1989). This is not the case in Egypt. The *zar* demons
cause mental and physical complaints, which make the woman inca-
pable of fulfilling her normal social role, including the bearing of children (Inhorn 1994: 199-201). The demons are therefore only indirectly responsible for infertility.

General description

I was lucky enough to make friends with Zahra, who is a well-known
zar leader in Cairo, and with Hassan, who is part of one of her permanent music groups. As a result I gained access to ceremonies where
Zahra was the leader. On occasion I was also able to accompany her

or Hassan to *zars* led by other leaders. *Sheikha* Zahra is a large, heavy black woman, whom everyone calls Zahra as-samra (Zahra the dark) on account of her dark skin. She learned the profession from her mother, who originally came from Sudan, but died years ago. Zahra lives with her family in a small self-built house upstairs on the roof of an apartment building in one of Cairo's popular districts.

The ceremony

Zahra has invited me to come to the *zar* that she has organized in a woman's home, who lives in a *hush* (a house made from a grave) in the city of the dead. It is not easy to find the house and when I arrive in the evening the *zar* has already begun. Zahra is sitting on the ground with a small group of women and laughs with pleasure when she sees me. I am immediately doused with incense by one of the women and then I am pushed onto a small space to sit down. The whole hush is used for the ceremony, that is to say a room with an area built on to it and a space that serves as a patio, but where three graves of deceased people stand too. There is not much light; here and there lamps are burning and a few candles and there is a thick cloud of *bukhur* (incense). The room is full to capacity with people, mainly women, but a number of men and children too. The *zar* bride is a woman of around fifty years of age in a long white *gallabiyya* (a sort of tunic). Besides her husband she has also brought a daughter and a few guests. She has a content, relaxed and slightly absent expression on her face. She has changed her headscarf and is wearing another *gallabiyya* and other ornaments. A candle is now pressed into everyone's hand and is lit. We first stand in a circle around the *zar* bride and afterwards form a *zaffa* (a ceremonial procession) as at a wedding. High, shrill tones ring out, produced by the women with the tongue, as at all festivities. The *sheikha* stops singing and the drumming also stops. She takes the bride by the hand and places her in the middle of the room. Two large turkeys are brought in. The *sheikha* first utters a few words, apologizing to the animals for their death. After that she says *allahu akbar* and then slaughters the animals in the ritual way. The birds are thrown into a large vat afterwards, with the lid on it, with much fluttering of wings, to bleed dry. For this the *sheikha* has first caught some blood from the cut throats in a dish.

This she now smears on the bride's forehead, cheeks and hands. This is a greeting to the demon master. The bottle of whisky that stood on the sacrificial table (*kursi*) is opened and glasses circulate to serve everyone. The daughter of the *zar* bride explains to me that the master who is possessing her mother is a *nasrani*. Whisky and other alcoholic drinks are forbidden in Islam, but in this case a demon, a Christian one, has given the instruction that whisky be drunk. In everyday life this would be against their religion. One cigarette after the other is lit up too, and the women smoke as much as they can (modern Egyptian women do smoke, but many do not do this in public or when many other people are present). Everyone enjoys the taste, the musicians play and there is much laughter. After some time plates of food are brought in and distributed. I now notice that at the back of the room a few women are sitting who are dressed less attractively and are not given any food. When I ask why this is so, I am told that they have not yet made a sacrifice and so are in fact still outsiders. After the break the music group changes. A *tambura* group has come in, eight men and women. They begin to play and in a short time a huge state of excitement is built up. Some of the women dance with rhythmic movements (*faqqar*). The heavy bodies are bent slightly forward, one shoulder a little higher than the other, the breathing heavy and panting. They dance, with a slightly turning movement that stays the same the whole time, until they come to the end of their strength and sit down again, exhausted. Still sitting on her chair, the woman next to me suddenly begins shaking and shuddering movements with her body. She stands up and joins in with the dancing women. Her daughter tells me, smiling, that the "master" has called. At this moment in front of my eyes an extraordinary spectacle develops. I see one woman busy with a large flame, like a fire-eater, while another, stretched out on the ground, creeps along with dancing motions. Yet another woman has tied a scarf around her hips and is dancing with swinging and swirling hip movements, with a long stick. Zahra too (the *sheikha*) is dancing vigorously with another woman. It looks as if the two of them are engaged in competition, to see who can keep it up the longest. Zahra dances dramatically, sometimes head down, sometimes head up. She grasps herself by the head and her face distorts as if in pain. Other women have come to stand around the two of them and have

now placed a black *tarha* (veil) over their heads. They stay dancing like this for a good twenty minutes to half an hour, ever
more vigorously, until it suddenly stops and Zahra flops down
onto a chair, panting heavily. Five minutes later she is walking
between the other women, laughing and fit. I decide to go
home. It is four o'clock in the morning and I promise Zahra I
will come back in a few hours, for this *zar* will continue for
another day and a night before everyone goes home.

A few days after this *zar* I go to visit Nura, a participant who invited
me during the ceremony to visit her. She lives with her family on the
second floor of a large apartment block in a lower-middle class district. When I come in she is sitting on the floor eating with two
daughters, a son and her sister. I am warmly invited, with broad gestures of welcome, to come and sit with them and join them in the
meal. After the meal, she, her sister and I go and sit on the balcony,
and with her sister's support she tells me about her *zar* experiences.

Nura

"When I was still a small child my mother dropped me on the
floor. This happened because of the jealousy of the *tahtaniyyin*
(demons who live underground). My mother says that from that
time on I was "clothed" by demons and suffered from *'asabiyya*
(nerves). When I was sixteen, I was married out to a rich man
and many people were jealous of me at that time. The man was
much older than me, and I was afraid of him. I went to live with
him in a flat and he was away the whole day. He went out early
in the morning and didn't come back until late in the evening. I
sat alone in that big apartment block all day long and then I got
sick, very sick, I had pains everywhere. This was because of *hasad*
(jealousy which causes someone to cast the evil eye). I cried all
day long and couldn't get out of bed. It was *halat nafsiyya* (an
expression for someone with psychological problems), I wanted
to die I was so lonely, I was so afraid in that big building.

The first time I had a private *zar* arranged for me was twenty
years ago; I took a friend with me that time. I had it done many
times after that, two months ago was the last time. I was feeling a
bit sick again and I had a sacrifice made again by *ukhti* Zahra
(my sister Zahra). I said to myself, *anna mit'awwida, ba'mil* (I know

what it is, so I'll do it). Zahra is very good. She worked for a long time with an old *sheikha,* who is dead now. She took a look at my *atar* (personal property used for divination) and told me who was possessing me. *Yawra Bey* is my master, for more than twenty years. He clothed me because I was so beautiful and I used to stand in front of the mirror so often. The king (the master) said "She is beautiful, I love her, I'll take her". When I am at the *zar* and I hear his music, he "takes" me and I feel it in my body. After I have danced, I feel calm again. I dance several times in an evening. I like it when he (*Yawra Bey*) comes down into me."

I ask Nura about the significance of some of the details I noticed during the *zar,* such as the woman dancing with the stick, and she answers "The woman is possessed by a *Si'idi* (demon from Upper Egypt). When he comes down she dances with the scarf and the stick, because that's how they do it in Upper Egypt." She tells me that everything has significance and explains that the woman who was dancing with the green head-scarf does it for her master, the green sultan. Green is the colour of Islam, but it is not clear whether this sultan has anything to do with Islam. Perhaps he is the equivalent of an Islamic saint, but neither the participants nor Zahra could tell me anything about this. Nura's own master, *Yawra Bey,* also wants green clothes; perhaps he and the green sultan are one and the same. "*Yawra Bey* is a demon who makes people tired and his father *Hakim Basha* goes dressed as a doctor, complete with stethoscope and a *fez.*[3] The woman who was dancing on the ground, almost in a lying position, did this for Gado, the master who has to do with the toilet (impure place). The woman who has such a master probably once fell on the floor in the toilet, so that the master got into her body. There is another master who also belongs with the toilet. His name is Saliha and the woman who has him as her master will always want to pour water over herself. The master who requires whisky from his "bride" is a foreigner and a Christian. *Umm Ghulam* is a *ghula* (a bad common demon) and that is the same demon as the *'arina* (*Qarina*). She belongs with the 'brothers and sisters' who live underground and is a danger to small children. El Gabalawi is a master who lives in the

---

[3] In the time of Mohammed Ali the *fez* was typically the clothing of civil servants; both *bey* and *basha/pasha* were previously used as official titles.

mountains." Nura herself also once made a sacrifice for this master in the mountains. At that time she was very tired and thought she was going to die. She also knows Sitt Kabira, an old, wise and important demon. I tell her that I saw that Zahra, the *sheikha*, danced for a good half hour without a break, with her body shaking violently and with her head and face completely hidden behind a veil. Nura explains that this is because her master is an Arab. "An Arab master always wants his 'bride' to dance veiled and wear golden rings with blue stones, just as Hussein, the grandson of the prophet and Islamic saint, always wants silver." Nura tells me that it depends on the *zar* bride how many music groups play on an evening. When she is possessed by a *tambura*, the *tambura* plays. If she is possessed by a *sudani*, then the *abu gheet* play, two *zar* music groups. So I learn that particular masters belong with particular music groups, but apart from their own name, they are called by the name of the music group.

I tell Nura I was unable to understand what was being sung and that everything was like "oohooh oohooh ooh, oho oho oh". She laughs and says "That's because you don't understand it. But the woman dancing to the music knows, because her master has come down into her."

The *zar* mimics the model of a general initiation rite, the marriage, whereby a change of status takes place and symbolic defloration (loss of virginity) occurs. But according to Nura a marriage does not really take place between the woman and the masters, *'biyifrahu w-biyidbahu w-bass* (they are having a party/are happy and sacrifice, that's all). She means that there are no sexual implications. But in everyday life women have real husbands who could sometimes get jealous of the masters.

I tell Nura I noticed that a *zar* like this costs a lot of money. I ask her how much she paid. She evades the question rather, and does not give a direct answer. "It all depends", she says, because "there are good *sheikha*s who really help you and there are *daggalin* (charlatans) who are only after your money. The price also depends on how long the *zar* is going to last, one, two or three days — the longer it goes on, the more it costs."

Nura has only been to *zar* and has never been to a session of Koran healing, but she considers it quite normal that the *jinn* are beaten by the healers there, to drive them out of the body. She

does not know the difference between the *jinn* and the *zar* masters, but thinks that in *jinn* it is a matter of bad demons, although
she knows from the Koran that there are good and bad, as well
as believing and unbelieving *jinn*, and then says, "*bismillah ar-rahman ar-rahim*" and "*dastur*" (two incantations that protect her
against *jinn*). "There are good and bad ones, some make you sick
and some don't, but most of them are good." A somewhat
ambiguous statement because someone goes to a *zar* in the first
place because she has become sick as a result of a master "clothing" her.

Nura's husband and eldest son know that she regularly attends the
zar. Both of them reject it. The son tells me that it would be enough if
his mother would read the Koran, but Nura takes no notice of their
criticism and like her sister, who also suffers from her nerves, she continues to go to the *zar*. She knows that the imams in the mosques also
condemn the *zar*, but she does not understand why, because she is not
doing anything bad.

In my opinion Nura misses the symbolism of the *zar*. She says that
the woman does not "really" marry the master, but "*biyifrahu w-biyidbahu*" (they have fun and slaughter/sacrifice). The word *farah* is typically used for a wedding party in Egypt, and *dabh* is sacrifice/offering.
At wedding parties there is a sacrifice and a *zaffa* (procession with
candles and music) is then very common. Nura makes no connection
between a wedding in the *zar* and a wedding in normal life. Zahra,
the *zar* leader, does not do this either. I make such a connection
because I have noticed that a significant part of life in Egypt is based
on marriage, family and children and this occupies a special place in
the lives of the great majority of Egyptian women (see also Rugh 1984
and Wikan 1980, 1996).[4] Without marriage parenthood is impossible
and without children life has no meaning. Children are symbolic cap-
ital and a compensation for all the problems one meets in life (Inhorn
1994: 27). A few Egyptian psychiatrists assured me that disturbances
of this pattern frequently manifest themselves in psychological problems. I am convinced that the emphasis on the wedding motif in the
zar symbolizes the social world of women in significant aspects; it is an
important metaphor in the relationship with demons.

---

[4] The Egyptian constitution of 1971, article 9, confirms this and says that the family is the basis of society and is founded on religion, morality and patriotism.

The demons mentioned by Nura correspond to those listed by Littmann (1950: 35-36) and Kriss and Kriss-Heinrich (1962: 185-187). It is noticeable that the possessed mimic certain characteristics that belong to a particular demon, but that this evidently does not have a direct connection with their own behaviour or illness. A Si'idic demon requires his "bride" to dance in the way customary in the Si'id (Upper Egypt), but why this should be so is unknown (the same is reported by Dols 1992: 289). Kriss and Kriss-Heinrich give an extensive discussion of the specific clothing the women have to wear to please and pacify their master. They also describe what I call the "fire dance", the Upper-Egyptian "stick dance" and the "Arabian dance", but they do not make any connections with specific illnesses either. These authors do record that the *zar* masters have both a positive and a negative side. The positive side consists in their being a sort of house/guardian spirit and the negative side is that they are conveyors of illnesses (1962: 156-159, 198-199). Littmann, who never personally attended a *zar*, writes that women cry, scream, strike themselves in the face and bang their heads against the wall, but he does not say why this happens (1950: 4). I myself have never seen such mindless behaviour at any *zar* (though I have seen it at Koran healings). Other researchers I have mentioned do not go into specific features of the demon masters.

Demons in the body make themselves known in a particular, standard way, and the body movements during the dance correspond among all the women (see my description of the ceremony above). The causes that lead a demon to invade the body are similarly standardized. Such causes as "standing in front of a mirror" or "falling in the bathroom" and so on, are commonly known. To a certain degree one can also speak of spontaneity. Nura does make a loose connection between her fall and being possessed when she was still a child, in order to indicate "that she has always had it". But I have frequently heard such explanations from other women. Some demons are associated with tiredness, headaches or stomach pains, but several demons are held responsible for the same symptoms. During the ceremony the possessed persons can express themselves openly without their behaviour being criticized by others and without their being held responsible for their illness. The possessed woman dances with the master when she feels him "come over her", i.e., she feels the spirit possessing her.

The work of the zar leader

In the description below I made a distinction between the private ceremony held for one woman in her own home and the public *zar*,
which is called *hadra*. In the case of the private *zar* the leader of the
ceremony is also the medium who, since she herself is "clothed" by a
demon, can help others to identify the possessing spirits. It is only
after this identification has taken place that the possessed person can
participate in the public *hadra*, a weekly ceremony for possessed
women. The function of the leader (*sheikha* or *kudya*) is "hereditary";
she is the mediator between the demon(s) and the sick person. She
can get on with all spirits and manipulate them. During the ceremony
she is decked out with all kinds of jewelry (especially large rings with
blue and red stones) and amulets (principally silver or gold pendants
with inscriptions from the Koran, such as the Fatiha and the Throne
verse) in order to appease the various spirits. A sick woman who is
seeking intercession on her behalf is called *arusa* (bride) and the ceremony is called *farah ma'a al-asyad* (wedding with the masters).

Zahra

> "I am 54 years old and have been working in the *zar* since I was
> ten. My mother was a *kudya* and held a *hadra* (meeting) each
> week in *Abu-l-Su'ud* (a place in old Cairo). My father and grand-
> father were both *zar sheikhs* too. There is nothing odd about this,
> because it happens that men are "taken" by a master and
> become *sheikhs*, make sacrifices and everything. Women usually
> go to a *kudya*, but although more women than men go to the *zar*,
> men sometimes come to me too. I have a *zar* sultan who belongs
> specially with me and he helps to determine what is wrong with
> the sick person. The sultan is not a *jinn*." Every time Zahra says
> "*jinn*" she immediately adds "*dastur*" to protect herself. "He is
> one of the *malayka ardiyya* (good demons, who are also called
> angels). It is not *jinn* — *dastur* — that help me; people are not
> allowed to deal with *jinn* — *dastur*. *Malayka ardiyya* live under-
> ground, but they are *min 'andi Allah* (from God), they are not *jinn*
> but *qurana'* (*qarins*). And God says that every person on earth has
> a *qarin* under the earth. The *qarin* and the 'sister under the earth'
> are the same thing." Zahra stresses that the *zar* masters are not
> the same as the beings usually called *jinn* and who are out to

scare people or bring them harm. Nor does she have any deal-
ings with this kind of being. There are other specialists for this,
who "open" the Koran or make *higab* (amulets).[5] I ask her if it is
the case that when a woman has *mass* or *lams ardiyya* ("touching"
by a demon), which is often spoken of in Koran healing, this
comes from the *jinn*. But she denies this and says that this sort of
thing comes from the *qarin* underground, who is angry at the
person. "The sister underground can get angry if hot water is
poured down the toilet at night or if you hit a cat. And she gets
really angry if you stand in front of a mirror or sing or shout in
the toilet." It then seems from her words that the *qarin* and the
kings/sultans of the *zar* are the same. Each master has a name of
his own and each one has his own speciality. "*Zar* is not always
held indoors. There are women who go to the mountains or the
sea to have slaughters (make sacrifices). It is not just *daqqa* (the
playing of drums and singing and dancing). It is much more
than that: *az-zar bahr wasi'a ba'a* (the *zar* is as wide as the sea). She
means by this that there are many ways of holding a *zar*.

In my experience it is a difficult question for many whether the "sister
underground" is a *giniyya*, *malayka* or a *qarina* (female *jinn*, angel, personal companion respectively). According to Inhorn (1994: 199), and
I agree with her, most poor women living in the cities are convinced
that the "sister underground" is at any rate not responsible for possession. For this *giniyya* is the supernatural image of the earthly person
and although there may be tensions and difficulties between the two,
she has no interest in a permanent possession of her earthly sister.

Zahra tells me that the evening before the *zar* she makes a *kursi*
(sacrificial table) on which she places three candles, roses, henna
and incense. What precisely should stand on the *kursi* has been
told to her in her sleep by the *malayka ardiyya*, but in any case all
the *zar* masters must be represented on the *kursi*. On this day the
sick person wears her *atar*. An *atar* consists of something personal
of the sick person, such as a headscarf, which is used by the *zar*
leader for divination; Zahra calls this "reading". She also wears a

---

[5] In both Badawi (1996), *A Dictionary of Egyptian Arabic* and Wehr (1980), *A Dictionary
of Modern Written Arabic*, *higab* is derived from a verb meaning cover up, separate off,
make invisible, hide and also veil. *Higab* means both veil and amulet in Egypt.

white *gallabiyya* and *tarha* (long tunic and a light veil). "After that she has to walk round the *kursi* three times and I sprinkle her with rose-water and douse her with incense. There is no music at this point. Sometimes it happens that I can't help the sick person because the master does not "come down". In that case I give the woman her *atar* back. The next day the sick person is greeted with drum music and the *zar* begins. After the sacrificial animals have been slaughtered, I smear the sick person with blood. She is not allowed to drink the blood, that is *haram* (forbidden)." I ask her if she then talks to the *qarin* of the sick woman, but she answers "I know everything through reading the *atar*. From the *atar* I know what is wrong with the sick person and then I perform the task given by the master(s). A woman is not always possessed by just one master or always by the same master. Sometimes the sultan himself does not come down and it can also be another master. The third and last day is also without music. At the end of the day I give the sick person a *sulha*, a reconciliation amulet made from a coin, which has been lying in the sacrificial blood, together with some salt, a piece of bread and some incense, tied up in a cloth. I tie this round her arm. She is not allowed to go out for a week, in case a *nazra* (evil glance/evil eye) falls on her. After seven days I go back to her and undo the *sulha* and say *ash-shifa' burhan* ('healing is proven'). I douse her with incense and we eat *ruzz bi-laban* (rice pudding) together."

The women who come to Zahra have generally made visits to various doctors for their *halat nafsiyya* or *'asabiyya* (psychological problems) but have been unable to get help anywhere. The doctor sends them away and says there is nothing wrong with them. They then come to her and "with God's help" they are healed. Most women seem to be possessed by *Yawra Bey* or *Hakim Basha*. These are masters that belong with Zahra and her group. These masters are mentioned by Nura in connection with great tiredness. After the *zar* the women go to the *hadra*, but the *zar* has to be repeated after one year. The costs for a *zar* range between two and three hundred pounds (approximately 30 to 45 pounds sterling/US$ 45 — 70), depending on the sacrificial animals. The women save up so as to be able to sacrifice again.

When I ask Zahra about the "specialities" of the *zar* masters, she tells me that Gado/Gato is the master specially associated with the toilet. In many houses the toilet consists of a "hole in the ground", which is often not connected to a sewer. I think this certainly has to do with connotations of the underworld, the spirits thought to live there, and with impurity. "The Red Sultan is very strong, he is not a Muslim or a Christian, he is an atheist and creates stomach pains. The White Sultan belongs with the angels, they are *shurafa'* (nobles), *di zayyi il-muslimin, zayyi il-'arab* (they are like Muslims, like Arabs).[6] The *Sitt al-Kabira* holds on to the head and makes the stomach swell up, the Sultan of the Sea holds on to the brains, while Christian *zar* masters always want something special to be slaughtered, such as black doves and sometimes pigs (forbidden for Muslims)."

To my question whether there is a connection between the planets and the *zar* masters, since this is claimed in some books of magic, she answers in the negative and adds, "I know all the *zar* songs: *beet Mamma, beet Basha, Rum Nagdi, Yuse, Abu Danfa', al-Gabalawi, de Wazir* and *al-Liwa', Yawra Bey, Hakim Basha, as-Safina, Sultan al-Bahr*, and so on. This is because I have been involved with the *zar* since I was ten."

Zahra knows the criticism applied to the *zar* from various quarters. It does not worry her, because she prays and fasts and is a good Muslim. "I inherited the *zar*, it is not something from our day. The people that say the *zar* is not good don't know anything about it. There are *sheikhs* who make amulets and talk to the *jinn*. That is bad, that is against Islam and a different way. The *zar* has nothing to do with this. I have nothing to do with magic (*sihr*) either, or the evil eye (*al-'ain*). That sort of thing has to be treated with *kitaba* ("opening" of the Koran). The *zar* is only concerned with things relating to the *qarina* and to do with falling, shouting or singing in the bathroom/toilet, standing in front of the mirror and things caused by the Sultan of the Sea. These are all things that tire the brain (cause psychological problems). There is magic, there is *zar*, and there is Koran healing. The *sheikhs*, the Koran healers, maintain that only their method of healing is good because they talk to the *jinn*, who are supposed never to come back again. But that is not true. In the *zar* I say to the sick person, "Shout away, feel free, carry on". Then she

---

[6] Perhaps she is also referring here to descendants of the Prophet, who are also called this.

calms down. The *zar* is *dhikr harim*. Everything is under God's authority." Zahra is here excusing the *zar* by comparing it with the *dhikr*; *dhikr* is a mystical religious experience of sufis during music and dancing. I do not agree on this point. It is true that some of the *zar* masters called upon are sufi saints, but the *dhikrs* that I have attended all start with hours of recitation of Koran verses. After that there is dancing, but the songs and the music are completely different. Moreover, in *dhikr* there is no question of calling upon demon masters; in fact the Prophet Mohammed himself is called upon and venerated.

In the course of my fieldwork in Egypt I noticed that all kinds of understandings of the world of devils and demons exist alongside each other. That is to say, almost all demons can alternate between being good and bad (see also Dols 1992:291). New phenomena are inserted as far as possible into existing categories. As already mentioned in the previous chapter, *jinn* is generally used for invisible beings. Good *jinn* are distinguished from bad by being called "earthly (underground) angels" (see also Inhorn 1994: 196-197). The *'afarit* are made of fire and according to popular belief they form a category of very mean demons who already lived on the earth many thousands of years before Adam. Unlike the *jinn*, who can have good qualities, these demons are always intent on harming people (Blackman 1927: 227-239; el-Sayed el-Aswad 1987: 236-237). An important group of supernatural beings is formed by the *tahtaniyyin* (the subterraneans) who are also called "brothers and sisters below the ground" and can be regarded as *doppelgänger* because they are similar to humans in all respects. They generally act to sort out injustices, but they can also turn against their earthly brother or sister. This happens especially if they are jealous (see also Inhorn 1994: 196-197). The *qarina* is also a (female) *doppelgänger* who lives underground. She is also called the "childbirth demon", held to be responsible especially for premature death in small children and babies. This demon is also often regarded as the same as the "sister under the earth" (Sengers 1994).

Alongside the various categories familiar predominantly among the lower social classes, but not among the higher classes who only know the demons mentioned in the Koran, there is another separate group of demons mentioned in manuals for magic. This category consists of seven important *jinn* princes, who are generally bad, and seven groups of good *jinn*, who are also called "angels". Under the influence of kabbalistic notions (Jewish secret doctrine and mysticism, which arose in the Middle Ages), these *jinn* and angels are associated with the seven days of the week and the seven planets. Generally this group is known only by men who can read and write and occupy themselves with magic.[7] Zahra the *zar* leader is familiar principally with *zar* demons and these, in my view, despite what Zahra herself maintains, are not to be classed with the underground beings that are called *jinn*, *'afarit*, *tahtaniyyin*, *malayka ardiyya* or *qarina*. This is also confirmed by Littmann (1950: 39, 44), who writes that the *jinn* have to do with all conceivable things that belong to human life, but that the *zar* masters occupy themselves exclusively with illnesses caused by possession. It is precisely because the *zar* demons have largely been adopted from other cultures that they form a separate group with separate names and deeds (Littmann 1950; Kriss & Kriss-Heinrich 1962).

In present-day Egypt the existence of demons and their deeds occupies many people. The sacred texts of the Koran are not interpreted in the same way by everyone. Moreover, the situation in this country (but this applies also to other Islamic countries) is that the oral culture is still very important because there are still very many illiterate people who are unable to read the Koran and therefore cannot participate in the same way in religious life as better developed and educated persons. The *jinn* and the angels of the Koran constitute the fixed core of supernatural beings which, as believers accept, were created by God. Around this there is a nebulous area of many other more or less malevolent beings that have become "modelled" by people (a reservoir of Babylonian-Assyrian, Greek and Christian notions, according to Kriss and Kriss-Heinrich, 1962: 14).

The asyad (the zar masters)

I use the words spirits, demons and masters interchangeably, but I have learned that where the *zar* is concerned, these beings are almost never referred to by the women as *jinn* but generally as *asyad* (masters). Some are called sultan or king. This seems to indicate a certain respect. When the word *jinn* is mentioned, moreover, an incantation (*dastur* or *bismillah ar-rahman ar-rahim*) is always pronounced as protec-

---

[7] See Canaan 1914: *Aberglaube und Volksmedizin im Lande der Bibel*, and 1929: *Dämonenglaube im Lande der Bibel*; Kriss & Kriss-Heinrich 1962: *Volksglauben im Bereich des Islam*; Winkler 1920: *Siegel und Charaktere in der Muhammedanischen Zauberei*.

tion. This reinforces my conviction that there is a difference between *jinn* and *asyad*. *Jinn* have the connotation of something bad, while the *asyad* are treated with a certain degree of friendliness, despite the fact that they too are supposed to be responsible for complaints and troubles. Outside the *zar* non-participants talk of all this with some arrogance, dismissing it as *khurafat* (superstition).

The *zar* spirits belong to particular dynasties, with a leader at their head (called the red, yellow, white or black king, *malik*, sultan or *pasha/basha*). The occupying spirits can be male as well as female and possess various names, personalities, professions and nationalities. Littmann (1950: 35-37) speaks of four important groups of demons, namely: spirits with personal names, nature spirits, country spirits and "transition spirits" that come from the realm of the *jinn*. Kriss and Kriss-Heinrich (1962: 145) speak of 66 *zar* spirits, the negative powers, and according to them this is comparable with the 99 "beautiful names of Allah", the positive powers. They too suggest that the spirits are classed according to rank and standing with a leader at their head. The division of spirits in Egypt would be as follows: regional spirits, nature spirits, Coptic spirits, a large group of Islamic spirits, representatives of professional groups and other "pragmatic" spirits. Following Littmann's example, they also add a number of spirits with personal names. The impression of both authors is that in Egypt, apart from the (Coptic) Christian and Islamic spirits, most of the *zar* spirits are "nature demons" and have a regional character. The other researchers into the *zar* in Egypt I have mentioned (Chapter 3) do not give any information about the demons.[8]

I do want to challenge something of the classification of the *zar* spirits by these authors. Certain of the characteristics they mention suggest that there was an underlying earlier division that has for the most part been lost. The spirits still familiar both to the *zar* leaders and the *zar* participants are: Sultan Mamma, Sitt al-Kabira (the great mother) and her sons Yuse (Yusuf) and Warayid, Umm al-Ghulam, the Sultan of the sea dwellers and his sister Safina, Rum Nagd and his sister Maruma, el Walid, Yawra Bey and his father Hakim Basha. Besides these we find 'Aweisha Lalla al-Maghribiyya (the Moroccan), as-Sudani (the Sudanese, who is also called al-Tambura), al-Makkawiyya (the Meccan), al-Habashi (the Ethiopian), as-Sa'udi (the

---

[8] In Omdurman (Sudan) the pantheon of demons seems clearer than in Egypt. See Böringer-Thärigen 1996: 121-146.

Saudi), as-Si'idi (an unnamed demon from Upper Egypt) and al-Gabalawi (the mountain demon). There is further mention of the White Sultan, the Red Sultan and the Yellow Sultan (the latter two are associated with fevers and tropically hot winds), Gado and Saliha (demons associated with impurity, e.g. the toilet), and an unnamed fire spirit. The (Coptic) Christian demons are: an-Nasrani (the Christian), Sultan ad-Deer (the sultan of the monastery) and the virgin Mary. The Islamic spirits are predominantly sufi saints: al-Badawi, al-Bayyumi, al-Dasuqi, Abdel Salam Darwish, 'Abd al-Qadir al-Jilani, and some members of the Prophet's family: Hassan and Hussein and the female saints sayyida Zeynab, sayyida Nafisa and sayyida 'Aisha. I often hear the names of these saints mentioned during the singing of the *zar* songs. It is not clear to me whether these are genuine *zar* demons as Kriss and Kriss-Heinrich say (1962: 147), or that they are named precisely to give protection against the other demons, as is the case in Ethiopia (1962: 199; see also Littmann 1950: 59). All the spirits, regardless of their origins, are alternately benevolent or malevolent. Islamic spirits can never be bad of course, since this would go against all religious convictions. Neither the *sheikha* nor the women I have spoken with are clear on this. I suspect that an emphasis on the Islamic spirits perhaps has to do with the pressure on women to behave at all costs in an Islamic way. Women know that the *zar* is heavily criticized and seek ways in which to let their own activities continue. The assumption of more Islamic elements could be such a way, consciously or unconsciously.

It is difficult to say what the origins are of the *zar* demons. Present-day participants do not know their origin and the authors mentioned above are of the opinion that the Egyptian *zar* is a melting pot of Arab and African belief in demons, so that the type and nature of the spirits is not sharply contoured (Kriss & Kriss-Heinrich 1962: 145). Kramer (1993) and Lewis (1969) write that the demons in African possession cults are generally outsiders, people who are admired or despised, or spirits that reflect historical experiences, such as persons from colonial times, for instance. According to both authors, the point in all cases is that the spirits reflect the experiences and emotions of "the other". Boddy (1988: 15; see also Böringer-Thärigen 1996: 64-69) has made similar observations and writes that in her research area (Hofriyat, Sudan) the spirits always belong to some other society and culture than their own and are always outsiders. The Egyptian *zar* spirits were doubtless once associated with particular situations and experiences too, but this is no longer known today. Only a culture-historical study would be able to provide insight into the origins of the demons.

The same applies to the incantations. Originally the chants were sung in the form of rounds; that is, the *zar* leader takes the lead and the *zar* participants repeat part of what she sings. This still happens in pretty much the same way. But apart from a few words here and there I was unable to understand the texts very well and was thus also unable to investigate their meaning. This is not strange, since the same thing was noted already by Blackman (1927), Zbinden (1953), Lewis (1969) and Gray (1969). Blackman wrote that in her time the meaning of the songs was no longer known. It was (and still is) the custom in Arab magic, furthermore, to pronounce or write down magic words in an incomprehensible language.[9] Sheikh Fathi in Cairo, with whom I often spoken about texts in books of sorcery, similarly called all "foreign" words "Syrian" or "Israelite" (Sengers 1994). Littmann (1950) copied a number of songs written down by his informer and I discussed some of these with Zahra, the *zar* leader mentioned above, and Hassan, the *tambura* player in her music group. Neither of them recognized the songs. This may mean that the songs have changed in the course of time or perhaps were never sung (possible each *zar* leader has her own "repertoire" too). Littmann translated written texts from 1911 and 1930 (which are probably older), but never heard the songs himself. Kriss and Kriss-Heinrich copied Littmann's texts and the songs they heard in their own *zar* experiences correspond to them. Other researchers say nothing about the texts. Three examples of *zar* songs I heard are:

---

[9] (a) Dols 1992: 268: *Majnun: The Madman in Medieval Islamic Society*; Taha Husein 1929: 122: *Al-Ayyam*, Winkler 1931: 193: *Salomo und die Karina*, and 1930: 30, 37: *Siegel und Charaktere in der Muhammedanischen Zauberei*, and Littmann 1950 VII: *Arabische Geisterbeschwörungen aus Ägypten*, all note that use is commonly made of incomprehensible words that are called "Syrian" or "Hebrew" expressions and are regarded as having secret and significant meanings.

(b) Dols (1992: 231) writes that Ibn Taymiyya (1263-1328), a hanbalistic theologian and legal adviser, who can perhaps be called the first "fundamentalist", was critical of sufism and of Muslims who joined in with Christian customs, burning incense and pronouncing incantations in order to neutralize the effects of the evil eye, magic and demons. Laoust writes that Ibn Taymiyya turned fiercely against impermissible "meanderings" in the faith. He wanted to follow only the Koran, *hadith* and *sunna*. He was not a champion of sufism, but never condemned it either. From his disciple Ibn Qayyim, whose medical insights are so important for present-day Koran healers, we know that he was influenced by sufism (EI2, vol. III, 821-822, 951-955). I have noticed that present-day fundamentalists like to refer to Ibn Taymiyya.

Leader: "O mother of Warayid"
Participants: "Come O *zar* bride"
Leader: "O woman of the Hijaz"
Participants: "Come mighty woman"

Leader: "O 'Aweisha Lalla"
Participants: "O Moroccan"
Leader: "O noble woman"
Participants: "She comes from the west"
Leader: "O 'Aweisha Lalla"
Participants: "O Moroccan"
Leader: "Welcome O lady"
Participants: "She comes from the west"

Leader: "O Mamma of the Right Guidance"
Participants: "O Mamma"
Leader: "The Perfect Full Moon"
Participants: "That is you O Mohammed"
Leader: "The *kursi* is set up"
Participants: "For Mamma"
Leader: "The candles are lit"
Participants: "For Mamma"

The songs that are song and which I have heard do not seem to differ greatly from Littmann's examples (1950). They are open-ended, incomplete and changing. But the music and the song "do" something with those present. The monotonous and repetitive singing of the *kudya* and the sound of the drums arouse regression, after which boundary-crossing into another state of consciousness is easier. It is a "sound-bath" which permeates everything and has an effect on the brainwaves. The mind is released and the individual falls into a state of trance (see also Finkler 1986: 637-638). At that moment it is as if the body is the real spectator and gesture, feeling and image are its language. A tension is built up, which is responded to by the participation of those present. The patients are "taken" and their bodies activated through their being inhabited by the master. The images evoked do not involve the women in a story and they are not meant for "contemplation". They do not lead to meaning and have no teleological goal. But it is precisely the lack of all this that gets the listeners involved.

Interpretation: zar as transition rite

As we touched upon in Chapter 3, Turner (1969) divides rituals into three phases: the separation phase, the liminal phase and the incorporation phase. These phases as so classified, are provided with fuller detail in the picture that follows.

The separation phase

The preparations for the *zar* constitute the separation phase. A feature of this phase is that the sick person is released from her group in a symbolic way. This part consists of three important moments. It begins with the sick person finding no relief from her complaints from healers or doctors she has consulted earlier and going to a *sheikha*. After a sort of admission conversation, the latter makes the diagnosis that in her case the problem is demons that for one reason or another have become angry with her and have invaded her body. By acknowledging the "occupation" of the body, the cause of the "conflict" is established and a way of restoring the relationships can be sought.

The next step is that the sick person has to hand the *sheikha* an *atar* (sign) of herself. This is generally a headscarf with some money tied up in the corner. The medium lays the scarf under her own pillow for three days and nights. During this time she asks her master (her own occupying spirit) to make the cause of her client's sickness known to her. She also wants to know which *asyad* (masters) have caused the sickness and what she must do to heal the person. That is to say, she wants to know how to pacify the *asyad* so that they leave the patient alone. Generally she is given instructions by her master to organize a *zar* in which a sacrifice is to be made. This is called *'aqd*, the contract between the possessed person and the master (the association with a marriage contract cannot completely be ruled out here; see also below, p. 117). Depending on the financial wherewithal of the patient, the sacrifice consists of a few white doves, a (generally) black chicken and a white cockerel, a turkey, a brown or black sheep or a goat. The *sheikha* then makes a *kursi*. This is a sacrificial table on which she sets out a number of candles, amulets, incense, specially prepared dishes, biscuits and other luxury items. Depending on the requirements set by the possessing demon alcohol and cigarettes may be added. In addition, she needs special items of clothing, which must be worn by her and the patient at the request of the spirits. She also must have at her disposal one or several music groups. After three days she knows who the demons are who are troubling the possessed person and she makes a "binding". She does this by knotting a coin in a cloth and tying it under the patient's left armpit. In a previously specially cleaned room three large candles are placed next to the sacrificial table, which are lit one hour before sundown. The patient spends the night in this room. The next morning she has to be dressed in a white *gallabiyya* (tunic). This is also how the *sheikha* herself is dressed, and she also has a white headscarf on and silver rings on her fingers and amulets around her neck (the sort of amulet depends on the requirements of the masters possessing the medium).

The liminal phase

In the liminal phase the patient is in a state of transition. She follows the instructions of the *zar* leader, who helps her to make the step to the status of cult initiate. The rituals are performed for one woman in her own home or at the home of the *sheikha*. The possessed person is accompanied by other women from her family and often also by her husband and her children. All attention is fixed on her and despite the crowd of people around her she remains the centre of attention throughout the whole of the ceremony. Also present is an important group of women spectators, who may or may not be possessed, and they come to "dance and talk" with their demon. This is certainly not cheap, because despite the fact that a substantial sum has been paid before the ceremony by the person who has commissioned it (depending on the means of the patient, two to three hundred pounds; in 1996/97 a pound was worth about twenty pence sterling), the others present have to pay the musicians for each dance (at a minimum of one pound per dance). Some of those present do not dance and just watch. This may be because they do not consider themselves to be possessed or because they have no money available for this (I have witnessed an argument that arose because a woman refused to be doused with incense for a second time because she would have to pay for it again). I do not know how much the *zar* leader is left with after a *zar* performance.[10] She has a large group of people

---

[10] On the payment of considerable amounts to the spiritual healer, Van Binsbergen (1999b) states: "… the money severs possible ties of lifelong dependence and transference which would otherwise develop; it is the one reminder that beyond the dream of

around her assisting her, who have to be paid too. Zahra, the *zar* leader I have described, seems to be able to make a living of it, but she confided in me that by comparison with earlier days when the *zar* was performed more frequently, her income now is much reduced. The audience present is important for the patient because this gives her support and at the same time recognition of her possession. The women "spectators" have dressed up for the occasion and wear a lot of perfume. These are requirements set by the occupying demons; the women have to please their own demon during the ceremony. Each *zar* leader works with fixed music groups (*firqa*). There are three different groups, which are active in turns during one ceremony and produce a completely different sound in each case: the *harim masri*, the *abu gheet* and the *tambura*. For each group different sorts of incense are used, too: for the first group this is mastic, aloes and Indian herbs; for the second, mastic, aloes and benzoin resin, and for the third aloes, galbanum and other aromatic spices. During the various parts of the ceremony the possessed person also wears different items of clothing and headscarves. The ceremony proper can also be divided into three phases by means of these ritual paraphernalia.

The ceremony always starts with extensive incensing of all those present (head, hands, trunk, and the legs under the skirts), who have to pay a specified amount for this (five pounds). After recitation of the *Fatiha* (the opening sura of the Koran) and a number of hymns of praise in honour of the Prophet and his companions, the "masters" are called upon by the *zar* leader (Zahra begins with "*ya asyad beet al-Mamma*" ["O masters of the house of *al-Mamma*"] and continues, "Welcome masters, dance with us O master, O sultan Mamma, welcome, etc."). She starts off the songs, which are answered by the musicians and the others present. After this the *harim masri* (literally: Egyptian women) usually begin to play, a music group made up entirely of older women. They play the *tabla*, a funnel-shaped drum held under the arm, and the *duff*, a large round drum held with one hand and beaten with the other. It is very important for the *sheikha* to know the correct names of the masters and the music that goes with them. During the singing of the incantations a master makes himself known by means of a "sign" that the possessed person recognizes and which makes her feel a strong inner urge to dance.

---

a self-contained personal microcosm which the therapy pretends to restore, lies a world of impersonal, universalised, value, calibrated and rendered infinitely exchangeable through the external, alien medium of money" (1999: 15).

After about two hours a short break follows and after that the *abu gheet* plays (probably named after the village to the north of Cairo where many *zar* musicians come from). This is a group of male musicians playing the *tabla, hana* and *nay* (drum, tambourine with little bells, and flute). The dancer giving the lead then also plays *as-saghat* (a sort of metal clappers fixed between the thumb and the index finger). The music of this group is melodious and the clappers make it sound quite light and cheerful, as appropriate at a "wedding" between the possessed woman and the master. During this part of the ceremony the sacrifice of the animals takes place. Usually this is poultry, such as chickens, cockerels and turkeys (sometimes also sheep, goats, and even camels), the beak and wings of which are cleaned by the *sheikha* and then incensed. The patient walks around or past the *kursi* seven times with the other offerings, while the *sheikha* and her helpers recite special formulas to adjure the *zar* spirits. The animals are slaughtered after this and a few drops of blood are sprinkled over the "tying" and the forehead of the possessed woman. (Occasionally the *sheikha* also smears part of the blood on the patient's head, elbows, thighs and belly.) The incense-burner goes through the room again and the *sheikha* calls upon the great masters with a special formula in which the Prophet and the names of Islamic saints are repeatedly uttered. After this ritual the company eats of the meal that has been prepared in the meantime, but this does not mean the end of the ceremony, since after a break the dancing continues.

After the break the *tambura*, a mixed group of men and women, plays. The *tambura* is a three, four, five or six-stringed lyre whose round soundbox is stretched over with goatskin, in which there are two openings called eyes (*'ain*). From the soundbox two wooden beams run diagonally upwards, connected together at various heights, roughly in the shape of a trapezium. The wooden beams and the cross connections are wrapped around with coloured ribbons, ropes of pearls and brushes and decorated with shells and amulets. The other instruments are: the *al-mazhar* (a hand-drum fifty centimetres in diameter and twelve centimetres high), the *tabla nuss* or *darabuqqa* (a cylindrical drum), the *al-marjas* (a drum beaten on both sides), the *tabla tambura* (a drum thirty centimetres in diameter which is beaten with a wooden stick, and the *ar-riqq* (a sort of tambourine). Groups like this have a *mangur*, a dance leader who wears a *mangur al-hawafir*, a thirty to forty-centimetre wide belt of goat nails fixed with small leather straps. By swinging the hips these produce a ringing sound. Dancing, and swinging his hips, he also plays the *as-saghat* (round metal clap-pers). By encouraging the women to dance he has to help them to get into an ecstatic state.[11] The *tambura* is the most important instrument in the group and its music is the most important of the evening. The *tambura* is considered to be inspired by the *asyad* (masters), who speak with the possessed by means of sounds. The music sounds heavy and dramatic, and whenever this group plays, the dancing participants get very excited. They dance facing the musicians, keeping their head and face covered with a *tarha* (a light transparent veil). Their upper bodies twist to and fro, the footwork being unimportant (the women scarcely move from the spot and the feet do not make special figures but more stamping on the spot movements). It is primarily the upper body that moves, twisting rhythmically. The eyes are closed and the faces express violent emotions. They keep on dancing until they liter-ally fall over. The *sheikha* then whispers a few words into the possessed persons' ears and blows rose oil into their faces, which makes them "wake up". The masters have left their body again and the women stay behind, exhausted but content. This moment is called "libera-tion", *ar-radwa'*. For a whole week the patient must sleep in the room where the ceremony has taken place. During this time her husband must keep away from her. This is by no means so strictly controlled as it used to be. These days the *sheikha* and her helpers, the musicians and guests leave after a day and a half to two days. When the *zar* is held outside the sick person's home, the sick person goes back to her own home when this part of the ceremony is over.

It should be noted that the *zar* is also attended by women who have no pathological history, but are still regarded as "clothed" because their behaviour does not correspond with cultural ideals and norms. This can be a whole variety of things, such as refusing to marry, behaving like a grouse, withdrawal, absentmindedness, confusion and in some cases childlessness.

---

[11] According to Kriss and Kriss-Heinrich (1962: 182) the word *tambura* relates only to the musical instrument in Egypt and not, as in Sudan, to the ceremony and every-thing that has to do with it. This is not my experience. In the *zars* I have attended, this part of the ceremony is also called *tambura*, and the reference is not merely to the instrument. In some Islamic countries the *tambura* is also called *simsimiyya* (Jenkins & Rovsing 1976; Shiloah 1995).

The incorporation phase (the hadra*)*

The incorporation phase begins with the second part of the dance session, when a "slaughter" (sacrifice) is performed for the masters. The sick woman's transition is now complete. She has been adopted into the cult group and will now go regularly to the *hadra* because her master "calls" her. The *hadra* is the public *zar*, at which other possessed women are also present (it is not held specially for one woman alone). These weekly gatherings are at the home of the *sheikha* or another *zar* leader and are organized at different localities within and outside Cairo (and elsewhere in Egypt). Some of these gatherings begin early in the afternoon, others not until around nine in the evening, going on until midnight. Here too, it is not the case that all the women present are possessed. Some come because they suspect this to be so, and if a woman gets an irresistible urge to get up and dance during the music (*daqqa*), this is viewed as a "sign" of a demon inside her. In order to be sure of this, however, and to be able to identify the demon, they must consult the *sheikha*. There are also women who come simply for social reasons or out of curiosity.

The function of the *kudya* (leader) in the *hadra* is limited to incensing the women and collecting a financial contribution of about five Egyptian pounds per person. In addition, the women pay the musicians one pound for each dance. The leader does not conduct any rituals to determine by which demon a woman is possessed, she does not sing any incantations and does not sacrifice any animals. The music is also much simpler here and consists of a group of women (*harim masri*) and a group of men (*abu gheet*). It is the female and male musicians that sing over the *zar* spirits. The *kudya* in the *hadra* seems to me more an "organizer" and "overseer" whose primary aim is to earn money than a "spiritual leader" who tracks down and pacifies evil spirits affecting women. The cosy character of the *hadra* ensures that it is like a *hafla* (party), as a woman told me. The fact that they can relax there will certainly have a therapeutic effect.

Personal experiences in the hadra

One of the *hadras* I regularly attend is held on the top floor of an almost derelict house in one of Cairo's old districts. It is quite a large, unfurnished room with two windows well above eye-level. Some old clothes lie around on the floor and the air is heavy with incense. On entering I am first doused with incense by the leader. I then go and sit down somewhere. The room is full of women sitting cross-legged together in groups on the ground. They drink tea, eat biscuits and fruit (the consumption of such little luxuries adds to the festive feeling) and chat and laugh together. The atmosphere is very relaxed. The music group consists of five older women whole play the instruments. I recognize the *nay* (bamboo flute without mouthpiece), *ri"* (*riqq*, tambourine with little tinkling bells), *tabla* (drum) and *saghat* (sort of round metallic clappers which make a ringing sound). The women's dance has little in common with what one mainly sees in Egypt, so-called "belly-dancing" with much swinging of the hips and elegant gestures with the arms and hands. It is more an on-the-spot rhythmic movement of the upper body and feet. In its use primarily of drums (*daqqa*) the music is reminiscent of music from black Africa. The music begins slowly, getting gradually stronger and ending in a climax of vigorous drumming.

After about an hour and a half there is a short break and the music group is relieved by a group of seven men. A few smiling women told me in advance that things really get going when the *rigala* (men) come and play. This is no exaggeration, since although the musical instruments stay the same, the male musicians make the music more exciting. Together with some of the women I dance in the vicinity of the group of musicians. Now and again one of them dances with us in encouragement. No one touches anyone else and everyone watches out that no one does anything that cannot be tolerated, i.e. that moral standards are not infringed. If a scarf should slip it is tied back in the hair, skirts are pulled down straight and smooth and any area of skin that is accidentally bared and rendered visible is immediately covered up again.[12] The women dance with their scarves pulled over their faces, and when later I ask a woman sitting next to me why that is so, she answers, "That way I am alone with my spirit." The dance is the "private conversation" between the woman and her spirit. She is a large, sturdy *baladi* woman, who tells me

---

[12] Messing (1959: 327) writes that in the Ethiopian *zar* each woman has two human "protectors" who protect the woman against injury, for example, during her possession trance. In the Egyptian *zar* too, family members stand around the woman in trance to catch her if she falls.

that she is possessed by a spirit which makes her suffer from headaches and aching limbs. She has a ready laugh and likes to talk. She comes here every week and her husband approves. Here she dances and "speaks" with her master. It is very relaxing, she says, and one can tell that she enjoys it, since she dances with abandon. Various songs are sung, many of which seem to be "religious" songs of some sort, telling of the greatness of Allah and the Prophet. Sometimes I can recognize the names of Muslim saints. Some of the women seem to know the songs, or parts of them, by heart and join in loudly. They do not dance to every song that is played. A woman tells me that each master reacts to a particular melody and that the women therefore know exactly which music to get up to dance to.

Bulbul (hadra-*attendee*)

Bulbul is a widow and lives alone, but she has two children. One of them, a daughter, died three years ago. Bulbul started going to *zars* twenty years ago. Always with *sheikh* Ibrahim in a small village outside Cairo where a *zar* is held every Friday afternoon (that is where I met Bulbul). She had "trouble with her nerves" and thus with her stomach. Ordinary medicines did not help and so she went to *sheikh* Ibrahim. She says she does not go for the *zar* itself, but the *sheikh* "opens the Koran" to her (i.e. he makes incantations). She also had the *sheikh* come to her home once, when an evil neighbour threatened to put a spell (*yiktib/sihr*) on her house. The *sheikh* then went through the house with incense, slaughtered a chicken in the bathroom (which he also took with him afterwards) and he ate a great deal of the special meal she had prepared. The spell was then undone. According to Bulbul the *sheikh* does not do magic or sorcery, but with the aid of the Koran he can "see" what is wrong with someone. These days, she says, the *zar* is no longer concerned with the *asyad*, but songs are sung for Allah and the saints (*sidi* Hussein, *sidi* Badawi, *sayyida* Zeinab, *sayyida* Nafisa and others). According to Bulbul, when women react to particular music, only then starting to dance, this is prompted by the body itself and is not because there is a spirit in it. Bulbul maintains that in her case she is interested only in the Koran reading and not in dancing with the masters. When I tell her I have clearly seen that the

dancing does her good, she admits that the *zar* makes her forget
the pain in her legs, and it is so cosy here ...

The ceremony has as it were reinvigorated the possessed woman and
healed her. But this does not last long, and this is because the *asyad*
have not been exorcized and have not disappeared forever. They
have only been temporarily pacified. A sick person once diagnosed as
"visited by a master" (clothed/occupied by a master) will always continue to suffer from it. The master calls her again and again, and
again and again she needs the help of the *sheikha* since she alone can
"see". Usually the way things work is that after the person concerned
has been adopted in the cult group, she goes regularly to dance in the
hadra. After a few years, if she has saved enough money, she will once
again have a "slaughter" performed, i.e. have her demons pacified.

Communitas

The *zar* can thus be divided into the three phases characteristic of a *rite
de passage*: separation, marginality and incorporation. Do Turner's views
of *communitas* (equality, protest, reflection, change etc.) also apply here?

I looked first of all to see if there might be any question of a protest
against the existing structure and the possibility of changing existing
situations, as claimed by Turner, but also by Boddy (1988; 1989), al-
Khuly (1996) and others. A possible comparison could be made with
what Fernea and Fernea write (1972; 1977) about saint-veneration in
Tunisia. They claim that women in Tunisia do indeed protest against
the existing structure by means of saint-veneration. This opinion is
shared by Mernissi (1975; 1977). The heavy involvement of women in
saint-veneration would be an expression of their dissatisfaction with
patriarchal society and a protest against their position in it. In the
sanctuaries women not only find space to express their grievances,
but this is even encouraged. Does anything change as a result in their
social situation outside the sanctuaries? No, because despite the fact
that they make every effort to engage supernatural powers to bend
the oppressive structure, they do not succeed; it has no effect on the
formal power structure (Mernissi 1977: 111-112).

There is a comparison to be drawn between what takes place in
saint-veneration in Tunisia and what happens in the *zar* in Egypt.
Among the women who attend the *zar*, there are perhaps a few for
whom illness and possession are an expression of protest against the

prevailing situation. There is also the possibility for conscious or unconscious manipulation of persons in the social environment, but there is no question of there being a "secret agenda" (Scott 1990). By contrast to what happens in saint-veneration in Tunisia, the *zar* masters are not asked to mediate in a given situation. Nor do they offer an alternative vision through which something can be set in motion in the women's thinking. If this were the case, then they would indeed be potentially explosive means of bringing about change. In my judgment, too, demon-possession has a powerful and challenging function in the context of the Egyptian *zar*, but for most women it does not include protest or resistance.

The next question is whether the *zar* has an effect on the existing power structure, as Turner says, or whether a particular situation is rather consolidated. Before giving an answer to this, I would look again at the events in the *zar*. In many ways the possessed person undergoes a status change within that context. First, the healing rituals in which the possessed person and significant others participate, are performed in the presence of as many family members and friends as possible. When a woman is acknowledged in her sick person's role, her status changes. She is treated with more respect and consideration, if only temporarily in most cases (for recognition of the sick person's role see also Boddy 1986; 1989; Morsy 1978; 1993). Another status change is that the woman "weds" the master possessing her. As in the everyday social situation an *'aqd* (contract) is made. The woman often calls her husband *sid* (singular of *asyad*), master, and she owes him complete obedience. This is also the case in the symbolic marriage with the demon. She has to meet all his wishes and requirements. The spirit world seems then to resemble the woman's everyday social world (see also Nelson 1971: 199). But do the events within the *zar* also lead to changes outside the *zar*? In my opinion this is not the case. The life of Egyptian women, particular in the lower social classes, relies on firm social ties, a clearly circumscribed environmental context and a tacit dependence on it in order to be able to function well in everyday life. If the harmony in this is disturbed, deep-seated emotional problems emerge. I suspect, and conversations with women confirm this suspicion, that most health complaints arise as a result of tensions in the environmental context, between the woman and her husband, between the woman and the family and between her and the broader society (I describe these situations in Chapter 7 below). The events in the *zar*, it is true, are "re-presentation" of the conditions of everyday life (Haldeman 1990: 49-57), but it does not necessarily lead to reflection on the circumstances and subsequently to changes in the world outside the *zar*. The "cure" in the *zar* is not intended for this purpose anyway; its goal is the reduction of tension. Through it the possessed person experiences a "liberation" and a "reversal of the evil" (improvement in the physical or psychological problems). But this is only temporary. In the woman's daily life outside the *zar*, in most cases no enduring and real change comes about. At best, in her social situation there is consideration for her "illness" (possession), but in due course people fall back into old patterns and the symptoms return too. This is reflected on a supernatural level in the fact that she is repeatedly "called" by her demon master (Finkler 1986: 631 also writes that an enduring feeling of wellbeing is linked with regular repetition of the healing rituals). My answer to the above question, whether there is any question of change or of consolidation of the existing structure, is that in the case of the *zar*, one must take account of the fact that both the existing structure and the position of women within it are confirmed by the women themselves: the *zar* is a way of maintaining the status quo.

And what is the situation with such aspects as comradeship, equality and the possibility of breaking through the limitations set by the everyday social structure, enabling reflection and "reorientation" vis-à-vis existing relationships (Turner 1974)? During the *zar* ceremony there is evidence of spontaneous and open *communitas*. Limitations of the everyday structure are removed, and there is toleration of free expression of what is normally considered reproachable behaviour, such as the use of alcohol and cigarettes, among other things. The dance leader whips the women up into a state of ecstasy in their dancing. Alienation and isolation appear to be resolved. But within the *zar* too, although there is an atmosphere of friendship and "shared pain", status differences remain noticeable, just like in social life outside. This is expressed first of all in the fact that a section of the "spectators" have not made a sacrifice and have therefore not been fully accepted into the cult group. Status is also expressed in the tokens of wealth set out on the *kursi* (sacrificial table) and in the slaughter of sacrificial animals. A substantial amount of money is needed in order to be able to organize a private *zar*, and so, despite their needs, this will be beyond the means of some women. Poor women often do not even have enough money to be able to dance and they do not partake of the meal offered to the guests during the ceremony either.

Another side-effect of the *zar* is that it gives certain women the opportunity to gain a higher status within the cult, one that differs markedly from their position in everyday life outside. The *zar* leader and, to a lesser degree, her helpers, are distinguished in status within the *zar*. The *zar* is also their living. Outside the cult group their work is not appreciated and they do not enjoy any social standing. So the extent to which the everyday structure is broken through within the *zar* is limited and there is no question of there being an opening into a new situation outside.

Similarly, I have doubts about participants' reflection on their own situation, as Turner expects is the case. Two social scientists who have done research into the *zar* in Egypt, suggest this possibility. Thus al-Khuly (1996: 11) writes that women have the opportunity during the ceremony to exchange ideas, express feelings and make suggestions. This can set ideas in motion that bring about another perspective on life. Nelson (1971: 205) speaks also of the emergence of an "alternative female worldview". How appropriate are their claims? In the "mimicking" of demons during the *zar* is there any question of reflexivity resulting in another experience of oneself? I think not. Events in social life drive the woman to the *zar*, but the demon's "tasks" which the possessed woman performs there have no direct connection with situations outside. There is no talking with others about personal experiences during the ceremony either. So I think that in the *zar* there is no question of reflection either, though there is of "blame-shifting". In Egypt I have observed that many in this society have a stronger inclination to project problems onto "outsiders" (*jinn*, *asyad*, magic and the evil eye) than to deal with things in an introspective way. Society is seen in relation to the spirits and the master is held responsible for everything that goes wrong in personal life. *Zar* works as follows: blame is laid outside the possessed person. She is confronted with factors from her own culture, objects, persons, relationship and environment, but she is never blamed for her own situation of distress. She may express aggression or wishes within the context of the ceremony, but the ultimate result is that she has to come to terms with the inescapable reality.

Nor do I agree with those researchers who say that changes take place in the life of the women because an important network is created by the *zar*, which allows them to make new relationships operating outside their daily lives (see Chapter 3). I have never noticed that women who attend the *zar* go and visit each other in daily life too.

Women are always constantly occupied with maintaining their honour and reputation. News of birth, marriage, death and other things
that cannot easily be kept hidden from others is exchanged freely, but
the less an outsider knows about intimate personal affairs, the better
(see also Early 1993; Rugh 1984; Wikan 1980; 1996). It has struck me
that the woman for whom the *zar* is organized comes with her own
group of "supporters". Most of the other women (the spectators) do
this too. They attend the *zar* with a daughter, sister or friend (it is not
customary for women to go somewhere on their own, since this can
damage their reputation). During the ceremony they stay together
and hardly any words are exchanged with other women, except for
superficial polite conversation. My observations are confirmed by
Finkler, who writes that healing rituals achieve rather the opposite of
social interaction because the belief that they are making contact with
spirits in trance requires by definition an introversion from the ritual
participant. This makes interaction work in a vertical direction,
between the participant and the supernatural, instead of a horizontal
direction between the participants (Finkler 1986: 636). Women I have
met in the course of various *zars* and *hadras* and whom I have visited
at home kept impressing on me beforehand the need not to talk about
the place where we first met (the *zar*) in the presence of others. They
often prefer people outside their own immediate family not to know
that they attend *zars*. It is certainly the case that besides the possessed
person for whom the ceremony is organized and besides the more or
less fixed group of fellow possessed persons and spectators, there is
also a "hard core" of women that more or less belong with a particular *zar* leader. Some assist her, while others "hang around". Each
week, even several times a week, they attend various *zar* meetings (to
some extent they can be compared with "groupies" who hang around
pop groups in the western world). In this case one can indeed speak of
a "network".

In the *hadra* things are different. Here it is rather easier to talk with
one another and because these meetings are organized and attended
by women on a weekly basis, this is a more or less fixed meeting place
for women outside the boundaries of their everyday existence.

Turner did research into quite a different type of society than I did.
He worked in country communities in Zambia, while I did my
research among women in the world city of Cairo. Turner's theory
suggests that liminality implies more possibilities than simply "abreaction" against suppressed effects (catharsis), namely a transition to

structural change. I have not noticed this to be a durable result of *zar* rituals in Egypt. Through the symbolic "marriage" with the master, it is more a case of a reinforcement of the existing situation of the possessed person than of change. So instead of transition rituals I would prefer to call the rituals in the *zar* "maintenance rituals". They do not lead to long-term change, but they do lead to a temporary discharge of psychological and/or social tension.

So if attendance at the *zar* does not bring about abiding change in women's roles in the everyday social world, what *does* the *zar* do? The primary goal in the *zar* is not to tell stories about reality. The ritual is not a tool for attaining social goals either. The different processes that are at work in the *zar* relate to a series of goals, namely coping with desires, passions and weaknesses. Secondary priorities are reciprocity and care for others. Further, the *zar* aims to strengthen the patients and the initiates.

A premise in the *zar* is a connection between person, society and cosmos. The rituals are oriented to the patient who has arranged the *zar*, her direct living environment and the spectators who are invited. It is a combination of symbolism, drama and therapy. The three aspects are equally important. By putting too much emphasis on one aspect, justice is not done to the two others: all three have a part to play.

The women I have observed in the *zar* and with whom I have conducted lengthy conversations, have problems with their nervous system, headaches, indeterminate pains in their arms and legs and "boiling blood". The pains they feel are absolutely not imagined and not intended to protest against injustice, express despair, withdraw from responsibilities or gain favours. With their sick role they do not gain much either, certainly not in the long term. In many cases it even adds pressure rather than alleviating it.

The symbolism of the *zar* communicates sentiments experienced elsewhere. Dissatisfaction can be expressed through the masters and through the masters secret desires can be admitted to, such as dancing, smoking and drinking: in short, escape from everyday life. Since the *zar* ceremony temporarily reduces stress, the symptoms can be reduced too. On the other hand, since the *zar* has a regulating effect, the social structure is in fact bolstered.

The researchers whose work I discussed in Chapter 3 lay too much emphasis, in my opinion, on the "functional" aspects of the ritual and thus they underplay other aspects, such as the therapeutic effects of the ritual and the significant experience for the *kudya*, the patient and the spectators. They also miss the fact that within the context of Islamic occult traditions the *zar* is less exotic than people think (cf. Gray 1969: 176). The non-ritual aspects are broadly equivalent to those of the religious (Koran) healers.

The atmosphere in Koran healing is completely different from that in the *zar*. Therapy with the Koran, as utilized by more commercially oriented healers, taps into a long tradition in which the holy book is used for healing from all kinds of sicknesses and ailments. As in the *zar*, a connection is assumed to exist between person, society and cosmos. The women who consult the Koran healers have the same ailments as the women who attend the *zar*. Their complaints are described by the healer as "touching" or "possession" by demons. Koran healers assume that particular Koran texts possess power and a specific light which work prophylactically against invasion by demons. And demons who have already entered a person can be driven out by this means. For this, recitation in a specific manner is required, known only to the healers. If the healer has the patient's confidence and works with conviction, he is in a position to change that person's experience or situation. Like the *zar* leader, the Koran healer articulates cultural symbols at a specific moment in time and as in her case, his success depends on his competence to organize and manipulate things in such a way that what ensues meets expectations.

CHAPTER FIVE

KORAN HEALING

Men or women who are "touched" (*mass* or *lams*) by the *jinn* or *'afarit*, or are "possessed" (*malbus/labs*) can be healed of these by means of a treatment with *ruqya*. *Ruqyas* are "magic spells" but in the case of Koran healing (Egyptian dialect: *'ilag bil-qur'an*) the reference is to extensive recitations of special verses from the Koran which offer protection against *jinn* and *'afarit*, sorcery/magic or the evil eye. The recitations are performed by a spiritual healer, often called *sheikh*, but a more official Egyptian term is *mu'alig bil-qur'an* (Koran healer). The treatment can take place at the patient's home or the healer's home, but often occurs in special "clinics for Islamic medicine" or in a room above or next to a particular mosque. The whole thing is then very reminiscent of group therapy since on average fifty to sixty women come to each *jalsa* (session). In some mosques there are as many as three sessions a day. If the therapy takes place in a clinic or next to the mosque, a rather small contribution is requested (around ten Egyptian pounds). Healers who work at home often seem to ask large sums for it, but I found it difficult to find out how large the amounts were.[1] Both men and women can suffer from touching or possession, but my experience is that it is predominantly women who are affected. From interviews and informal conversations with women I have come to the conclusion that the concern is with a wide variety of social, economic and sexual problems which lead to mental instability and physical problems, all of which the healer puts down to "touching" or "possession" and are treated by means of *ruqya*.

The function of Koran healer is, one might say, a new profession. By "new" I mean that there have always been persons who have tried to help people with the aid of the Koran, but now it is a matter of "professional healers". Rather poorly educated persons have discovered a gap in the market which allows them to earn a decent living as healers. Their art is not based on scientific medical knowledge but on a particular interpretation of religion. I shall return to this.

---

[1] Sabir Shawkat, an Egyptian journalist, wrote in *al-Jann wa al-Jamilat* (The *Jinn* and the Egyptian 'Stars'/ Celebrities, Cairo 1995), that some contemporary Koran healers/sorcerers earn large sums of money.

In accordance with the *hadith* (traditions of the Prophet), the most important instigators of sickness are devils, demons and the evil eye, while in prophetic medicine God is seen as the most important instigator (see Chapter 2). For the present-day Koran healer, devils and demons, equally, are the most important instigators of illness. A large proportion of their treatments displays similarities with principles from prophetic medicine. The ideas of the mediaeval doctor Ibn al-Qayyim, mentioned above, are particularly influential on them. Their patients are primarily, but not exclusively, women from the lower social classes, for which the treatment has a low threshold since their culture as it were calls for this sort of healing. From childhood they have learned that the holy words of the Koran contain *baraka* (blessing/grace) and offer protection against *jinn*.

No one knows the precise number of healers, but according to the Egyptian press, in Cairo alone there are more than three hundred healers, who practise in mosques, clinics or at home. I have attended the meetings of ten healers on a regular basis. I would point out that a clear distinction has to be made between "healing with the aid of the Koran" by non-professional, non-commercial healers who help people by virtue of their religious conviction, and "Koran healing" by professional, commercial healers for whom this is a living. Here I am talking about the latter category. Although any practising Muslim will readily agree that the Koran brings healing, since this is said in sura *al-Isra'* (17): 82, which reads, "And We reveal of the Quran that which is a healing and a mercy to the believers", nonetheless in the eyes of many people Koran healing goes too far in the form in which it is found in mosques and "Islamic clinics". They generally do not know precisely what takes place at such a session of Koran healing. When they hear of it, they think that it is only "stupid and undeveloped" people who participate, but that is far from being the case.

General description

The building I have just entered is situated in a narrow street in one of Cairo's many popular districts and on the outside it looks nothing like a mosque. The front entrance is teeming with women. When I get upstairs I go to the *sheikh*, the one who is leading this meeting. He is a man with a friendly face, who is wearing a white *gallabiyya* and a loosely buttoned headscarf. I am very welcome, he says, and he introduces me to his "assistants". These are five men, also dressed in *gallabiyyas*, and an equal number of women dressed from head to toe in black, heavily veiled. Later I will see what the functions of these assistants are. This room, but also the room I first came into, is quite large. There are green mats on the floor and chairs all along the walls. The *sheikh* says that I should watch carefully, and if I have questions I should just come to him. The hall is now slowly filling up with women, who sit down on the chairs. I go and sit among them. The session begins with the *sheikh* telling the women that there are certain rules they must adhere to. In Koran healing they must wear absolutely no amulets on their person and there must be none on the wall at home either. God is the Healer, and they must rely on him and not on amulets. After that he lists the ills and infirmities caused by *ginn* (*jinn*), which can be healed by recitation of the Koran.

The *sheikh* begins with a recitation of the Fatiha, the opening sura of the Koran. The women listen, eyes downcast. One of the male assistants then takes over the microphone from the *sheikh* and projects at great speed and with a very compelling and loud voice a flood of Koran texts over their heads. It is all so fast that I cannot possibly understand what he is saying. Some women quickly go into a sort of trance. The assistants keep a close eye on these women, and as soon as one of them begins to twist her head or to flail about with her arms, they hurriedly go over to her and wipe the sweat from her forehead with a paper handkerchief or straighten out the cloth that is meant to cover her legs which may have got a little out of place. Suddenly a woman begins to beat about wildly with her arms, cries out and falls on the ground with a bump.[2] The assistant *sheikh* goes and sits next to her and screams into her ear at the top of his voice, "*bismillah, bismillah, bismillah*" (calling upon God), followed by a series of Koran texts. He also screams in her ear at the demon "*ukhrug, ukhrug!*" (get out, go away!). All around me there is now loud screaming and moaning and squirming of bodies on the ground. The *sheikh's* assistants run hurriedly from one case to another, while he himself watches contentedly. I walk over to a woman

---

[2] Dols (1992: 278) writes that falling on the ground is seen as a clear sign of possession by an inimical *jinn*.

lying on the ground. Her face is distorted as if in pain, her body is squirming about and she is uttering loud, shrill shrieks. The *sheikh's* assistant sits next to her and recites Koran verses into her ear; one of the veiled women has covered her with a blanket and is holding her tightly. After a little while the assistant orders her to lift her arm and move the finger where the demon is at that moment. Unexpectedly he pricks her finger with a pin and presses a drop of deep red blood out of it. The woman shrieks and then calms down. The assistant talks to her a little longer and then moves on to the next case. The woman stays lying down for a minute or two and then I help her to a chair, where she stays sitting, apparently exhausted.

Gradually the "treated" women go, leaving only the women who, hanging in their chairs, are still wrestling with the demons that are possessing their bodies, who evidently do not give up so easily. One by one these women are treated separately in the hall adjacent. I go over too and watch what happens to a young woman I sat talking with for a while earlier on. She is lying on the ground, covered up by one of the veiled women. The assistant loudly shouts *bismillahs* in her ear and recites Koran verses. Now and again she seems to wake up to some degree from her trance and he asks her how she feels. Her answer is always "I can't feel anything", whereupon the assistant recites louder and calls upon God. At one point she also has her finger pricked, after which she squirms around on the floor. The assistant does not seem happy with the result and orders her to stand up. She does this and stands in front of him, swaying. When the assistant keeps shouting Koran texts and "get out, get out" in her ear, she suddenly falls over backwards onto the floor with a bump. The assistant stays sitting next to her, praying, until she gets up of her own accord and sits down on a chair. He admonishes her to say more prayers and otherwise leaves her alone.

The call to evening prayer rings out and the *sheikh* and his assistants withdraw to pray. Most of the women that remain in the hall do the same. I take the opportunity to leave.

This *sheikh* conducts three prayer meetings for women afflicted by demons each Saturday afternoon (and on Wednesday afternoons a session for men). Through the reciting of the Holy Koran, the *jinn* are driven back out of their bodies. Below I give an account of this *sheikh's* views in interview form. In another part of Cairo, predominantly a people's district, I attend the prayer meetings of *sheikh* Al-Mu'attar, which also have the aim of expelling the *shayatin* (devils) and *jinn* (demons) from people. The *sheikh* is a friendly old man who holds his practice in an "Islamic clinic". The clinic is housed in a six-storey building. There is a mosque, a Koran school, a library, a study and the *sheikh*'s surgery. Housed in the same building are also a number of regular doctors with all kinds of specializations. The *sheikh* says that these doctors regularly refer patients to him. The *sheikh*'s surgery is for private consultations; a noticeboard announces: "For women only". For "group work" there is a room one storey higher. In this room, roughly ten metres long and six metres wide, men and women are treated at the same time.

> In the middle hangs a shabby green rag which serves as a curtain separating the men from the women. The men sit close together on one side of the curtain, the women on the other. Everyone sits cross-legged on the floor. Here and there a mother has a small child on lap. *Sheikh* Al-Mu'attar has sat down on a chair at the top end of the hall in the middle, so that he can observe both the men's and women's sections. He holds a long stick in his hand. On both the men's and the women's sides sits an attendant, who also holds a long stick in his hands. These chaperones are each situated in the middle of "their" section, with their back to the curtain. I sit in the women's section, but sufficiently close to the curtain that I can follow pretty well what is going on on the men's side.
>
> As I have noticed before at this sort of meeting, the women keep an eye on each other. Has an area of skin got exposed, has a lock of hair crept out from under her scarf, is everyone joining in properly with the others? The women are constantly looking around, to attend to each other's "improprieties". The *sheikh* and the "chaperones" do the same, but as they do so they project power and authority. The *sheikh* keeps hitting the wall to the left and right of the curtain with his stick, to encourage women to correct a lock of hair, straighten a skirt, or to pull down a sleeve that has ridden up a bit. He thus encourages a man or woman to raise their voice a little more in the recitation of Koran verses and pious sayings. The prayer healing consists primarily in the communal recitation aloud of Koran verses and pious sayings.

Sheikh Al-Mu'attar, followed by his attendants, sets the tone, the rhythm and the volume in which everything is done. The women on the one side of the curtain and the men on the other, do their best to do things just as the *sheikh* indicates. Doesn't it sound good enough? Isn't it loud enough? Smack! ... The stick strikes the wall or the head of the person who is "off". There is no break. One verse after the other, and one saying after the other roll out. The continual repetition of the verses and the way in which the *sheikh* and his helpers check how it is all done gives the whole thing the feel of an old-fashioned *kuttab* (Koran school where children learn the Koran by heart by repeating texts).

La ilaha illa llaah (there is no God but Allah) sounds out at full volume from a good hundred throats. Suddenly a woman begins to scream. She stands up, waves her hands in the air and grasps hold of her head, which is shaking violently to and fro. The attendant tries to grab hold of her, but she hits him away from her, screaming loudly. He finally manages to get hold of her and to put her on the ground next to him. When the *sheikh* admonishes her to stop screaming, she sets to all the more loudly. He stands up, admonishes her again and then catches her head, shoulders and legs with vigorous swipes of his stick. He hits her so hard that his stick can't take it and breaks into two pieces. While he is letting these blows rain down on her, he screams loudly "*ukhrug, ukhrug*" (get out, get out!) at the bad spirit in the woman. The other women go and sit in a circle around the crying and wailing woman. With raised finger and pointing at her reproachfully, they shout pious texts as loud as they can, not directed at her but at the *jinn* in her body. After some time she calms down, but now others are beginning to shout too. Directly in front of me two *baladi* women are sitting who have a paralysed little boy of about seven years of age with them. With abandon they shout into his ear and make the child keep spitting into a handkerchief. Then I see that there are women who keep spitting too, and it dawns on me that this is "spitting out" the evil spirit.·

On the other side of the curtain, in the men's section, things are happening too. I hear repeating shouting and I then see that the *sheikh* is turning to that side to give instructions to his helper. By pushing the curtain up a bit I look cautiously to see what is going on, hoping that the *sheikh* will not notice my "disobedi-

ence". I see a man squirming on the ground. It certainly looks as
if he is struggling with his demons. He too receives vigorous
blows from the attendant. The healing session continues until
afternoon prayer is announced in the mosque.

These are two examples of *'ilag bil-qur'an* (Koran healing) in Cairo, as
held as group meetings. There are, however, also healers who have
their practice at home. I have attended such a private meeting a number of times and have observed that their ways of working do not
deviate in any significant way from what I have described above.

The expulsion procedures as I have observed them, are standardized and have to do with direct communication between the
sheikh/exorcist and the demon (the Arabic word for exorcist is *mu'azzim*, but these persons call themselves healers, *mu'alig*). The healer tries
in the first place to get his patients into a state of trance. Unlike
shamans, who go into a trance themselves in order to determine their
client's sickness (see for instance Desjarlais 1992), this does not happen with the Koran healer. After the possessed person has gone into
trance, the healer/exorcist calls up the demon and quizzes him. Usually the questions concern such matters as: what is your name, are
you alone or are there other demons with you, why have you possessed the person, when did you do so, how long do you plan to stay,
and what is your faith? If the demon turns out not to be Muslim, he is
asked if he wants to convert. Later in this account I give an example
of such an interview with demons.

During the interview the patient seems passive and absent, and her
answers come with difficulty and in fits and starts. The possessed person answers the question but it is the demon who is held to be speaking through her lips. The exorcist interrupts his questions with
screams into the patient's ear to encourage the demon to leave the
body, and sometimes he uses physical violence (beatings with a stick)
and threats.

Demons who refuse to leave the body are "burned" by the recitation of special Koran verses. Some healers have told me and shown
me that they have developed a special ointment which they apply to
the patient's wrists and forehead. The composition of the ointment is
supposed to burn the demons. Often the healer also presses forcefully
on the "openings" in the head (the throat glands, the temples, at the
top of the forehead and in the fontanel; I shall return to "bodily orifices" later). The purpose of this is to force the demon(s) to descend to

other parts of the body. After the exorcist has decided he has enough
information about the demon and the latter has agreed to leave the
body, he pricks the patient's finger with a pin and presses a drop of
blood out at that point. The patient releases a scream and wakes up
out of the trance. Usually she is tired and says she cannot remember
anything of what has happened (amnesia). The finger is not the only
place the demon can leave the body from. The toes are also mentioned and the eyes. If the demon wants to leave through the eyes,
this is a big risk because blindness can be the result. So the demon
must be forced to move from the head to a lower point in the body.[3]
To finish off the treatment those concerned stay for an hour or longer
with headphones on and sit listening to cassettes playing Koran
recitation.

The sick (al-marda)

Case 1

Fatima is thirty and unmarried. She comes from the landed middle
class and lives with her mother and sister. I met Fatima at an admission session with a Koran healer. This Koran healer has a practice at
home but his treatment corresponds with what I have seen in the
"group practices". The following report has been put together from
several conversations I had with Fatima.

> "Since the age of seventeen I have heard voices when lying in
> bed. Babies crying, women's voices, and animal noises such as
> the barking of dogs. As a result I was unable to sleep at night for
> a long time, and I used to just walk around the house a bit. Dur-
> ing the day I was not bothered by it, everything was OK then.
> Things got steadily worse and I withdrew from my family and
> friends. I wanted to work and went in search of a job. Whenever
> I applied somewhere that a job was on offer, I was told that they

---

[3] The idea that demons have to leave the body through a drop of blood is based on
a *hadith*, which says that "demons go through the veins like a blood-clot". *Hadiths* are
sayings or traditions of the Prophet. From the question whether traditions were also
"genuine" there developed tradition-research based on *isnad*, i.e. that each tradent is
investigated to see if he had really met the authority in whose name he speaks,
whether he was reliable or that he was perhaps known as someone with a good or a
poor memory. By means of these critical steps, the chaff (unreliable traditions) was
separated from the grain (reliable traditions) (see Raven 1995; Robson 1971).

did not need anyone. Even if I had all the necessary requirements, I was still turned down. Things went exactly the same
way when a man came to ask for my hand. Everything went well
and we set a date for the marriage. Suddenly the boy changed
his mind and was "gone with the wind". I went to America
when I was twenty-five and exactly the same thing happened
there as here. I had a good job, but I never got the salary that I
should really have been paid. When the Gulf crisis started, I
came home again.

One day I started running after my mother with a knife. Now
it seems as if it was all a dream. A neighbour downstairs told my
mother I was not normal and that she should take me to someone who would help me. That person was *sheikh* Abu Musa, who
helps people with the Koran. My mother went to him first to
talk to him and after that she took me with her. Abu Musa saw
that I was troubled by *jinn* that were living in me and were jealous. For my treatment he would start by praying and then do
tanwim maghnatisi (hypnosis). He said, "If I go and pray for the
first time and the *jinn* come, then they will beat you, so don't be
afraid." And he was right, because when I was lying in bed at
night, a very tall figure came and he beat me terribly. I tried to
scream, but no sound came out of my throat. It really wasn't a
dream, because I could see the figure! My mother called the
sheikh and told him that someone was beating me. He said that I
should go and sleep next to my mother, and that I should just
say *Allah, Allah*. When I woke up the following morning I was
covered in bruises. Then I went back to the *sheikh* for hypnosis.
He told me that I was not to wear any gold and nothing
coloured red. I was not to come near to water, such as a river or
the sea. I was not to come near to cemeteries either, not to step
over blood and not to go into a church, because, the *sheikh* said,
two of the *jinn* who were besetting me were Christians. I did
what he said and I went to hypnosis every day. I felt that things
were starting to change. I got friends again and I joined in with
normal life again.

The *sheikh* had told me that the *jinn* would return during the
treatment. And that's what happened. They looked like people
and walked on two legs, but they had a green leathery skin, like
lizards. Even their faces were green, like leather, and they had a
tail. I told them I did not belong with them, that I wanted to

lead a normal human life and wanted nothing to do with them. They went away, but afterwards they came back with different faces and they looked like snakes. It was like a dream. During the hypnosis Abu Musa called up a *jinn* called *sheikh* Abdallah. I could not communicate with him very well because he was one of the higher *sheikh*s who spoke to me in high Arabic and I don't understand that very well.[4] So he called up another *jinn* called *sheikh* Abu Mohammed. This was a young man and he was easy to talk to. Each time I was under hypnosis, this Abu Mohammed came, and I said the prayers together with him. This *sheikh* also called up the *jinn* who were inside me and talked to them. The *jinn* inside me were a *rumi* (Greek orthodox), a *misihi* (Coptic Christian), a *buzi* (Buddhist) and a water *jinn* (*zar* master). There were four of them. There was no Muslim *jinn*. He was able to drive two of them out. The other two, he said, I had to see them through the face of someone I knew. One came with the face of an uncle of mine, and the other came with the face of my grand-father. I was not afraid of them. I was treated by Abu Musa for a year; in the beginning every day, afterwards once a week. The first few times I came he gave me rosewater to drink, but I never had medicines, only prayers were said. Abu Musa says now that I am *diniyya w-la dunyawiyya* (faithful and not "worldly") and that means that I am a good believer. I believe only in God and I don't bother myself with things that are against God's com-mandments."

The *jinn* the Koran healers are concerned with are sometimes very close to notions of demons as mentioned in the Koran, but often they also overlap with the demons from popular belief, who belong to the *tahtaniyyin* (the subterrestrials), and they even overlap with the *zar* mas-ters (as in the story above). Fatima's visions of demons correspond to current views: demons sometimes resemble humans, but their skin is a strange colour and is leathery, and they have a tail. Lizards, scorpions and snakes are typically the embodiment of demons. Evil spirits are also often tall and beat their victims or throttle them. Three of the four demons mentioned above belong to a different religion, although

---

[4] "Higher *sheikh*" here means "higher in the demonic ranking" since Abu Musa too works with demons whose help he calls upon in healing his patients (thus, speaking in healers' terms, he is really using the "not-permitted path").

this was the only time in my experience that a Buddhist *jinn* was involved. I suspect that this was inspired by this Koran healer himself, because in my conversation with him I noticed that he had some vague knowledge of eastern religions. Usually the non-Islamic *jinn* are Christians and sometimes Jews.

The description Fatima gives of the symptoms of her possession is a standard one: she hears voices, is troubled by insomnia, withdraws from family and friends, her engagement is suddenly broken and her feeling is one of general malaise. The *sheikh*'s advice is that Fatima should not wear gold or anything red, not step over blood and not come close to water, a cemetery or a church. My interpretation of this is that devout Muslims are not allowed to wear gold because this belongs with "the provision of the life of this world; and Allah is He with Whom is the good goal (of life)" (*al-'Imran* [3]: 12) (they do not wear golden wedding rings either). She is not to wear red because the colour red is associated with the demon called the "red sultan". This one belongs with the *zar* masters and can be very mean. She is probably not allowed to come into the vicinity of water because one of the demons is a water demon (also a *zar* master). In Upper Egypt in particular it is believed that demons living in the water (the Nile) are the souls of the deceased (they are generally called *'afarit*). People who come close to the river can be pulled into the depths by the spirits. I do not know whether this is also the idea behind the *sheikh*'s advice to Fatima. Blood and cemeteries are impure. The church clearly is connected with the Christian demons that are possessing Fatima and the story runs that Christians (and Jews) aim to draw Muslims away from their faith. The indirect advice to Fatima is to keep more to the Islamic lifestyle.

Case 2

Sharifa is twenty-five years old and single. I met her together with her mother at a *sheikh*'s house and afterwards I conducted various conversations with her. Sharifa had previously been to another *sheikh* before she consulted this one. What struck me at this initial conversation was that the *sheikh* first asked for general information about her work, the family at home, whether she was engaged to be married, and so on. After that he moved on quite quickly to "diagnostic" questions like, "Are you sleeping well, how often do you dream, what do you see in your dreams, do you see strange people, do you see animals and insects?" and so on. He was directing things in a particular direction by such questions, and from the beginning I had the feeling that he was angling for the "demon direction". I have noticed that such questions belong to the standard vocabulary of healers/exorcists. The *sheikh* can observe his patient during the conversation, he learns too how she reacts to everyday problems, by which means he can also tell whether he is going to be able to heal the "sick" person or not. Clever healers have learned to withdraw in good time from situations they cannot deal with.

Sharifa started to talk about her "strange" experiences as if of her own accord. It seems she has a clear problem, and that is men. She has already been engaged five times, but things have never yet got as far as marriage because the future husband always goes off beforehand. It seems that all the men were chosen for her, first by both parents and later just by the mother, when her father died. This is not really a strange state of affairs since Egyptian parents are actively involved in the search for partners for their children. But Sharifa was not content with the situation for various reasons. From one fiancé she received too little in the way of *shabqa* (mandatory engagement present consisting of a gold ring, necklace, bracelet or earrings), and the other made no effort to find a flat that the couple could live in later. The third and following fiancés did not fit the bill either, for similar reasons. When I asked Sharifa if she would not have preferred to look for a husband for herself and whether this was perhaps the reason for the failure of the engagements, at first she cried and then she laughed in relief because of the understanding I showed for her situation. The fact that her engagements were broken several times gives her a bad image, and she is aware of that. It makes her less attractive on the marriage market, because it is very common for people to interpret the undesired breaking of engagements as possession by a demon who is himself in love with the girl and so uses every possible means to chase off potential marriage candidates and to force sexual fantasies onto the victim. And the underlying reason for the visit to the *sheikh* is to chase off the demon out of her body. It is perfectly normal in Egypt for a mother to take her daughter along to a *sheikh* in such a case. In non-western countries healing has to do not only with relations between the healer and the patient, but also with the interaction between healer, patient and the family.

"Two years ago my mother took me to a *sheikh* for the first time, to ask him what was wrong with me. At that time I could not

walk very well and I felt strange and frightened. He told my
mother that I had fallen on the doorstep when I was two years
old. My mother didn't remember it at first, but afterwards she
did. The *sheikh* said that my case was not a matter of *malbusa*
("clothing") but *haffit malayka* (touching by an angel). I don't
know what that is precisely, but they say that in the foundations
of the house and under doorsteps live the souls of dead people
and they can hit you, that is *haffit malayka*. It's the *tahtaniyyin*, the
"subterrestrials". The *sheikh* said that it happened a long time
ago and so there was not much that could be done about it. He
gave me some oil and *bukhur* (incense) and said that I should pray
a lot. One day I went to my father's grave. I sat there crying and
I asked him why he went away and left me with problems, and
why I was still not married. That day I had my period, but I had
also dressed up nice and smart and was wearing make-up. That
night I dreamt that my father said, "Come on, take off your
clothes, I want to have sex with you." It was not real, it was in
my dream! I shouted, "No, that's not on, don't do that, I'm your
daughter." But he said that I should not be afraid and that he
would not tell my mother or anyone else. Then he did it with me
and afterwards, when it was over, his whole face changed. He
suddenly changed into a *shaytan* (devil). It was a *shaytan* who had
appeared in the person of my father. I woke up and was very
frightened. I told my mother and she said, "That comes from
thinking of your problems all the time and putting yourself
under pressure." But the dreams kept coming back every night
from then on, for about two months. I wake up at night and find
I have no underwear on and I have scratches all over my body,
on my arms, my face … and it looks as if someone has left teeth-
marks in my legs as well. I'm covered in bruises. This always
happens at night and during the day everything is OK. But one
day I had a really strange feeling. From then on I wanted to
have sex with everyone. If I saw a boy all I could think about
was that I wanted to sleep with him. I was so ashamed because
I'm not that type. It says in the Koran that a woman must be
chaste and that sex is only allowed if you are married. So I went
to the *sheikh* again and told him all that had happened. I asked
him if he would help me. I had to tell him everything first. He
asked if I had the feeling that I wanted to have sex in the morning, or that I wanted to stand naked in front of the mirror and

make *harakat ginsiyya* (sexy movements) and wanted to dance and
sing. I said yes, because when I am alone at home I do that sort
of thing. He also asked if I have bruises in the morning, if my
underwear is off and if there are wet patches on the sheets. Then
he said that he knew what he had to do and he opened a *mandal*
to look (divination by reading water or oil). He told me exactly
when I was at my father's grave and that I had my period then.
He said, "You are clothed by a *ginn*. This *ginn* is a Christian and
the first time he came in the form of your father, but after the
sex he changed into his own normal form, a *ginn*." The *sheikh*
made me remove from my bedroom all toys and photos from
my childhood. The mirror had to go too and I am absolutely not
allowed to look into a mirror anywhere else. I am only allowed
to wear *hagat tawila* (long skirts = "Islamic clothing") and no
ordinary skirts or miniskirts. I am not allowed to talk to boys
either. He gave me incense that smells really bad, *rihit hammam*
(toilet-smell). I go to him once a week, but he says prayers for me
every night from his own home, and I can feel that. I paid a
thousand pounds. But that is not for the treatment, that is free. I
just had to pay for the incense. The incense is very expensive
because it comes all the way from Yemen, but my mother pays
for it all. Now things are going a bit better for me."

Sharifa's problems seem to go much deeper than she, her mother,
and possibly the *sheikh* too really suspect. Are we talking incest, secret
yearnings for the father, suppressed sexual feelings? These are pretty
well taboo subjects in Egypt. Sharifa chose to go to her father's grave
when she was menstruating. On the level of popular perception the
transgression here lies in the fact that an impure person visits an
impure place. It is not for me to draw psychoanalytical conclusions
from Sharifa's stories, but I can imagine that this act, felt to be a
"sin", caused the further collapse of herself. Perhaps it is also a matter
of unconscious desires for sex with the most forbidden category, the
father.

In Sharifa's story we meet in addition standard views of demons.
Thus falling occupies an important place in demonology, especially
where it is a matter of when, where and how the individual fell.
Doorsteps and bathrooms are among the most dangerous places
where someone can fall and this almost always results in possession.
The cause of this is that these are the places where demons prefer to

stay. It often seems to be a sin when a woman stands in front of a mirror, or dances and sings. Does this have to do with lust or with the
experiencing of one's own physicality? I have very often heard that
women are not allowed to look in mirrors, especially not if they are in
vulnerable situations, such as pregnancy, but also possession. And a
beautiful woman becomes "vulnerable" if she looks in a mirror.
Women's explanations of this get no further than "the *jinn* can strike
then". In any case the mirror, like any reflecting surface, is an ancient
divination instrument that leads the women into their unconscious. In
orthodox and fundamentalist circles song and dance are viewed as
unsuitable for an Islamic lifestyle.[5] Sharifa has to remove the photos
from her childhood. This may have to do with rejection of childhood
and acceptance of disciplined womanhood. This is plausible since she
is also encouraged to wear Islamic clothing. Whether the incense really smelt so bad, I cannot tell. Healers work with a scale of attributes,
rituals and popular views of the influence of demons and the cause
and healing of physical and mental problems. It is possible that the
so-called bad-smelling incense belongs in this context.

For the diagnosis "*you are possessed by a jinn*", the healer gives a
name to unconscious conflicts in the patient and thereby makes them
manageable. He is empathetic, warm, supportive and at the same time
authoritarian in the interaction with her. The idiom of communication between healer and patient is the articulation of personal problems in combined expressions from popular culture (cosmological and
sociological). Explanation of the situation in demonological terms provides a meaningful framework that is understood by the patient and is
sanctioned by an appeal to the sacred source, the Koran.

The Koran healer (al-mu'alig bil-qur'an)

Generally speaking, Koran healers are not old men with long beards,
but rather young men with long beards, of around thirty or forty
years of age. Some of them wear "oriental" clothes (*gallabiyya* and
'imma/ 'imama) and others wear western clothing.[6] Most healers admit

---

[5] No specific instructions are given in the Koran regarding music and song. Koran
commentators have different opinions on this. Scholars seeking support in the *Hadith*
think that the Prophet had no objection to music and song (Shiloah 1995: 32-33).

[6] To make a turban, Egyptian men take a white or coloured skullcap or a fez-like
head covering and wrap a long woollen or cotton scarf around it, or a long narrow
cloth made of very fine cotton.

that they have not had the benefit of a scientific education. Nor do they have any education in Islamic law or theology. They do claim to be *hafizin* of the Koran and the *sunna*, that is that they have memorized both.[7] They only discovered their "gift" in the course of a personal crisis. They gained insight into and knowledge of the secret verses and suras in the Koran, which opened up their "treasures" for them (Finkler also writes that healers have often gone through a personal crisis/illness of their own, after which the roles are reversed: the sick person becomes the healer, 1986: 631, 639). They all claim to be able to drive out the *jinn* and the *'afarit* from the victim's body. The well-known and important healers have divided up greater Cairo into districts (Bulaq, al-Haram, al-Marj, Hilwan, etc.) and they each have their own large groups of patients. Many began practising as an aid in one of the mosques, which made it easy for them to get into contact with sick people. Some claim to work together with psychiatrists. The latter are supposed to send the patients they cannot treat themselves on to healers, who in turn send on patients to psychiatrists whenever they cannot help them because their illnesses are not caused by *jinn*.

The only conditions a healer must meet is that he must know and be able to recite the verses in the Koran that bring healing. Most healers are men. One woman has come very much to the fore through all the publicity in the media (*Akhbar al-Hawadith* 15 September 1994 and *al-Musawwar* 30 September 1994). This is Huriyya. But despite the fact that she is now well known and says she is able to drive out all *'afarit*, she is not accepted by male colleagues. The reason for this is that she is illiterate and has not memorized the Koran. For most healers, the focus is on healing from *jinn* by Koran recitation. There are a few who claim to be able to drive out *jinn* with electricity, magnets or other aids such as cupping (vacuum-pulled glass bowls are placed on the body to draw out pains) or with home-made ointments and pills. Some say they are able to heal cancer or aids. *Sheikh* Mahdi is a healer who tops them all with his *jinn*. He claims to have contact with Saalii, the "queen of the *jinn*".

---

[7] *Sunna*, "that which is recommended". A distinction is made between five sorts of deeds: *wajib* (compulsory), *sunna* (recommended), *halal* (permitted), *makruh* (to be rejected) and *haram* (forbidden). The fundamentalists view themselves as the only true *sunni*. They want to purify Islam of later interpretations and additions. *Sunnis* ("they who follow the teaching of the Prophet") is also a term used to indicate a distinction from *shi'ites* ("those who are followers of 'Ali (the son-in-law of the Prophet). Egyptians are *sunnis*.

She has control over two million *jinn* whom she has placed at his disposal to heal every conceivable illness, both those with a physical cause and those with a psychological or spiritual cause. He does not heal with the Koran, but with the aid of these *jinn*. *Sheikh* Sanusi (he has nothing to do with the Sanusi brotherhood in Libya), a cousin of his, heals with the aid of angels *(malayka ardiyya)*. These are good demons, which are also called angels and "live under the earth" *(Akhbar al-Hawadith* 6 October 1994). There is animosity between the cousins, and by indicating that Mahdi uses *jinn* while he himself uses angels, Sanusi makes a distinction between the "permitted" and the "not-permitted" path (see Chapter 2). Both healers encourage their patients to turn their backs on modern medical science with its hospitals and instead to come to their practice in order to be healed of possession by demons. In recent years they have had considerable success with their call. Thousands of people have streamed every day from near and far to the villages where they both have their practices (about two hours' drive from Cairo). For each "case", Sanusi says he asks only five to ten Egyptian pounds (75 pence to £ 1.50 sterling), money that has to serve for the construction of an "Islamic" hospital in his own village. Mahdi says he makes available his knowledge of the *jinn* without personal gain in the service of the sick; that is his deal with the "queen". The sum asked by Sanusi seems particularly low, since in Cairo even the simplest healer asks more.[8] I have also visited these healers myself, and have talked to them. Sanusi's work in particular can be compared with healing by the "laying-on of hands", as is known also in Europe. He boasts of being a member of the "International Association of Astrologers" which is based in Paris (several healers claim this and a few have shown me a "diploma"). Two hours away from them lives another well-known healer: *sheikh* Saad Yusuf Mahmud Abu Aziz, who, like a few others, has written a book: "The Islamic Alternative to the Undoing of Sorcery and Exorcism from Touching by Devils" (Cairo

---

[8] (a) So the two cousins heal with the aid of *jinn*. See also: Kriss & Kriss-Heinrich, 1960: 14. They write that believing (Muslim) *jinn* can also be servants of saints and have access to secret powers with which they can heal sick people.

(b) Prices range from ten Egyptian pounds (around £1.50 sterling) to well above a thousand. Most healers claim to ask nothing for their services, but this is certainly not true. That they do not admit to this is because it is not generally considered a good thing to ask money for "God's word" (see also Mommersteeg 1996). I suspect, moreover, that some healers are paid by the Moslim League in Mecca, but this is difficult to confirm.

1994). Their methods correspond in general terms with those of other healers and his book does not offer new insights. I shall return to the content of a number of books later.

A very well-known healer, Abu Salim, set out his ideas and methods in an interview. I went to his sessions for some considerable time. He is an engaging personality and authoritarian at the same time. This healer also stimulated me to come to his sessions so that I could make Koran healing known in Europe too.

"People come to me after they have first been to all sorts of doctors and are desperate because their medicines have not helped" (the "failure" of regular doctors to heal a sickness is very frequently the prompt for someone to visit a spiritual healer: see also Finkler 1986: 639). "I always begin by telling people that Koran healing can do no damage and that God has great power and can do everything. I then warn people against *jinn* and *shaytan*. I tell them too that they must trust in God alone and must not use amulets or other things to protect themselves. Only God has power. I talk with *jinn* and warn them that they must leave the bodies of their victims. Some people go into a trance or a really deep sleep during my recitation of *ruqyas* (special Koran verses). Later they often have no recollection of what has happened. I make a distinction between persons who are possessed by *jinn* and those who are affected by magic or the *qarin* (the personal demon of each human being). They are given different treatment. My assistants speak Koran verses into the ears of these people. They keep that up until such a person begins to act very nervously and aggressively and begins to utter incomprehensible sounds — that is the work of the *jinn*. My assistant then commands the *jinn* to leave the body. If he does not, then he is burnt by the effects of the Koran. Very often the *jinn* do not want to leave and you notice that because the person gets restless, stands up and starts thrashing about or screaming loudly. It is the *jinn* or *shaytan* in the person that does that, who screams through his tongue or makes him make strange movements. The sick person doesn't know anything about this, because he is in a state of trance. There are special verses in the Koran that make the *jinn* and the *shaytan* burn. The sick person doesn't feel this, or rather later on they don't know anything about it. I don't beat the sick people either to drive out the *jinn*, the Koran drives them out, because the Koran is healing, *asl-inn il-qur'an shifa'*.[9]

There are two sorts of illness, physical and spiritual. I treat spiritual illnesses, but in some physical sicknesses *jinn* play a part too. Doctors know that and admit that there are no medicines for some sicknesses, only the Koran helps with these. Through *mass* and *labs* (touching and clothing) by a *shaytan* all sorts of complaints arise. I can help people with most of these complaints. The Koran heals all sicknesses caused by *jinn*, namely: paralysis, temporary blindness, bleeding, hearing problems, infertility, hysteria, pain in the body or in the joints for which doctors can find no cause, headaches and many other things. The Koran calms the spirit and the body, which allows the person to quieten down and his illness is healed.

There are two sorts of *jinn*: *shayatin* and *'afarit*. Some *jinn* are Muslims, some are Christians and some are unbelievers. Some have masked faces and some go into someone's body. They can do that because the person concerned has a weak personality, is weak in faith or an unbeliever, is very sad, cries without reason, or is very angry. But on the other hand if the person has a strong faith in God and has the habit of always reading the Koran, then the *jinn* will never attack him.

There is talk of different attacks by *jinn*. In the first case it enters the whole body. In the second case it only goes into certain parts, such as the legs, arms or the tongue. In the third case the *jinn* stays in the body for a long time, but not for ever. In the fourth case it comes very briefly and quickly, as in *mass* (touching) during nightmares. Through my experience I know where in the body the *jinn* is; in the eyes, in the heart, in the belly, in the stomach, in the womb, in the hands. The *jinn* always makes its presence felt. Because I talk with the sick people and above all ask them about their dreams, I know what is wrong with them. Dreams in which all sorts of insects, snakes or other beings appear are very important for the diagnosis of *mass* (touching), *labs* (possession), *hasad* (evil eye), *'amal* and *sihr* (magic). The con-

---

[9] This conversation took place in May 1996. Abu Salim is a pseudonym. According to reports in the press (1995) he held sessions in which as many as four hundred persons took part at a time. His practice was closed down by the authorities in 1997 because one of his male assistants had hit a woman in order to drive out the demons. Her family went to the police, but there was no court case as a result.

ditions that must be met in order to heal with the Koran consist, first that the healer is a devout person and second that the sick person is a good Muslim. He has to believe in one God, not do anything bad and be convinced that only God can heal him.

I have been doing Koran healing for twelve years now. I have acquired a lot of knowledge from books on *at-tibb an-nabawi* (prophetic medicine), from books on Islam, from *al-kutub al-samawiyya* by al-Bukhari and Muslim (tradition scholars, ninth century), but also from Christian and Jewish books and very old books about *sunna* (customs of the Prophet). Funnily enough, in the West many, many studies have been made on demons, far more than in the East, and in America a lot of research has been done into Koran healing too.

There are priests and others who say that they can drive out demons with the Bible or the Torah, and in the *zar* it is done with music and dancing. But that is really quite different from Koran healing. What happens in the *zar*, by the way, is superstition. What happens in the *dhikr* (sufi ritual) is the same as in the *zar*: they do not pray, they just say anything. What herbalists do is heal with plants. That is different, that is good, it has been scientifically proven. There are also healers who say they heal with the help of the *jinn*. This does happen, but this is not good. A Muslim must stay away from the *jinn*, whether it is a matter of healing or not, that's what it says in the Koran. The difference between all these methods and Koran healing is that the Koran itself is healing."[10]

Sheikh Abu Salim is a "man of God" and he constantly emphasizes that he only calls upon the Word of God in order to heal people. He

---

[10] The Hay'at al-I'jaz al-'Ilmi is an institute that is established in Mecca and is connected with the Moslim League. The organization says it gives financial support to scientific projects that show that the Koran, *sunna* and *hadith* contain signs and indications that can be applied in the case of physical and mental illness. In the book, "Proposed Medical Research Projects Derived from the Koran and Sunna", published by them (Mecca 1992: 1-56), Abdul-Aziz Kamel writes that the healing of illnesses is a three-dimensional activity that must be tackled on the physical, moral and psychological levels. Any deviation in one of these aspects is regarded in Islam as illness requiring treatment. In view of the fact that there is a strong correlation between faith and healing, treatment with the Koran is recommended in the case of physical, psychological and spiritual illness. The references to illnesses and recommendations for healing broadly correspond with what Koran healers say, with the exception that nowhere in this book are the *jinn* mentioned as a cause of sickness.

thereby legitimates himself, at the same time distancing himself from "the not-permitted path" as practised, in his view, by magicians, sorcerers, sufis and *zar* leaders.[11] At the beginning of each session he emphasizes that the women must not wear any amulets (*higab-hugub*). In principle, the wearing of Koran texts is not forbidden, but the writing of texts on little pieces of paper is associated with magic and sufism. Abu Salim is very much aware of the fact that his work is situated on the boundaries of what is generally acceptable and so he consciously seeks for symbols that distinguish him as a person from the other group of healers. He claims to behave in conformity with the *sunna*. So he dresses in a white *gallabiyya* with *'imma* (long shirt and "turban") and has a beard. This is the way in which the Prophet is supposed to have been dressed, but it is also the way in which Muslim activists dress in Egypt.

Unlike the *zar*, in which the rituals are predominantly performed by women for women, Koran healing is typically a male affair; men perform rituals to heal women. The modern Koran healer is to be viewed as a free entrepreneur, dealing in illnesses, his most important customers being women.

The Koran healer as a separate professional group

The "men of religion" are generally called *sheikh* (plural *shuyukh*). This is a title that is also used for persons in particular administrative functions in the villages and in small towns and in order to show respect, especially to older people (in the feminine form, *sheikha*, also used for older women). In the religious context, alongside *sheikh* also *imam* is used for the person who leads the ritual prayer or is head of a mosque, *khatib* for a preacher (especially on Fridays) and *wa'iz* for a sort of freelance professional preacher who is not connected to any one mosque in particular, but comes under a sub-department of the al-Azhar (Gaffney 1994). "Men of religion" must possess *'ilm* (knowledge), in particular knowledge of the Koran, *hadith*, *sunna* and the

---

[11] The Koran healer (*mu'alig bil-qur'an*) wants above all to distinguish himself from the sufi healer (*sheikh bil-baraka*). This is a conflict on an abstract theological plane: in theory in Islam there is no possibility of mediation between the believer and God. Sufis are accused (by the orthodox and fundamentalists) with corrupting the Islamic message, with placing themselves between humans and God and of being interested only in occult knowledge. The average Egyptian does not make a strict distinction between sufi healers and Koran healers.

shari'a (Islamic law) (in connection with this see also Eickelmaan 1989: 304-315).

The *sheikhs*/Koran healers who are occupied with the relationship between people and supernatural powers often pretend to belong to a particular mosque. In reality most of them are "free entrepreneurs" who gain their clients through word-of-mouth recommendations and also ask money for it (often a great deal of money) (see also Finkler 1986: 635). Most healers have not studied at the *al-Azhar* either, but they do claim to be *hafiz*, i.e. that they have learned the Koran by heart and have thereby gained respect. (There is no control over this either from the *al-Azhar* or on the part of the government.) These *mu'aligin bil-qur'an* (Koran healers) do not generally belong to a sufi order (mystical order), of which persons who heal are often called *shuyukh bil-baraka* because they possess the power to bless.[12] With their beards and *gallabiyyas*, in attitude and behaviour they most closely resemble the "fundamentalists", who also prefer to dress like this (Gaffney 1994).

To be able to exercise the profession of Koran healer, it is regarded as a condition that you must know the Koran by heart and be able to recite the verses. Knowledge of the Koran is typically something that belongs with men. Women generally do not have this knowledge because they are behind in the realm of formal education and thus also have had little or no access to formal Koran instruction. In Egypt Koran healers form an "elite of men" who have a certain amount of power. The *sheikhs* of Koran healing radiate this power and self-confidence. In addition they have a number of codes of behaviour that are intended to produce an effect. Among these is that because they must remain "pure", they must not touch a woman during the treatment. They transfer their special powers to the patient via a chain of touchings via the husband or the brother. Sometimes they use plastic gloves so as not to "contaminate" themselves by touching a woman. They tell the women that they are beset by *jinn* because she has not behaved in accordance with Islamic teachings, which is the reason she is now suffering from "nerves", sickness, pain, bleedings, dramatic personality disorder (hysteria), confusion, insomnia, epileptic fits, etc. During

---

[12] Collin, EI, vol. I, 1960, 1032, defines *baraka* as "Beneficent force, of divine origin, which causes superabundance in the physical sphere and prosperity and happiness in the psychic order". See also: Kriss & Kriss-Heinrich 1960: 4-6. They write that *baraka* is a sort of magical power which is transferred from the saint to his children and grandchildren.

the treatment women have to recite Koran verses aloud. If they do not do this sufficiently well, they receive reprimands or are taken on one side and given a serious talking-to. If the demons keep up their resistance (she does not "feel" anything in such cases), they are beaten with a stick.

Transactions between healer and patient

Above I discussed a number of aspects of Koran healing, which clearly illustrate how the healing sessions generally run and what are the problems for which sick persons visit a Koran healer. As in the case of the *zar*, the process of Koran healing runs in three phases: first the problem is given a culturally legitimated name, and then this cultural name is manipulated as a symbolic form outside the patient, after which a relief of the symptoms is achieved and a new label, healing, is given.

It emerges from the conversation with the healer Abu Salim that he does not doubt his own powers and forces, which, in his opinion, ordinary doctors do not possess. But he always speaks of his strong faith in God's power and work, in which he himself is only an instrument. Regular doctors, he says, can only approach illnesses via western medical science and he sees an essential difference here. Spiritual illnesses, such as possession, are not normal physical deviations, for which modern medical science often does offer a solution. Spiritual illnesses are caused in a supernatural way and can therefore only be healed in a spiritual way. As in the *zar*, the healer-patient transactions at the initial session are oriented towards psychosocial aspects of the sickness, such as earlier experiences, behaviour, family relationships and financial problems. Most healers treat non-life-threatening ailments, psychosomatic and psychological complaints, and interpersonal problems where social and cultural problems are an important component. Intelligent healers know from experience whether they can cope with the problems of a particular patient. If they suspect that this is not the case, they send him/her on to a specialist or hospital.[13] Just like the regular doctor, who often uses difficult words and terms

---

[13] Koran healers do not regard themselves as competitors to the regular doctors. In general they are pretty well informed as to what biomedicine has to offer and refer clients when they suspect that they will not be able to help them. Regular doctors know much less about what traditional healers do: see the Egyptian daily and weekly papers of 1994 and my conversation with Dr. Al-Madani in Chapter 5.

in front of the patient, the healer makes use of a "professional" (demon) jargon, which however is easier to understand than the medical terminology used by the regular doctor, since it is closer to the patient's own world of thought and experience. Furthermore the patient has a need for personal and meaningful explanations in relation to his or her health. The Koran healer is skilled in manipulating the explanations and he makes a big thing of his experience in order to come over as authoritative. Since the healer replaces negatively valued models and metaphors with the positively valued ones of the Koran, the patients have the feeling that they themselves can contribute to overcoming their sickness. This, like the rituals that the healer performs during his healing sessions, contributes to the psychotherapeutic effect in the healer-patient relationship.

In Koran healing there is special emphasis on personal responsibility. That is to say, the patient herself is to blame for the emergence of her illness. From newspaper articles, books and personal conversations I have been able to establish that Koran healers all convey more or less the same message to women: "You must be a good Muslim, behave appropriately in relation to food and drink, say your prayers regularly, dress 'Islamically' (for some healers this means completely veiled if at all possible), act modestly, stay indoors and regard caring for your husband and children as your main task, commissioned by God." If you have a good "Islamic" lifestyle like this, nothing can overcome you because you are protected against the *jinn*, because they do not like good Muslims. One of the best-known healers in Cairo says, "Devils and demons only live in a bad person who does not purify himself and pray." That is to say that if you are sick and the diagnosis is being touched or (worse) possession, this is all your own fault, because you should have kept up a good Islamic lifestyle. In my opinion this constitutes the biggest difference from *zar* healing. In *zar* the sick person is never blamed for the misfortune that overcomes her; it is always, and in all circumstances, the demon master that is responsible.

Jinn are responsible for misfortune and sickness which affect women in particular. Koran healers (like *zar* leaders) have their own notions of the ins and outs of these beings.

Jinn and healing

Demons are not personified in Koran healing in the same ways as in the *zar*. An exception to this is that a very few healers do name the *qarin(a)*, an indication that can be regarded as a "personal name". It is certainly part of the healing session that the healer asks for the name of the *jinn*. Without knowing his name he cannot drive him out. Healers say that they keep strictly to the Koran, but although *jinn* are mentioned in the Koran, it is a big step to the interpretation of the healer: he ascribes will and power to them and he classifies them in degrees of malevolence. The *jinn* of the Koran healers are not like the *jinn* as described in magic books, nor the *asyad* (spirits) of the *zar*. Nor are they coupled to the ancestors. Very frequently the demons belong to another religion. In such cases they are (usually) Coptic priests or Jews.

The *jinn* who cause "touching" or "possession" and with whom the Koran healers are concerned, seem to show more resemblances to the *jinn* of the Koran, magic and *zar*; they have properties of all three groups. Very frequently *jinn* want to marry a woman. If the person concerned does not respond to his advances, he becomes difficult and starts bothering her, which produces *'asabiyya* or *halat nafsiyya* (nervousness). *Lams* and *mass* are "touching" by a demon or devil, which produce minor psychological or physical problems; *labs* "clothing" (possession) causes serious psychological and physical complaints and can even incite people to murder.

In the main, *jinn* cause spiritual illnesses (*amrad ruhiyya*), which can give rise to physical complaints which, the healers maintain, can only be healed with the Koran. There is no connection between a named illness or psychological disorder and a named *jinn* who is responsible for it. Illnesses that arise as a result of organic irregularities cannot be healed by Koran recitation, although everyone can always find comfort and healing in the Koran.

There is, however, an explicit causal connection between magic and *jinn*. Through an individual having magic carried out to the disadvantage of another person, *jinn* can enter the body of that victim. To drive the *jinn* out again special capacities are required, such as a "gift from God" or a "pact" that is made with the devil. Most healers base themselves on the first quality (the gift from God), but the second category also exists, though people tend to talk about this less, as it is the "not-permitted path". The first category declares that in all circumstances it is God himself who does the healing, the second belongs to the group of sorcerers who rely on secret knowledge which they have at their disposal through their own personal demon (this is similar to what the *zar* leader claims). We are confronted here by an important question: what are the limits of what is acceptable within Islam? In other words, what is magic, and what is not magic?

Symptoms of spiritual illness ascribed to jinn and magic

In writing about the symptoms of spiritual illness I have taken as a basis conversations with healers and compared their stories with information from the books that deal with touching, possession, *jinn* and Koran healing.[14] It emerges from the literature that evil super-natural powers are responsible for many sicknesses that appear to be purely organic. The symptoms are not caused in such cases by an organic disorder but by *jinn* which have entered the body through an "opening" and have caused possession. Epilepsy is always mentioned as an example. This illness can have physical causes, but it can also be caused by *jinn* which have penetrated the brain, the heart and the central nervous system.[15] So it is very important to be able to distinguish between them. If it is a matter of an organic disorder, the help of a doctor or specialist must be called in and at the same time one must trust in the help of God and special prayers must be said.[16] If on the other hand it is a matter of spiritually caused illness, then the help of a doctor or specialist will be ineffective because these illnesses are caused by demons, magic, the evil eye or devilry. For this sort of illness only *ruqya* helps, that is certain verses of the Koran which are recited by a spiritual healer in a specific way.

Koran healers in Egypt talk of four causes of illness. First, physical complaints which arise through physical characteristics. Second,

---

[14] The books in question are: *I'jaz al-Qur'an fi 'Ilaj al-sihr, wa al-hasad, wa mass al-shay-tan* (The miracles of the Koran in the healing of sorcery, the evil eye, and touching by the devil), by Dr. Mohammad Mahmoud abd-Allah, lecturer in Koranic studies at the *al-Azhar* University; *Dalil al-mu'alijin bi l-qur'an al-karim* (Manual for healers with the Holy Koran) by Dr. Rabad Mohammad Sama'ha, graduate of the Islamic Research Institute of the *al-Azhar*, *Al-mass wa al-sihr wa al-hasad: al-asbab, al-a'rad, al-wiqaya, al-'ilaj* (Touching, sorcery and the evil eye: causes, symptoms, protection and healing) by Dr. Said A. Nomeir, a doctor; and *Al-badil al-islam li-fukk al-sihr wa tard al-mnass al-shaytani* (The Islamic alternative to the undoing of sorcery and the driving out of touching by devils), by Saad Yusuf Mahmud Abu Aziz, a Koran healer.

[15] Epilepsy can have organic as well as psychological components. In medieval Europe too, mental illnesses and epilepsy were ascribed to the invasion of the body by demons.

[16] From the Middle Ages on, the following mental illnesses were known: epilepsy, madness, rage, delirium, damage to mental faculties and the mind, forgetfulness, bestiality, insomnia, lethargy, noises in the head, dizziness, swellings and various sorts of headache (medical handbook by at-Tabari [240/855], noted in Dols 1992: 115).

physical complaints that arise through supernatural powers. Third, mental diseases which arise through a pathological disturbance of the mental faculties. Fourth, psychic complaints that arise through the work of supernatural forces. This division is entirely in accordance with the guidelines for "prophetic medicine" discussed in Chapter 2.

Factors held to lead to demon possession are: disobedience to God by skipping prayers, forgetting a number of *raka'at* (prostrations), performing the prayers without attention or having intrusive thoughts which mean the prayers have to be interrupted. Other factors are: extreme emotional situations, such as anger, deep melancholy or an overpowering fear. But a harsh and cruel upbringing or certain circumstances caused by serious social problems or war can also play a role. A frequently mentioned further cause is that a *jinn* has fallen in love with a person and tries with all its strength to keep that person for itself. Causing injury to a *jinn* is also often mentioned. This can be deliberate damage through the use of amulets to burn the *jinn* unjustly, or without reason, and unconscious damage by throwing stones into dark places, urinating in holes in the ground (places where the *jinn* live), or making loud noises which disturb the *jinn* in the places they live. Suddenly entering a forsaken place without first naming God's name or saying a prayer, or falling suddenly without immediately naming God's name, are also particularly fraught with risks. There may be some question of hereditary components which make some people extra susceptible to attracting "possession". So in the case of a patient with unclear pathological symptoms it is necessary to look into the further circumstances. The negative symptoms of demon possession may, for instance, also be found among other family members. In such cases it is advisable for all family members to follow the same healing programme.

Names, categories and diagnosis of possession

There are various names for sorcery/magic, the most important of which are *sihr* and *'amal*. The two words are used interchangeably for what anthropologists call sorcery and (black) magic. Various sorts of *sihr* or *'amal* are known both to experts in this field and to "ordinary" people. These are, in order: *sihr al-tafriq*, which is meant to cause a separation between a man and his wife, a father and his son or a brother and his sister; *sihr al-marad*, which is meant to cause sickness and disabilities in the body; *sihr al-mahabba*, which is meant to make a

young man marry a particular girl against his will (or vice versa), and
sihr al-'ishq, which is meant to evoke passionate love. Specialists in
magical practices distinguish further *tathbit mulk al-hakim*, magic to
obtain a feeling of power, *tahqiq gharad maddi*, sorcery to obtain material gain, and *tahqiq gharad ma'nawi*, sorcery to gain prestige.

The healers distinguish four categories of behaviour which indicate
that magic is at work. The first category is to recognize the following
phenomena: the patient stares, changes accent/use of language
and/or alters in physical strength. In this case the patient loses consciousness and is not aware of his own reactions, words or deeds. In
cases of the second category the patient is not aware of his surroundings; he is like someone dreaming and only partially remembers any of
it and has no control over his words and/or actions. The third category comprises cases in which the patient knows what he is doing or saying, but has no control over it. Patients in the fourth category, finally,
do not lose consciousness, remain aware of what is happening and
have complete control of their words and actions. This is very common and these cases may be associated with three sorts of weeping fits:
weeping without wanting to, weeping when tears come from the sides
or the middle of the eyes, and weeping in which the tears taste bitter.
These tears differ from normal tears, which usually are salty in taste.
Sometimes the weeping is coupled with involuntary laughter, with a
lack of feeling, stiffness or a feeling of heaviness in the body.

Besides this the healer explains the supernatural cause of mental
and physical complaints on the basis of a number of indicators. In
particular, dreams, vague physical and mental complaints and sudden changes in behaviour are important indications that *jinn* have
entered a patient's body. The most important indicators are: dreams
about snakes, scorpions and animals such as dogs, cats, buffaloes or
camels. Dreams in which one falls from high places, or walks in cemeteries and forsaken places. Dreams in which one walks through water
or blood. Dreams about spirits and strange-looking people. Repeatedly recurring dreams that cause fear, or in which one sees accidents
happen or perceives the illness or death of someone. Talking in one's
sleep, making growling noises, crying, whistling or laughing, grinding
one's teeth, or sleep-walking. General restlessness, excessive mastur-
bation and nightmares are also an indication. Pain in one or more
organs, which is not helped by medicine; headaches for which no
physical cause can be found, heavy menstruation that gives rise to
physical weakness, depression, frustration, a feeling of asphyxiation,

palpitations, dizziness, haziness, speech impediments, absent-mindedness, spastic movements or cramps, unconsciousness, hallucinations, loss of control of the limbs or unusual stiffness while there is no indication of overtiredness or a physical cause, other odd feelings in part, or the whole, of the body. Sudden aversion to one's spouse, children or family. Animosity, hatred, attempts at seduction, suspicion, distrust, doubt, melancholy. Uncontrollable explosions of anger, sudden unusual forgetfulness, sudden physical laziness with extreme lethargy. Devilish, frightening thoughts about committing terrible sins, such as criminal acts and adultery. Paranoid feelings, fantasy images, a marked flickering in the eyes, or inability to look people straight in the eye without wanting to look away (bewitched and possessed persons also frequently have two different eyes). Touching and possession by one or more demons are also discernible in incommunicativeness and apathy, a married woman's state of *marbuta* (being "bound"), which makes her unable or unwilling to have sexual intercourse with her husband, and *rabt* (impotence of a man). Finally, when penetration of a virgin is difficult or impossible, or when harmony is broken between a man and a woman.

Know your enemy

For good treatment it is not only necessary that the healer is able to recite the right verses from the Koran, but he must also know his "opponent". The latter is actually the primary requisite. To this end he enters into a conversation with the demon in which he questions it as to its name, faith and motivations. If the identity of the demon is known, the healer/ exorcist can then command the demon to leave the possessed person's body. If the *jinn* does not heed this call, the healer can achieve the same thing through the torture, burning or killing of the *jinn*.[17] In illustration I shall give an account of two conversations which *sheikh* Khalid al-Tunsi had with demons. The conversations were published in the newspaper *al-Uruba* in 1993, with the title, "Confessions of the *jinn* as confessed to *sheikh* al-Tunsi". The journalists Mahmoud Khalil and Mohammed Husn, from this news-

---

[17] The commanding of the demon is already described in the New Testament, Luke 7.26-33 and Mark 5.7-13. See further W. van Binsbergen & F. Wiggermann (1997) on magic in ancient Mesopotamia and G. Luck (1985) on magic and the occult in Graeco-Roman antiquity.

paper, were present at the *sheikh's* "interview" with the *jinn*. In a personal conversation with them (1994) they confirmed to me that they
had indeed heard the *jinn* speak through the mouth of this person.

Case 1
A twenty-one-year-old woman, who went into a church in her dream.
When she woke up she no longer wanted her parents to call her *'Abir*,
because from now on her name is *Kanisa* (Church). She is constantly
in a state of excitement and rows with everyone who comes near to
her. She is depressive and barricades the front door so that no one
can enter or leave the house. The *sheikh* speaks to the *jinn* inside her.

> *Sheikh*: "Who are you? How old are you? Who sent you? Are you
> a priest? Get out of 'Abir's body."
> The *jinn* answers that his name is *Kanisa* and the name of his
> mother is Maryam (Mary).
> *Jinn*: "No I will not go away."
> The *sheikh* recites Koran verses to punish the *jinn*.
> *Jinn*: "Get lost with the Koran. I will not leave her body."
> *Sheikh*: "Is the Koran good?"
> *Jinn*: "Yes, the Koran is good."
> *Sheikh*: "Why don't you want me to recite verses then?"
> *Jinn*: "Because that punishes me."
> The *sheikh* again recites a few verses.
> *Sheikh*: "Go away or I will burn you."
> The *sheikh* then gives the woman some water to drink and reads
> the Koran. She answers that the water tastes of medicine and
> that she feels better.

Case 2
A woman in her late fifties, who has been "inhabited" by a *jinn* for the
past thirty-six years. She has already been to various doctors and has
spent a fortune. She has now come to the *sheikh* to ask for his help. In
her case too, the *sheikh* starts by enquiring into the *jinn*'s background.
It turns out that he is a young *jinn* (twenty-seven years old) who is
looking for his father. Unfortunately his father has previously been
burned by the *sheikh* because he was inhabiting someone too.

> *Sheikh*: "Your father was an infidel. Do you want to be burnt
> too?"

The *jinn* maintains that he wants to see his father, who he says was a Christian.

Sheikh: "How did you get into the woman's body?"

Jinn: "I don't know, my father took me with him."

Sheikh: "Do you have a mother too?"

Jinn: "I don't know."

The *sheikh* commands him to depart and asks him if he will accept Islam so that he can go to heaven. If he does not do this he will burn and end up in hell.

Jinn: "Must I burn because I am an infidel?"

Sheikh: "That is what the Koran says."

The *jinn* asks where he is to go if he leaves the body.

Sheikh: "Convert to Islam, show repentance to Allah and you will not go into the fire. If you convert you can go to the other faithful *jinn* in Mecca."

The *jinn* wants to convert and chooses to be called Mohammed from now on. As a sign of repentance and penitence he has to repeat the verses that the *sheikh* recites, ask God for forgiveness and say two *shahadat* (confessions). The *sheikh* takes one of the woman's hands and asks the *jinn* to sit in the woman's fingertip. He then pricks the woman's finger with a needle, and dark blood flows from it. The *jinn* then leaves her body. Immediately afterwards the woman feels relaxed and better.

I myself experienced a *jinn* speaking through a woman's mouth at a session with *sheikh* Alaa, at least this is how the *sheikh* interpreted it to me.

I have noticed that Koran healers say with remarkable frequency that many *jinn* are Christians and place "un-Islamic" demands on women, such as dancing, wearing short skirts and performing sexual acts. Some *jinn* also forbid listening to the Koran and saying prayers. In addition, there are stories in circulation claiming that by means of their *jinn* Christians are busy with a campaign of conversion directed at Muslims (see also al-Khuly 1996). Is it coincidence or are the healers an extension of fundamentalist groups who think that women must be "re-islamicized"? It appears so, because possessed women who seek treatment from a Koran healer experience enormous pressure to dress "Islamically", to pray more, be more pious and read the Koran more regularly.

Methods of treatment of possession caused by magic/sorcery

When a healer suspects a case of possession (whether caused by magic
or not), then he can carry out his treatment in several ways. First,
through *ruqya w-ta'awizat*, recitation of the Koran and calling on
Allah, directing requests to him in the confidence that he is the Only
Healer who can expose evil and who is the solution to everything.
Second, through *ilag ad-da' bid-da'* (healing of sorcery by sorcery).
Since the healer knows the secret powers of the suras, he has power
over the devil and can use it to fight the illness jointly. This sort of
healing is actually forbidden since humans are not allowed to work
together with *jinn* and devils (see Chapter 2). But I have noticed a certain degree of tolerance for this among some "bona fide" healers. The
healers I describe say they are doing *'ilag bil-qur'an* (healing with the
Koran). They certainly call themselves bona fide, even though they
also "talk" with *jinn* in their patients' bodies. This is officially condemned, but not by them since they also call upon Allah as the Great
Healer and use Koran verses for healing. There are also healers who
do not use the Koran and who have made a "contract" with the devil
or *jinn* who helps them in their work. They are called sorcerers and
are reprehensible.

Demon possession is mentioned in the Koran (e.g. in *al-Mu'minun*
[23]: 25 and *Saba'* [34]: 8, 46), but no demon-expulsions are mentioned that can be compared with the exorcisms of Jesus. But I have
often heard stories of exorcisms performed by the Prophet, like the
story of a little boy that was brought to him because he was possessed
by a demon. The Prophet prayed for him and stroked his chest, after
which the boy spewed up a creature that was the demon (compare
my report on the prayer meeting with *sheikh* al-Mu'attar, above). This
story of the Prophet and the little boy is very old and comes from the
Sunan (*hadith* collection by al-Darimi [797-868: Raven 1995: 18;
Leemhuis [1989: 22] calls the collection *musnad*). This story originates
later than the Koran, but by adducing the example of the Prophet, it
is shown that there is a tolerant attitude towards this form of healing.
The criterion is always that for all sorts of sorcery/magic refuge must
be sought with God.[18]

---

[18] I was curious as to the opinion of the al-Azhar on healers and Koran healing and
so went for advice to Dr. Abdul Aziz Ezat Abdul Jalil, mentioned above, who wrote
down his answer for me: "Koran healing is allowed, but healing is certainly not one

Men, jinn *and* magic

Although my research was oriented to women and possession, now and again I did have chance to be present at a healing session for men and thereby to learn something about men and possession. Most healers could not be persuaded to let me attend healing sessions for men (with the exception of the mixed sitting with *sheikh* al-Mu'attar described earlier). My (female) presence would create too much disruption. I was able to make an appointment with a well-known *sheikh* and be present at one of his treatments. On the day of my visit there were two gentlemen. One of them was being treated by the *sheikh* for his sickness and the other was wanting to learn the profession of Koran healer from the *sheikh*.

Case 1

The sick person is a fifty-seven year old man. From his speech I can tell that he has had a good education. He is a member of the board of directors in a firm. He is being treated by the *sheikh* for nervous tension. He has consulted many doctors for his complaints, specialists in psychic illnesses. They were unable to make him better. So that is why, he says, he has come to this *sheikh*. The *sheikh* listens to his complaints and problems and then reads and recites a number of verses from the Koran for him. This calms him.

"My illness has a long history and is caused by *jinn*. My problems, which led to my sickness, were also caused by *jinn*. It is *mass*

---

of the primary functions of the Koran. The Koran serves as a guide for the life of Muslims, that is the most important function of the Holy Book. For Koran healing certain criteria must be met, such as the requirement that the healers must have a pure and devout heart and that the sick persons must be strong in character and faith. Both need to know that only Allah can heal." He quotes Ibn al-Qayyim: "Healing with the Koran must be seen as a war, in which the enemy can only be vanquished if the weapon is effective and the arm strong. If either one of these factors is missing the fight will not be won. In the case of Koran healing this means that both the sick person and the healer must believe in the power of God."

According to Dr. Abdul Aziz Ezat Abdul Jalil, opinion is divided among Islamic scholars regarding the use of incantation (*ruqya*): "But the general view is that incantation is permitted as long as Allah alone is called upon, the incantations are not done in an incomprehensible language and do not contain blasphemy, and that they are pronounced in the deepest conviction that they only have any effect with the permission of God." In the appendix I give a concise introduction to the use of *ruqya* and the actions that have to be performed together with them.

(touching) by a *jinn*." I ask him how he knows this. "If a case of illness is not the result of physical disorders and has nothing to do with what you have eaten, then in ninety percent of cases it is a question of touching by *jinn*, or the devil has entered your body. The regular doctors gave me medicines, but they did not help." I ask him if it is possible that there are other causes for his condition, besides those that he has already mentioned, such as problems at home. "If, as in my case, there is no history of physical disorders, no other problems, and if there is no question of complaints that can be attributed to food, then it absolutely has to be *mass* from *jinn*." I tell him that I saw him a few days before also, and ask how often he comes to the *sheikh*. "A few times a week. I have probably been five or six times now and I feel quite a bit better already."

Case 2

A sixty-year-old man. I have seen him here before and I ask if he is also being treated by the *sheikh*. He comes to learn from the *sheikh*, not because he is sick, he tells me. He hopes he too will be able to heal people in the future. I say that it is usually *hafizin* (people who have memorized the Koran) who perform Koran healing. Is he a *hafiz* too?

> "Of course I am." He points out that a distinction must be made between *amrad ʿaqliyya*, mental sicknesses, and *amrad ruhiyya*, spiritual sicknesses. "For the treatment you need to know exactly what you are dealing with, and most doctors, who have only had a scientific education, do not know the difference. Nor do they know what the symptoms of spiritual sickness are, which are expressed in headaches, confusion and inability to think clearly, personality changes, and so on. Spiritual sicknesses must be treated by a *sheikh*. Sicknesses of the spirit that are caused by physical disorders or problems belong with the regular doctors and psychiatrists." I ask him how anyone can know for sure whether it is a matter of an "ordinary" illness or a "spiritual" illness. "That is the big problem, because they are very similar. 'Ordinary' psychological disorders do not respond to Koran healing, and conversely spiritual illnesses do not respond to regular medicine.[19] The person suffering from a

---

[19] In psychology this is called proof by evidence.

spiritual illness sees all kinds of animals in his dreams, especially cats, and that is a sign that he is spiritually sick." I ask if spiritual sickness comes from sorcery. "That is possible, but it can also come from the 'evil eye', or from *al-'ishq*, the passionate love of a *jinn* that wants to marry a human being." I ask him whether he knows why there has been so much more interest in Koran healing in the past two or three years. "This is because people are under more and more pressure. People have also departed from the true Islamic way of life. The result of this is psychic disorders. People must turn back to Allah." I ask him if Egyptians were in a better condition three years ago. "It is true that three years ago there was hardly any talk of Koran healing. I do not know why that is so." I say that I have heard that there are *sheikh*s who heal with the Koran alone, but that among them there are also some who use the *jinn* for healing. That I have read in the newspaper of a *sheikh* who says that among the *jinn* there are doctors, advocates and many other "professional *jinn*", all of whom he uses at specific moments. Is this a *daggal* (swindler)? "This is a 'rotten apple' among the *sheikh*s. It is forbidden to enter into a deal with the *jinn* and to use them in the treatment of illnesses."

I tell the two gentlemen that I think the *zar* can also have a healing effect. Both shake their heads dismissively and say there is nothing to it. "*Zar* is 'pharaonic'. The *jinn* are not really cast out in the *zar*, but only 'bound'." I say that in the *zar* the name of Allah is also recited, so why should it not be good? "In Koran recitation the angels listen and in the *zar* the *jinn* listen. There is war between the angels and the *jinn*. That is why the *jinn* do not properly disappear through the *zar*, but they do through Koran healing."

Sheikh Abdel Khaliq al-Atar sits down with us and says that he will show me how he heals. He then begins with Koran recitation, which takes ten minutes. The sick man and the "student" pray along with him, with their arms raised. Then everyone goes home.

Rabt (impotence)

Dr. Adel Mohammed al-Madani is a renowned psychiatrist in Cairo, who is interested in "popular illnesses", in particular in *rabt* (impotence among men), which is caused by *jinn* and healed by "traditional" healers. He has researched this and told me that by far the most popular and most widespread healing method for impotence (56.6%) is the "undoing" (*yifukk*) of magical formulas by a traditional healer.

According to al-Madani a very large proportion of recently married young men suffer from impotence. The fact that before marriage men are not allowed to enter into any sexual relationships and the putting off of marriage for economic reasons until later in life, cause especially great pressure. When the wedding day has finally arrived, the young man has to "perform" and deflower his bride practically in full view of the whole assembled family. *Rabt* may also be a cover for homosexuality, which in Islamic societies, Egypt included, is regarded as a great sin.

Other conclusions from his research are that economic factors play a key role. Most men who believe in impotence through *jinn* belong to the lower income classes. These men rarely visit regular doctors with their problems in view of the high costs for consultations, medicines, transport to visit the doctors, and so on. Moreover, traditional healers live predominantly in the lower income-bracket districts and are well known there too. In addition, the healer uses idiomatic language closer to that of ordinary people than that of scientifically trained doctors. These healers enjoy greater confidence among the people than regular doctors and psychologically they wield greater influence over their clients. So they are bound to be consulted more readily precisely for psychological problems since their "psychological language" is more familiar than that of scientifically trained psychiatrists. For persons suffering from impotence it is, furthermore, a great relief when they are told that they themselves are not responsible for their "impotence" but that external forces have a hand in it and that it can affect anyone.

According to al-Madani, confidence in traditional healers is not limited to the lowest classes. People from other social classes also consult a spiritual healer from time to time. He himself calls for better, unprejudiced research into the knowledge and skills of "popular" healers and where appropriate for them to be "topped-up" with scientific knowledge about the causes of physical and mental complaints. My experience, and this was confirmed by Dr. al-Madani, is that men are much more likely to take their problems to a *sheikh* who undoes magic or a healer who heals with the Koran, than to visit a *zar*. Although men do attend, the *zar* is regarded as women's territory.

Interpretation: Koran healing as transition rite

Can the same analytical terms be applied to Koran healing as to the *zar*? I think that this is indeed possible, even if the rituals are somewhat less explicit and rather more difficult to describe than in the *zar*.[20]

The initial interview with the Koran healer is comparable with the ritual preparations and diagnoses by the *zar* leader. The sick person goes to the healer, who declares that this is a case of demon possession. The sick person is "accepted" and relations have to be restored, not with the *jinn* (or "masters") but with God, who in turn will provide healing. I call this part of the procedure the preliminal or separation phase, because the person in question is "separated" from a situation in which the "conflict" arose. The liminal phase begins at the moment that the sick person starts attending the sessions of Koran recitation. Just as in the *zar* this has the goal of coming into contact with the supernatural forces that are oppressing him or her, that is to say the *jinn* that have entered the body. No amulets here, or incense, music or dancing. The rituals consist in intense listening to and the repetition of recitations of special Koran verses.

The Koran is recited on many different occasions, from the inauguration of a new mosque, the opening of a new shoe shop or snackbar to a *sahra diniyya* (special religious memorial services). In Egypt there are many prominent Koran-reciters who have developed their own style. Frequently they are sponsored by the media and cassettes are published with their *qira'at* (recitations). The religious radio station *Ida'at al-Qur'an al-Karim* broadcasts nothing but Koran recitals in *murattal* and *mujawwad* style, all day long. The first style is devout and private, the second is a musical style favoured by professional cantors and is to be heard especially during the *salat al-juma'a* (Friday prayers). During Ramadan (the Islamic month of fasting) and on religious holidays the media broadcast the recitation of special Koran verses. As a

---

[20] See Chapter 3 for the theoretical background of rituals in healing cults and Chapter 4 for the application of this terminological apparatus by Van Gennep and Turner to the components of the *zar*.

component of *rites de passage* Koran recitation plays a prominent role
in memorial services for the deceased. The sound of Koran recitation
is to be heard day and night, in the street, in taxis, in shops, in
mosques and in private homes. This is the daily background music in
Egypt, the heart of the liturgy and the spirit of official and social life.
The Koran has central place in Islamic society. The significance of
this is reflected not least by means of the tradition of recitation (Nelson 1985).

Koran verses contain, the healers say, a special power and light,
which can be applied by experts (such as themselves) in the healing of
illnesses. I myself have experienced that it is possible to be moved by
the specific rhythmic and melodic elements of the recitation of the
verses. This applies all the more to the possessed women (and men)
who attend the *jalasat* (sessions) in the expectation that this will in fact
happen. Through the pervasive and very loud way in which the
recitations take place, the persons concerned undergo an alteration in
consciousness that can be described as trance. In this condition the
jinn responsible for their misfortune manifests itself. The healers
manipulate this experience in such a way that a climax is reached,
after which the tensions that have built up disappear and a feeling of
relief sets in.

The incorporation phase begins after the healer has ordered the
woman to come back regularly and in particular when she responds
to his exhortation to lead a "more Islamic" life, after which she will
never again be bothered by *jinn*. If she goes and dresses and lives in
accordance with the new guidelines received from the *sheikh*/healer
then one may speak of incorporation into a new "cult group".

Turner's ideas of *communitas*, of a new situation that continues to
work outside the *jalasat*, producing comradeship, equality, reflection
and reorientation in existing relationships, norms and values, do not
in my opinion apply to Koran healing, any more than they do to the
zar. The session with the Koran healer, is not meant to bring this
about, any more than in the *zar*. The opposite is the case — the treatment leads to maintenance of the status quo.

In the case of possession one can look further than social and religious
explanations alone, namely towards the significance of the body in a
specific situation. With our bodies we experience and interpret the
world and society, which in turn leave their mark on our bodies. The
human body is in all regards a cultural product that exists in a specific

context, in which it is an active subject, shaped by social impulses and history (McGuire 1990: 285). Like Devisch (1993) I believe that the human body itself, as the embodiment of cultural traditions, can bring about healing. Hence my comments on the *bricolage* that is used by healers in *zar* and Koran healing.[21]

---

[21] By *bricolage* I mean the many "aids" used to bring about a particular effect. Creyghton (1981:37), following the example of Lévi-Strauss (1963), calls people who have not had the benefit of a formal medical training but are still occupied with medicine, *bricoleurs* ("do-it-yourselfers"). She writes that this sort of person is to be found in all societies at all times. They work in the "treasuries" of their culture where they find meanings, old customs and knowledge which they adapt to new circumstances.

CHAPTER SIX

POSSESSION AS A CENTRAL ELEMENT
IN LOCAL COSMOLOGY

In Chapter 3 I showed how Devisch (1993) unravels and interprets
the means and processes that play an active role in the healing practices of his research group. From this perspective he looks at space-
time dimensions and the different therapeutic relationships, such as
those with the body, the family and society. My view of things agrees
with his in a number of respects. Like him, I am of the opinion that
the interpretation of the cause of an illness begins with the hypothesis
that there is a meaningful resonance between the body, interaction
with one's nearest and dearest and society. Symptom and sickness are
viewed as disruptions of the life of the person concerned and also of
the person's physical, social, moral and cosmological context. The *zar*
leader and the Koran healer try to drive the sickness out of the body
by tracking down, mastering and removing the conflict from which
the patient is suffering. With a variety of means they attack the cause
of the disturbance, turn it around and rehabilitate the individual
within the family and/or living environment.

In all cultures there is a connection between sickness and the subjective and cultural experiences of the individual. So I preface my discussion of *zar* and Koran healing with an exposition of the local cosmological structure. In both healing cults traditions and skills are cre-
atively interwoven with aspects from the various areas of life. The rituals are oriented towards physical experience and build a bridge
between body, cosmos, group and society.

In Egypt it is believed that the instigators of possession are non-
human beings that live under the ground and are able under certain
conditions to penetrate the body through "openings". In order properly to draw out the significance of this physical aspect, the section
that follows is entirely devoted to the experience of physicality. I
examine the experience of womanhood in the culture within this
research group and the specific vulnerability of the female body
through the presence of bodily openings. After that follows a discussion of understandings of gender, the physical experience of the *zar*
rituals in music and dance, and of the recitation of the Holy Scripture
in Koran healing. I shall then indicate differences and agreements

between the two methods of healing, and look into the symbolic material. I conclude with a treatment of *zar* and Koran healing in relation to sufi brotherhoods and saints' tombs.

In the cosmological thinking of the women in my research the world is populated by countless supernatural beings: angels, devils, *jinn* and "brothers and sisters underground".

Angels are made of particles of light. They represent good, are often God's helpers and live in the seven heavens. Devils are described in less good terms, but everyone knows that *Iblis*, himself a fallen angel, is the *Shaytan* (devil) and the chief of countless hosts of *shayatin*, the devil's malign helpers. *Jinn* are made of particles of fire and form a world parallel to our own. They live under the ground in families or tribes. Some are very powerful, others weak. They are often malevolent. In Egypt *jinn* are sometimes confused with the *ikhwat that al-ard*, the brothers and sisters underground, who are invisible *doppelgänger* of humans. When these "brothers and sisters" get angry or jealous, they can cause harm and illness, but in the main they do not. There resides a certain logic in the distinction between *jinn* and the "brothers and sisters", since the latter are the image of the human being and everything evil they inflict on humans, they also do to themselves.

Women are considered to be less strong in their faith, moreover they are impure for a number of days each month (see also Sabbah 1984). Impurity wields a strong magnetic influence on *jinn*. To these two supposed weak points among women comes a third, namely the fact that they have more bodily openings. *Zar* leaders, Koran healers and the women themselves have an opinion of "bodily openings". From conversations with them I have put together the following view of the body.

Vulnerability

The body

The body is divided into three parts: the head, the trunk (with the belly, stomach, intestines, liver and kidneys) and the legs. The trunk (*gism*) is the central part of the whole body. The head and the legs "clothe" (*yilbis*) the trunk. The most important weak points of the body are in the transition areas of the body: on both sides of the neck, under both arms and in both groins (the lymph glands). They are held to be "openings", but they can swell up during illness and the swelling is then called *beeda* (egg). The *beeda* then has the function of a stopper or a cork that prevents bacteria from penetrating the body through the openings (weak points) to vulnerable parts and causing injury there. The head has a large number of openings through which the *jinn* can both step into and leave the invisible (internal) body. There are five openings in the skull, namely: at the front and at the back of the skull (the large and the small fontanel), the temples and a spot on the top of the head. Then there is the mouth, the most visible "opening" of the body and the doorway through which the body takes in food and air and through which it produces sounds by way of the tongue. The moisture from the mouth (saliva) of ordinary people is impure, but that of holy men and pious men has *baraka* (power to bless). The eye socket is an opening that houses the eye. The eye is a symbol of good and evil. It is the place in which evil can reside independent of the person who has such an eye. This phenomenon is called "the evil eye", which is feared not only in Egypt but also elsewhere (Garrison Arensberg, 1976; Spooner 1970). Some people also speak of an "eye" on the forehead between the eyes. This eye is called *basar* and it is connected with a place on the same level as the heart, which is called *basira*. This is a sort of spiritual eye with which subjective phenomena can be perceived. It is also called the seat of *firasa* (intuition). The nose is an important organ that on one hand is impure because of its excretions and on the other hand positive because it can perceive God's miracles in nature. The ear is often called an opening through which the devil and the demons *biywishwish* (whisper) and put bad ideas and thoughts in a person's head.[1] But The Word also enters by the ear, as in listening to Koran recitation. I shall return to the special significance of eye, ear, nose and mouth in relation to The Word.

The area around the genitals and the anus is "open" and especially impure and shameful. All excretions from the lower part of the body, semen, menstrual blood, urine and faeces, are impure. On the other hand excretions from the upper part of the body, such as the saliva of holy men, but also mother's milk, are very commonly regarded as pure and are used in healing.

The woman differs in particular because of the "openness" of her

[1] Compare al-Suyuti, Cairo, n.d., but probably from the pen of Sanawbari, 1412: *al-Rahma fi al-tibb wa al-hikma*.

vagina, through which she is especially vulnerable to demons. Evil spirits often come into the body through this route. Hence it is *sunna* (customs and actions in the tradition of the Prophet) that when a man has sex with his wife, he keeps his body covered. The devil is then unable to see him and slip into the woman's body through the vagina. The vagina is also the opening through which menstrual blood leaves the body. This is *damm fasad* (rotten blood); it is negative and can cause injury to other parts of the body.

"Unclean blood" is also the blood that flows during childbirth and the woman is therefore impure for forty days (*fatrit an-nafasa'*), after which comes *damm tahara* (purifying blood). There is also an important difference between light blood and dark blood. Dark blood is "dirty"; it is unclean and heavy. It flows through the body with some difficulty and is thus the cause of illnesses. Light blood is "clean" blood that provides for good health and a balanced mood. Egyptians also say a cheerful and lively person has *damm khafif*, that is, "light" blood. In general blood has a positive meaning and a negative meaning. In a positive sense it means "life"; "man is created from a blood-clot" (sura *al-'Alaq* [96]: 2). The negative sense is that blood is the route through which *jinn* can move through the human body (the Prophet said that the Devil also moves through a person like a trickle of blood or a blood-clot, and blood is therefore impure).

The significance of the womb is ambiguous. On the one hand it is compared with a grave and a grave is impure (el-Sayed el-Aswad 1987), but on the other hand the womb is the source of all life and the connecting vital stream of body to family to society. During childbirth the pelvis is "opened". The woman must purify herself ritually with water, which "closes" the pelvis again. This occurs forty days after giving birth. The back can also be "open" and is then the cause of miscarriages. The ovaries are partially negative by virtue of their different tasks: the right ovary produces children and the left one menstrual blood. A certain hidden value is attributed to left and right. Right is positive and is associated with masculinity and children. Left is negative and is connected with menstrual blood. The menstrual period or the forty days after childbirth are dangerous times since one is then especially vulnerable through the opening of the body through which blood flows.

Dimensions in time and space

Besides having to do with an open body, the incursion of evil spirits also has to do with vulnerability through "openings" in time and place. The time after sunset is particularly dangerous. It is better not to pour hot water down the toilet in the evening, because it can frighten the underground inhabitants and make them angry and vengeful. Actions before the rising of the new moon also holds special dangers, because by not keeping to particular rules one can expose oneself to *mushahara/kabsa*. This is a particular type of sorcery which results in infertility or a deficiency in the mother's milk after childbirth. This can endanger the infant's life (Inhorn 1994; Sengers 1994).

After sunset it is dangerous to be found in particular places: a lonely and forsaken place, a ruin, a graveyard, a boggy or stinking place, or by water such as a river, lake, or sea. It is known that *jinn* live here and wander about in the darkness. But also a *furn baladi*, an old-fashioned oven made of stones and earth, which one finds in the countryside, is dangerous because *jinn* are made of fire, are originally fire spirits and therefore like to live in and near fire.

From stories told me by the people I have talked with, I have learned that in the home it is in particular the toilet with adjoining bathroom and the place next to it (*al-bahraya*) that are the most dangerous places. The toilet is especially *nagis* (impure, through excrement and the washing away off semen and menstrual blood). Moreover it is a place that has a connection to the "underground world". So before entering a bathroom or toilet one must first say *bismillah* (in the name of God) or *a'uzu mil-khubs wa-l-khabayis* (God protect me against all impurity) in order to be protected against the *jinn*.

The doorstep or threshold of a house is dangerous because *jinn* often live underneath them, as also a staircase in a house or a place under a staircase. Is there a parallel between the entrance to the house and the routes into a person? No one expressed a clear opinion about this, but in stairwells there is often a handprint on the walls made with the blood of a sacrificial animal, to avert evil.

Emotion/fright

Emotions and fright cause dangerous "openings". Crying or being sad in the *hammam* (bathroom/toilet) is particularly dangerous, according to the women, because this increases the risk of getting possessed. Fright creates a symbolic opening through which the *jinn* can go in or out. Fright in combination with a beating is even more dangerous, especially if one falls on the floor in the *hammam*. Since the person is then empty, separated or uncoupled, an opening is created through which *jinn* can easily enter.

Each individual person is surrounded by a field of light. For a pious person this light field is very strong, so that the *jinn* cannot approach him. Because of the power of this light they even have to look away from him. For a person with a weak light field (less strong in their faith) the *jinn* are constantly in the area, lying in wait for a chance to take possession of the body. A light field is not a firm substance, but vague and full of cracks. Beneath the first light field there is a second field that forms a strong attraction for *jinn*. As such as a person has a strong emotional experience (anger, great sorrow, shock), this has serious consequences for the person's vulnerability. The cracks in the first field widen, so that the *jinn* can enter through them and be pulled automatically through the second field. In the case of women, the light field is generally weak.

Semiotic structure

Oppositions

In Arabic the soul is called *nafs* or *ruh*. These terms characterize the two sides of the Islamic understanding of the soul. *Nafs* is associated with flowing blood, psyche, individuality (ego), desire and eroticism.[2] It is the symbol of the female principle that has to be broken in order to admit the "Light of Mohammed", that is permeated by divine spirit. In mystical doctrine the believer must follow the "path of purification". He does this by breaking with his human qualities, that is to say by cleansing himself of *nafs*. As a member of a *tariqa* ("path") he tries to perfect himself by *ruh*, which stands directly opposite *'aql* (worldly intellect). *Ruh* is associated with spirit and the male principle. Just as *nafs* is present in the blood, *ruh* resides in the male sex organs. It is notable that demons are often called *ruhani* instead of *jinn* and that spiritually caused illnesses are *marad ruhani* (Morsy 1978). Through the opposition between life and death (pure and impure) and in part

---

[2] Amin (1953: 167) also speaks of *nafs/nafas* as "breath with an evil force" in roughly the same way as the "evil eye".

because blood and the sex organs are equally impure, *nafs* and *ruh* have both a positive and a negative connotation.

Another important anatomical opposition is that between head and feet, which has symbolic parallels in the visible and invisible cosmos and in the human body. One can also speak of an opposition between the visible and the invisible (internal) body. Rituals which concern the body, or actions against pains or sicknesses, are carried out on the visible body in order to create an effect on the invisible body. In religious healing this is particularly noticeable. It is not only among my Egyptian conversation partners that the body and bodily openings have special significance, as this is also often the case in other cultures (cf. Desjarlais 1992; Devisch 1993; Becker 1995). The body is not only open to invasion by demons but also open to The Word.

Word and body

In relation to spiritual illnesses reference is often made to the connection between *basar* and *basira* (the spiritual eye and the place near the heart). It is the duty of each upright person to strive for a straight line that runs from the spiritual eye to the place near the heart. That is the path to and from God, and the path to yourself. It is the path of the *mu'min* (faithful). An important cause of sickness is the condition of being *mish-mu'min* (not *mu'min*). Someone in this condition would have no love in his heart but be oriented to material things instead of God. Such a person is empty, and emptiness makes you weak. As a result of his weakness he is easy prey for the *jinn*. In the case of women the problem is not so much that they do not believe but that their faith is insufficient or too weak, which makes them especially vulnerable.

The senses play an important role in the "consumption" of music and The Word. This applies in particular to the music and dancing in the *zar* ritual. The *zar* masters make themselves known through a particular melody which goes in through the ear, stimulating the body in the dance. The women thus come into contact with their deepest feelings and enter into conversation with their "master". Koran healers on the other hand do not use any music but trust in The Word. Their only weapon against *jinn*, they say, is the Koran. The eye reads The Word, the tongue recites The Word and the ear listens to the Holy Words. They penetrate deep into the body, where they summon the *jinn* and expel or burn them.

The mouth can also drink the sacred texts, when they have first been dissolved in water. If they are burned together with incense, the person afflicted by *jinn* can breathe in the therapeutic words. These last two methods, however, are close to what magicians/sorcerers do and so they are rejected by healers who say they are following the "Right Path", because these practices, in their view, destroy God's word.

Apart from the interaction between Word and body through the senses, there is also interaction with the moving body in prayer. Not only is the recitation of the sacred words important, but also the combination of the words with body movements during the prayers. The movements of the body are strictly prescribed and correspond with the meaning of the spoken text. For a faithful Muslim prayer is thus simultaneously both an internal practice and an (external) physical exercise.

Body movements also have to do with the way in which one enters a consecrated place. A mosque (positive space) is entered with the right foot first, while speaking words of blessing. By contrast, places associated with *jinn* (such as the bathroom or toilet) are entered with the left foot first, while speaking words intended to avert evil.

The multi-faceted role of music

Music can be experienced in many ways, physiologically, psychologically, emotionally and aesthetically. One can "make" music and "feel" music. Music is primarily perceived through the ears, but musical vibrations are wave movements that are tangible and often also visible (Beaulieu, 1987). An example of this is that when the strings of an instrument are touched one can feel sound vibrating. When singing a song, one not only makes sound but one also experiences the sound physically. There is not only an external sensitivity to music, but also an internal sensitivity, it is absorbed by the whole body. That is also the case when the *kudya* sings the incantations and the musicians in the *zar* beat the drums and play the *tambura*, or when the *sheikh* recites the Koran verses. Those present feel the sound through their skin vibrating in their body and in the head. It has a physical impact on them and causes a sensory change in their consciousness.

On a psychological level music changes the existential experience simultaneously in time and space. The music made in the *zar* and the specific melody of the Koran recitation must be regarded as varied ways of altering consciousness of time and space. Because music is emotionally charged, it brings a person into a special relationship with his or her own feelings and the outside world. A feeling of total bonding emerges with one's own "I" and with the world.

Some researchers think that music has a hypnotic effect on the nervous system. People talk of "the monotonous sound of the drum", or "obsessively rhythmic repetition". But music does not always lead to trance. Music through which one goes into trance during the ceremony does not have the same effect outside the ceremony. This is because the psychic stimulus is missing, namely the association with a particular day and a particular place. A number of factors are therefore missing. It is the total situation that leads to music causing trance. Is this perhaps a case of "conditioned reflex"? If the production of trance is dependent on other external factors, then it is not.

Others talk of the neurophysiological effect of certain sounds in music (low-frequency vibrations). The combination of drums, dance and song would bring about a process of dissociation of the consciousness. Moreover, particular movements, such as turning the head and neck around, are responsible for a disturbance of the inner ear, while at the same time one may observe that there is "over-saturation". Rouget (1985) gives a detailed treatment of various theories on music and trance and comes to the conclusion that no single theory has proper scientific support. In his view, the power of music alone is not responsible for the fact that the individual goes into trance. Neither music nor dancing mechanically or automatically causes trance (after all spectators and listeners do not go into trance). The most important additional factor is that trance has to be desired.

In the East, since time immemorial healing practices have made use of empathetic music, in which the patient is stimulated to move the head rhythmically up and down (Khan 1923; Sargant 1974). This was the case in particular when the complaints appeared to be psychological in nature and were regarded as due to obsession or the effects of magic. This unleashed the patient's emotions and allowed him to talk about his secret complaints, which had until then been hidden through fear, conventions and social norms. So the healer was in a position to track down and deal with the cause of the patient's sickness.

Gender

Also important alongside the way in which the women in my research think about their bodily openings, is the way in which they learn, from childhood, how the relationship is between the body and the world around them. In Egyptian society (but elsewhere too) subtle practices are used to subordinate the female body (see also Kapferer 1983: 100-110). A few examples: Koran healers and pious men "protect" themselves by covering their hands against coming into contact with the female body. A woman is not allowed to express her emotions and she must not interrupt her husband. Without male company or permission she is not allowed to go out on the street. There are areas specially reserved for women in buses, trains and the metro. There are special ticket offices for women (and in some Islamic countries separate entrances) in government buildings and mosques. The woman's body is there for her husband's pleasure and for the bearing of his children (*al-Baqara* [2]: 223). In the eyes of many men, her mind is inferior to a man's mind. The woman is thought to be without *'aql* (reason/understanding) or at any rate to have less of it than men. Moreover, she has too many emotions, which hinders rational thought. That is why God has made men to be "maintainers of women" (*al-Nisa'* [4]: 34).[3] In western societies identity is connected with an interpersonal process and social interaction (McGuire 1990). The situation is different in most Islamic societies. A woman identifies herself in relation to the family to which she belongs, or the wider circle of relatives. There is no difference between her body and her identity. If the I-feeling is threatened, this has implications for her physical and psychological wellbeing (see also Boddy 1989). There are many references in the Koran to the place, position and "correct" behaviour of the woman. For the ignorant, malevolent and religious fanatics it is simple by use of these religious duties to keep the woman under one's thumb, especially when the women concerned have had little education and have little in the way of economic possibilities.

---

[3] Reason/understanding forms the connection between the visible (natural) and the invisible (supernatural), the body and the soul, the individual and society. In order to be a full member of society a Muslim (read: man) must have his full reason/understanding at his disposal. Women have less reason/understanding than men. They are therefore less than full members of society.

Zar and Koran healing

Bricolage

How can the ritual drama have a healing effect on the physical body
and on emotions? What does it "do" in order to heal the patient? In
my view, the music and dancing in *zar* and the recitation in Koran
healing are important factors in this. The body and the imagination
are stimulated into play. The sick person steps beyond the physical,
social and cosmological boundaries, which frees her from the state of
possession and reconnects her with a meaningful and empowering
social order.

The healing ritual in the *zar* draws upon a *bricolage* of aids, which
have directly to do with "physicality". This begins with the *atar*, which
generally consists of a small personal and used piece of clothing
belonging to the sick person, such as a headscarf, which helps the
leader to make a "bond", i.e. contact, with the occupying demon. At
the beginning of the *zar* the woman are extensively incensed: the
head, the arms, the body and along the legs as far as under the skirts.
Incense is thought to have *baraka* (power to bless), it smells good and
after some time a heavy, sultry air hangs in the room which those present find conducive towards a particular mood. The women have perfumed themselves heavily and have put on their best clothes. They
are decked out as "brides" and are adorned with jewellery. This suggests that something quite special is going to happen.

At a *zar* of any real size three different music groups will play. They
play in succession. The music differs strongly between them, but it is
clear that they are working towards a climax; from the *harim masri*
(women's group) to the *abu gheet* (men's group) to the *tambura* (mixed
group) the music gets more and more dramatic. This is also the case
in each separate group: the music begins slowly, becomes more vigorous and ends in a climax. The women's dancing, too, becomes more
vigorous and exhausting as the evening progresses and goes on into
the night, until the patient finally, quite literally, drops.

The pattern of the dancing is not fixed in advance and some women
have a preference for a particular tune which permits them to "enter
into conversation" more easily or more intensively with their possessing demon. The dance leader (*mangur*) whips the women up with the
rhythmic swinging of his hips, the ringing of the little bells around his
middle and the sound of his *saghat* (round metal clappers), to such an
extent that they go into a state of trance during the dancing.

Through the singing and dancing form is given to emotional and physical experiences and the possessing demon gains an identity: the sick dance for the Upper-Egyptian, the stethoscope dance for *Yawra Bey* or his father *Hakim Basha*, the squirming movement across the floor for master Gado of the impure places, and the veil dance for the Saudi master. The patient and the demon have become one, and the dance articulates deep feelings of fear, oppression, care and individual emotion. The "curse" that rests on the sick woman is transformed in the dance into a friendly relationship with the master. Her family and the spectators participate in this. It is a declaration of their solidarity with the sick person, but at the same time the dancing is also for pleasure, relaxation and the expression of individual feelings and desires. Rhythm, tempo, movement, intonation and melody are employed in a process that strengthens body and mind. Dance and song transport the body beyond its own boundaries and living world. *Zar* is a lusty, collective celebration of the body and an expression of solidarity in which a blockage is removed through the resolution of a conflict situation. This produces healing.

The term *bricolage* applies to Koran healing just as well as to *zar*. Everything the healers use to distinguish themselves can be indicated as such: their exterior (the *gallabiyya*, turban and beard), their "knowledge of the Koran", their "God-given gift of healing others" and their upright and pious life-style. For most healers The Word (the Koran) is the most important instrument in the healing. Some of them also use a whole range of aids such as ointments, magnetic bowls and such like, or they write sacred verses on pieces of paper that must be burned and breathed in or dissolved in water and drunk. Others again occupy themselves with cupping (the placing of heated glass bowls on the body to track down and heal ailments), or cauterization (the burning out of wounds).

As in *zar*, in Koran healing an initial introductory interview takes place (though this is less like an "initiation" than is the case in *zar*). The healer talks with the patient and identifies the problems she is wrestling with, after which he determines that the problem lies with a malevolent *jinn* which needs to be driven out. The *jinn* leaves the body only after pressure has been put on it to do so. That is why it is "worked on" by the healer through the ears. The healer interrogates it in order to determine its identity. Through the recitation of The Word the demon will then convert, flee or go up in smoke.

The *jinn* must leave the body through a prick with a needle in a finger or a toe (an "opening" is made). When *jinn* are unwilling it is not uncommon for the body to be beaten with sticks. During the healing sessions I have noticed that the sick person makes spastic movements with arms and legs, and sometimes with the whole body during the recitation. The sick person is, moreover, encouraged to hit out, shout, run through the treatment room or beat on the wall with her fists. This is all interpreted as the reactions of the resistant demon. The ritual of Koran healing, as in *zar*, exists in order to bring about certain effects: it leads to a point of catharsis and abreaction, removing the blockage. The evil spirit is driven out, the conflict situation is resolved and the patient gets better. That is to say that by means of the healing drama the sick person has got her own body going again, which has produced the possibility of overcoming problems and sickness, and she has become one with her family and society, and a new meaningful situation has come into being. Although the first step to a Koran healer is usually taken in the company of a family member, the family is not necessarily present at the ritual. The patient is, however, very strongly aware of a supporting group. The other women present are all co-sufferers. In addition, she is convinced, and is supported in this belief, that she is essentially doing something positive, constructive and Islamic, which has the approval of the whole community of the faithful.

The healer works upon the sick person's inner world, on sensual and physical forms of contact and on social and existential involvement among the group and in the patient's world. There is reconnection with feelings, desires, physical awareness and internal forces. Just as the negative influence of the demons penetrated through the bodily openings, so now the positive forces reach her. The body itself becomes the instrument of healing. Rhythm, song and dance in *zar*, but also the specific melody of the Koran recitation, connect the patient with her own body and its sensual perceptions, with her cultural traditions and her world of life, through which the healing process is activated and stimulated. In the identification of the demons and the indication of the way to healing, clarity is created and hope given. The patient overcomes her resentment and guilt feelings and regains the vitality to work through her problems and cares. In connection with this, Devisch (1993: 264) speaks of "weaving". In healing cults, he suggests, the art of healing consists of weaving, reweaving and interweaving of three elements: the physical body, the family or group and the society. During the ritual the generative forces within and between the many activities, movements and dimensions of body, group and world are rewoven into a harmonious whole. As an instrument in this the body is itself the most important factor, which converts meaning, structuring and energies between physical, social and cosmological fields from negative ones to positive ones.

Zar and Koran healing each form a practical method of intertwining the body with the group and society, with the spoken word (but not The Word) being less important than rhythm, dance, adornment of the body, distantiation and trance. The ritual therapy creates a very special atmosphere in which the ludicrous and the serious are mixed, in which the outward signs of inner conflicts are stimulated and in which boundaries are crossed in order to find the way back to the normative. On a personal level one might speak here of a special "therapy"; on the group level one might speak of cultural continuity and significance.

Differences and agreements between zar and Koran healing

The most important differences between *zar* and Koran healing consist in the fact that the first is a healing cult in which predominantly women hold sway and *pacify* the besetting demons, and that Koran healing is an *exorcism* cult which is dominated by men and in which women are subordinate. In Koran healing an appeal is made to religion on the basis of a fundamentalist interpretation of the Koran. The religious views are not necessarily the same as those of the afflicted women, but society appears to be moving in the direction of greater religiosity and as they adapt to this, they hope through working on themselves, i.e. by leading a "better" Islamic lifestyle, to gain relief from their ailments. In the social values scale Koran healing has the status of "legitimate" over against the *zar* as "illegitimate", i.e. "un-Islamic".

In atmosphere the *zar* and Koran healing are as different as night and day. First of all, the cosiness of the *zar* (and the *hadra*) is completely absent in Koran healing. Koran healing is exorcism and this means force. The healer (*sheikh*) dominates the *jinn* instead of the *jinn* dictating its wishes and demands to the possessed person, as happens in the *zar*. Koran healing involves an appeal to a stricter Islamic lifestyle. The soul must be purified so that the demon will leave its victim forever. That is the goal. The victim will be permanently healed, as long as she or he keeps to the Islamic religious regulations and lifestyle. The atmosphere is harsh and strict. The women must keep their whole body covered, preferably the face too. They are not allowed to wear henna or make-up, jewellery or amulets. This is completely opposite to the *zar* ceremony, in which the women's *asyad* (masters) demand precisely that they are smartly dressed, adorn themselves with jewellery and use perfume. A woman who has once participated in a *zar* ritual will always have to keep coming back, since, as they say, "her master keeps calling her". But women like to come, because the *zar* is a cheerful event. They dance with their spirit, they abandon themselves physically and mentally to the music and they dress up as if it were a wedding.

As in the *zar* music contains a "signal" for the spirits to manifest themselves, so is Koran recitation the *sheikh*'s instrument to call up the possessing spirit. In the *zar* the music of the drums and the leader's singing are loud and penetrating, which brings about a state of mind. In Koran healing the same goal is followed. The Koran healer does not regard himself as the *medium* (as the *zar* leader does) who can help others through his own experience. He is the *instrument* who, through his pious behaviour, has received from God the gift of healing. The demons which the Koran healers expel strongly resemble the demons that are pacified in the *zar*, since though they have other names and manifest themselves in a different way, they all cause possession, resulting in the same illnesses. In their method of treatment healers place strong emphasis on religion and they argue that their treatment is so effective that the demons disappear forever, while the treatment in the *zar* only has a temporary effect.

The resistance and the rebellion, true patterns of disorder, are suppressed in Koran healing and the women are subjected to the disciplinary institutions of society. The treatment of the Koran healers reflects trends in thinking like those in daily life: women have problems because they are weak in the faith, which makes them more susceptible than men to the attacks of evil forces. If they change their lifestyle and orient themselves more to God and true doctrine, they will automatically be protected against the dark powers. On the other hand the demon masters of the *zar* openly display their physical desires and in the ritual they incite the women to indulge in luxury, the wearing of beautiful clothes and jewellery, the use of perfume and the smoking of cigarettes and the drinking of alcoholic drinks.

Zar and Koran healing both give the individual the possibility of justifying problematic behaviour deemed otherwise unacceptable according to dominant norms, and to bring an individual illness or complaint into the open and make it public. Both methods of healing use a "dramatic" approach for this. Because both healer and patient believe in the same cosmology, the personal problem is expressed in terms of the supernatural. Happy and unhappy personal situations are linked with the activities of persons who operate by means of magic and the evil eye, and with supernatural middlemen who cause the touching and possession. Both means of healing thereby foster belief in the occult.

In both *zar* and Koran healing one may speak of a demon as a "possessing element", whose general aim is to cause harm to the possessed women. The state of possession occurs involuntarily and affects individuals, not a group. During the healing rituals there can be changes to the level of consciousness, facial expression and sometimes voice. I have found no clear indications of insensitivity to pain, as some Koran healers claim, but in Koran healing I have indeed noticed muscular spasms. Koran healers in particular maintain that women have no recollection afterwards of what has occurred (amnesia).

As a non-medical person I can make no judgments with regard to any possible connections with hysteria (as in "soul sickness" or "nervous disorders"). In view of the fact that dramatic personality disorder (hysteria) is historically associated with a wide variety of behaviour patterns, this is a concept that can easily be misleading. So I see no reason to brand the women I have observed in these two, so very different healing rituals, as "hysterical".[4] Demon possession, as treated in *zar* and Koran healing, is in my opinion best viewed as a pattern of interpersonal behaviour that is learned, shaped and maintained in and by a particular social context. Lambek (1989) speaks in this connection of "a representation of the self given shape by social factors", which corresponds to implicit and explicit views of what "being possessed" is and which is judged by those concerned and significant others to be "events and actions that happen outside the control of the possessed person". In the cases of possession with which I am familiar, I have the

---

[4] Finkler (1986: 632) writes that there is no reason at all to regard the healers or the ritual participants as psychopathological. Kleinman (1980: 214), cited by Finkler, says of the healers that "most were remarkable individuals who possessed strong personalities and many adaptive coping skills". My findings lead me to agree with these statements.

impression that the primary situation is one of stress followed by a pathological reaction. Possessed women seek healing for this, whether of their own accord, or on the incitement of their direct environment, in *zar* or Koran healing (see also Jilek 1989; Kemp 1989).

Criticism of the zar

Fundamentalists (and orthodox Muslims) have no sympathy for the *zar* ceremony, since it is performed at a time and in a place that are specially devoted to it, where men are admitted but can wield no authority. Despite the overarching patriarchy of Egyptian society, in this ceremony women fulfil the role of both ritual specialist and participant. This may be one of the reasons why the *zar* is regarded by fundamentalist Muslims as dangerous.

Another point is that the *zar* breaks through religious dogmas: "negotiations" are held with demons. This acknowledges the power of these beings, and for fundamentalists (and orthodox Muslims) this is equivalent to what sorcerers do, who also make a "contract" with devils and demons. Critics of the *zar* also mention the immorality/prostitution and adultery (*fujr* and *zina*) that are supposed to take place during the ceremony. I have never noticed any such thing, and al-Khuly (1996: 16) shares my view. There is indeed a charged atmosphere during the ceremony. This is a result of the stirring music, the seductive hip-swinging of the dance leader, the rhythmic movement of female bodies in the dance, the heavy perfumed air with the sweet smell of incense from the burners and the jangling and sparkling of jewellery — all things that are not supposed to belong in a pious Islamic lifestyle.

The middle and higher classes in particular see the *zar* as at odds with their concept of social development and/or Islamic values. Koran healing is socially more acceptable because it is legitimated by its appeal to the Holy Koran. Despite the fact that strong resistance to Koran healing has emerged through the media, and healers are often depicted in an unfavourable light because they use the Koran for their own ends, the emphasis on the strict Islamic teaching has led to this form of healing becoming very popular in a short space of time, and each week hundred of women jostle together to be admitted to the treatment by the *sheikhs*.[5]

---

[5] Leemhuis (personal communication) thinks that there is a connection between the popularity of this healing method and orthodoxy's recognition of the suddenly

The symbolic material: effectiveness of the rituals

Views of health and sickness are connected with cultural, political and moral values (Van der Geest & Nijhof 1989; Helman 1984; Kelinman 1980). A western-educated doctor or psychiatrist who treats a patient will in most cases declare him or her to be cured if particular complaints disappear. The patient can be of the opinion that this is not so and that it is now high time to visit a spiritual healer.[6] I support my research with explanations of sickness and healing as given by the women and the healers. These are explanations in which terms for sickness and especially of healing are often not coherently ordered.

Turner (1986) calls the "rituals of affliction" of the Ndembu (northwest Zambia) "meaningful stories" that tell us something of the social structure through which people gain insight and are spurred on to social acts.[7] Devisch (1993) has a different view. For him, healing rituals go further than "stories" and he thinks that precisely rhythm, dance and song are the most important ways to kick-start the healing forces in the body.

On the *zar* ceremony I wrote that the songs are practically incomprehensible and that their meaning is even largely unknown to many women. In my view the therapeutic effects can therefore not be directly derived from the text of the songs, something that Koran healers do claim concerning the Koran texts. They suggest that the texts have a force and a specific light which only "initiates" understand, and which send the demons packing or burn them up.

In Egypt personal calamity is often expressed in somatic terms (Morsy 1978). The women who attend the *zar* or Koran healing are

---

popular book by al-Shibli, which measures out the existence of *jinn* in all their ins and outs. This book, in his view, is playing a key role in the revival of public acceptance of the *jinn*. Al-Sibli is often cited in all sorts of publications as giving the orthodox point of view. First publication in Cairo in 1908, with reprints in 1983, 1988 and 1990 or 1991.

[6] Each form of medical thinking is a social-cultural construction. That is to say that these are views and treatment methods that have been developed by people. From a theoretical perspective the various views and healing methods are equally valid. Van der Geest and Nijhof (1989: 3) are of the opinion that western medical significations have played a dominant role for a long time (too long) and have too long been regarded as the only true representations of reality. They argue that sociologists and anthropologists should study the social reality of sickness and health care as a construction of meanings.

[7] Cf. Tennekens 1982: 113. The term "rituals of affliction" derives from Turner: a healing ritual whose goal is to drive out demons and to adopt the "victim" in a cult.

in general aware of a sequence of generally strongly emotional events preceding their illness, which were the consequence of a real trauma. Healers and *zar* leaders "translate" these events into a "demonic pattern". That is to say, in a pattern marked by the intervention of supernatural beings who have misused a temporary weakness of the body. The explanatory model thus rests on a mixture of the real traumatic experience with the "demonic pattern". The healing in the *zar* occurs through the "pacification of the master". The song of the *kudya* does not itself bring healing, but it does refer to "hidden sources" and "secret knowledge", namely to her relationship with the masters. In Koran healing the same pattern occurs. The healers claim to have secret powers and forces at their disposal, which give them the ability with the aid of Koran recitation to drive out the demons. In both cases the therapeutic treatment can be viewed as a process of rebirth and resocialization for the patient.

Schieffelin (1969: 59-62, 81) researched spiritist seances among the Kaluli of Papua New Guinea and writes that the effectiveness of rituals is dependent on what is caused by the "performance" of the symbolic material, i.e. through the way in which this "material" is articulated and brought to life. If the ritual "works", during the performance an indeterminate change takes place in the quality of the experience or situation of the participant. He also suggests that this aspect of socially reproduced reality cannot be reduced simply to text, structure or symbolic manipulation (see also Devisch 1993). The performance of the rituals itself plays an important part in this. Each performance differs from the other in the social circumstances and the motivation of the participants. The performance can run according to the standard or be improvised. In all cases it provides participants with an ordered series of expectations, so that they have the feeling than they are progressing in a particular direction. In order to achieve certain effects the leader of the ceremony can decide to make use of aids such as instruments, music, singing or special sounds, or not to use them. The way in which this is done may be programmed, or not. Further, the leader in each case must constantly maintain and guide the quality of the interaction with the participants.

In the *zar* the process runs as follows: the sick person seeks help from the *kudya* (*zar* leader), who in turn calls in the help of her masters to gain insight into the situation of the person concerned and to receive instructions regarding preparations for the ritual. In order to help the patient gain a picture of her own situation, preparatory rites are performed by the *kudya*, after which the healing ceremony follows. She maintains control over all the parts of the process: the selection of the songs that belong with each master, the way in which the songs are sung, periods of silence, moments that the spirits manifest themselves, requirements that the masters make, the slaughtering of the sacrificial animals, and so on. She and the patient work together on a basis of trust and the *kudya* must be and remain credible in all circumstances. She calls up the masters and articulates cultural symbols at a specific moment in time. If she succeeds in "grasping" this specific moment, the ritual will work. The leader thus has great responsibility. The success of the whole thing depends on her competence in organizing and manipulating things in such a way that what occurs meets the expectations of the participants (see also Van Binsbergen 1981; Finkler 1986).

The therapy with the Koran, as applied by modern commercially oriented healers, capitalizes on a long tradition in which the Holy Book is used in the healing of all sorts of sickness and ailments. Here too the assumption is that there is a connection between person, body, society and cosmos. Since only Koran healers are supposed to know the special form of the recitation necessary to harness the power and light of the verses against the demons, this can be termed their "hidden sources" and "secret knowledge". In Koran healing it is also the case that its effectiveness is dependent on the vivification of the symbolic material. If the healer has the confidence of the patient and works convincingly, he is in a position to change her experience or situation. His most important aid in this is the patient's ultimate confidence that God's word will always help.

Women have told me that in the case of both healing methods, afterwards they were tired out and did not feel any immediate physical improvement. Gradually things got better and they felt lighter, more relaxed and relieved. The pain slowly left the body. I think the unfortunate fact that the sickness might return in due course indicates limitations. If the person feels better because the tensions have been removed, and a feeling of wellbeing has come in their place, then this means that the demon that had become an enemy is made a "friend" once again, or, as in Koran healing, has been driven out. But if there is no resolution of the underlying conflicts and tensions that are the cause of the malaise in the first instance, then the sickness will in due course revert to the previous condition. The relapse is not seen by the patients as due to any incompetence of the healer, since it is generally known that demons are fickle by nature and do not easily let go of their victims. Devisch too (1933: 244-245) writes that from the perspective of the cult the return of the symptoms is not viewed as a failure. If the result is less than was expected, then this is attributed to a series of other possible factors. The return of the sickness is interpreted as a sign of the fickleness of the demons, as in the case of Nura:

> Nura relates that as a child she suffered from nervousness, caused by her mother having dropped her on the ground. This is the first explanation for her being "clothed" by a demon. As a young woman, married to a much older man and at home alone all day, she feels lonely. In Egyptian society people do not like to be alone. All one's joys and sorrows are shared with one's close family. Nura goes into depression. In Nura's etiology in which supernatural forces play a role, some direct and indirect important causes for her possession are now mentioned: in her childhood she fell on the ground, the ground is impure, and under the ground live demons who probably got angry because they were disturbed when she fell, and their revenge on her is "clothing". When demons have once taken possession of a person, they are difficult to drive out. Sometimes they do not manifest themselves for years. But when Nura is married and lives without her family, she is afflicted by *halat nafsiyya*, i.e. depression and fits of weeping. This is in itself one of the most important situations exploited by demons to manifest themselves once again. Nura adds that she was beautiful and often stood in front of the mirror; master *Yawra Bey* saw this, fell in love with her and decided to clothe her once again.

The negligence of Nura's mother when she was still a baby, and Nura's sadness and loneliness as *arusa* (bride) are objectified, brought into the open and shaped into the symptom "clothed by master *Yawra Bey*". Later, from time to time Nura suffers again from sadness and/or tensions, which are then attributed to the fickleness of the demon. She has a slaughter carried out for her again. The rituals that are performed explicitly pacify the master Yawra Bey and implicitly Nura's tensions are relieved. Nervousness and pains disappear, sadness and loneliness are resolved: as a cultural construction the *zar* works.

Nura consulted a *zar* leader and became a regular attendee of the *zar* meetings. Other women in similar circumstances might perhaps have opted for Koran healing. Some go to both forms of healing. The choice is often a matter of chance or is the result of the input of family or friends with similar experience or knowledge about these healing cults.[8]

In *zar* and Koran healing a fantasy world is created in which the masters and the *jinn* play important roles. Do the participants regard the whole thing as a "dramatic performance"? No, certainly not, since this is not a production of "pretend situations". In their eyes the world is inhabited by spirits and some persons can come into contact with them, such as the *zar* leader who does it with the masters, and the Koran healer who does it with the *jinn*. The whole thing can be incomprehensible to outsiders and can possibly be viewed as fantasy, but for the participants it has meaning.

Zar and Koran healing in relation to Sufi brotherhoods and graves of the saints

I think that for various reasons a distinction must be made between the practice of *dhikr* (sufi ritual) and the visiting of saints' graves on the one hand, and *zar* and Koran healing on the other. The sufi ritual, the *dhikr*, is performed out of religious motives. Through singing and dancing the Prophet and the saints are praised and "the hearts opened" to God. Healing does play a role among the sufi brotherhoods — they have of course always been busy with the "undoing" of magic and sorcery, but women and men go to the *dhikr* primarily because the dancing "liberates" them and by doing this they give honour to God and the Prophet. Saints' graves are closely connected with the brotherhoods, but in Egypt they are visited mainly in order to pray for healing from sickness or injury caused by the evil eye or magic, or to be healed of infertility (Brandt 1994; Early 1993). No contact with spirits is involved, though there is contact with the saints. The methods and aims of the three means of healing (*zar*, Koran healing and *dhikr*) overlap, but in *zar*, and, it seems to me, in Koran healing too the contact with the demons is in central position while in the *dhikr* the concern is with contact with God, the Prophet and the saints.

---

[8] Some psychiatrists in Egypt told me that the depression Nura was suffering from as a young woman, married out and needing to adapt to the new situation in life is very common among young women.

The situation with sufi brotherhoods and healing appears to be somewhat different in Morocco compared with Egypt, since here healing cults are indeed linked to religious brotherhoods.[9] In his book, *The Hamadsha*, Crapanzano gives a description of a Moroccan religious (sufi) brotherhood, which venerates the saints Sidi 'Ali ben Hamdush and Sidi Ahmad Dghughi. This brotherhood is known primarily as a healing cult. Its members go into trance and mutilate themselves in order to please the possessing female demon *'Aysha Qandisha*, who is responsible for physical and/or psychological complaints. There is what might be termed a symbiotic relationship with her. In a ritual dance (*hadra*) she is "pacified" with incense, music, particular food, special clothing and rituals (Crapanzano 1973: 158-159). This corresponds to what happens in the Egyptian *zar*, though here there is never any question of self-mutilation, but is different from what occurs during the rituals of the sufi brotherhoods. The members of the religious brotherhoods praise and glorify God and the Prophet in prayer, song and dance, and try to lead a pious life. They do not "pacify" demons in the way this happens in Morocco. They do expel them if necessary.

So there are a number of agreements between the *Hamadsha* cult (and other similar brotherhoods related to North African Maraboutism) and the Egyptian *zar* cult. The main difference between the two cults consists in the fact that the *zar* is not inspired by nor practised with preconceived or justified religious motives. The *zar*

---

[9] Besides the avenue of western medicine, in Morocco there is also a wide choice of different non-scientific healing methods. The options here are the visiting of saints' graves, the *faqih*, which works with Koran texts and amulets, and the *sharif* (*shurafa*), a healer who belongs to a religious brotherhood. He heals with *baraka* (divine blessing or grace), with particular technical knowledge for the treatment of specific illnesses (burning, blood-letting or cupping) or by means of the expulsion of demons. As in Egypt, there is perceived to be a dualistic division into natural and supernatural sicknesses. The first category has an organic cause and the second is brought about by *junun* (Moroccan for *jinn*), the evil eye or magic. The sick person's choice of which healer to go to seems not to be made by the sick person but through such motives as the money available, the experience of family members or friends, and whether one is a member of a particular brotherhood or not. Besides some demons with known names, such as the *ghwal* and the female demon *'Aysha Qandisha*, the Moroccan demons have the same characteristics as elsewhere in the Islamic world (Bakker 1993; Crapanzano 1973; Doutté 1908/1984; Westermarck 1926). Since 'Aysha Qandish has to be "pacified" again and again, there is no question of exorcism here and it is more a case of a sort of "patroness" of this brotherhood. Expulsion then only applies to other demons. Dols (1992: 292) therefore wonders whether the *Hamadsha* order can really be classed as a sufi brotherhood.

is compared with "un-Islamic practices", while brotherhoods like the Hamadsha are legitimated as "Islamic".[10] Nor does Koran healing have any relation to sufi brotherhoods and the visitation and veneration of saints' graves. Rather the opposite. Koran healing appears to be fundamentalistically oriented. Indeed, though inspired and practised by and with religious motives, the veneration of holy men and brotherhoods is expressly rejected by this ideology. That is not to say that all Koran healers are fundamentalists. This is difficult to gauge, one might add. Some legitimate themselves over against fundamentalists by appealing to the Koran and *hadith*, while others are nothing but charlatans (attention will be given to these in Chapter 7). Koran healers regard themselves as the only true healers who can really heal sicknesses because they use God's word. They present themselves as "pure" Islamic.

An Egyptian woman who feels herself possessed by a demon and is suffering from all kinds of ailments as a result, expresses more than just that. Possession is linked with a large number of social worries: infertility, sexual attractiveness and uncertainty about the marriage relationship, children or family, economic problems, and so on. The woman identifies with this through her body, and through her body she experiences sorrow and pain, but also pleasure and joy. The experiences of the body are social experiences in which learned roles are formed by the social context. These cares are dealt with in Chapter 7, the sociographic chapter. Here I let women speak for themselves. The cases I have collected are situated in the framework of contemporary Egyptian society, giving the reader an insight into the socially constructed self-image and the socio-cultural context in which possession occurs, and also into the way in which personal experience of possession is expressed within standardized cultural terms.

---

[10] In the *zar* the dance generally has central place. Zahra the *zar* leader compares the *zar* with the sufi *dhikr* and Böringer-Thäringen (1996: 155-156) also sees connections. I suspect that the *zar* may have some degree of religious meaning for some, but that for most people this is something situated to one side of their religious convictions. Hence they see no problem with attending the meetings.

CHAPTER 7

A KALEIDOSCOPIC PICTURE OF EGYPTIAN SOCIETY

These are the voices of women who live in poverty, who have told me about their circumstances, their disappointments, their dreams and their reality. These stories form the starting-point in the search for the connection between living conditions, social relationships and what is known as possession. They are the result of informal interviews, conversations and observation. I have not attempted to reproduce in the text the dialogue between myself and the subject during the fieldwork. Nor do I supply the whole story in each case, or all the stories. For one thing, stories were not told in one breath. Sometimes I had to return several times, and the essential thing I wanted to know was "wrapped" in a multitude of words. Second, there was a great deal of repetition. Not only did I often hear more or less the same perspectives on possession, as this seems to similar expression among most women, in nervousness, insomnia, strange dreams and odd pains, but also the causes are largely the same.

Baladi women generally tell their stories in quite a racy style. It surprised me rather that they were not embarrassed about telling me their stories in great detail, with precise information about situations and about reactions to the events. If more persons were present, the accounts often were reminiscent of a "deliberation" in which the others interpreted, applauded, asked questions or resorted to "cultural argumentation" (Early 1985).

Telling of their own experiences seemed to have a therapeutic effect on the women, since they could share their concern about particular situations with others, who in turn sympathize and empathize with them. This therapeutic effect does not of course apply specifically to these women, because in western psychotherapeutic treatments too, catharsis through telling their story is often important for the healing of the patient. The "cathartic value" however also applies to the hearers, since through listening to and participating in the story they experience similar sorts of problems anew, which produces an interaction with those present.

Earlier I discussed al-Khuly's research and mentioned that she thinks the *zar* has to do with the way in which women deal with daily conflicts, and the negotiating strategies they use in their own environ-

ment and in public. She writes (1996: 11) that during the healing rituals of *hadra* — and *zar* — women can make suggestions and express
feelings that would not be possible in the everyday context. Nelson's
view (1971: 205) is in some regards similar to al-Khuly's. She is of the
opinion that an "alternative female worldview" can emerge. I lean
towards another opinion than these two researchers, at least in the
context they are referring to. However I believe that the emergence of
an alternative picture is possible in the situations as described above,
i.e. in the situation of recounting personal stories, in the safety of
one's own home with a small group of sympathizers who often have
to deal with similar problems themselves. So the stories can be a creative force and play a mediating role in the formation of a new reality. In the telling, the culture is described and interpreted. At the same
time individual experiences are incorporated, which could produce
another perspective on the norms and values. This could lead to
abandonment of the strict role pattern, so that space is created for
new possibilities and a better mastery of one's own situation. This
comes close to Turner's *communitas*, but the circumstances within
which it occurs are different.

Each individual needs social acceptance to be able to survive and
this is especially significant in societies in which there is intense social
control and where personal relationships are very important, as in
Egypt. Women therefore strongly emphasize the presentation of
themselves. "Appropriate" behaviour, like "inappropriate" behaviour, is defined in terms of female tasks (cf. Wikan 1996). In this society it is also the case that problems are often interpreted as being the
result of jealousy, envy, magic and the influence of non-human
beings. Self-criticism or reflection are evident only to a much smaller
degree.

Out of all the different stories of women I have made a choice in
order to let diverse characters have their say and to illuminate the circumstances that led to possession. These are not "life stories", but
each story is indeed the personal story of a single individual. In the
case of all these women there are divergent views of what counts as a
problem. There are even differences on this point between social (sub)
groups in the same society.

I noted earlier that the perspective of *baladi* women is often dismissed as irrelevant. In the first place by men, who think that women
lie, deceive and talk a lot of nonsense. In the second place by the
more well-to-do section of the Egyptian population, who think that

baladi women "only complain, and do nothing to change their situation". I disagree with both views. Men largely withdraw from the everyday cares that women have in keeping their heads above water, and the well-to-do part of the population often knows nothing of the intense poverty that is to be found in the popular districts. Nor do they know the *baladi* women's determination to cope with life and to help their children get on in the world.

Not only is the experience of poverty and other problems linked with culture, but the extent to which this can be talked about is culturally determined. The possibilities and crisis situations the women tell of are problems which they experience as such in their culture, but which can come over as "strange and incomprehensible" to people from higher social classes in their own society and to westerners. So I have sketched a "context" around the stories I have constructed, built from data found in newspaper articles, sociographic literature and/or my own observation, all of which have directly to do with the subjects touched upon by the women. The context is intended to clarify how the women's subculture is in different ways integrated into the overarching culture and how each one plays a part in society in her own unique way. It is, I think, essentially important to understand these women's experiences, their world and their decisions. So I endeavour to create a picture which will give the reader some idea of what things are like in the slum districts of Cairo and what are the possible links with possession. I use the word "subculture" because the situation of the women I describe must not be taken to be a stereotypical Egyptian society. Subculture indicates that their class context is integrated in different ways into the culture of Egyptian society as a whole.

From the women's stories I throw light on one or more aspects. It is not the case that each story gives a separate analysis of the personal problem. My intention is to sketch a kaleidoscopic picture of Egyptian society and of the environment in which the women of my stories live. It is only in passing that I touch once more upon the two healing ceremonies described above, since attention is here concentrated on the socio-economic context. It will, however, become clear how the cultural programming of sickness, body and belief in demons dominates the lives of these women. In the main I also leave the experiences of Turner or Devisch out of consideration, since the societies in which they conducted their research are on a smaller scale than a world city such as Cairo. Sickness and healing in their research group are wrapped up in the pattern of the whole life group and the role and work of the healer are clearly mapped out. In Cairo spiritual healing is extremely common, but it does not have the same social recognition as in the societies they describe.

Fatiha

"I was seventeen when I was married out by my parents and my husband was forty. My father and mother had said, "He is a civil servant and you will have a good life." When you're young and your father and mother say that, what can you do? So I said yes, and I was pleased with the beautiful clothes I got and with the *shabka* (an engagement present in the form of a gold bracelet or ring). But it turned out that I was not his first and only wife. At that moment I didn't care, because the woman didn't really exist, as far as I was concerned. Besides, I was young and he, my husband, was always with me. His other wife did live in the same house and after a while it made me cry the whole time. So my husband said he would rent another flat for me so that I could relax. I moved and he let the other woman stay living in that apartment. What I didn't know was that he was visiting her behind my back. He spent his nights with me and in the daytime he went to her. When I found out about this, I got really nervous and problems arose. I was not happy and wanted to go out to work, to be out of the house. But I couldn't find any work because I had never finished elementary school. So first I had to go back to school. And so I did, to the *al-'ibtida'i* (elementary school). I didn't tell them I was married, because they would certainly have made comments. Then my daughter was born. I left her with my mother all day, since I had to go to school, and I only went to her to breastfeed her. When she was a year old I wanted a divorce. After the divorce I went to live with my parents. In the meantime I had found work and paid for my daughter and myself. But my father was always arguing about money and when my daughter was crying or sick, no one looked out for her. I worked all day and I had no idea what was going on. After a while I wanted to get married again. There were men who wanted to marry me, but no one wanted to have my daughter as well. Then my ex-husband turned up again and he wanted me

back, for the child's sake. He talked to my father about it and he
said I should go back, so I did. But my husband had in the
meantime taken on another wife. I didn't of course know that
until I was back with him. In the meantime I have three daughters, but my husband prefers sons to daughters. So in the daytime he lives with the other woman and her children in a big
house and I sit here with my three children in the one living
room with one bedroom. He does leave money for the housekeeping, but there is no love. He doesn't even say anything to his
children. When he gets up in the morning he goes off and stays
away all day. He only comes home to sleep. I would like to get
divorced again, but when I just had one daughter I couldn't
cope with my family ... and now I have three! So I just don't
think about it.

One time he had incurred debts, because one of the other
wife's sons had to get married, and he took my money. I was
furious with him! But my nerves were so frayed and every day I
felt more and more suffocated, and I just couldn't breathe any
more. So then I went to a Koran *sheikh*. He said that it came
through *mass* (touching by a demon) and that I should pray a lot,
because the *'afarit* (demons) can easily get into a woman's body if
she is sad. For a time I went to him every week and then started
wearing the *niqab* (full veil). That is better, because if someone
knows I am married to an old man and I myself am still so
young, they start thinking, "She's fair game." The *sheikh* thought
the *niqab* was better too, because he told me, "A woman in your
circumstances, alone, *must* veil herself because that protects her."
I prayed a great deal and now I feel better. From that time on I
also went to lessons (religious lessons with the organization,
"Muslim Sisters"). The lessons were about Islam and the Traditions of the Prophet. They were all young women giving the
lessons, with university degrees. They also came to you at home
to explain the faith and if you had problems they would help
you, even if you needed money. They also helped you to find
work so that you had money to live on. It is important to have
work, because then you are not so dependent on other people.
But it is difficult to find work, because not everyone wants to
take on a *munaqqaba* (fully veiled woman). I have to take the veil
off then, and that is *haram* (not good). Now I don't go around
with unveiled women either, because it is not possible to pray

and recite the Koran and at the same time do things that offend Allah. Because women that walk around so dolled up, with exposed face and perfume, they are loose women.

When there were problems in the district here, the lessons were prohibited.[1] They say that the Muslim Brothers beat people up here in this area, but I don't believe it, we don't do that sort of thing. It is the case that if the Brothers hear that there is a party somewhere, they go there and say it is forbidden to have a (belly-) dancer dance. If people go ahead and do it, then they hit out. But that is good, because God has said that immorality must be punished, and a half-naked dancer like that is bad, or am I wrong?

The Brothers are not like other men. When they pick a wife then she must know God and they bring their children up to know God, right from the start. They pay attention to morality. Other men choose a woman because she is good-looking, but after the wedding everything changes and then he leaves her in the lurch. God has created the woman to serve the man, but not just to be his maidservant and have his children. God has created the woman as woman and the man as man. The woman is for the home and for her children, but not only to cook and do the washing. The woman has the most important work, the bringing-up of the children, and that is not an easy job. Islam is not against women going to school and studying, but if they only think of work and earning money, and not of their children or their job at home, then that is awful! The brothers and sisters of *al-mugtama' al-islami* (the Islamic Brotherhood), bring up their children differently, knowing God. They do not go to the cinema and don't buy videos to watch films at home. I know there are also documentaries and religious programmes on television that you can learn from, but most people watch the other programmes, don't they? The devil is everywhere. And on television they show films that are immoral. I don't have a television myself because I have learned from the Brothers how I can protect my children."

---

[1] In December 1992 there were armed confrontations between the state security forces and radical Islamic activists. The leader of the *Jama'a al-Islamiyya* (a radical political Islamic organization) had openly announced that his organization formed a "state within the state", where his views of Islam held sway. The members of this group burned down various churches and shops, terrorized the neighbourhood and forced Coptic women to wear "Islamic" clothing.

Interpretation

Striking, in Fatiha's story, are the following: her obedience to her parents, husband, *sheikh*, and at a later stage the ideology of the Muslim Brothers. Further, her unhappy marriage, the visit to the Koran healer and her decision to adopt the veil. The spiritual and physical obedience of a girl or wife to father, brothers and male family members is generally viewed as a virtue. This ideal extends even beyond the direct circle to the broader society, and in Fatiha's case to the *sheikh* and Brotherhood.

I would summarize Fatiha's story as follows: she is unhappy and is apparently unable to do anything to change this. She is getting physical complaints, her "nerves are frayed", she has a feeling of asphyxiation and feels sad. She goes to a Koran healer with her complaints and tells her story. Both are well aware of her less than ideal living conditions, but the healer confirms that demons have invaded the body because she was sad, and that is why she does not feel well. The healer's interpretation can be called "classic" in cases of possession and coincides fully with the cosmological views of the patient herself. In the "therapy" he puts a stop to the evil and Fatiha feels better.

If we revisit Fatiha's story with Turner's ideas in mind, then it seems that during the liminality changes occurred, through which a new situation arose for her and a reorientation towards existing relationships, norms and values took place. To a certain degree this is indeed what happened, but it did not lead to permanent changes in her living conditions: her life merely became more bearable.

In the chapter on Koran healing I wrote that the healer is a representative of the social order, who invites the patient to take a new look at her life and that his therapy aims to suppress resistance and rebellion and to subject women to the disciplinary institutions of society. But, though there are no social changes, there may well be internal changes through which the woman can once again cope with life. This is because the living situation is structured anew, and the network within her environment is restored (what Devisch calls "weaving" and "interweaving", by which means, according to him, "the vital current" gets going again). In Fatiha's case this means that she is presented with other norms and values and comes to a re-evaluation of her own situation. By means of the therapy she gets to know the brothers and sisters of *al-mugtama' al-islami* (the Islamic Brotherhood) and she joins this Brotherhood. She adopts the ideology of the "brothers and sisters" and is inspired to adopt the full veil. The latter is an important step in her life and one of the solutions that women seek as an escape from their problems (I shall comment on this later). So one can speak of particular changes in Fatiha's life, because on a symbolic level this means that from now on her body and femininity are screened from society and at the same time from demons, because these malevolent beings do not descend on a pious woman who keeps to the rules of Islam. On a social level, however, not much changes, she accepts her living conditions, but helped by her connection with the Brotherhood a new integration into the daily social world takes place and she feels strengthened, both physically and mentally.

For Fatiha's unhappy married life it is important to know that in principle an Egyptian woman can have set down in her marriage contract, before the wedding, what rights she has and does not have. This also applies to the right to refuse if the spouse wants to take more than one wife. But because of social customs, such as the belief that it is not good to negotiate about and discuss such things in advance, and also frequently through ignorance of the fact that rights can be set down, women make too little use of this possibility.[2]

Family rights

In Egypt strong emphasis is placed on marriage. The minimum permitted marriageable age for girls is sixteen (for men, eighteen), but in rural areas a few years ago forty-four percent of girls were still marrying under the legally permitted age (the checking of age is not watertight). In the past twenty years, in urban areas in particular things have changed and girls here marry more frequently than they used to, when they are older than sixteen. The national average in 1994 was twenty-two. Twenty-three percent of women between forty and fifty years of age have experienced divorce or have been widowed, and thirty-eight percent of women in the age group around fifty have been married more than once (Coptic Christians, who comprise about ten percent of the population, are not allowed to divorce, according to their religious laws).

In the middle and lower classes, marriages between cousins are still

---

[2] A survey by CAPMAS (The Central Agency for Public Mobilization and Statistics) (1993), shows that only 20 percent of women are familiar with the right to registration.

encouraged.[3] Common too are arranged marriages ("sensible marriages" between sons and daughters of friends, acquaintances and
business partners). This very often means that the prospective bride
and groom scarcely know each other. Leila El Hamamsy (1994), who
researched the socio-cultural factors influential in marriages of young
girls, writes that forty-seven percent of the girls in her research area
(Sharkiyya and Aswan) married a man selected by their father and
that twenty-four percent of the girls had not been asked their opinion
beforehand. It is also common for young girls to be married out to
much older rich men who have been married a number of times
before and have children. These days "love marriages" between
young people who have met and fallen in love at university or at
work, are occurring with increasing frequency, especially in the middle class. But the family still has the final say.

Living together unmarried and sex before marriage are absolutely
taboo. A girl who believes that her lover will marry her if they have had
sexual intercourse before the marriage, will usually be disappointed.
The average Egyptian man wants to have his fun, but he will always
marry a virgin! Besides cultural views of virginity, religious (Muslim and
Coptic) considerations play a particularly significant role. An unmarried girl and a married woman must be chaste and demure. The fundamentalist ideology, which is constantly gaining ground, emphasizes this
even more. Religion dictates that the man should also behave chastely,
but virility is a cultural ideal, and active sexual behaviour is part of this.

The marriage contract

According to Islamic custom, marriage is a contract. Both parties can
set down their conditions in it. In the *Personal Statute* (law no. 100,
1985), relations between Muslims are set down, from engagement,
marriage and divorce, to the death of one of the partners, the mutual
responsibilities of the marriage partners and those of the parents in
relation to the children. The stipulations relating to marriage and
divorce are borrowed from the Islamic religion and therefore do not
apply to non-Muslims. Non-Muslims are subject to the rules of their
own religions or sects (for conflicts within mixed marriages, the *Personal Statute* does indeed apply).

---

[3] Twenty-nine percent: first preference cross cousins, second preference parallel
cousins (Rugh 1985: 111-116).

The marriage contract is a civil contract in which both parties can set down their requirements. An essential clause in the contract relates to the dowry (*mahr*), an amount that the bridegroom pays to the bride as a sum of money, in one transaction. A second payment can be made to the woman in the case of divorce or the decease of the husband (paid by the family: the *mu'akhkhar al-sadaq*, i.e. "deferred" dowry; Early 1985). At the engagement, furthermore, the prospective groom gives his fiancée a gift in gold (*shabka*). The bridegroom is responsible for the couple's accommodation. The bride and her family are expected to take care of the furniture and household articles. It can happen that poor families ask the husband to pay the dowry before the wedding ceremony so that the bride can buy the necessary things (Rugh 1984). The possessions brought into the marriage by the bride and groom and goods acquired during the marriage (land, house, permanent articles) are also registered (*aima* or *lista*).

Marriage contracts must be signed in the presence of a notary (the *ma'zun*, a civil servant who joins people in marriage and registers divorces), but if this does not take place for any reason, the contract still applies. An unregistered marriage contract is called *'urfi*. Such a contract does not give a woman the same rights as a registered contract. For instance, she then has no right to alimony in the case of divorce, no right to her husband's pension on his death and she has to take various legal steps to confirm custody of her children. An *'urfi* can be made between two persons without much ado. It is used primarily when entering into a "temporary marriage"; in other words sexual rights can be granted in it without there being corresponding (marriage) responsibilities.

Right to work

Although the right to go out to work is set down in the constitution and is thus not dependent on the husband's permission, it is advisable for women to have this set down in the marriage contract. It often turns out that in the case of divorce the husband protests against the paying of alimony because he was "against her going out to work". In practice, it seems that many women do not know this, nor indeed the fact that they do not need their husband's permission to go out!

Divorce

The husband automatically has the right to *qisma* (divorce) without having to give any reason. It is sufficient to say to his wife, without witnesses, "Go away; you are divorced". He does have to have this officially recorded by the *ma'zun*. A woman has to have the right to divorce (*talaq*) set down in the contract. She can also include in the contract that she has the right to divorce without the mediation of the court, but this does not detract from the fact that the husband has the right to unilateral divorce whenever it suits him.[4]

In Egypt, Muslim men are allowed to marry four women, but the number of polygamous marriages is in steep decline. In cases where the husband marries a second (or third, or fourth) wife, the wife can, if she suffers material or moral injury as a result, seek divorce on the basis of Law no. 100/1985. Inclusion of a "no second wife" clause in the marriage contract relieves her of the onus of proving "injury through the second marriage". Under the previous Personal Statue (family law), the husband could marry a second wife without informing his first wife about it. He could also divorce the first wife without her knowledge. Since 1985 a wife must be informed of each following marriage and in the case of divorce she must receive a copy of the divorce form.

Women also have the right to divorce in cases where (1) the husband has left her for longer than a year, (2) the husband has to serve a prison sentence longer than three years, (3) the husband no longer maintains her financially, (4) the husband is suffering from an incurable disease (e.g. leprosy or madness) and she was not aware of this at the time she entered into the marriage, (5) there is social and natural incompatibility, (6) from a social and/or cultural point of view cohabitation is impossible, for instance because of ill-treatment by the husband or the taking of a second wife, and (7) on account of sexual shortcomings on the part of the husband, such as impotence or sterility.

The wife must keep to the *'idda*, the legally prescribed probationary period during which she is not allowed to remarry after a divorce or the decease of the husband (i.e. three menstrual periods or until after giving birth; *al-Baqara* [2]: 229; *al-Talaq* [65]: 5).

---

[4] A new law (March 2000) provides for the possibility of a unilateral declaration of divorce (*khul'*), waiving financial rights. *Al-Ahram Weekly* no. 472, 9-15 March 2000, p. 1, reported that the courts had already received a hundred applications.

There are two forms of divorce: "reversible" and "irreversible" and registration of them has to take place in the presence of the *ma'zun* within thirty days. "Reversible" means that the marriage is not dissolved until the *'idda* has passed. The husband can undo the divorce without the wife's agreement. "Irreversible" is not dependent on the *'idda* and must be clearly registered as "irreversible". In the case of divorce the wife has the right to one year of *'idda*-alimony or a two-year *mut'a* alimony set on the basis of the husband's financial and social position, the duration of the marriage and the reasons for the divorce. The *Mu'akhkhar al-Sadaq* (deferred dowry), the conditions for which are included in the marriage contract, is paid out at the time of the divorce or upon the decease of the husband.

Custody of children after divorce

After a divorce the children stay with their mother until the age of ten (or if so determined by the comt until the age of fifteen years) and girls until the age of twenty years (or if so determined by the court until their marriage).

Both parents have visiting rights. A husband who divorces his wife is responsible for the housing of his ex-wife and children. If he does not have other accommodation than their joint home, he must leave it for use by his ex-wife and children as long as she has custody of the children. In the case of remarriage by the mother, she loses custody. Until the custody of children is officially transferred to the father, in such cases it goes to the maternal or paternal grandmother.

Social status of the wife through her children

To remain unmarried is just as unattractive an option for the average Egyptian woman as remaining childless. It is not "feminine" and not "masculine" to have no children. Although people now know that childlessness can also be the man's "fault", it is generally the wife who is blamed.

On average an Egyptian woman spends fifteen years of her life bearing children (between the first and the last child, El-Hamamsy 1994). It is considered ideal for the first pregnancy to follow immediately after the wedding. Thirty-eight percent of women between twenty-five and thirty years of age have their first child before the age of twenty. The average number of children (in 1992) is 3.9 per family.

Programmes intended to promote the reduction of the number of children to a maximum of two are broadcast on radio and television. But Egyptian men often take the view that the use of a condom is not "masculine" and so the problem is transferred to the wife. Only two percent of men and forty-seven percent of women use contraceptives (the woman must have her husband's permission for this). But Egyptians regard each child as a gift from God (*min 'and-Allah*) and have no objection to a large family.

Inheritance rights on the death of the husband

Under Islamic and Egyptian law a wife has a right to her husband's possessions and conversely the husband has a right to part of his wife's possessions. But there are considerable differences between the sexes as regards the division of the inheritance. Relatively speaking, the husband inherits twice as much of his wife's legacy as the wife inherits on her husband's death. This inequality is defended on the basis of the difference in responsibilities between husband and wife. The husband can have it notarized that his wife inherits a large proportion of his possessions. In general on her husband's death the wife receives a quarter of his possessions if there are no children, and if there are children, one eighth. The husband inherits half of his wife's possessions if there are no children, and one quarter if there are children (Rugh 1984).

Clothing

Above I wrote that Fatiha decided to take on the veil. In the first instance, she herself says, this was in order to feel protected, and maintain her good reputation, and only secondly out of religious conviction.

What does "Islamic clothing" mean? For Fatiha and many other women it means screening off on a symbolic level and protection on a social level, since they see themselves as now "embraced" by the Islamic community, which does not necessarily mean involvement with the fundamentalist Muslim Brotherhood (as in Fatiha's case). It has to do with an inner conviction and women often talk about "being ready" or "being in a position" to take on the veil. The wearer indicates that she has crossed a "boundary": she announces publicly that she is a believer. The acceptance of the veil also gives many the hope of gaining a socially improved life through leading a more pious life. But beyond Islamic society there are, generally speaking, plenty of misunderstandings, such as: what kind of clothing is that, is it compulsory for Muslim women to wear it? In the West the veil is often seen as a symbol of the oppression of women. If "the West" were to quiz these women about it, it would — to many people's amazement — hear the opposite, namely that the veil liberates and protects women in a fast-changing world.

Although the ancient Egyptian civilization (ca. 3100 BCE to the Greek conquests in 333 BCE) was a male-dominated society, women enjoyed considerable personal freedom. They did not veil themselves and did not live in separation from the men. It was only when Egypt came under "European power", i.e. under the Greeks and Romans, who did veil their women, that the status of women changed and there was a noticeable regression, which increased further after the Islamic conquest of Egypt.

From verses in the Koran it could be deduced that the veiling of women was not customary in the time of the Prophet. Men are indeed encouraged to maintain a distance between themselves and the Prophet's wives (al-Ahzab [33]: 53). This verse was to be repeatedly reinterpreted in the future and deepened out. During the Abbasidic period in particular (750-1258) the veiling and separating of women in harems became customary. A number of practices for women, given legal and religious sanction, were regarded increasingly as typically Islamic and have remained in force to our own day (Ahmed 1992).

In nineteenth-century Egypt it was primarily urban women from the middle and upper classes that veiled themselves and lived a separated lifestyle. These were both Muslim women and women from the minority groups (Copts, Jews, Syrian Christians). Veiling was more a class-related affair than a matter of religion or ethnicity.

Around the turn of the century religious and ethnic affiliation were important determinants of the social behaviour of women in the middle and upper classes. It is women from the minority groups who, under the influence of European ideas, discard the veil. Islamic women had more problems with the discarding of the veil because veiling and separation were viewed as part of their religion. But not everyone agreed with this. Qasim Amin, for instance, an Egyptian intellectual, who published *The Liberation of the Woman* (1899) and *The New Woman* (1900). In both books he fiercely opposes veiling and the separation of the woman. He viewed these things as reprehensible and related to other forms of oppression in society. Amin also made a plea for education for women and the right to economic independence through paid work. This does not mean that he was a champion of equal rights for men and women. The Egyptian woman was not ready for this, in his view. The fact that Amin wanted to show that veiling and separation were not Islamic regulations, provoked massive resistance among men (and women) who wanted to continue to uphold these practices. Under the leadership of such feminists as Huda Sha'rawi, Nabawiya Musa and many others, Islamic women gradually moved over to discarding the face veil, covering only the hair with a scarf. In accordance with Islamic regulations, they continued to wear modest clothing. Both Amin and the Egyptian feminists of his day were fiercely criticized. Most women, however, remained totally veiled until the 1920s (Ahmed 1992; Badran 1996).

During the Nasser regime (1952-1970), social mobility was encouraged and women went and followed better and higher courses of education. As a result many were able to gain position in the government bureaucracy (in feature films of the Nasser period women appear in the main in "European" clothes). Originally it was mainly middle-class women with an academic degree that went to work in government offices (*muwazzafat*). These days it is predominantly young women from the lower middle class with a secondary education. In general they do less important work (administration, receptionist work, photocopying). The salaries are not high, but the work does have a certain status. For a long time the wearing of Western clothing has gone along with this status. Less well-educated women who work in factories or as *shaghghalas* (cleaners), or have a small shop or business in the street, dress mainly in the *baladi* ("popular") style. This applies also to women who work on the land (the majority of working women). They have never gone veiled because this is impractical for their work.

Roughly speaking, one can now divide women's clothing into three main styles: typically Egyptian "popular clothing" (*sha'bi/baladi*), worn by women from the "traditional" social classes in the city and the villages; a sort of "international" (*afrangi*, foreign/western) clothing worn by the urban middle and upper classes; and *zay islami* ("Islamic" clothing), which crosses class boundaries.

The average "popular woman" owns no more than a few items of clothing. Perhaps she will on holidays such as the *mulid an-nabi* (the Prophet's birthday) or the month of Ramadan (Islamic month of fasting) get money from her husband to buy material for a new *fustan* (dress) which will be sewn by herself or a neighbour or acquaintance. This *fustan* has three important elements: a (usually) florid basic dress, similar to an old-fashioned high-cut western European nightdress, which reaches to the ankles and has long sleeves. On top of that, when she goes out, for reasons of modesty she wears a *gallabiyya samra*, a long black "over"-dress in more or less the same style as the "under" dress. On the head she ties a coloured or plain *sharb* (scarf) which covers the hair, and over that goes a *tarha*, a black transparent veil-like top scarf. By no means all women wear the *tarha*. The dress material is usually cotton or a slightly heavier material for the winter; the over-dress is generally made of a synthetic material. Old women and widows usually go completely in black. Young girls go in a western dress or in a similar nightdress-like dress with a scarf tied around the head, and when they go to school they wear a school uniform and in some cases a headscarf, depending on how religious the family is. The clothing of Coptic women does not differ greatly from that of Muslim women. Women from the popular districts do not wear the veil, but sometimes a woman pulls part of the *tarha* over her face. In Cairo the *milaya laff* is also still to be seen as outer clothing. This is a long black cloth that is wrapped around the head, shoulders and the body. When walking the woman pulls the outside end of the cloth tightly around the body and lets the end hang over her arm. Unlike the *fustan*, which has a wide cut and covers the body, the *milaya laff* reveals many contours of the body because of the way it is worn. In smaller towns and villages in the Nile delta and Upper Egypt, variations are possible on the clothing described above (Rugh 1986).

There is not a great deal to be said about the western clothing (*afrangi*) of women in the upper classes. Their clothing varies and is predominantly in the same style as in Europe or America. Depending on the wearer's view of religion, she will cover or not cover her head outdoors. These women often travel abroad and have been participating in the work force for many years. They occupy high administrative posts, are university teachers or have their own business. Their lives run pretty much as those of other women of their level in western countries, though perhaps their husband and children have a more central place in their existence than is the case among western "career women" (Mohsen 1985; Sullivan 1986).

Since the 1970s a new sort of "Islamic" clothing (*zayy islami/zayy shari'a*) has been seen in the streets of the large towns, which has gradually increased and spread into the villages. It is the clothing of many women who go to school, university or work each day, and it crosses class boundaries. It consists of a long, generally loosely hanging high-cut dress with long sleeves and a scarf which covers the hair and neck. But there are also women who still wear their skirts to the calves, or dress in jeans and wear a scarf all the same.

There is a great deal of variation in the scarf and it is susceptible to fashion. Indoors the hair is covered by a smaller scarf tied around the head, leaving the neck free; depending on how religious people are, in the presence of men who do not belong to the household, a full head-covering may also be worn indoors. The head covering can to some extent resemble a nun's cap. It then falls over the forehead, so that all the hair is covered, and reaches to the shoulders or the midriff, but leaves the face free. The scarf and the wide clothing are very impor-tant, because women must cover up their "adornment" (*zina*), the hair and the breasts, which according to Islamic conceptions make the woman sexually attractive. These rules are based on the Koran (sura *al-Ahzab* [22]: 59): "O Prophet! say to your wives and your daughters and the women of the believers that they let down upon them their over-garments; this will be more proper, that they may be known, and thus they will not be given trouble; and Allah is Forgiving, Merci-ful." Saajidah Abdus Sattar (1987: 91), a Dutch Muslim woman, writes that the intention of this instruction becomes clear if one bears in mind the clothing that was customary among women in the time of the Prophet. At that time women wore a long, loosely hanging piece of clothing with a deep opening on the front, which facilitated the feeding of babies. On the head a *khimara* was worn, a long hanging headscarf which covered the hair on the head and hung down the back. One end of the headscarf had to be used to cover the breasts, which would otherwise have been visible. The Koranic instruction would mean that Muslim women would be identifiable as such by this means. For this they must dress in such a way that the typical female body shapes are disguised. The point of this is to protect oneself and one's environment against prohibited contacts.

There is a good deal of variation in this "Islamic" clothing. Women who dress in long skirts and a scarf over their heads, call themselves *muhaggabat* (covered women). The term derives from the word *higab*, which means curtain, covering, screen and even amulet. But there is also a stricter form which developed under the influence of funda-mentalism. These women call themselves *munaqqabat* (veiled women).

This standard fundamentalist clothing consists of a dress down to the ankles (*gilbab*), high-cut and with long sleeves. The somewhat thicker cotton or woollen materials are sober in colour (brown, dark blue, grey). The head covering is similar to the nun's cap, as described above, but some wearers also cover their face with a veil (*niqab*) which leaves a small opening for the eyes, over which a pair of sunglasses or often a transparent veil is worn. Generally the whole thing is finished off with gloves and stockings. The fundamentalist view of how a moral woman should dress is based on sura *al-Ahzab* (33): 53: "And when you ask of them (any of the Prophet's wives) any goods, ask of them from behind a curtain (*higab*); this is purer for your hearts and (for) their hearts." The standard versions of "Islamic clothing" mentioned above reflect to some extent differences in interpretation of the Koran verses cited. There are no specific instructions from the *al-Azhar*, for instance (the most important religious institution in Egypt) as to how Islamic clothing should look. Each subcultural group can set up its own guidelines for it. If one disregards the example of Abdus Sattar mentioned above, there are no historical models of "Islamic" clothing either. Gaffney (1994) calls this a "new self-declared religious ensemble for expressing values and meanings".

The question arises why women have, since the 1970s, been returning to veiling and separation. No clear answer can be given to this. In the first place there is great variation in the extent to which this is the case. Second, there is also great variation in the national and urban context. Women from the lower middle and middle class, who preferred to dress in a "European" way twenty years ago because it underlined their newly acquired freedom to go out to work, are generally precisely the ones who now go veiled. The "modern" identity brings with it that they must find a way of keeping their place in the labour market because the money is sorely needed to keep the household going. Linked with this is the fact that they are more exposed, and more frequently so, to the looks and remarks of men in the street and on the work floor. Their own husbands become jealous and this gives rise to conflicts at home. Women who wear the *higab* (headscarf) and the long skirts often say that they do this because men respect a *muhaggaba* more. It says of the wearer: "I am a Muslim woman, and therefore a respectable woman, so stay away from me." In some cases it is a matter of a self-imposed stricter identification with Islamic norms and values. An example of this is Fatiha, the woman in my account.

Rugh (1986) writes that a study by the National Centre for Social and Criminological Studies in Cairo has shown that sixty percent of all school-educated women in the study wear "Islamic clothing". Forty percent of these say they do it for the sake of modesty and costs, twenty-five percent that they do so because it is fashionable or in order to save hairdressing money, and five percent are of the opinion that Islamic clothing protects one against the undesired advances of men. The rest did not give a reason.

As regards the question of veiling, religious fundamentalism also plays a role. The veiled woman is a decent and respected woman, they say, and unveiled women are made to feel guilty. Not only are they supposedly indecent, but they are also accused of being non-believers. It is supposed to be an unveiled woman's own fault if she is bothered by men. Fear that through lack of knowledge of the holy books one might commit sacrilege keeps many from resisting them. People prefer to go with the flow.[5] Rugh (1986) and Macleod (1991) write that the face veil has practically disappeared in Egypt. I would contest this. Ten years ago scarcely any fully veiled women were to be seen in the streets of Cairo. I now see more women who have adopted the full veil, and when I sit in Cairo's underground and look around me, I see hardly any women who are not at least wearing a headscarf.

As is evident from the context stories, it is not strange that Fatiha was married out by her parents as a young girl to a considerably older man. I have encountered the same living conditions as Fatiha's several times with other women. The husband has to manage to divide up his time and income between several wives; in most cases all the wives suffer as a result. Fatiha was gradually suffocating. By going back to school she tries to create her chances on the labour market, but she only partially succeeds in this and only for a short time. There are no "social safety-nets" in Egypt and as a result of her limited social and economic possibilities Fatiha cannot free herself from the loveless situation and go and live independently of her husband with her children. A new perspective occurs in the form of association with the Muslim Brothers, which gives her the chance to keep herself together mentally. Marital problems and an economic situation without prospects are often the lot of poor women. This is also the case for Salma, the woman in my next account.

---

[5] Abul Nagain, Patriarchy ... Islamism or the State? in: *People's Rights, Women's Rights*, 2.8.1996.

Salma

Salma lives with her children in a two-room flat. The impression is one of deep poverty. The walls are unpainted and bare. The floor is of stone. Apart from a single chair there is no furniture. A large bed stands in one room. Items of clothing, shoes and pieces of bread are lying around everywhere. Salma sits on the ground and has a sick child at her breast, and three girls (her daughters) sit around her. The eldest daughter is at school. It is a sad sight altogether.

"I am thirty-two and I married when I was twenty. My husband is ten years older than me. He does not come from the same family as me. I met him when he saw me with some friends. He wanted to marry me and asked for my father's permission. He was in favour. My future husband arranged for a flat and the *shabka* (engagement gift), and then we had a wedding celebration and I was married. I now have five children, four girls and a boy. The eldest is eleven, and I don't want any more, I'm sick. This happened because I had a fight with my husband. He hit me and then I fell in the bathroom and the *jinn* crept into me. I have been sick since then. Since I fell down, I have had constant pain in my belly and my head. This is *lamsa ardiyya* (touching by an underground being), that's what a *sheikh* told me. This *sheikh* burnt incense for me, but that's all he did. So I went with a woman I knew to another, a Copt. This woman had told me that he could undo sorcery. This Christian man started to pray with me, but I got a lot sicker from that moment on. I had dreams and nightmares. In these dreams I saw all kinds of people and all sorts of things. The woman who took me with her, turned out to be having an affair with my husband and that's why she wanted me to go to this Christian man. This Christian doesn't heal at all, far from it — he does *'amal* (black magic) and she paid him a lot of money for it. I don't know how much. They cooked that up together. Before that woman came into our lives my husband was very good to me, but since then everything has changed. He spends a lot of money out of the house, but I don't know if he gives her money. He is a plumber and makes a good living. He leaves some money for the children, but nothing for me. This has been going on for three years. I don't know if he is still going with the woman, I don't ask him any-

thing. I have put him out of my head. He comes and goes whenever he likes. He sleeps in the other room. He gives the children
some money, says nothing, and goes off again. In the meantime
I have had a son, and he is now a year old. That is normal for us
(men insist on their "marital rights"). I don't want a divorce, that
is *'eeb* (bad/shameful), and in any case, where would I go? And
the children? They need a father, a mother is not the same as a
father. Besides, a mother is not as strong and strict as a father. I
still dream about these strange things, and I still see all those
people in my sleep. They laugh, but I can't understand why. My
spirit is tired and sick. I want rest. I have bought medicines, but
when I take them I get really scared. So I had a *sheikh* come here.
I paid him a hundred pounds (£13/$20). He told me I had to
drink a full glass of salt water in one go. After that he read the
Koran and at the same time an earthquake broke out in my
body. I fell on my knees and had to vomit terribly. I was very
nervous, I cried and screamed. And afterwards, *bismillah ar-rahman ar-rahim* (in the name of the Merciful One) the *sheikh* said
that I was bewitched and that I had spewed out the *jinn* (demon)
when I vomited. But it didn't help and I went to yet another
sheikh. He gave me holy water and incense and I was to drink the
water and burn the incense in the afternoons. I had to pay him
twenty-five pounds, but this didn't help either. Perhaps it has
something to do with this house, I don't know. In some houses
demons live and they can get disturbed and then they start bothering people. Some *sheikhs* give incense and some give a scripture
amulet (usually folded-up Koran texts and "magic letters"). But I
threw them away because I can't read and I want something
that works fast. My husband says nothing about it. He doesn't
speak to me at all any more, by the way. He comes in at twelve
o'clock at night, goes to bed, and that's that. He used to come
and bring me a glass of water, but that's all over."

Interpretation

Material poverty came about in Salma's life after the crisis situation
with her husband. She did know times when she had sufficient means,
but after he had a relationship with another woman, he turned his
back on her. He still pays for the children, but no longer for her. Fatiha's and Salma's stories are broadly similar. Both women had unhap-

py experiences with their husband. It seems as if their problems multiply and, seeing no way out, they get overwrought and fall victim to physical and mental problems. The reactions of the two women differ. Fatiha finds comfort and support with the organization of the Muslim Brothers and Sisters and takes up the veil. She follows religious lessons and adopts the fundamentalist ideology of the group, which changes her perspective. Not that the quality of her life has improved so much, but she is no longer on her own.

In her marriage, Salma is dependent on her husband for her material support and status. In return for the man's input stands the wife's traditional duty to "deliver" care, sexuality and children. Men have an unequal power position through their exclusive right to polygamy and differences in civil rights. The ideological justification of this unequal relationship offers women little in the way of physical and mental perspectives. Their life runs in a spiral of problems. The mental tensions caused by the poverty have an effect on the marital situation and pull them down deeper and deeper. Salma's situation of poverty is very depressing, but she gave me the impression that she was suffering mainly from the humiliation of her husband's indifference to her wellbeing. She is banished completely out of his social life, despite the fact that he still visits her sometimes at night and demands his "rights". She is discouraged and thinks divorce is not an option, because this is 'eeb (shameful), and where can she go? Quite evidently she is not getting support from her family either, who are often a woman's last hope. Children are often the reason in such a tense situation why women are inclined to put up with a bad marriage and humiliations and fall into the role of the victim.

For women who lack protection from the family and who are confronted with extreme poverty and humiliation, which gives them "frayed nerves", the traditional healer is often the only way out. A visit to a psychologist or psychiatrist is often too much of a step, both culturally and often also financially. Salma too seeks help and from her story it seems that she has visited a whole series of healers without any benefit.

Explanations about healers, such as Salma's, are always "explanations in retrospect", but they do indicate a social reality. In the case of the Christian *sheikh* who bewitches her instead of healing her, I recognize stories I have often heard about Coptic priests in particular. It is said that they practise the nastiest sort of black magic. There is a tendency to blame them as the instigators of a great deal of natural and

supernatural evil. This is certainly the case in the district where Salma
lives, where fundamentalists, who encourage this kind of tale-telling,
are strongly represented.

As I said earlier, it is striking how many women are bothered by
demons after they have experienced a violent shock, have been beat-
en or have fallen in the bathroom. My experience is that many
women think it is normal to be beaten by their husband. I shall return
to this later. Women from Salma's social class often have had not
school education, which greatly limits their economic options.

Education

From the time of Abdel Nasser (1952-1970) Egypt can point to great
progress in the area of schooling. In this period poverty was regarded
as the central problem that could be solved by giving people access to
basic amenities, in particular land and education. An education law
came in and the aim was that by 1970 each Egyptian citizen should at
least be able to follow an elementary education. A large number of
new schools were built and enrolments in elementary education
increased. In the six-to-eleven age-group this was forty percent in
1953 and by 1985 it had increased to eighty-five percent. But despite
the fact that public schools were free (a financial contribution is now
required), great inequality continued to exist between boys and girls
in the area of education. A large number of girls that attend elementary school leave school prematurely to go to work or because their
parents do not see the point of it; 5.4 percent do not finish elementary
school until later in life (see Fatiha's example). Among women one
can speak of secondary illiteracy, i.e. that they only follow the elementary school for a few years, and then get married or get a job. They
lose the knowledge they gained at school, which means that in many
cases they get no further than being able to write a simple signature
(CAPMAS 1992).

At all levels of public education schools have too many students,
too few facilities and inadequately trained personnel, who, furthermore, are underpaid. Any Egyptian family that can afford it at all will
thus send their children to private schools. Families that cannot afford
it send their children to public schools, where the level of education is
so low that they start their careers on the labour market with a disadvantage that it is difficult to catch up from (Kamphoefner 1996).
Korayem (1996: 56) writes that many poor families cannot afford the

costs of children's education and that this is an important reason for them to leave school prematurely. Another important factor for premature school-leaving is the fact that children have no interest in what education offers them and they prefer to go to work. Poverty and a poor education system lead to child labour, which is common in Egyptian society.

In 1991 59.2 percent of adult Egyptian women were still illiterate and 35.5 percent of adult males (CAPMAS 1992). This situation is improving only slowly. Illiteracy is the result of poverty, inequality and injustice. It is the most important characteristic of poor women and in many cases the barometer of their social problems. Many studies of the position of women in Egypt note the influence of gender in education and in the labour market. Kamphoefner (1996) made a study in 1986 among illiterate women, asking them their opinion about schooling. She wondered whether ability to read and write does indeed make a big difference to women from the lower income groups. The women in her research said they did not suffer much from their lack of schooling. Most of them are able to read numbers and are very good and quick at working out prices in their heads. So on the market and in the shops they manage pretty well and if official papers have to be filled in they ask someone who can do that. The vast majority of women said they did want as high as possible an education for their children, including their daughters. But the cultural ideal is not for a girl to study for a career. The girl studies in order to get higher on the social ladder through marriage. The expectation is that well-educated girls can have a "better" (i.e. economically better) marriage. The dominant traditionally determined role of the sexes is still that the girl marries and has children and for this she does not need to go to school. The researcher concludes that unless ability to read and write is connected with gaining an income, women from the lower social groups see no point in a school education for themselves (Kamphoefner 1996: 97-98). The point is that at the moment no direct economic advantages are to be gained from a school education. It takes great effort for women from the lower classes to be able to follow a course of education. The time they spend on it detracts from the time they have to do household work or to go in search of things to buy for the family. Although the traditional role of the husband consists in providing for the income, the contribution of women in the form of the channelling of goods and services to the household is essential (Hoodfar 1996b). If they want to use their school knowledge

for a job, they are away from home too much and too often to be able
to build networks that help them survive. Women who do enter the
labour market often end up with poorly paid jobs and what they earn
does not compensate for what they lose through their absence from
home. Moreover they have a double job, because the housekeeping
waits for them at home and ... a wife who cannot take adequate care
of her family loses prestige, respect and power. This is what Fatiha
too was trying to say and it is the opinion of many women from her
class. In general the view applies that a woman cannot do two things
well at the same time, be a good wife/mother/homemaker and hold
down a job. In the upper classes things are different. These women
have a better education and thus a chance of better jobs and more
money, so that they can delegate their household tasks and shopping
to their maids.

Economic participation: indicators

In Cairo, 35.4 percent of families live in poverty and 6 percent in
extreme poverty (Korayem 1996). Unemployment levels in Egypt are
high. According to the (most recent available) data of 1990 (CAP-
MAS 1993a), the total potential workforce in Egypt is 15.7 million, of
a total population of 53.6 million. 1.3 million of this potential workforce was unemployed. In 1996 the number of unemployed was estimated at between 2 and 3 million people (13-20%).

In urban areas, the government and the civil service are the largest
employers in practically all economic activities (their role is less
important in rural areas). Since the time of Nasser each graduate was
guaranteed a job by the government, which resulted in a surplus of
personnel. The World Bank's advice is therefore that this law should
be scrapped. If this does occur, many will lose their jobs and the
unemployment figures will shoot up.

Of women in the age-group 20-39, 49 percent are in paid employment; in the age-group 40-59 35 percent are in paid employment;
and in the age-group 60-64 22.4 percent have a job. 39.6 percent of
working women are illiterate; 3.3 percent can read and write a little; 5
percent have completed elementary education, 26.6 percent have a
second school education; 8.2 percent have had tertiary education and
16 percent have an academic education. In practice this means that
the largest group of women (the illiterate and those who can read and
write a little or have had an elementary education) are in a very poor

position on the labour market. In the main they work as domestic help in richer Egyptian households or in the informal sector (by informal sector I mean "activities that do not fall under the recognition and regulation of the government"; Singerman 1996). Women with a secondary school education often work in the low-paid government jobs. The possibilities for highly educated women are greater. Women who live in a large city have generally benefited from more school education and have more chance of paid employment than women in the villages and in the countryside (Fouad 1994).

Men are traditionally viewed as the ones who care for the family and make decisions on the size of the family and the pattern of expenditure. The cultural ideal is that after her wedding a wife stays at home and takes care of the children and the household. So there are noticeable differences between the sexes in the labour market, not only among those with an elementary education but also among those with a secondary and tertiary education. Compared with 73.6 percent of men with an academic education, 26.4 percent of women with a similar education work, and compared with 66.8 percent of men with a secondary education, 33.3 percent of women work. If a woman wants to work, this will be done against the protests of her husband or her family. In a family where there is sufficient income a woman should not go out to work. If she does do this, then this is "loss of face" for the husband. Korayem (1996: 59) writes that in financially difficult situations women sell their wedding gifts or look for a job for one of their children. In poor families it is far from uncommon for the husband to be unemployed while the wife keeps the family with her work.

If economic circumstances dictate, men can be forced to take more than one job. Officials, for instance, who "traditionally" have a low salary (the government often pays lower salaries than in the private sector), have a second job in the evenings or at night as a taxi driver. Their wives sometimes try to earn a little too as *shaghghala* (cleaners). In general this work is frowned upon by women from the middle and lower-middle classes.

Single women who are not supported financially by an ex-husband (or father) must find a way of earning their living entirely on their own. Old-age provisions (pensions) are generally low for people who have worked in the civil service, or in (the few) companies that have a pension scheme of their own. The so-called Sadat pension and social security (Ministry of Social Affairs) are supposed to provide the poor with a minimum income. This is not the case, however. In 1988/98 the legally set pension was ten pounds a month, approximately £1.30/$ 2.00 (World Bank 1991c). So children often have to help their parents to make ends meet in their old age. Sons in particular are important for a mother in this respect.

Although 26 percent of all working women in urban areas and 47 percent of women in rural areas say they work to supplement their family budget, they can count on very little help with the household from their husbands. In addition, there are hardly any crèches. Working women therefore rely on help from the grandmother, mother or sister to look after the children (see the example of Fatiha). In low-income circumstances women have to make do without the many conveniences that women have elsewhere. No modern household appliances and no modern supermarkets where everything is ready to use. Women must therefore spend much of their time cleaning (in Cairo the wind blows thick layers of desert dust into the house every day), washing (in this class the whole family's clothing is washed by hand), shopping (articles have to be bought in different small shops), preparing food (there are few pre-packed or prepared articles). Many women have to carry water up the steps to their flat every day. Is it any wonder that they are always *ta'bana* (tired)? While most women complain of chronic tiredness, husbands complain that their wives leave for work too early or come home too late. In addition they are accused of neglecting their work at home and the care of the children through going out to work (Fouad 1994; Korayem 1996).

Men have much more social leeway than women. They also spend more money on themselves than women do. They often sit for hours in the coffee-house with their friends, smoking a *shisha* (water-pipe). This costs money. Women have to see to it that they keep the household going on a modest income. "Relaxation" generally means no more than drinking a glass of tea with a member of the family.

Health care

Do women like Salma go to traditional healers because this is cheaper? No, because although most healers say they provide their services free, I have often heard women mention large sums of money that they have managed somehow to scrape together. But this is less noticeable than it might be because the payments are generally in small instalments and it only turns out in retrospect that the healer has been expensive. Money is not the only criterion. Much more important are cultural ideas that an "ordinary" doctor cannot see the difference between complaints caused by organic disorders and complaints caused by *jinn* and *'afarit* (demons). Things are a bit different in respect of psychiatric help. In the first place because there is a stigma attached to this ("you must be really crazy if you go to one of those doctors"). Secondly because this is usually expensive, which is too great an obstacle to poor people in particular. Thirdly, it counts for a great deal that, in these social classes in particular, many psychological disorders are interpreted as possession, which can only be healed in a spiritual way (see al-Sendiony 1974).

In recent decades a great deal has improved in the area of health care for women and children in Egypt. Infant and child mortality rates have dropped considerably, but deaths during childbirth are still very high (on average 184 in 100,000). Government spending on health care increased from 148.4 million Egyptian pounds in 1980/81 to 691.4 million pounds in 1989/90. But salaries in health care have also risen and this is where most of the money goes (96.4%, cf. World Bank 1991c). The government now saves money on what (since Nasser) were originally free national health services (doctors, specialists, clinics and hospitals) by charging patients a small amount, or indirectly by having them buy medicine themselves. Since the price of medicines has risen sharply in recent years, it has to be said that the costs of health care for the poor have gone up. In addition, in the course of the 1980s the population increased at the rate of 2.8 percent per year. As a result, in real terms the government's per-capita investment in the health service has not increased but decreased. Poor people therefore put off visits to a doctor or consultant as long as possible and first try a "traditional" healer (Korayem 1996: 55). I have also observed that people deviate from the recommended dose of medicine, thereby making it "last longer". One of the women in my research never went to the doctor's during official surgery hours but accosted him in the street and then got a prescription without charge. It is not uncommon for people to stand near chemists' and ask passers-by for a contribution to the purchase of medicines.

Malnutrition is relatively widespread among both adults and children in Egypt: 24.4 percent of children (boys and girls) under five are malnourished to some degree; 3.2 percent of boys in this age-group and 3.3 percent of girls are too thin; 9.1 percent of boys and 9.3 percent of girls are clearly below the average weight applicable to their age-group. Malnutrition reduces the productivity of adults and the learning capacity of children (cf. Korayem 1994). Through malnutrition and physical and mental neglect, it can happen that girls like *umm* Mastafa are bothered by demons already at a young age.

Umm Mustafa

Umm Mustafa is the wife of a healer, *sheikh* Mustafa. He is an unpleasant man who is constantly shouting at his wife and children. In a newspaper article (*Akhbar al-Hawadith*, 1994) he claims to be the only true Koran healer, who obtained his secrets from a few *jinn* who whispered to him how he should heal people. This happened when his wife was sick with *sara'* (epilepsy). He is the healer who made Salma drink salt-water to make her spew out the *jinn*. When I visited him, he was very cagey about his knowledge, but I have also heard from other women he has treated stories about drinking salt-water, or of his putting a spoon in the patient's throat to make her retch (and spit out the *jinn*). I had the following conversation with his wife when he was not at home.

> "I do not originally come from Cairo. I only came here after I was married. My parents were *fallahin* (peasants) with a small parcel of land. There were four of us children. As a small child I had to help my mother with the housework of course, but I also worked on the land. I have been bothered by *jinn* for a long, long time. It began one day when my mother bit me in the back. My mother had just finished baking bread and I had to help her to spread out the loaves on the floor of the room (freshly baked *'ees baladi*, the local type of flat loaves, are spread out to steam); The sheep started eating the bread (small animals run around freely inside the house as well as outdoors) and so I slapped one of the sheep. My mother got very cross and bit me in the back. She said, 'Animals can't talk and so you mustn't hit them.' I got a real shock and afterwards I was always crying. At night I used to hear all sorts of noises, animal noises and human noises. I had no feeling left in my body and all I could do was sleep all day. They organized a *zar* for me then. My mother took me there because she wanted to know what was wrong with me. But the *kudya* (*zar* leader) couldn't find anything wrong with me and we

went away again. Then my father had a *sheikh* come, one who 'opens up the Book' (a healer who works divination with the Koran). He said I had a Muslim *jinn* and faithful *'ifrit* (Muslim demons) living in me, but he said, 'I won't say anything about it because it is secret.' I had to be shut up in a dark room for four days, so that I couldn't see anyone and couldn't talk to anyone. At night the *jinn* came to me and they put the light on for me. I was not to be scared because they would stay with me and they said, 'We will protect you.' I also saw the *jinn, bismillah ar rahman ar-rahim* ('in the name of Allah, the Merciful One' — an expression for protection). These were Muslim *jinn* from Saudi Arabia, and from all over, and from all sorts of other countries. I wasn't at all scared because they had said they would protect me if anyone should hit me. After four days everything was OK again and I had no more trouble."

"I got married at seventeen, to a cousin on my father's side. His parents and mine had arranged it. Actually, he wanted to marry another girl, but her parents were against it. I was not asked anything. That is not good. They should have asked, "What do you think of it?" When I was just married, my husband often hit me. Especially before I had any children. I have six children now. He hit me all over the place, just like that, without any reason. It was not because I didn't get the food ready, or didn't clean the house. He went to work, and when he came back he hit me, just like that. I tried to look nice for when he came home. Then he looked at me like this, but actually he didn't want to look. He came into the house and screamed, "I can't look at you, you're so ugly." When he looked at me he saw the face of an ape, he said, and then he hit me. I didn't understand what was wrong with me. If I was so ugly, why did he marry me in the first place? Later a *sheikh* told me that this had to do with *sihr al-mahabba* (love magic). We never went out, nor with the children later. But he himself was out every evening, with his friends. To start with we lived here in this district in a one-room flat near the railway line. My husband was without work for a long time, and after that he did casual work for an electrician. We had no money at all and the first child came quickly." She points to a girl and says, "She is *al-bikriyya* (the first-born). He smoked hashish, he had problems. He never used to come home until late in the evening and then demanded sex with me. I

refused because he had often beaten me that morning. Then he
got mad and hit me all over the place. 'It's my right,' he used to
scream them. There were times when I went to sit in front of the
neighbour's door because he didn't dare shout or hit me there.
My problems started up again and the *jinn* came back. But after
a while the *tahtaniyyin* (underground dwellers) got angry with my
husband because he was beating me. They told him that I was
malbusa (possessed by *jinn*). And then they told him, 'If you don't
stop hitting her, we will punish you, we'll blind you.' Then he
got really scared and didn't hit me any more. After that he went
and read all sorts of books about *jinn* and the Koran, and he
started healing people of *jinn* himself."

Interpretation

As a child, *umm* Mustafa had a terrible shock, and she was also beaten.
On marrying, she finds herself in an impossible marital situation with
her husband. It is a case of real rejection and mistreatment. Salma too,
the woman in the previous story, suffered rejection and humiliation,
but *umm* Mustafa seems to pass it off, as it were, by offering a supernatural explanation. The aetiology, according to the *sheikh* she asked for
help, is that there is a demon involved with her, who has fallen in love
with her, and because she is unobtainable, he makes her as ugly as an
ape every time her husband looks at her, so that he has a shock and
rejects her. The mechanism of blame-shifting is the same as in a state
of powerlessness when as a child she was locked up alone in a room for
four days because of possession and the *jinn* visited her. The *jinn*, who
turned out to be Muslims, then play a protective role: they put the
light on for her, comfort her and keep her company. Later too, when
her husband keeps hitting her, the demons come back to protect her
and they warn him to leave her alone. Culturally the beating of
women is justified and it is based on sura *al-Nisa'* (4): 34: "(as to) those
on whose part you fear desertion, admonish them, and leave them
alone in the sleeping-places and beat them; then if they obey you, do
not seek a way against them." For a woman in *umm* Mustafa's position,
it is difficult to blame her husband for a beating which she (from his
point of view, and perhaps also from hers) deserves. So she justifies
herself and her husband's behaviour in various ways in the form of
actions by demons. It is a ready-made cultural mechanism for blame-
shifting, which is very commonly used. A factor in this, undoubtedly, is

the fact that reflection and self-examination are not encouraged in these circles. *Umm* Mustafa's husband finally experiences a positive influence from the *jinn*, because he starts reading books and becomes a healer himself. As a result of this new profession his status is enhanced, even if only within the limited circle of the possessed, and it provides him with a new source of income (cf. Finkler 1986: 633-634).

Many Egyptians reject the explanations for misfortune given. They regard it as superstition and contrary to true Islam. For poor *baladi* women, the mystical powers mean a way to have confidence in their fate and it gives them the space to "manipulate" this lot: what is interpreted by outsiders as superstition and fatalism is an active strategy as far as these women are concerned.

Beating and magical fear

The beating of children and women is found all over the world. In my conversations with Egyptian women it struck me that beating is often taken for granted. Whenever I ask whether they have ever thought of hitting back or defending themselves in some other way, they always answer in the negative. It is *'eeb* (bad), I am told, for a woman to hit her husband back. Why, I ask, is he allowed to hit her? "*Alashan huwa ragil*", "Because he is a man." A man, women said, can hit his wife if she is disobedient, if she has not cooked the meal, if he cannot find his shoes, and very importantly, if he wants sex with her and she does not want it. Islam quite expressly recognizes sex as a need that must be satisfied in both sexes, but the emphasis lies on satisfaction of the man's needs: "It is his right (*haqqu*)."

There is also the cultural view in Egypt that women are unable to control their sexual urges. Such talk about women is very frequently adduced as a reason for the circumcision of girls; they are supposed to be able to control themselves better then.[6] Particularly in lower social circles, beating is taken for granted as something based on the Koran. Is this in fact the case? The Koran does say that men are the overseers of women and that they are allowed to punish women when they are disobedient, but the Koran also encourages good and just treatment of women.

---

[6] 82 percent of women in Egypt are circumcised: according to a report of the NGO Forum on Women in Beijing (1995), 60 percent of women and 59 percent of men think that this is as it should be.

Like standing in front of a mirror and falling in the bathroom, the experience of a violent emotional shock is also often the cause of possession. Not only in Egypt, but also in other Islamic countries, this is called "shock" (*tarba/khadda*), the reference being both to the causer and the healer of evil. In my travels through various Islamic countries I was able to buy various sorts of "shock bowls" (*tasit al-khadda*). These are copper bowls or flat dishes in which Koran texts are engraved. By putting water in the bowls and then drinking it, one can heal the evil (the water takes up the blessing — *baraka* — of the sacred texts). Emotional shock as the instigator of sickness and other evils was already known in Antiquity and is familiar in other parts of the world. In Latin America, for instance, this is called "magical fear", *espanto* or *susto* (both words can be translated as "shock" and "fear").

Two sorts of fear may be distinguished, first the "ordinary" sort of fear, for incidents that occasion fear (such as being afraid of failing one's driving test), but which has no effect on the soul and has no psychological consequences. Fear in the second context always relates to a sickness or an abnormal physical condition. Gillin (1948) writes that "magical fear" in communities in Guatemala and Peru manifests itself in a person through symptoms of depression, withdrawal from normal life and from responsibilities, and signs which apparently indicate a temporary collapse of the organization of the ego. The cultural explanation in those countries where "magical fear" is recognized, is that the person concerned has lost his or her soul. At a moment of great fear the soul has escaped from a person's body. The organism becomes greatly weakened as a result, which allows *aires* (bad winds/spirits) to enter the body and to cause sickness and/or some other kind of misfortune. By tracking down the escaped soul and the performance of all sorts of rituals, the soul is brought back into the body and the victim is healed (see also Desjarlais 1992). In several respects the causes and symptoms described above resemble those mentioned by my conversation partners in connection with touching or possession. Hence following Gillin I shall also refer to their shock/fear as "magical fear".

According to the *jinn* belief in Egypt, every individual is in principle susceptible to possession or touching by demons, but the degree of vulnerability varies. Women and children are more vulnerable than men (see also Messing 1959). I have written above that certain places and situations may also play a role, since they can, as it were, "invite" the *jinn*. I have often heard women say that after they had had a bad shock or fallen, they fell victim to all sorts of complaints. Morsy (1978;

1993) also writes that in Egypt fear is an important aetiological category: fear makes the body sensitive to illness. *Makhlu'* is a person who is "empty" and "uncoupled" and finds himself or herself in an emotional state of shock, which affects the nervous system. In the case of shock a person is symbolically "opened", dislocated, "fallen apart", which allows the *jinn* to enter the body (see Chapters 5 and 6). Among the women in my research group "shock" was often caused by their being beaten by their father, husband or brother. Almost immediately afterwards the victim was subject to strange dreams, swollen face, pains in the belly or the head, deafness, trouble with nerves, or apathy. Gillin (1948) writes that *susto* is associated with the same complaints. In his research area the remedy in such cases consists of magical procedures that are carried out by a shaman who has to recapture the soul and bring it back to its owner's body.

Also found in Egypt is the belief that the *ruh* (soul) can leave the body (el-Sayed el-Aswad 1987), but this is the case on a person's death. I have never heard of it in another connection, although people do speak of being "empty". But *susto* in Latin America and demon possession in Egypt have in common that the victim has got into an emotional state through which spirits can go into and out of the body through body openings.

Violence against women

As in other countries, violence in the home is a problem in Egypt that has as yet being little studied. Physical violence against women is dismissed in Egyptian society, but it is taken for granted, and is very common, especially in the lower classes. In particular women who have no strong protection through their own family, have little chance of escaping this violence, despite legal rights to report their husband to the police (Khattab 1992; Mohsen 1985; Tadros 1998). In 1995 the Al-Nadim Centre for the Management and Rehabilitation of Victims of Violence and the New Women Research Centre in Cairo conducted a large national study of the use of violence against women. Attention was focused on violence in the home, in the street and at work. Five hundred women and one hundred men from various socio-economic classes, levels of education and age-groups were questioned. The same questions were asked of men and women. The answers given by the men confirm the women's answers regarding the sort of violence they experience in life and their fear of it.

The research shows that 66 percent of the women have encountered insults at work, 70 percent of which are sexual in nature (from
sexual propositions to various forms of intimidation). In 23 percent of
cases the women were left with feelings of agitation, fear and depression. Despite their negative feelings these women carry on with their
work because they need the money for their families.

Almost all the women said that they had been accosted in the
street; 54.1 percent spoke of verbal abuse and 37.5 percent spoke also
of abuse involving physical contact. 39 percent of women gave a positive answer to the question whether they regarded assault as a real
risk for themselves. 70 percent of the men also gave a positive answer
to the question whether they though assault might overcome one of
their female family members or neighbours. What women complain
about most is annoyances they experience in the street on the part of
men who deliberately bump into them, "accidentally" touch or pinch
them, press their bodies against them in the overcrowded buses, and
so on. So some take an ambivalent view of mobility outdoors and in
one's own neighbourhood. On one hand it gives them new opportu-
nities of gaining income and on the other hand many wonder
whether it is "correct" for an Islamic woman to walk the streets so
freely. The massive shift to the wearing of "Islamic clothing" has a
great deal to do with this, according to Macleod (1996). She is of the
opinion that this form of dress has less to do with fundamentalist
Islamic ideas than with the "conquest" of new space for women in the
world outside the home. Islamic dress apparently gives women the
opportunity to move freely while at the same time remaining respected.

83 percent of the women and 94 percent of the men questioned
said they knew families in which sons beat their mothers; 96 percent
of the women had heard of brothers who beat their sisters; 83 percent
of the women knew families that marry off their daughters without
their agreement; 95 percent had heard of families who had married
their daughters out to much older men. Women said they were aware
of the emotional effects that this has on the girls. 23 percent said that
the girls felt like merchandise; 11 percent said that what has been
done to them is unjust; 19 percent said that girls feel miserable and
depressive as a result. 64 percent of the women and 68 percent of the
men said they had heard of cases of incestuous assault. In most cases
the abuse involved a father, brother or step-father. Concern for the
reputation of the family of the victim and the victim herself conspire

to ensure that cases are rarely reported (see also al-Saadawi 1979). These figures indicate that it is not a matter of isolated cases.

When asked what women regard as an act of violence on the part of their husband, the man's dominant attitude came overwhelmingly to the fore, as well as his demand that one should always agree with him. In addition his right to forbid her to go out, to sexual intercourse, to discipline her, to determine how many children there will be and his right to marry several women. 61 percent of women in the research group gave a positive answer to the question whether they had ever themselves been the victim of any form of violence on the part of their husbands.

The cultural view that men are the boss of women is also evident in the answers of the male respondents: 64 percent think that the man has the right to impose his will on his wife, 46 percent think that he always has the right to sexual intercourse (even if this is against her will) and 70 percent think that he has the right to hit his wife.

Although the research took place predominantly among men and women from the less educated groups, violence against women is not limited to this group: 9 percent of the women who say they have been beaten by their husband, and 35 percent of the men who say they have hit their wives, possess an academic degree.[7] Violence against women is thus not limited to the poor and uneducated classes (the research into violence against women was conducted in order to make recommendations at the NGO Forum on Women, 1995).

On the position of the woman in Egypt one can say that at home there is a system that by complex cultural mechanisms in combination with religious views still ascribes power to the man. The separation of women, gender differences in the division of labour and male dominance in decision-making are some of the factors that influence women's personal freedom and options. This applies to their health, their customs and habits or their work. In a broader context political and legal systems and institutions reinforce these mechanisms further. A trend to a stricter interpretation of religion has not improved the situation of women in the past twenty years. There are, moreover, few organizations that pay attention to the needs of women. Most

---

[7] In a personal conversation with me Dr. Marlyn Tadros (Human Rights Organization, Cairo, November 1996) spoke of her horror at a court verdict: a woman from the lower classes had submitted a request for divorce because her husband was constantly beating her. The court refused to grant the request on the grounds "that violence is culturally accepted among women from her class".

existing (government) organizations fall short of the mark when it comes to meeting the needs of women. Dr. Shereen Abul Naga, lecturer at the Cairo University and feminist, accuses the Mubarak government of opportunism as far as matters related to the position of women are concerned. The state and the Islamists (fundamentalists), she says, both misuse the woman. When it is a question of power then the state is happy to sacrifice the woman. Through the media the impression is awakened that it is working for the improvement of the position of women, but in practice attention reaches no further than the problem of illiteracy in the countryside. The Islamists in turn use religious and cultural values that support and encourage violence against women.[8]

Fundamentalism

In the framework of this study it is not possible to give an extensive discussion of the fundamentalist movement in Egypt (also called the "Islamist" movement). That would be too ambitious. I shall therefore restrict myself to some brief comments since the subject has come up a number of times thus far. An "Islamist" is someone who combines his devotion to Islam with political activism. In Egypt one can speak of pluralism in relation to Islamist movements. That is to say that there is not one group or movement that represents the whole society, but several. The Muslim Brotherhood (*al-Ikhwan al-Muslimun*), which was set up by Hassan al-Banna in 1928 (and developed from a long tradition of Islamic reform movements), is probably the most popular of these. From its beginnings to the present day this Brotherhood has exercised great influence on Egyptian society and politics. The aim of all Islamist movements is the establishment of an "Islamic state". The way in which they want to do this is varied. The Muslim Brotherhood is known for its cooperativeness. It tries to realize its goals by, among other things, education, the stimulation of an (Islamic) consciousness and social services. The *al-Jihad* and the *al-Jama'a al-Islamiyya* on the other hand have a militant approach. They are opposed to the state and its institutions. The *al-Takfir wa al-Hijra* has an approach directed first of all towards social reform and after that to reform of the political system. The Muslim Brotherhood is currently the most important opposition group against Mubarak's ruling National Democratic Par-

---

[8] Patriarchy ... Islam or the State? in: *People's Rights, Women's Rights*, 2.8.1996.

ty (NDP). During the Sadat government the *Jama'a Islamiyya* was the group with the greatest support among students.

With the assassination of President Sadat (6 October 1981), a greater recourse to terrorism develops. Since 1986 there have been regular political assassination attempts. Militant activism has been primarily oriented against the state in recent decades. Its target has often been tourism, as a symbol of foreign support for the regime. But the victims have not only been foreign tourists; there have also been many deaths among the Egyptian population (mainly Christians in Upper Egypt). The clear presence of militant Islamic movements was met with a violent reaction from the Mubarak government. Human rights groups report that in 1997 twenty thousand presumed militant activists were detained in Egyptian prisons.

Militant activities do not enjoy great support among the population, but the activities of the Brotherhood and other non-violent Islamic organizations do have such support. Their popularity has two important causes. First, through the failure of the government, meaning (among other things): corruption, maladministration, inefficiency and repression. Second, the readiness of Islamic movements to tackle unemployment, poverty, inflation, illiteracy and other things regarded as due to government neglect. From 1943 already the leader of the Muslim Brothers, Hassan al-Bana, had given its members the task of paying attention to the health of people in the villages and the towns. Young members were encouraged to make the population aware of the significance of hygiene, and that they should start making use of modern medical science. From 1994 the organization set up its own policlinics, hospitals and schools. The Brotherhood is currently (as are other organizations) active as an NGO (non-governmental organization) alongside or in mosques. The organizations of "social Islam" exercise great influence on the lives of people in the poor districts in particular. Alongside these NGO's small and larger Islamist social care orgnizations (*jam'iyyat khayriyya*) are spread all over the country. They provide an extensive network of services, such as free clinics and hospitals, but other activities are also organized. These include "little classes" for women, where alongside information on the Koran and *hadith* they also get support on a social level (see Fatiha's account in this chapter). One might say that "social Islam" is at pains to jump into the breach where the government has defaulted in helping the poor. The picture of the Islamist organizations should not, on the other hand, be seen to onesidedly and optimistically, since there are also many examples of corrupt and inefficient Islamist organizations. A great deal of attention is paid to this in the Egyptian press (for instance the scandals surrounding Islamist investment companies that have relieved thousands of people of their money).

Until the 1970s the greatest support for the Muslim Brotherhood came from intellectuals and the middle class. As the years have gone by, the profile of members of the militant movements has especially changed. Their members are younger, come predominantly from lower-income environments, live in the slum districts (certain "poor" districts, such as Imbaba in the Guiza area, are known for their great support for the militant movements) and have less education than their "Brothers" of the previous generation(s). In the 1970s the average age of an activist was between twenty-five and twenty-seven years and 64 percent had a university education or a tertiary school diploma. Currently this is twenty-one years of age, and only 30 percent now have followed higher education. Many young people have the feeling that modern Egyptian society does nothing for them. They think that a stricter Islamic lifestyle would be able to change the general social situation in Egypt. They are not trying to turn the clock back, but are looking for new ways to adjust the Islamic paradigm to contemporary conditions.

Islam is as dominant today as Nasserism was in the 1960s. The Islamic Alliance, the new political organization of the Brotherhood, now operates under the slogan *Al-Islam huwa al-Hall* ("Islam is the solution") and appears to be finding resonance with more and more people. This has helped lead to a great official Islamicization of public life in Egypt. Thus in 1980 the *Shari'a* (Islamic law) became the basis of Egyptian legislation (but was not declared the only source because of the concerns of the Coptic section of the population), and in 1987 the civil code was changed, which led to a deterioration in the position of women, since certain laws were "rescinded". Weeklies and daily newspapers receive letters from readers with questions concerning personal devotion and on radio and television lively discussions are held on Islamic questions. The wearing of religiously approved clothing is stimulated and is now ubiquitous. (The "man in the street" is encouraged to keep to the letter of the Koran and to the performance of religion in daily activities. Prayer rooms have been set up in public buildings. Each election produces more religious candidates. Egypt is nominally a democracy with a multi-party system, but the Mubarak regime fears the Brotherhood and tries in all possible ways to hinder its participation in the government. This led to various violent incidents in the 1995 elections. Although the state party (NDP) maintained its monopoly in the government, in the elections of trade union leaders (*niqabat*) of lawyers, doctors, engineers and journalists the Islamist candidates (primarily Muslim Brothers) emerged overwhelmingly as winners of the vote.

The Islamist movements are still distinguished by their inflexible and intolerant attitude towards others. To mention a few examples: the publicist Farag Fauda, who was murdered, the assassination attempt on the Nobel prize-winner Nagib Mahfuz and the accusation of the scientist Nasr Hamed Abu Zaid, who is supposedly an apostate. But the "war" is continuing. It simmers under the surface of Egyptian society. Mubarak's limited liberalization and partial implementation of democracy has not yet brought any improvement of living conditions for the vast majority of people. Despair, poverty and helplessness are for part of the population a source of inspiration to change Islam into an ideology which, through justifying violent acts, is regarded by many as a distortion of Islam. Islam has become the principal challenge for the Mubarak government.[9]

Umm Harbi

A difficult economic situation forces families to send their children out at a young age to earn a little money. In Egypt there is the culturally idealized notion that, because they are so desired, children are always surrounded with love, but the following account by *umm* Harbi shows another reality.

> "I was born in the *Si'id*, that is the south of Egypt. My father was also a *si'idi*, but my mother was a *fallaha* (someone from the countryside) from the Delta. There were three of us at home, three girls, and I was the youngest. I was still very small when my mother died. I can hardly remember her. My father remarried shortly after that and I called the woman "mother". But people told me that she was not my mother and that my mother

---

[9] According to many, e.g. Nasr Abu Zaid, there is no difference in principle between the "political Isalmists" and the "social Islamists" (Guenena 1986, 1996; Hiro 1988; Ibrahim 1980; Joffé 1996; Sillivan & Sana Abed-Kotob 1999).

was dead. The new woman was not nice. She beat us with a stick and we got no more to eat than a piece of bread or some vegetables cooked in water. My grandma, father's mother, gave us things to eat and was very kind to us. Without her we would definitely have died. I had to go to work when I was about seven years old. The work was somewhere far away from home and my sisters and I always went there for two months at a time. We were picked up by car and we took our own food with us — well, if you can call it food, because we didn't have much more than a bit of bread and cheese. Our work was on a cotton plantation. I had to pick the caterpillars off the cotton so that they couldn't eat up the leaves. I worked all day on the land. From morning till so late in the evening that you couldn't see the caterpillars any more. Then we went to the shack that we had built ourselves with some branches next to the irrigation canal, where the three of us lived. We used to wash ourselves a bit in the canal and went to sleep. Through doing this my eldest sister, Sabah, was bothered by the *'afarit* (demons), which are *jinn* that live in the canal. When you have your *dawra* (period) you are not allowed to go to the water because they get angry and go inside you, but she did that. She was sick for a long time and actually the *'afarit* still haven't left her."

"In any case, after four days our food had all gone and we had nothing left, and no money to buy anything. I cried with hunger and my sisters tried to comfort me. To get something to eat we went begging along the other shacks and a few houses standing near the cotton fields. The people who owned the cotton fields were themselves very rich of course, but they didn't give us anything. From other people working on the fields we got something to eat now and again and they gave us a blanket to sleep under. We worked like that for two months in a row and then we went back briefly to father's house. He took the money off us that we had earned and we were beaten. My grandma, my father's mother, was very cross about it and told him he was crazy to do that — that he made his three daughters work so hard, took their money and then didn't even give them anything to eat. But my father took no notice. He had two sons by the new wife and they were given good food to eat, meat, chicken, vegetables. We are girls and we could eat stones! When I was a bit older, a neighbour came along who said that there were lots of people in Cairo who wanted young girls to do the cleaning. So I went to Cairo with the neighbour, who was from our family. I was about ten or eleven when I came to work for a famous actor in Zamalek (an upper-middle class district). I had to work very hard, but I really enjoyed it because all kinds of people visited him and the people were really quite nice to me and I was given very good food to eat. My father came to Cairo every three months to pick up my salary, and if he was not happy with something I got another thrashing. At that time you earned at most three pounds a month and he gave the money to his wife for his sons. Girls don't count here. One time my boss said, 'Why don't you hide next time he comes? If your father asks me where you are, I'll tell him you don't work here any more.' So I did that. I hid all day long and I didn't even dare look out of the window or stand on the balcony, I was so scared that he might see me. When my father couldn't find me, he went away and I never saw him again."

Interpretation

Umm Harbi is a solid, sturdy woman. At a young age she went to work and that made her strong. But things were different for her sister. I met Sabah at both the *zar* and Koran healing, always looking for healing from the *'afarit*. *Umm* Harbi reports that her sister was menstruating when she went close to the irrigation canal where *'afarit* of course live. They became angry, because she broke a double taboo: she comes close to the water, where demons live, in a state of great impurity (her period). So actually it is her own fault that she got "clothed", and that is how she comes to be looking everywhere for help in pacifying or exorcizing the demons.

Children and child labour

Child labour, it is generally agreed, is an impediment to human development. Despite legal provisions, however, there are large numbers of children in Egypt between the ages of six and fourteen who are forced to work. The number of working children under fifteen was estimated in 1984 at one and a half to two million. In 1995 68.3 percent of boys and 38.2 percent of girls under twelve were economically active. The number of working girls in the countryside is greater than in the urban areas and they start work at a younger age. In the towns girls more frequently go to school than in the villages, so that the moment they start paid employment is postponed for a few years. In the villages there are few alternatives to work on the land. It is still customary for rich city families to "adopt" a girl from the country. Such a child comes into the family and in most cases she becomes the children's "maid". The number of young girls from the country that have paid domestic work, or who do unpaid work under the label of "adoption", is not recorded. Injury or abuse at work is not generally reported. This also applies to sexual abuse. The strong family ties keep incidents within the home. Dominant values and public attitudes foster secrecy (CAPMAS 1992).

In Egyptian society children are very much desired, even if there are in fact too many mouths to feed. The mother's role is strongly idealized and the role of children in relation to their mother also. It scarcely needs saying that the ideals are far from always met. *Umm* Harbi said that her father loved his sons by the second wife more than his daughters by his first wife. Sons are much loved and are thus often the decisive factor when it is a matter of extending the family (in practice this means that people keep going until they have a son). Research has shown that there are strong gender preferences in relation to children. Egyptian women have no particular preference for a boy or a girl as long as they already have a son or if as yet they have no children. But when children are there, 60 percent of mothers with only daughters and 42 percent with more daughters than sons have a preference for a son when the family is to be extended. This is also the case when there are as many sons as there are daughters.

It is also a cultural ideal that the daughter marries early and preferably has her first child nine months later. Seven percent of city women and fifty percent of country women have a preference for a marriage when the girl is young. The legally permitted age for girls is sixteen, but it is not uncommon for a girl to be married off at a younger age. The education of the mother evidently plays a role in the determination of the marriageable age; 40 percent of illiterate mothers and 9 percent of mothers with a completed elementary education indicate a preference for marriage at a young age. Marrying off at a young age has a great deal to do with sexuality and the honour of the family. Girls and women are supposed not to be able to curb their sexual urges. So if people marry young their sex urges are suitably channelled and the family honour cannot be besmirched by the "dishonourable" behaviour of the girl (Egyptian Medical Women's Association EMWA 1995 and CAPMAS & UNICEF 1992, 1995). In order to curb sexual lust, clitoridectomy (*tahara*: the full or partial excision of the external female genitals) is considered appropriate.

Circumcision (tahara) and virginity

Female circumcision (*tahara*) is a topic that has caused a good deal of commotion in recent years. In the west and in Egypt itself, the (im)moral character of female circumcision is under discussion by women in the modern and economically better-off classes. Opponents regard the operation as a mutilation of the female body and as a form of sexual oppression. Proponents of course view it as a necessity. Still today more than three-quarters of all women in Egypt have been circumcised (*People's Rights, Women's Rights,* June 1998). The great majority of the women concerned are from the economically lower classes and from the countryside.

Four reasons are generally given for circumcision. First, a moral reason: it suppresses sexual lust among virgins, it curbs lust among married women (so that they do not bother their husbands) and divorced women and widows can cope better with their abstinence. Second, an aesthetic reason: a circumcised woman is supposed to be more beautiful (the external genitals are associated with masculinity). Third, a religious reason: it purifies the girl. Fourth: it is supposed to be an Islamic tradition. The latter reason is supposed to be based on a saying of the Prophet, who is supposed to have said, "Perform circumcision, but do not go too far in it." Opponents however always point out that female circumcision was not originally an Islamic custom and is not practised in all Islamic countries. All the women I have talked with were circumcised and have also had their daughters circumcised or plan to do so when the time comes. The expressions that crop up in this context are: "It is ugly", "it will carry on growing", "men don't want uncircumcised women because 'it' looks like the male organ".

Problems, but also the extent to which problems are openly discussed, are culturally determined. Thus great value is attached in all Islamic countries to the virginity of the girl before marriage. It is known, but scarcely open to discussion, that the loss of the hymen can occur through for instance a medical operation, or that the hymen itself can be entirely absent without a girl having lost her virginity. The girl may also have been the victim of sexual aggression in the street or within the family. According to Saadawi (1979), the latter possibility is far from inconceivable in Egyptian society, where sexual needs have to be suppressed until after the wedding ceremony. *Iman* is one of those women who married young.

Iman

"I was still under thirteen when I got married. My husband was twenty-four and he was a cousin of mine. Because I was still too young I had to ask for permission, I had to have a form filled in and go to the *ma'zun* (registrar of marriages) with two photos. If anything were to happen, for instance if I should die because I was still so young, then they had a photo of me. When I got married I was completely alone, no father and no mother with me. I had no idea what it meant to be married. The first time he wanted sex with me I refused, because I was terribly scared. I pushed him away and screamed *'eeb 'aleik!* (You should be ashamed of yourself!). He said I shouldn't hit him because he was my husband and that all married people did 'it'. But I kept refusing when he came and lay next to me. One evening he put hashish in my tea and then it happened without me knowing. The following day I cried and cried because I just kept bleeding. Because it didn't stop and I kept fainting, I had to go to the hospital. They were really angry there because I was still much too young to have sex. They asked me where my husband was, but his mother, who came with me, told the doctor he was away. They gave me an injection and medicine. But when I slept with my husband I didn't like it because it was painful. Everyone told me that this was normal in the beginning and it was no shame that my husband wanted it, but if I didn't want it, then that was a sin. The pain wasn't getting any better, so I went to a *sheikh*. He said that Girgis, a Christian *jinn*, was living in me. He did not want my husband to make love to me because he wanted me himself. The *sheikh* drove him out, but I don't know how. With *bukhur* (incense) and with the Koran, he said. I was about fifteen when I had my first child. I gave birth alone at home with the *daya*, the midwife. A year later my second child came. In all I had four sons and a daughter. I had to work hard to provide food for them all and send them to school. My husband worked somewhere in a workshop where they made sheets and he only earned very little. We had a one-room flat in Bulaq, a well-known popular district in Cairo. I worked all day in people's homes as a domestic help and when I came home in the evening I did washing for other people. I earned twenty-five piaster that way (a hundred piaster is one pound, about £ 0.13/$ 0.20) and sometimes they paid a bit extra. When my first son was born, I bought a pram and when I went to work in the morning I put my son in it and took him with me to work. I did the same with all my children. I have always taken good care of my children. If I had money I bought chicken, macaroni, vegetables and tomatoes, so at least they could eat well. Everything I earned went on food. When they were older I sent them to school. I never went to school myself, but my children did! My husband did go to school and he could read and write. But he didn't think it was necessary for his children. He thought it was a waste of money, he said, if I had to buy something for school, an exercise book or a pen, or something like that. In those days you had to buy everything yourself. I said to him, 'What do you want, do we have to let them stay ignorant? I want them to go to school.' A few good people who saw that I worked hard and sent my children to school, helped me out now and again. They gave me a bit of money or some clothes. I let all my children marry young. My daughter was fifteen when she got married and my sons about nineteen or twenty. When my sons got married I was able to give them a bit of money a little at a time. I had saved for them in the *gama'iyya*.[10] Their children were all born here at my place and I took care of food and drink. I now also take care of their children when they are sick. But after all I have done for them, they are not good sons. Their wives are nice enough, but

---

[10] A *gama'iyya* is an informal savings club set up by a number of women. Each of them gives a small weekly or monthly amount to the leader—*ra'isa*. When time has passed each member in turn can cash in the whole amount. This method of saving is very common.

recently my eldest son gave me a beating and gave me verbal abuse. Their father has done nothing for them. He never took any notice of anything, he just led his own life. He is not a good man. He comes and goes as he likes, but he hardly brings in any money and on top of that he knocks me about. But it is not the custom here to divorce. It brings shame if a woman leaves her husband. And if a husband dies his wife has to marry again straight away. It brings shame to stay unmarried."

Interpretation

I have often heard similar stories to Iman's of women losing their virginity. Also of hashish or alcohol being used to dope the girl so that she offers less resistance. It is quite understandable that young girls do not want to sleep with a man they do not know, or hardly know. Their whole life long they have been told that their body is both impure and very much desired by men and that they must therefore defend themselves so that the honour of the family is not besmirched.

It is difficult to check whether Iman's deflowering really occurred as described (and whether things still happen this way), but since I have heard it many times, I cannot exclude the possibility. The *sheikh* refers to *sihr al-mahabba*, i.e. "love magic", by a Christian *jinn* (see Chapter 5). Here again we have the same mechanism of blame-shifting I mentioned earlier. The girl is frightened and sex is painful (owing to the young husband's clumsiness?). She is powerless, because sex is compulsory — after all, she is married. The mechanism means that she herself is not to blame and her young husband is justified in his sexual demands: it is all the work of demons. It is clear that Iman had enduring physical problems following the deflowering. She told me that she spent a long time at her aunt's/mother-in-law's because she was an orphan. It was she who decided on the marriage between the twelve-year-old girl and her own son. This sort of thing is not uncommon, but Iman was still very young and at the *ma'zun* and later at the hospital they had to keep quiet about her true age. Why did she make the child marry so young? Perhaps the mother had noticed that her son found the girl extremely sexually attractive? In such cases things move on quickly to marriage so as to avoid possible public shame as a result of assault and rape. It is possible that the information available is incomplete, because anything to do with sexuality is not easily talked about within the cultural context. During my fieldwork I have often met situations when I had to rely on my own intuition and lengthy experience in interaction with women. I pay attention to linguistic expressions, the way in which stories are told, the body language and value judgments of my conversation partners and try to reproduce these as completely and faithfully as possible, but despite my good intentions it is possible that distortions can arise. In order to limit this sort of effect as much as possible, I have made it a habit not only to speak with the people concerned at different times, unexpectedly, and from different angles on the same crucial, difficult or unclear point, but also to use "awkward" topics in a "game" with others, in which I try to discover whether "such situations" *might be* possible. In this way my conversations and participation with the women produce a greater flow of information and better insight into their cultural orientation.

Iman tells us that she had to do everything on her own and that her husband never took any notice of what was going on. I have often heard comments like this from women. An outsider might get the impression that the husband and wife live parallel lives alongside each other, but this is not entirely true. His role, too, is not always easy. It is certainly the case that men live in an "outside" world and women in an "indoor" world. Women live with their children, men need friends in order to be men. And he needs money for this, because it is not at home that he meets his friends but in the coffee-house. There he has to drink something and smoke a *shisha* (water-pipe). This is money he takes away from his family. But without it he is not a real man.

Father and mother: the struggle to survive

A question I have often asked women is what they think is the most important thing in marriage. The answers were almost always the same: "that he doesn't hit" and "that he takes good care of his family". In Egyptian culture the marriage is a contract, you give something and you get something in return. Many young men and women who enter into that contract do so for pragmatic reasons. Love? That comes later. Once she is married and has children, it is the mother's task to bring up the children and to teach them respect for their father. Gender roles are strongly in evidence in the upbringing, the strict and authoritarian father figure versus the gentle and loving mother figure. The mother sees herself ideally as the central person in the life of her children, treating them in a gentle and loving way. The father emphasizes obedience and a great deal of beating is used in the process. This often makes children afraid of their father. It is not the case that smacking children is socially unacceptable. Corporal punishment is said to be good for children, because it teaches them respect and obedience. Small children are often spoilt by the mother, but when children grow up they start being more demanding and, like children everywhere in the world, they want money to buy clothes and do fun things with. The parents are then confronted with the impossibility of giving them what they want. The culture prescribes that the father takes care of the income and that the mother does the housework, is available to him sexually, brings up the children and teaches them respect for their father. But men from the lower classes are frequently unable, or insufficiently able, to fulfil their task and this leads to considerable tensions within the family. Wife and children are economically extremely dependent on the husband and father, and material contributions from the man are seen as an expression of his love for them. I have often heard men say that they do what they can, and I have already described above how more and more men have not just one but two or three jobs. Some work sixty to seventy hours a week. But their work is poorly paid if, for instance, they work for the government or are unskilled labourers. Men who work in the private sector are often a bit better off. In many poor families there are daily arguments about money. Money for food, money to clothe the children with and money to send them to school. The mother, up to her neck in worries, tells the children that their father is no good because he has not seen to it that they have everything they need. The poor economic situation moves many men to seek a way out in migration. The family's standard of living does improve a notch as a result, but migration also have its negative sides, as in the case of Huda.

Huda

Huda is thirty years old and has three children. The eldest child is a girl of eleven and the youngest is six. I met her in a village just outside Cairo. She was there to visit a *sheikh* who was the subject of a great deal of attention from the press a number of years ago. His "repertoire" is as extensive as his fame. Not only does he heal psychological complaints, but also heart problems, rheumatism and diabetes. He says he spends the money he earns through healing on good causes, such as the building of a mosque just in front of his house (there is indeed a half-finished structure there). Huda's husband works in Saudi Arabia and so one of her brothers keeps her company. She tells me that the sickness she has cannot be healed by an ordinary doctor because it is *marad ruhani* (spiritual illness), and that only Koran healing can help because only God can heal her sickness. When I ask what is wrong with her, she tells me that she cannot move properly, she has pain in her arms, strange dreams and is extremely nervous. She has been suffering from this for the past six years and has been to all possible doctors and hospitals, but no one was able to do anything for her. She was given cortisone as a medicine. I hear from the *sheikh*'s "assistant" that when Huda first came to him, she could hardly walk. She was dragging herself along and kept falling over. Huda tells me:

> "But the medicine didn't help and the doctors said "It's a strange case". But I am still ill and am in pain. Perhaps this is "touching" by a *jinn*, but the *sheikh* didn't say anything about that. He prays, but healing comes from God. I am suffering from touching by a *jinn*, I feel that that is what it is. I have pain everywhere, in my legs, in my back, everywhere. But the doctors can't find anything. I have been here nine times already. I pray to God and He has given me his blessing. I feel better. I have been ill because of tensions between myself and my family. There were problems with my brothers, with my parents and with my children. My husband is away, and I live on my own, and I don't get any help from my family, and they are cross with me, and my husband isn't with me. I have no one to talk to. And then I cried, and then the *gann* came. I saw the *gann* at night. In the middle of the night I felt something sitting on my bed. He sat on my legs and he moved over my whole body, and he looked at me, like this (she demonstrates). I saw him. But when I got up to put the light on, he disappeared. In the beginning, just after my husband had left, everything went well until I got into an argument with my in-laws. After that with my brothers, my parents and my children. It got worse and worse. I am a nervous type and everything knocks me off balance. I feel a pressure inside me. My husband has been gone for ten years. That is difficult. The children, their school, the home, everything lands on my

plate. I was nervous, ever since he left. That is because I don't
like change. When he used to come home every evening he used
to sit with me and I could talk to him. When he went away I got
depressed. That has grown over the years. Ten years on your
own is a long time, but what can I do?

Interpretation

As is once again evident here from the conversation, women are sometimes well aware of a sequence of events which have knocked them off
balance. Each case of demon touching or possession is preceded by
sorrow or another oppressive situation which "prepares" the body for
invasion by demons. In Huda's case it is not a spiral of poverty that
drags her down, but a spiral of inequality between herself, her family
and her relations. Huda's husband works in Saudi Arabia and after a
number of years she can no longer cope with being on her own.

Between 1974 and 1984 alone, almost three million Egyptians emigrated to the Arab oil states (Saudi Arabia, Kuwait, Iraq). Most
migrants were unskilled or semi-skilled male workers, who left their
families behind in Egypt to go and work temporarily elsewhere. Emi-
gration is regarded by the government as an important boost for the
Egyptian economy, because it relieves the labour market and it has
the advantage of bringing in important foreign currency through the
migrants' money transfers. For the worker who emigrated it meant a
chance for a few years to earn ten to twenty times as much as in his
own country.

From the second half of the 1980s onwards, there has been a
change in migration, because after the drop in oil prices a different
policy has been followed in the Gulf states. In that period around four
hundred thousand workers returned to Egypt. After the opening of
the Libyan labour market many left for that country. Not for long,
however, because the Gulf crisis broke out. Hundreds of thousands of
Egyptians had to return home from the various migration countries.
Many returned regretfully and had to set about finding a place in the
Egyptian labour market once again.

The consequences of migration

The decision to leave for other parts is generally taken out of economic considerations and most women support their husband's decision

at the beginning, because one can then expect a better life in one's own country after a few years. Most men who decide to migrate may be divided into two groups: first, the unmarried young men who need the money to finance their wedding, which is (too) expensive for people from the poorer quarters too; second, married men who already have a number of children. Fear that the marriage will fall apart as a result of the migration because as yet there are no children stops many a just-married couple taking the step.

In general the men do not enjoy life in the rich oil states, because they are far away from wife, children and the family, and because apart from work "there is nothing to do" (especially Saudis and Kuwaitis come to Egypt because there is more amusement there than in their own country). In addition, the inhabitants of the "host country" look down on the migrants and the authorities treat them in an unfriendly way. If political tensions develop between host countries and Egypt, the migrants are expelled from the country without redress. Libya has done this several times and after the Gulf crisis Saudi Arabia and Kuwait did the same. Often the migrant has to leave the country at a moment's notice, leaving behind his few possessions (Hoodfar 1996a).

Migration has important consequences for the wives that are left behind. One-parent families have come into being with the mother as the head of the family. This of course has implications for women and children in Egyptian society, both during their husband's/father's absence and after his return. Since it is regarded both by men and women in Egypt (and other Islamic countries) as socially incorrect for a woman to live alone, women in the country who remain after their husband's departure, often return to their own family for a while or go and live with the in-laws. In the cities they often stay with their children in their own home or one of their brothers or sisters temporarily moves in with them. Young women in particular do not enjoy coming back under the "control" of their father or mother (-in-law). When the wife becomes the head of the family, this involves her having to do her husband's tasks as well as her own usual ones. She thus has greater responsibility for family expenditure, has to learn to cope on her own with money, and if necessary must deal with the authorities on her own. She also has to give guidance to the children and worry about her husband, whether he will return when his time abroad is over. For women in the country, this also means that they must often take on their husband's duties on the land (Hoodfar 1996a).

Particularly in the first months after her husband's departure, the wife is under great strain, largely because she is constantly watched by family, friends and neighbours. Women who have no job of their own are often left with a small amount of money from their husband and they then have to wait for his bank transfers. Women who do have a job of their own are expected to manage the household with their own money until the husband returns with his earnings. Such financial arrangements mean a (temporary) change in the roles because according to Islam and Egyptian culture the husband is viewed as the breadwinner. Another important change in the lives of these women is that they gain greater freedom within the household to divide up their time as they themselves would wish. In other words they do not have to be at their husband's beck and call.

The absence of the father of course has an effect on the children too. Although in lower-income environments in particular the father is away from home a lot in order to provide for his family — often from early in the morning until around ten o'clock at night — and his role in the children's upbringing generally goes little further than dishing out thrashings, nonetheless he is at hand to turn up now and again and discipline the children. In migrant households young daughters often find things more difficult than before because alongside going to school they also have more work to do in the household. Sons often feel freer as a result of the father's absence, but this also makes them more difficult to handle for the mother, who cannot keep them under her thumb. Very often they "terrorize" their mother and sisters because they take over the man's role and "rule the roost". On the other hand some families become more democratic because the mother discusses things more with her children and takes account of their opinions when taking decisions.

In the past, families used to live more together than they do today. Women whose husband has migrated have to rely on their neighbours more than they used to do, if their family lives some distance away. In particular in areas where people with lower incomes live, the help of neighbours and solidarity are very important (Korayem 1996). Wives whose husbands have migrated have more time for social contacts in the neighbourhood as a result of their absence. There are of course also cases, like Huda's, where wives cannot cope with all this new independence and who become alienated from family and neighbours through an accumulation of uncertainties and tensions. Often women are also afraid that when their husband returns with money the whole wider family will want to profit from it. In Egypt it is customary for relatives to help each other out financially. Returning migrants are expected to have become rich and thus to have no problem in handing out money. Unskilled workers do earn more in the oil states than at home, but they certainly do not return with so much money that they can indeed hand it out.

Economic consequences for families

Hoodfar (1996a) observes that lower-class women whose husbands have migrated have more say in the way the money that is earned is to be spent than women from the middle and upper classes. Lower-class women try to buy durable goods for the house with the money transferred to them by their husbands, or to invest in a piece of land so that they can build on it later. In the towns people also often invest in the purchase of a *taksi b-in-nafar* (a taxi that takes a particular route and where each passenger pays for his or her part of the journey) or a *kushk* (a wooden kiosk of the type found on the street corners everywhere, where cigarettes, soft drinks or food are usually sold). After his return the husband will be able to earn his living that way. In the countryside land is bought so as to be able to build onto one's property.

Husbands of wives in the middle and upper classes, unlike the husbands in the first group, do not regularly transfer money but save it up for their return. The situation here is that before the migration the household was financed by his earnings and that she was able to do what she liked with her earnings (if any). The migration reverses the roles and she becomes the breadwinner and he can do what he wants with his earnings. These women also have less say in the investment of money earned abroad. After his return it often proves difficult to pick up again and continue the traditional roles of the husband as breadwinner and the wife as a dependant.

The cultural consequences and influence of migration on gender roles

Egyptian girls are brought up to take on the jobs that need doing in the home. Within the marriage their most valuable role is that of mother. Motherhood is also the basis for (economic) security, power and status. Boys on the other hand are socialized by the roles of father and breadwinner. From childhood on girls are taught to take care of

their reputation so that they will be able to find a good marriage partner later on: they are not to transgress the norms of their sex and
must be subordinate to men. In the past twenty years the traditional
role of women has been emphasized even more strongly from fundamentalist quarters. But the absence of the husband for many years
means in practice that women take on the responsibilities that traditionally rest with men. Women from the lower classes in particular
become very assertive because they have to defend their family's
interests. For some women, like Huda, migration and staying behind
alone mean confusions and tension, which puts a strain on their
health. For others it means a change of self-image because they discover that they are quite able to take on responsibilities. In both cases
it will in due course mean a change in the relationship with the husband, the children, relations and acquaintances.[11]

Migration can also have other consequences for the lives of
women. In the oil states there is much stricter segregation and a much
stricter code of moral behaviour than in Egypt. Many men who
return to Egypt want to keep to the attitudes to women that hold sway
in the oil states, and require their wives to take on the veil, give up
their work outside the home and start to live a stricter "Islamic life".
In Egypt this is mockingly called "petro-Islam".

Hoodfar (1996a) has investigated whether migration has led to a
feminization of the Egyptian family or to a reinforcement of traditional female roles. Her findings are that although women are placed in
an unconventional situation through migration and have to function
as the head of the household, this has not led to structural changes.
The traditional ideology of marriage, in which the husband is the
breadwinner and the wife is the financially dependent spouse and
mother, has remained unchanged.

Reda' (and others): visit of the jinn

Huda, the woman in the previous account, is visited at night by *a jinn*
and she claims that this is the cause of her physical malaise. I have
also been told stories of *jinn* persuading a woman to leave her husband. This *jinn* would then be jealous that the woman is married to an

---

[11] Early 1993; Hoodfar 1996a/b; Korayem 1996; El-Messiri 1978; Wikan 1980,
1996.

"earthly" man. He then does all he can to cause arguments between the partners because he wants to marry the woman himself. Conversely there are also female *jinn* who want to marry the "earthly" husband.

Reda' is thirty-seven years old, and married with five children; the eldest is eighteen and the youngest twelve. She was not born in Cairo but comes from another large town in Egypt. She relates:

"I had been married for about a year and had in the meantime given birth to my first little girl, but was not yet pregnant with a second child. One day I was lying asleep and then I suddenly saw a very beautiful being, who asked me, 'Are you asleep?' I said yes, and he asked me to sit next to me. It was very strange. I was asleep, but I had the feeling that I wasn't asleep. It was more as if I was awake, or rather half awake and half asleep. This being who was talking to me was a really good-looking man and I just stared at him wide-eyed. I was amazed and wondered what was happening and who this person was. Suddenly this apparition touched me, and I couldn't say a word. When my husband came home and we went to bed to sleep, the being came again and said, 'Leave your husband. It's better if you don't sleep with him. Lie anywhere you like, but not next to him.' I asked him why I shouldn't do that, but all he said was, 'Don't do it.' I got up and my husband said, 'What are you doing, why are you getting up?' I told him I was too hot and wanted to lie somewhere else. So I went and sat outside. Then I saw the being come up to me again and sit down next to me. He talked to me, and said lovely things to me. We spent a long time chatting together. I wasn't afraid, but my hair did stand on end. The being told me, 'I'm not going to hurt you, but you mustn't sleep with him', and he pointed towards my husband. I felt completely in his power. If my husband said something to me, then the being blew into my ear (*widani bi-tsaffar wi bitwishwish*) so that I could not understand my husband's words. I'm really serious! I could constantly feel his breath in my ear and it was as if my body was lifted up by him. I kept having more and more arguments with my husband and he beat me because I didn't want anything to do with him. When my mother-in-law came, I told her everything. But she didn't believe me. My mother-in-law used to stay with me quite often and she used to sleep in the other room on the children's bed.

One time she felt that someone was smoking cigarettes in the room. She said nothing, but she felt that there was someone there. She could feel him breathing. When she went to the bathroom to wash she felt that someone was going with her. Once when my little girl was crying I saw the being pick her up, put a pillow under her head and put her down under the table. I saw that he was concerned, but still I got scared. I picked up my daughter and ran away. The being always came at night and he asked me why I was so afraid, and he said, "I heard your daughter crying and so I tried to console her."

"This being lived with me for a long, long time. He was a really good-looking man and I just couldn't forget his face and the way he looked. You can't imagine how kind he was. When he came he kept on talking to me and I kept listening. He didn't do anything bad. Everything he did was good. But he was jealous when I slept with my husband. Then he said, 'Don't go and lie next to your husband', and then he pinched me until I was black and blue all over. He was jealous because I had a husband. I showed the bruises to my mother-in-law and my mother and said to them, 'Look what he did. All these bruises are because I slept with my husband.' The reason for all this was that he wanted to be married to me himself. My husband didn't believe a word of it and said I was superstitious. It was only when his mother told him she had seen him too, and that he was really true, that he believed it! It was the strong love of a *ginni*. If a *ginni* falls in love with you, then he does everything for you and follows you everywhere! Naturally I didn't want to marry him. I wanted children and an ordinary husband. I didn't want to be married to someone who lives underground! This being was certainly not a *qarina* or an *ukht*. It was something else, it was a *ginni*. The *ukht* and the *qarina* don't do anything bad. For instance, if you go to the toilet, or you scream when you're giving birth, then the *ukht* says, 'No!' And if, for instance, you smack your child, then the *ukht* says, 'No!' If I cry at night or can't sleep, then she says, 'No!' *Qarina* and *ukht* from underground lead you to good things! But if you yourself do evil or bad things, it is only then that she does bad things too. If you do something bad to someone and they are against it "underground", then they punish you, otherwise they don't. This *ginni* lived with me in that house for five years, but I first saw him when I had been living there for two years. After that we moved. Right away from there! And then I never saw him again."

Interpretation

What "message" is being conveyed here? That wives do not enjoy being with their husbands? That the husband is not kind to his wife and, to the accompaniment of beatings, demands "his" rights, in a context in which it is a sin to refuse? Or is it more general, a fantasy of beauty, love, care in husband/wife relationships? In an Islamic society the husband has an inalienable right to sexual intercourse with his wife and can demand it of her. Romantic love is often not involved. Married couples show no affection for each other in public. In the tiny, cramped flats there is no room for privacy and the sex act has to happen quickly and clandestinely. Women do not reproach their husbands for demanding sex, because that is simply not in their line of thinking: after all, the Koran says that they are "the field of their husband" and they have internalized this. In direct opposition to this, however, is the general image among men that women cannot control themselves sexually. Close examination of the stories told me by women shows that there is no question of any lack of self-control. What I find in the stories of the amorous *jinn* is a yearning for love and tenderness. The *jinn* is always a good-looking man, who is kind and tender, comes and lies next to the woman and caresses her, and gets angry and aggressive if the husband beats his wife and demands sex. The topic of "*jinn* who want to marry earthly beings" is not new (see e.g. Leemhuis 1993). But Egyptian anthropologists and a number of psychiatrists I have talked with about my findings, say that the phenomenon of Christian *jinn* has become widespread only in the past six or seven years or so. These *jinn* primarily want sex with the women and incite them to perform "un-Islamic" acts.

Kadhra is twenty and works in a lawyer's office:
> "I have a Christian *jinn* living in me. He wants to marry me and says I must go out dancing and wear short skirts. He doesn't want me to pray and wear the veil."

Leila is thirty, married, but without children:
> "My *jinn* is a priest and he has been living in me for the past six years. When I go to bed, he comes and lies next to me. He

touches me and is really kind. He says that he wants to have children with me. He doesn't like me reading the Koran, but I do it
anyway."

Umm Mohammed is forty-five and has three children:

"I can't have sex with my husband and so he beat me and kicked
me. Once he grabbed me by the throat, and I wasn't able to
speak for a long time afterwards. The *jinn* who lives in me is
called Girgis (George) and he is very good-looking. The *sheikh*
told my husband that this is because of the *jinn* and now he
understands and doesn't hit me any more."

Women know that their sexuality is linked to the Koranic view that
the man is the guardian of the woman and they respect the sacred
words. Although discord shines through at a number of points in their
stories, they also confirmed several times that "this and that" is that
way because that's what it says in the Koran and because the husband is, after all, a man (*'alashan huwa ragil*).

In this chapter I have concentrated on the question of how *baladi*
women experience life in practice and how they bring their experiences to expression in symbols. I have written in a narrative style and
expressly chosen to put the "subject's" viewpoint in central place and
not to burden the reader with complex theories. The topics in the cases discussed remain close to the cultural question of possession and
healing, while the topics in the context are borrowed from social categories. Through this working method I have been able to supply a
large amount of cultural information. My interest is not in the analysis of individual situations but in setting out the main problems, difficulties and social impediments experienced by my conversation partners in successive stages in their lives. By making use of available
sociographic literature, at the same time I show the interaction
between the way things are done in practice and social structures and
I offer an insight into cultural programming of illness, body and belief
in demons. My verdict is that *baladi* women are not passive victims
but actively participating individuals who have their own view of reality and try to bring it to expression.

CHAPTER EIGHT

CONCLUDING OBSERVATIONS

In Egypt, biomedical health care forms but one possibility in a wide range for people confronted with health problems. Ethnomedical specialists are on hand in abundance and are extensively consulted both by the rural and the urban population. In this study I have concentrated on the question how people deal with mental and physical health problems caused, according to the cultural interpretation, by the invasion of *jinn/asyad* (demons), and in what ways healing is sought. My working method consists in giving a picture of two of the many healing practices occupied with the world of spirits — the *zar* ceremony and Koran healing — and to look into how these forms of traditional health care are viewed in particular by women from the economically lower classes.

Cairo is the location selected for the research, because alongside inhabitants born and bred in this city of millions, migrants from all parts of the country have taken up residence. It was thus possible to gain a picture of views shared not only by the indigenous Cairo population but also by people who have migrated to the metropolis from the country. The thought-forms and world of life that I describe are thus to be interpreted more broadly than simply within the context of a city such as Cairo. The same applies to the social classes in which the research was conducted. To be sure, views of supernatural causes of misfortune and sickness are stronger in the lower classes than in the higher, but experience has taught me that these ideas are not limited to one single social layer. A certain degree of fear of demons exists among all layers of the population.

I allow women to speak for themselves. I do this with the goal of giving the reader the knowledge needed to be able to enter into the world I describe. I do not claim that I "know" or "represent" these women in my ethnography: it simply means that they have let me have a glimpse into their lives. The stories they have told me have been selected, cut into pieces, edited as a text and supplied with a quantity of data from the literature and from my own observations, placed in the context of Egyptian society. I have endeavoured to give as accurate as possible an account and a discussion of their world of experience.

The social experiences with these women have been supplemented with conversations with *zar* leaders, Koran healers and others. The goal here was to investigate the content of demon possession. I studied the organizational structure of these "specialists", the hierarchy, education, background, prestige and remuneration. I looked into the roles of possessed and non-possessed persons: What people ask a healer for help and why? What illnesses are treated, what course does the treatment take and what are its effects? Finally I gave attention to possible tensions between local cultural ideals and real situations.

Participation and observation were supplemented with bibliographic research (Arab and western sources) into views about demons and education about Islam in Egypt. In addition I looked at historical connections between demon belief in other cultures, the pre-Islamic period, contemporary formal Islam and the local variety. I paid attention to the background of magicians, sorcerers, magic and prophetic medicine. This was constantly related to cultural-anthropological and sociological studies of possession and explanations of behaviour associated with it. My own experiences in relation to *zar* and Koran healing were compared with descriptions by Egyptian and western researchers.

The method

My premise for this study was to stay as close as possible to the world of experience of my participants. This explains the rather peripheral place of theoretical assessments and the great attention to the description and interpretation of communicative events. This meant in practice that I spent hundreds of hours with women in their homes, or sitting on the front doorstep while we drank very sweet tea and chatted about everything that was happening in the neighbourhood. I went to birth and wedding parties and I mourned when someone in the family died. I visited doctors and accompanied them to the *kudya* (*zar* leader) or *sheikh* (Koran healer). When they went to the *zar* ceremony or to sessions of Koran healing, I joined in with them in the dancing or prayers. Along the way I posed my questions, about all kinds of things, but not unsystematically, because these were oriented towards getting to know them and their world. Sometimes I recorded parts of the conversations with a small cassette-recorder. I sometimes used comments and imagery in order, by a roundabout route, to get people to "open up" and get that person to talk. All these stories form the basis of my account.

Asking questions and "living together" is the central aspect of ethnography. So it may appear to be a question of "being there". That is in fact the case, but "to have been there" is not enough: if participatory observation is to have any point, sufficient specificity has to be brought into play on the spot, in the existing situation. The ethnographer must have the right social skills and considerable facility in the local language. He or she must be creative and flexible and be able to adapt to sometimes strange, difficult or unhygienic circumstances. In all cases the ethnographer must be able to see things in perspective and constantly take due account of his or her own role in the foreign environment and of his or her own reactions to the whole thing.

Did all this work out well for me? No, sometimes it didn't, and sometimes it did. I experienced many moments of tiredness and loneliness and of doubt about whether I was going about things the right way, and whether there was any point to it all. Ethnography is an absolute social experience with "the other", who is a bosom-friend at times, but at other times is an alienating practitioner of incomprehensible practices and religious views.

After, or alongside the fieldwork experience comes the question of how to set all this down on paper. The data produced in the process are unique, but how is this to be translated for the reader? How to I turn my cultural knowledge into anthropological knowledge? I have asked myself this question (as so many anthropologists have done) time and time again. I believe that I have formed anthropological knowledge through "taking apart" my experiences and putting them together again in words in such a way that I share the "alien" world with the reader.

The subject

The women I write about encounter physical and/or psychological problems. According to the healers they consult these are caused by demons that have invaded their body. This is called "touching" or "clothing". The invasion of supernatural beings can occur through magic or the evil eye. It can also be the result of a condition of violent emotions or through supposed religious weakness in the person concerned. In order to regain good health the spirits must be pacified in a spiritual way or be driven out. This occurs in *zar* ceremonies or during Koran healing sessions.

The first healing practice that I describe is the *zar*, the aim of which is to pacify the demons. This happens in the course of extensive ceremonies that may last for several days. In most cases the leader of the ceremony says that her knowledge and skills are inherited. That is to say that the "secret sources" are a tradition handed down from generation to generation. She is the medium between the possessing spirit(s) and the sick person. The spirits are called *asyad*, "masters". They belong to particular dynasties and have their own ranks and stations. There are regional spirits, natural spirits, Coptic and other Christian, Jewish and Islamic spirits and sometimes spirits represent particular professional groups. It is important for the leader of the rituals to know all the spirits, to know how to deal with them and to be able to manipulate them. The ceremonies take place at the leader's home or the sick person's home. They are (almost) entirely concentrated on women and it is also primarily women that are responsible for the leadership and the organization. It is sometimes the case that men are leaders of *zar* groups, but in the main they are only musicians.

The *zar* leader is told by her own "master" what demon has entered the person concerned and she interprets the requirements the possessed person must meet. After this the grand ceremony begins with dancing and music. Each leader works with more or less fixed music groups. The music is very important because each spirit has its own melody, which is recognized by the possessed person as the "signal" from the demon to manifest itself. The music of the drums and the singing of the leader are loud and penetrating. The possessed person dances, goes into trance and "speaks" with her "master". The dancing is quite exhausting, but has a regenerating effect. The person concerned feels that she can once again cope with her life. The healing is always temporary, however, because she must keep on regularly attending the ceremonies of the cult group in order to humour the spirit, and at some point she will have to make another sacrifice.

The *zar* ceremony is regarded by many outsiders as something un-Islamic and reprehensible. The women are familiar with this criticism, but they keep it up. Not only on account of the healing effect, but also for the sake of a good time. They see themselves as good Muslims because alongside their attendance at the *zar* they do not neglect their religious duties.

A similarly controversial method of healing for possession is *'ilaj bil-qur'an* (Koran healing), which is carried out by persons who in common parlance are called *sheikh*. Most of them have become healers after a personal crisis or illness. In Koran healing there is no talk of "masters" but of *jinn*. These are the non-human beings that once were created by God out of fire, but which have a preference for underground and/or impure places. They may be unbelievers, Christians, Jews or Muslims, but almost always their aim is to bring people misfortune. Koran healers talk of "spiritual illnesses" that are caused by *jinn* and they use the Holy Book to drive these spirits out of the sick person's body once and for all, in *exorcism*. In certain Koran verses there is supposed to be a particular power and light familiar only to initiates. On account of a worthy life they have been given the gift by God to apply the "secret sources" in the diagnosis and healing of sicknesses. Koran healing takes place at a mosque, in "Islamic clinics" or privately at the healer's house or in a possessed person's home. The healers offer quite a range of services. Their "customers" are predominantly women.

Spiritual illnesses arise, the healers say, as a result of being entered by demons at a moment that the person is not oriented towards Allah, which has placed her (or him) in a state of unbelief. In most cases there is talk of it being the person's "own fault". This is in contrast to explanations in the *zar*, where the possessed person is never directly given the blame.

According to the local concept of humanity, women are specially prone to attracting the attentions of *jinn*, because they are weaker in reasoning than men and stronger in emotions. In addition, women are impure for a number of days of the month or after the birth of a child. In the state of impurity they are not allowed to pray and this too weakens their resistance to demons, which can then slip into their bodies through "openings". Further, it is generally supposed that women are weaker in the faith and are more easily misled.

Koran recitation is the instrument used by the *sheikh*. The reciting has to take place in accordance with special stipulations, in which rhythm, pitch and accentuation are very important. It sends patients into a state of trance and the *jinn* manifests himself. He is questioned by the healer and after that burned or exorcized. As in the *zar*, finally, the women are expected to adapt their lifestyle. They are encouraged to lead a more Islamic life, in which veiling, modesty and subordination to the husband apply.

It is also the case with Koran healers that not everyone agrees with their practices. They are accused of using the Holy Book to their own ends. Despite these reservations their number has sharply increased in recent years, both in urban and in rural areas. Often they have large numbers of patients and they are not afraid to ask considerable sums for their services.

Sequence

The results of my research have been set out as follows in this study: in Chapters 1 and 7 I tried to show what the content of the "women's world" looks like. Women assume a different social position from men. This is the product of relationships, experiences, sources of help, and so on. Gender plays a significant role in daily life. The accessibility of material and non-material sources is also important. Sometimes a rift develops between individual behaviour and what the culture prescribes. This gives rise to stress, which some people are better able to deal with than others. Some people are better able to handle themselves and to adapt to the expectations placed on them. To some extent this explains why one woman becomes "possessed" and another does not. It is certainly the case that possession is relatively more common among women than men. This has partly to do with the fact that the position of men, even if it is not very high in social terms, is still better than that of women in a comparable situation. It seems to me that it is impossible and inappropriate to give a general typification of *baladiyyat* (popular women). Each woman has her own view of things and her own circumstances. I show that these women have their own take on reality and deal in a creative way with sickness, adversity, problems and relationships.

In Chapter 2 I relate how the present-day world of experience in relation to demons is structured. I do this in order to give the reader some insight into the world of thought of the people I am writing about. As a result, the subjects treated after that can be more easily situated in the overarching cosmological structure. It will become clear to the reader that the notions and associated practices are certainly not as un-Islamic or exotic as is sometimes supposed.

In Chapter 3 I have set out a theoretical framework. I discuss successively a number of generally anthropological theoretical approaches of research into possession and comment on a number of studies that have been conducted in Islamic Sudan and in Egypt. My aim in this is to indicate the routes I take to arriving at statements that can be made about the rituals in the healing practices I have studied and the theoretical support I have sought in ordering my insights and perceptions. I give an account of the way in which I make use of the ideas of Van Binsbergen (1981), Devisch (1993) and Turner (1967. 1969, 1974) in my ethnography.

In Chapters 4 and 5 I describe in detail the *zar* and Koran healing rituals and give an account of how *zar* leaders, Koran healers and possessed persons deal with possession and healing.

In the *zar* the leader comes into interaction with the demon masters and she has to know their "language" (the music) and their characteristics in order to be able to manipulate them. Koran healers condemn this and say that consorting with demons means taking the "not-permitted path". In my opinion these apparently fundamentalistic Koran healers in fact do the same thing, though in a different way, because they too acknowledge the power of the *jinn* and move into interaction with them.

In support of their claim that they are truly Islamic, most Koran healers avoid applying any other means than God's word, the Koran. I discovered that the modern commercially oriented Koran healers maintain a mishmash of orthodox and popular notions about demons and related practices in order to attract and impress their patients. They have their own interpretation of the Koran verses and in particular their own interpretation of the *jinn* and the mischief that they can create. But because they are men (and in this society men presume to have a monopoly on religion) and because in everything they do they refer to the Koran and legitimate their practices by it, they lay themselves open to less criticism than the *zar* leaders. In order to analyze the rituals in the two healing methods, I use Turner's concepts. I do not, like him, believe that the possibility of structural change arises for the participants in the course of the performance of the rituals. In both healing methods efforts are not directed towards this goal but to the maintenance of the status quo.

In Chapter 6 it becomes clear why women are thought to be more accessible than men to demons. The connection between possession and the various notions of vulnerability through body openings, space-time dimensions, a nasty shock and emotion is clear after analysis of the relationship between the possessed person, body, cosmos and society. Development of this using subcultural understandings of feminine characteristics offers the possibility not only to unravel women's views but also those of men. In the same chapter I look into ritual drama. Here I come to the insight that *zar* and Koran healing do not differ from each other as much as is assumed by some people in Egyptian society. Both practices use cultural traditions and values through which, each in their own way, bear a specific significance. The basic principle is common to both healing methods: trance, catharsis, abreaction and reversal of evil.

Most researchers I have discussed in the anthropological theoretical part of this study place too much emphasis, in my view, on one or more "instrumental" aspects of possession behaviour. I acknowledge that possession can be a means for certain people to express their personal unhappiness, to work it through and open it up for discussion, or to shift blame beyond one's own person or group. But there is more than that, namely the meaningful experience that the rituals have for the participants. The music and dance in the *zar* ritual and the symbolic power of The Word in the recitation in Koran healing allow the possessed person to transcend physical, cosmological and social boundaries. The sick person merges with the demon in the creative acting out of the ritual drama, in which memories and experiences are brought to expression. The intense experience of this process leads to a renewed ordering and empowering connection with the living environment. The "therapeutic" group (the group of supporters) offers a safe space for self-healing for this to take place.

I conclude Chapter 6 with a treatment of *zar* and Koran healing in relation to sufi brotherhoods and their healing methods. In my view the *zar* should be viewed separately from the sufi ritual, the *dhikr*. The two ceremonies have different backgrounds and histories and are carried out with a variety of motives. Koran healers in general have no connection with the mystical sufi orders. Most Koran healers have an understanding of demons that does not fully coincide in fact with that of fundamentalists. Nonetheless, I believe that this healing method may possibly be used as an answer to the "odious" *zar* and as a way of "re-Islamicizing" women (i.e. teaching them a fundamentalistic attitude to life). The emphasis on a purely Islamic lifestyle and accusations in the direction of the Copts suggesting that Christian demons keep Muslim women from their (religious) duties, are very commonly expressed.

Demons and possession in Egypt (but also in many other Islamic countries) are a cultural legitimated means of explaining sickness and of shifting blame to factors outside one's own group. The daily cares cannot always be easily solved and the search for a "cultural explanation" occurs in order to smooth over the discrepancy between what actually occurs and what one would prefer to happen. This strategy is not some weak defence but a dynamic option that is produced by a rich and energetic culture.

CONCISE MANUAL FOR THE USE OF THE HOLY KORAN AGAINST MAGIC AND SORCERY

In the course of my fieldwork I talked with various *sheikhs* and healers and "Koran experts" about *jinn*, sorcery, "possession" and "touching" and the physical and mental disorders that can come from them. The average Koran healer's "repertoire" is rather more extensive than I have been able to indicate in this study. This appendix is intended as a supplement to this. It is a summary of what Koran healers have told me about illnesses caused by *jinn* and contains data brought together from various books that deal with this subject. The conversations with the healers were conducted in Egyptian Arabic. The compilation (see bibliography) was translated from standard Arabic. For the Koran texts I made use of the English translation by M.H. Shakir.

Jinn, the devil and sorcerers

Jinn is a name applicable to all sorts of demons. The father of all the devils is *Iblis*. This word derives from *iflis*, which means bankruptcy and failure. Iblis was once obedient to God and did good deeds, but he became proud and thought that he no longer needed to be obedient to God; he went "bankrupt", as it were, in his good deeds and as punishment he was turned into a devil (sura *al-Kahf* [18]: 50). All devils belong to the family of Iblis. Devils are bad and so are their deeds; their work is to lead people astray and tempt them, making them commit sins and become disobedient to God. God has described in the Koran the eternal enmity between Iblis and his descendants and Adam and his descendants (sura *Ta-Ha* [20]: 117). Not only was this enmity confirmed by Iblis, but he also indicated from which directions he would come to lead people astray. In sura *al-A'raf* [7]: 1 four directions are indicated for this: right, left, in front and behind. He will not come from above, because only God comes from above; he will not come from below, because that place is only for slaves. The *jinn* were created before humans and they are known to have special abilities which humans do not have. They were created out of fire, can assume various forms and are quicker than the wind. But God has also charged them with certain limitations, which they transgress on pain of immediate death. If God were to let the *jinn* have their way, and specially the great *jinn* called the *Marid/Marada* of the devils (a special sort of recalcitrant *jinn* or bad spirits), then they would annihilate the human race. God is the only ruler of the universe and he has created everything and everyone. This means that the *jinn* can do nothing without his permission.

There are various sorts of *jinn*: unbelieving *jinn*, good, bad, corrupt and Muslim *jinn*. The devil is always an unbelieving *jinn*. This is confirmed both by the Koran and by the *jinn* themselves in sura *al-Jinn* (72): 11, 14: "Some of us are good and others of us are below that, and some of us are those who submit, and some of us are the deviators; so whoever submits, these aim at the right way" (i.e. if they become Muslim).

Each person has a *jinn*, even the Prophet, who said, *"ma min ahad illa wa lahu shaytan* (everyone has a *shaytan*) *wa li shaytan* (and I have a *shaytan*)"*. The *jinn* of the Prophet was Muslim, however.

The difference between angels and jinn

There are three worlds: that of the *jinn*, that of the angels and that of humans. They can only move in each other's worlds with the permission of Allah. Angels are made of light and everything they do is good. *Jinn*/devils are made of fire and everything they do is bad. Angels and devils possess the ability to change shape. Angels only take on the shape of good things such as birds. *Jinn* on the other hand take on the form of low beings, such as dogs, cats, snakes, and so on. This occurs in particular if they have to help in sorcery and magic. The sorcerer uses the services of a servant-*jinn*, whom he commissions to do something bad, or to cause problems between a man and his wife, a father and his son, a man and his brother. The *jinn* assumes the form of a cat, for instance, and does what he is told to do. Angels are a sort of heavenly soldiers. Some angels are chosen by God to be prophets or to do good deeds (sura *al-Hajj* [22]: 75). They are never disobedient to God.

Jinn have no knowledge of hidden things

The Koran rejects the idea that *jinn* are able to predict the future or have knowledge of hidden things. Sura *Saba'* 34:14 has to do with the death of Solomon. The *jinn* were subordinate to him. Together with the winds and the birds they had to help him and follow his orders. Solomon gave the *jinn* the task of digging a number of seas, and leaning on his stick, he watched. They worked hard to please him and out of fear for his anger and his punishment. The *jinn* were astonished when they discovered that when the worms had entirely eaten up Solomon's stick and he fell on the ground, he had been dead for a year. They had not noticed the fact that he had died and that was embarrassing to them because they claimed to know about everything. So it turns out that *jinn* do not know hidden things and cannot determine fate, nor do they dispose of life, death or resurrection. Only Allah knows hidden things.

Different sorts of jinn

Sura *al-Rahman* 55: 14 and 15 tells us that *jinn* were created out of fire and humans out of clay. From the order given in the Koran, we may deduce that humans are superior to *jinn* (sura *al-Hijr* 15: 26), but that the *jinn* are older than humans because they were created earlier (sura *al-Hijr* 15: 27): "And the jinn We created before, of intensely hot fire."

The attributes of the *jinn* are stronger than those of humans, but there are limits: Allah maintains control over them because otherwise they would annihilate mankind: Allah holds the whole thing in balance. Sorcerers can make use of the *jinn* to their own ends. For the performance of magic specifically the bad *jinn* are applied, who are *kafir* (unbelieving), *fasiq* (sinful) and *mushrik* (polytheistic), the same qualities that the sorcerer himself has too.

Names and attributes of jinn and the places they are found

The general name is *jinn* (*ginni*), but a *jinn* that always lives in people's houses is called *amir* (prince/leader). In the presence of small children *jinn* are often called *arwah* (winds/spirits). If the *jinn* is a bad spirit he is called *shaytan* and if he is very nasty to humans he is called *'ifrit*. The *jinn* prefer to stay in the bathroom, toilet, rubbish heaps and in other impure places, such as cemeteries and out-of-the-way, dilapidated and empty houses. They are also found in markets and amusement places. The sorcerer goes to these ungodly places in order to meet the *jinn* and to make agreements with them about their collaboration. It is important that an "empty house" need not necessarily be "empty of people". A place is also "empty" if God's name is not mentioned there (*dhikr* Allah) and no one prays there. So anyone entering one of the above-mentioned places must first say *bismillah* before entering it, because then it is no longer "empty of God". Through recitation of the Koran the *jinn* can be driven out and protection can be obtained (sura *al-Mu'minun* 23: 97-98), but only Allah can destroy the *jinn*. So healers who claim to burn the *jinn* do not do so themselves — it comes about by means of the light of the Koran, which burns them.

Sorcerers and sorcery

Sorcery came into being when the angels Harut and Marut came down from heaven to Babylon and the devils performed magic throughout the kingdom of Solomon. The Koran notes in sura *al-Baqara* (2): 102: "And they followed what the Shaitans chanted of sorcery in the reign of Sulaiman [Solomon], and Sulaiman was not an unbeliever, but the Shaitans disbelieved, they taught men sorcery and that was sent down to the two angels at Babel, Harut and Marut". Solomon and the two angels were thus the first to use sorcery (contemporary Koran healers always appeal to Solomon if anyone expresses doubts about the existence of sorcery).

The word *sihr* (sorcery) is an abbreviation of "*sirr haram*" (forbidden secret), the healers say, and it is so called because of the following fact: whenever the sorcerer carries out his work in secret, he can hide his acts from human eyes, but not from God. Sorcery is forbidden (*haram*) because by performing it one is disobedient to the Creator. It is a sin worse than murder and the second of the seven mortal sins mentioned by the Prophet, which must be avoided:

1. Giving God a companion
2. practising sorcery
3. committing suicide
4. using an orphan's money
5. practising usury

6. avoiding the day of war

7. slandering faithful women

Sins that are absolutely unforgivable are: Giving God a companion
and causing someone harm. And this is precisely what is at issue in
sorcery: power is given to the devil and a person harms his fellow
human being.

The devil and the sorcerer

All sorcery is a cooperation between the devilish human (the sorcerer)
and the devilish *jinn* (the sorcerer's servant-*jinn*). In working his magic
the sorcerer calls in the help of the *jinn* (sura *al-Jinn* [72]: 6), which can
be in the form to which they agree. The servant-*jinn* in turn often uses
the *qarin* of a certain person (the fixed demon that belongs with each
person) to carry out the tasks required by the sorcerer. *Jinn* not only
differ in religion (Muslim, Christian, Jewish), but also belong to different hierarchically organized groups with their own leaders (*muluk*). A
good sorcerer knows which *jinn* he is working with, but if he makes a
mistake, it can happen that *jinn* belonging to different groups conflict
with each other, which will unavoidably lead to the death of the
"patient". Sorcery is the result of a relationship between the devilish
person and his pact-partner the devilish *jinn*, but usually such a relationship does not exist. It is the sorcerer who makes such a pact. He is
the human devil par excellence, who is assisted by *the* Devil. The sorcerer who wants to use the devilish *jinn* first sets up a contract with
him concerning the conditions, such as: the *jinn* will not deceive him,
will not divulge his secrets to another and will not disregard his
orders. The sorcerer in turn fasts for a certain time to please the devil
and after that sacrifices to the devil and in the name of the devil. This
is absolutely forbidden, since fasting and sacrifice can only occur in
the name of God.

That the sorcerer has a devilish disposition is also evident from the
fact that he writes Koran verses in an impure way, i.e. he writes the
Fatiha (the opening sura) back to front, writes with menstrual blood or
with the blood of birds indicated by the *jinn* and sacrificed. In addition
he always has a ritually impure body and impure clothing which he
wears inside out, he tears pages out of the Koran which he puts in his
sandals and wears them to go into the toilet and he washes his genitals
with milk and touches the Koran afterwards. The devil incites the

sorcerer to commit lewd acts, after which he must write these amulets and talismans with the sperm from his acts.

The sorcerer and the *jinn* meet in secret places where they go with strange means of transport. The sorcerer is an unbeliever and sorcery is a deed of unbelief. Anyone who tries to learn sorcery and who enters into a pact with the devil is a polytheist. Whoever stays with the Highest Truth will have all his sins forgiven, except for polytheism and doing harm to fellow human beings.

Guidelines for healing of magic/sorcery

There are various "prescriptions" for the many afflictions caused by the pact between the devilish person and his partner the devilish *jinn*, consisting of a combination of *ruqyas*, which may be recited by the healer or applied as "do-it-yourself" medicine.

1. *Sihr al-marad* — *sorcery that produces illness*

This sort of magic is suspected whenever there are pains in one of the organs (especially vague pains in the arms or legs) without there being any question of pathological irregularities, of partial or complete paralysis, headaches, the non-functioning of one of the senses, such as feeling, smelling, hearing, or ringing in the ears and bleedings. Treatment: recitation of the *al-Shifa'* verses (Koran verses that speak about healing), namely sura *al-Tawba* (9): 14, *al-Shu'ara* (26): 80, *al-Nahl* (16): 69, *Yunus* (10): 57, *Fussilat* (41): 44 and *al-Isra'* (17): 82. In addition, the bewitched person must for seven days, morning and evening, drink water over which the Koran verses *al-Falaq* (113) and *al-Nas* (114) and verse 102 of *al-Baqara* (2) have been pronounced, and wash with the rest. If the person concerned has been bewitched as a result of something he has drunk, he will have stomach-ache for seven days. If the spell has not been lifted after seven days, he must listen to a cassette-tape recording of *Ayat al-Kursi* (*al-Baqara* [2]: 255) three times a day for one month. After that he performs a test to see if the spell is broken. If that is not the case, then he must listen to a recording of the suras *al-Saffat* (37), *Yunus* (10), *al-Dukhan* (44) and *al-Jinn* (72) three times a day for three weeks. He can also record the *Ayat al-Kursi* and sura *al-Saffat* seventy times and listen to them three times a day. After this the healer will recite *al-Fatiha* (1), *al-Falaq* (113) and *al-Nas* (114) and then

recite seven times: "And We reveal of the Quran that which is a healing and a mercy to the believers" (sura *al-Isra'* [17]: 82). After that the
healer must say seven times, "In the name of Allah, I read this formula for you that Allah might heal you of all sicknesses and protect you
against all spirits and the evil eye; in truth Allah heals you". After this
the patient must say seven times, "Allah, Lord of the world, release
me from pain, heal me because Thou art the Healer, no healing is
better than Thy healing". Depending on the condition of the patient,
this prayer must be said for a period of forty days or more.

Other options are:
- The sick person must say seven times *al-Fatiha* (1) and *Ayat al-Kursi*
  (2): 255 and *al-Falaq* (113) and *al-Nas* (114), and say, "The Koran
  brings healing and blessing for the faithful."
- Write the six verses of *al-Shifa'* on a bowl, fill it with water and
  drink from it three times.
- For headache the healer must read *Ayat al-Kursi* (2): 255, *al-Ikhlas*
  (112) and *al-Falaq* (113) and *al-Nas* (114) seven times over the head
  of the patient. It is also possible to recite these suras over nutmeg
  oil or olive oil and massage the patient with it.
- For loss of one of the senses the following suras must be recorded
  on a cassette-tape: seven times *al-Fatiha* (1), seven times *Ayat al-Kursi*
  (2): 255, seven times *al-Falaq* (113) and *al-Nas* (114), once *al-Jinn*
  (72) and once *al-Dukhan* (44). The sick person must listen to this
  tape three times a day while calling upon God and asking him for
  support. In addition he must say one hundred times, "There is no
  power nor might except with Allah" and one hundred times, "God
  is forgiveness and He is the Faithful One". All this must be done
  before the morning prayers, at which point "There is no God but
  God" must be said, and one hundred times "He disposes of life and
  death and he has power over everything". Massage with poppy-
  seed oil over which the suras mentioned have been pronounced is
  also excellent.
- In cases of sickness through anxiety, one writes the *al-Shifa'* verses
  with saffron on a piece of paper held over a bowl of water, after
  which one adds some bee's honey and has the patient drink this on
  an empty stomach for three days.
- Women's bleedings which are not menstrual (*sihr al-tanzif*) are
  caused by the sorcerer who has instructed his servant-*jinn* to enter
  the woman's body through the veins. The recommended treatment

is to recite the *ruqya* three times, also recommended in the case of "*sihr al-tafriq*" (divorce sorcery; see below). She must also drink boiled *hummus* (chickpeas) with gum arabic and *baladi* (peasant) butter. The recipe is: 1 gram of gum arabic plus 1 cup of mashed chickpeas; cook together, place in a bowl and add a spoonful of *baladi* (peasant) butter; to be drunk from morning and evening.

2. *Rabt in a man (magic which causes impotence and problems in sexual intercourse)*

Rabt is the worst sort of magic, because it aims to derail marriages. Since it goes together with symptoms of "touching" by *jinn* he cannot be alleviated by medicine. The *jinn* causes *rabt* in a man on account of the fact that he himself is in love with the man's wife. He therefore inhibits the man's ability to have sexual intercourse with her. In this situation the wife must follow the programme of treatment applicable to "touching by *jinn*". In order to heal *rabt* completely the best thing is to treat both marriage partners at the same time. There are three causes for the man being unable to have sexual intercourse with his wife: because he has an incomplete erection, no erection at all, or has a premature orgasm. All three cases do not have a physical cause but arise by the devil bewitching that part of the man's brain that is responsible for sexual excitement and sends signals to the sex organs. The devil prevents the sending of the signals, which means that no or insufficient blood is pumped to the penis and an erection is made problematic.

For *rabt* in a woman there are five causes: she involuntarily closes her legs together, so that the husband cannot penetrate; the *jinn* bewitches her and manipulates the nerves in the brain that are responsible for sexual excitement during the sex act (it is as if her body is under the influence of drugs, so that she does not become moist, making penetration difficult and causing the act to fail); she suffers from bleeding during the sex act (this differs from bleeding caused by magic as noted above); there are obstructions preventing the husband from having intercourse with her; the husband is unable to find his wife's vagina.

In the treatment of *al-marbut* (the "one bound" by *rabt*) there is a choice from the following options:
– Take seven green leaves from the honey-locust and pound them

fine; add water and pound until the whole is mixed together. *Ayat al-Kursi* (2): 255 must be recited over the bowl containing the mixture and after that the last verse of sura *al-Baqara* (2). Take care that the amount of water is sufficient to drink from it and to wash with it three times.

– Take a [ritually] cleaned dish and write in it with saffron sura *la-Baqara* (2); swill it around and wash the body of the "bound" person with that water, saying "in the name of Allah".

– Leave chickpeas (*hummus*) to soak in water for three nights, then write sura *al-Ikhlas* (112) seven times and sura *al-Qadr* (97) twenty-five times. Put this together in a clean dish and mix it with water from the *hummus*: drink it and wash the body with it, saying, "in the name of Allah".

– Write on the left and the right thigh bone, on the forehead and on the back of the "bound" persons, "There is no God but God and Mohammed is his messenger" and from sura *al-An'am* (6): "And with Him are the keys of the unseen treasures — none knows them but He; and He knows what is in the land and the sea, and there falls not a leaf but He knows it, nor a grain in the darkness of the earth, nor anything green nor dry but (it is all) in a clear book."

– Write the same verse with saffron on the inside of a dish and then fill it with water, saying at the same time: "in the name of Allah; from Allah to Allah; nothing is greater than Allah; there is no power nor might but with Allah; He is the Just One". Recite this seven times over the dish of water and then give it to the "bound" person to drink, and to wash from it.

– Before going to bed the ritual washing must be performed (*al-wudu*). After that the *Ayat al-Kursi* (2): 255 and the suras *al-Ikhlas* (112), *al-Falaq* (113) and *al-Nas* (114) must be read. After that spit into the palms of the hands and rub three times over the whole body.

– The *Ayat al-Kursi* (2): 255 is recorded on a cassette-tape and suras *al-Ikhlas* (112), *al-Falaq* (113) and *al-Nas* (114), and these are listened to once a day. One can also read this *ruqya* over water, from which one drinks once a day and washes every three days. After morning prayers one also says one hundred times, "There is no God but God, He is the only God and there is none like Him."

In all the remedies mentioned above the treatment is maintained for a month, until the symptoms of *rabt* have disappeared.

3. *Sorcery that causes apathy*

Record the following suras on three cassette-tapes: *al-Fatiha* (1), *al-Baqara* (2), *al-'Imran* (3), *Yasin* (36), *al-Saffat* (37), *al-Dukhan* (44), *al-Dhariyat* (51), *al-Hashr* (59), *al-Ma'arij* (70), *al-Ghashiya* (88), *al-Zalzala* (99), *al-Qari'a* (101) and *al-Mu'awwidhatan* (113, 144). The afflicted person must listen to the first cassette in the morning, the second in the afternoon, and the third 45 minutes before bedtime. In addition the affected person must drink water over which the special *ruqyas* against sorcery have been pronounced.

4. *Sorcery that makes one hear voices*

Symptoms of this sort of magic include suspicion and doubt about friends and loved ones. This can take on such proportions that it leads to madness. The affected person can choose from the following treatments:

- He must perform the ritual cleansing (*al-wudu'*) and read *Ayat al-Kursi* (2): 255 and *al-Mu'awwidhatan* (113, 144) before going to bed. He must also spit into the palms of his hands and then rub them three times over his whole body.
- Before going to sleep the suras *al-Saffat* (37) and *al-Dukhan* (44) must be read or listened to, sura *al-Baqara* (2) must be read or listened to three days in a row, in the evenings and mornings the following prayer must be said seven times: "God is my protector, He is the only God, He is the Lord of the High Throne."
- The last two verses of sura *al-Baqara* must be read before going to bed.
- Before going to bed pray: "In the name of Allah, I lay myself beside him (to sleep), forgive me my sins, destroy my devil, set me free and bless me with Thy mercy." Also listen to a cassette recording of suras *Fussilat* (41), *al-Fath* (48) and *al-Jinn* (72) three times a day for a month.

5. *Sara' (epilepsy and forms of it)*

Epilepsy can have a spiritual or a physical cause and can arise through the influence of bad, low spirits (*al-arwah al-ardiyya al-khabitha*) or through certain gases in the stomach which go to the central nervous system and through a deficiency in the oxygen-circulation in the blood which means that the central nervous system in the brain is not sufficiently supplied. For the first of these causes the best medicine is the expulsion of the bad *jinn* by calling upon Allah and constant recitation of the Koran (the high spirit Allah conquers the bad spirit the *jinn*). For the second cause mentioned one has to go to a (medical) doctor. For protection in general from *sara'* the best thing is praying, reciting the Koran and trusting in God. It is also recommended to record the following suras on a cassette-tape: seven times *Ayat al-Kursi* (2): 255; seven times sura *al-Falaq* (113) and *al-Nas* (114); once sura *al-Jinn* (72), once sura *al-Dukhan* (44) and listen to it three times a day, calling upon God and asking for His support.

6. Sihr al-Tafriq or "labs" (sorcery of divorce or "clothing")

This sort of sorcery is noticeable if someone suddenly feels an aversion to someone which leads to their separation: father and son, brother and sister, husband and wife. An example of this is the situation in which a wife suddenly is revolted by her husband and thinks that he is extremely ugly. It is also possible to feeling a sudden revulsion for the place in which one lives. *Tafriq* is thus a matter of sudden changes of love into hate, sudden big fights about nothing, or of no longer being able to be forgiving. All this is caused by the magic of a sorcerer who has used the special devilish servant-*jinn*. The constant calling upon God (*dhikr Allah*) offers special protection against this and it makes the *jinn* disappear. The reciting of the following suras above the head and in the ears of the afflicted person is important. Keep to the correct sequence and say after each sura: "I seek my refuge in Allah from the cursed devil": sura *al-Kursi* (2): 255; *al-Baqara* (2): 5, 102, 164, 255, 275, 276; *al-'Imran* (3): 17-19; *al-A'raf* (7): 44-46, 117, 122; *Yunus* (10): 71-72; *Ta-Ha* (20): 69; *al-Mu'minun* (23): 115, 117; *al-Saffat* (37): 1-10; *al-Ahqaf* (46): 29, 32; *al-Rahman* (55): 33, 32; *al-Hashr* (59): 21, 24; *al-Ikhlas* (112); in its entirely, *al-Jinn* (72): 1-9.

The *sheikh*/healer who helps the affected person must protect himself with the Koran, saying, "There is no God but God", and reciting *Ayat al-Kursi* (2): 255 seven times. If the *jinn* speaks through the lips of the affected person, a verse must be recited seven times from: *al-Baqara* (20), *al-'Imran* (3) and *al-Jinn* (72) and after that the *jinn* must be asked: What is your name, what is your religion, from which country are you, what do you want of this sick person?

If the *jinn* proves not to be a Muslim, ask him to convert. If he is a

Muslim explain to him that what he is doing is against the religion, that he is allowing himself to be used as a servant by the sorcerer, and that he must leave the body of the affected person. In addition, ask him if he is alone and if he has assistants. If he has assistants, ask him to bring them with him and ask them the same questions. During the treatment with *ruqya* the patient will feel a powerful headache, shake violently or become dizzy. If the *jinn* will not leave the body, then be patient and friendly towards him. However, if he stands by his refusal, then Ibn al-Qayyim (14th-century physician and Koran scholar) recommends that he be beaten out of the sick person's body, more Koran verses being recited afterwards. If the sick person begins to shake or become dizzy, this is a good sign. If he falls, this is the sign that the *jinn* is in him. If he does not fall down, then do the *ruqya* another three times and ask the same questions again and recite more Koran verses. It is also a good thing to record suras *al-Saffat* (37), *Yunus* (10), *al-Dukhan* (44) and *al-Jinn* (72) on a cassette-tape and have the sick person listen to it three times a day for three weeks, and "if Allah wills" he/she will be healed. If the patient does not feel anything during the *ruqya* it is possible that no magic has been performed on him, but that he still has the same problems or symptoms as someone to whom that has indeed happened. In that case the best thing is to repeat the *ruqya*. If he does not yet feel anything after that, then record suras *Yunus* (10), *al-Dukhan* (44) and *al-Jinn* (72) on a cassette-tape and have the sick person listen to it three times a day for a month. In addition he must say three hundred times, "I seek my refuge in God", and three hundred times, "There is no power nor might but with God". He or she must also ritually wash before going to bed (*wudu'*), read the *Ayat al-Kursi* (2): 255 and say *bismillah* before everything he or she does (*tasmiya*).

7. Sihr al-mahabba (love sorcery)

The symptoms of love sorcery include an exaggerated feeling of love and affection, or a desire for a great deal of sexual intercourse, abandoning oneself blindly to it. This sort of magic is used by one of the two marriage partners, for instance if the bride is very beautiful, very rich and more important than the groom, who is poor. Because he has no control over her as a result, he has magic performed, which makes the woman look at him only and want him only (the reverse can also apply). The same sort of magic can be done without people being married. For instance, when a man wants to marry a woman who is already promised to someone else, he has the magic done so that she will not marry the groom to whom she is "promised".

A choice can be made from the following treatments:
- Read and recite seven times the Koran verses mentioned above for *sihr al-tafriq* except for verse 102 of *al-Baqara* (2), replacing this with sura *al-Taghabun* (64): 14, 115 and 166.
- If the person in question has no feeling in his limbs, has a headache, pain in the chest which makes him feel he is suffocating, or violent stomach-ache, the following verses must also be recited above water and be given him to drink: *Yunus* (10): 81, 82 and *al-A'raf* (7): 117, 118, 119-122. If afterwards he spews up something yellow, red or black, the magic will be over; if this does not happen, do the above again over water and have him drink it three days in a row.
- Recite suras *Ta-Ha* (20): 69; *Ayat al-Kursi* (2): 255 and *al-Baqara* (2): 255 seven times over a bowl of water, and then the affected person drinks it three days in a row on an empty stomach.
- Read the *ruqya* which is especially intended for sorcery, but instead of verse 102 of sura *al-Baqara* (2), verses 14, 15 and 16 of sura *al-Taghabun* (64) must be read. The affected person feels pain in the stomach, a heavy feeling in his limbs, headache and depression. If he has drunk something over which a magic formula has been pronounced, he may also be nauseous. Suras *al-Falaq* (113) and *al-Nas* (114) plus *Ayat al-Kursi* (2): 255 must then be recited for him seven times over water, after which he is to drink it. If the affected person then spews up something yellow, red or black, the sorcery is broken. If this does not happen, he must continue for three weeks with drinking this water, accompanying this by reading verses 81 and 82 of *Yunus* (10), verses 117 to 122 of *al-A'raf* (7) and verse 69 of *Ta-Ha* (20).

Naturally the person who has had the magic performed must absolutely not know that these counter-measures have been taken. In addition, the healer must protect himself by constant recitation of the Koran and calling upon Allah.

8. *Takhyil (hallucinations/delusions)*

As a result of this sort of magic the affected person sees stationary objects move or moving objects stand still; large objects become small or small objects become large; ugly things become beautiful and beautiful things ugly, and so on. In short, everything looks different from reality. The therapy aims at the expulsion of the devil, through the summons to prayer, the requesting of God's help, the reading of *Ayat al-Kursi*, the reading of the Koran, naming God and praising Him by saying *Subhana Allah* (*dikhr* and *tasbih*), saying *bismillahs* (*al-tas-miya*) and ritual cleansing (*at-tasallah bil-wudu'*). The naming of God's name gives rest to the heart.

9. *Taraf min al-junun (someone who is affected by the jinn which gives him a form of madness, a "screw loose")*

This comes from jealousy and envy (*hasad*). The sorcerer uses the ser-vant-*jinn* to make the affected person lose his mind, so that for instance he can no longer concentrate, hesitates, loses his orientation, can no longer make decisions and can no longer regulate his affairs. Furthermore, he is suspicious about everything, afraid of the people around him, and he believes that the people he normally loves are his enemies. He also displays an inclination to tear his clothes. This sort of magic is performed by "writing" on the head of a snake or fish: in such a case the affected person also suffers from disturbed sleep. The *jinn* that help with this sort of magic are unbelieving *jinn* (*kafir*) and this is the worst sort of magic, because it is "black magic": the person who "has the writing done" has no trace of good in his heart.

Treatment by means of the following *ruqyas* is very effective:

– For one month, twice a day (can be extended to three months or longer), the affected person must listen to a cassette-tape with suras *al-Baqara* (2), *Hud* (11), *al-Hijr* (15), *al-Saffat* (37), *al-Rahman* (55), *al-Mulk* (67), *al-Jinn* (71), *al-A'la* (87), *al-Zalzala* (99), *al-Humaza* (104) and *al-Mu'awwidhatan* (113, 114). The affected person must also drink the water over which these *ruqyas* have been read.

– Write the *Ayat al-Shifa'* with saffron on a clean dish, fill it with water and have the patient drink from it three times while simultaneously seven pious sayings are pronounced, concluding with a *bismillah*.

– Fill a dish with water and write on it with saffron the *Ayat al-Kursi* (2): 255 and seven times sura *al-Falaq* (113) and *al-Nas* (114). Say

Allahu Akbar in the patient's ear and have him drink from the water
and wash with it for three days. The patient must also pray each
day and recite *Ayat al-Kursi* (2): 255, sura *al-Ikhlas* (112) and suras *al-Falaq* (113) and *al-Nas* (114) three times a day.

The person affected by *taraf min al-junun* must furthermore write down
seven Koran verses and carry them with him. In addition, it is possible to record the following suras on a cassette-tape to which the
affected person listens three times a day: four verses from the beginning and three from the end of *al-Baqara* (2), *Ayat al-Kursi* (2): 255,
ten verses from the beginning of *al-Saffat* (37), *al-Jinn* (72), *al-Zalzala* (99),
al-Falaq (113) and *al-Nas* (114). These verses can also be recited over a
bowl of water, after which the patient drinks from it and washes him-
self/herself from it while saying, "if Allah wills".

10. *Sihr ta'til al-jawaz (prevention of the marriage)*

Someone asks a sorcerer to arrange for "such-and-such a girl",
"daughter of so-and-so", not to marry. It is predominantly unbelievers and jealous people who ask for this sort of magic to be "written".
The sorcerer asks for the girl's name and that of her mother, or the
father's and his mother's. The sorcerer uses his servant-*jinn* for this
sort of magic. He enters the woman's body and arranges for her to
develop an abhorrence of marriage and to refuse any proposal of
marriage (the reverse is also possible, i.e. in relation to a man). Treatment: read three times the *ruqya* that is used for *sihr al-tafriq* (divorce),
and record on a cassette-tape: *Ayat al-Kursi* (2): 255, the first verses of
al-Saffat (37), *al-Jinn* (72) and sura *al-Falaq* (113) and *al-Nas* (114). The
patient must listen to this three times a day. It is also possible to learn
by heart the verses used in the healing of *sihr al-junun* (madness) or to
read verse 102 of sura *al-Baqara* (2) over water, after which the patient
drinks the water and washes with it.

11. *Mass (touching by jinn)*

There are four sorts of "touching" by *jinn*: visions (*mass al-taif*), whispering and devilish inspiration (*al-waswasa wa al-nazgh*), contact with
the *jinn* (*al-ittisal*), deviations and fear (*al-tazayyugh wa al-rahba*).
– Visions are caused by a person being surrounded and blocked by
   the devil, who sends special vibrations towards him, which give

him invisible forces and make him feel torn in a conflict between power and counter-power. In most cases this ends in confusion and forgetfulness, pains in the chest and frustration. In some cases it ends in stupidity and listlessness. This type of *mass* influences the memory, the will and the intelligence; it leads to eccentricity, odd behaviour and strange utterances. God has said that if the devil sends *mass al-taif* to a person, this always happens to people who are polytheists and do not have God in their thoughts or call on His name. The devil has no power over those who remember God and call on Him.

- Whispering and devilish inspiration occur through devilish vibrations being sent to the chest and the soul. This causes doubts about religion and leads to fantasies about the Creator, i.e. the affected person starts thinking differently about the creation, finding it unimportant. Ultimately he will give God equals and partners, and will ascribe a wife and a son to God. Through whispering and devilish inspiration he turns away from worshipping God and no longer prays; that is to say, because of his doubts he neglects his duties (and becomes apostate).

- Contact is a matter of a relationship between the *jinn* and the human. This is the most extreme, most dangerous and most damaging form of *mass*. That is to say that the *jinn* and the human want to be together (marry). This contravenes Allah's rules, because he has made them different from each other — each of them has his own basic features and characteristics, which are entirely different from each other.

- Through deviations and fear (*al-tazayyugh wa al-rahba*) the afflicted person starts to see things differently than they are in reality, or he sees things that are not there, which makes him very fearful. In this case mass is used by the devil, who in a flash deceitfully changes the shape of everything.

In the first place one can protect oneself against mass by naming the name of Allah. "Touching" cannot happen unless one has neglected to call upon God. Second, very protective is the reading, attentively listening to and meditation on the Koran, because this drives away the devil. Third, it is necessary to give up friendship with the devil and to concentrate on friendship with Allah. He is the Creator and the Protector of His creation; have faith in the word of the Most High. In addition, the reading of the Koran is not only a protection against the *jinn*, it is also an invisible shield which makes the believer stronger.

12. *Hasad and wiqaya (jealousy and protection against it)*

The first sin is jealousy and the one who caused it in the first place (*Fatih bab al-hasad*) was Iblis. He seduced Adam, which meant he had to leave paradise. *Hasad* is caused by no notice being taken of Allah in people's hearts. A jealous person sends "the eye" to another person who has blessings, afflicting that person with misfortune. The "evil eye" is thus the instrument of jealousy and envy. A *hadith* says: "In truth the evil eye can drive a man to his grave" (there are many *hadiths* which mention the existence of "the eye": by the Prophet, Muslim, Abu Huraira, A'isha etc.). The jealous person can radiate a special force from his/her eye, which harms another person. The prophet also said that a person must seek refuge in Allah from the *jinn* and the eye of the human. One can also commit *hasad* with the aid of bad spirits. The bad spirit of the jealous person is glad if it can harm the other person. The jealous person can affect someone without that person noticing and that is precisely the root of the evil. It is also possible for someone to be "affected" without "the look" applying. *Hasad* can come both from humans and from *jinn* and comes about through jealousy and envy. It can damage the senses, but also the spirit. In protection one recites the suras *al-Falaq* (113) and *al-Nas* (114) or one asks the jealous person to wash in a dish of water and then to throw it over the victim in one go. The afflicted person can also wash with it: the face, the hands, elbows, knees, limbs and the feet and the sex organs. He will also get his energy back as if he had never been affected by *hasad*.

The expulsion of the jinn from the body

General rule: read to the patient: "I seek my refuge in Allah against the dreadful devil"; read seven times: *Ayat al-Kursi* (2): 255 and say: "There is no God but God" and "He decides on life and death" and "God has no equal". If the devil refuses to leave the body, read seven times *al-Zalzala* (99) and if he still refuses read seven times the beginning verses of *al-Saffat* (37: 1-10) and then *Ayat al-Kursi*. It is also good to accompany the *ruqya* with massaging the body with rose water. Do this three times in the evening after the *maghrib* prayer.

Help and protection come from the Koran through reading suras 113 and 114 (*mu'awwidhatan*), the *Fatiha* (the opening sura) and *Ayat al-Kursi* (*al-Baqara* [2]: 255). Further, one must repeat the words of the Prophet: "I seek support from the words of Allah from his anger and his punishment, and from the evil of his servants (humans) and from seductions by the devils when they appear." The afflicted persons must also say: "I seek support from Allah the Merciful, and there is nothing higher than He." There are also many *ruqyas* and *tahsinat* [pious sayings] that one can recite to protect oneself against *jinn*, devils, *'afarit* and so on. For a person afflicted by "the eye" it is recommended also to say "and there is no power or might except with Allah" and the suras *al-Falaq* (113) and *al-Nas* (114).

Marriage between jinn and humans

Are there any references to a marriage between humans and *jinn* in the Koran and the *sunna*? Yes, the healers say, because the Almighty says in *al-Isra'* (17): 64: "And beguile whomsoever of them you can with your voice, and collect against them your forces riding and on foot, *and share with them in wealth and children, and hold out promises to them*". Precisely this part of verse 64 (my italics) is used by them to prove that there can indeed be such a marriage. There are, moreover, many stories of Abu Bakr and contemporaries of the Prophet who refer to a marriage between a *jinn* and a human or to the existence of *jinn*, as in the following story: Omar Ibn al-Khattab (one of the four upright kalifs) had to give a verdict in the matter of the case of a woman whose husband disappeared without trace after his evening prayers. This kalif asked her to wait for her husband for four years and if he was still not back, she would be permitted to remarry. But her husband came back and told Omar Ibn al-Khattab that he had been taken captive by *jinn* during a fight between Muslim and unbelieving *jinn* and because he was a believer he was compelled to spend many years with them. So it had been a good decision to have the woman wait four years for her husband's return.

In general it is said that the *jinn* can cause epilepsy and other sicknesses out of sexual lusts, passion and infatuation with a person, and if sexual intercourse takes place between a *jinn* and a human, children can be born of it. The *jinn* who wants sexual intercourse with a human can do so because he/she can change shape, take on human

form, and be beautiful or ugly, just as he wishes. In the cases of a
female *jinn* the man would think he is dealing with a loving, beautiful
and perfectly normal woman.

Is a marriage between *jinn* and humans legitimate? This is a question that has occupied minds for centuries. Some earlier religious
scholars regarded such marriages as illegitimate and impossible. The
question of pregnancy (caused by a *jinn*) has also occupied them.
Some considered this impossible and forbade a marriage between
humans and *jinn* on the grounds of the fact that Allah made them different. Koran scholars refer in this matter to sura *al-Rum* (30): 21:
"And one of His signs is that He created mates for you from your-
selves that you may find rest in them, and He put between you love
and compassion; most surely there are signs in this for a people who
reflect." In other words, Allah wants humans to marry humans and
because human beings and *jinn* are created different, such a marriage
is impossible. According to the book of al-Shibli (*Kitab akam al-marjan fi
ahkam al-jann*, cited in Leemhuis 1989: 21), some earlier authorities
thought that a marriage between *jinnis* and humans was indeed possible, but illegitimate. Others, including al-Shibli himself, thought it
was possible but abhorrent. Some others thought that it was permitted only in certain circumstances, such as a long journey through the
desert (ibid.: 25-27).

What do the children of a human and a *jinn* look like? People say
that the children of a *jinn* man and a human wife are visible to
humans. On the other hand children of a human man and a *jinn* wife
(*jinniyya*) are not visible. Boys born of a marriage between a *jinn/jin-
niyya* and a human are supposed to have a strong female inclinations
(be effeminate). If a man has sexual intercourse with his wife without
naming God's name or keeping his body covered (see the judgment of
sheikh Fathi in Chapter 2), then the risk of a child by a *shaytan* or a *jinn*
is also very great.

Old topic, new life. The topic of "marriage between *jinn* and humans"
is already very ancient, but it is noteworthy that it has recently been
given a new lease of life by Koran healers. I myself have observed in
the course of Koran healing sessions that women are often given the
diagnosis that a *jinn* wants to marry her and is causing problems as a
result. Several times I have been told stories of marriages between
humans and *jinn* and I have noticed that these stories are taken very
seriously. In the Egyptian press stories of this sort of marriage also

appear frequently. Thus the *Egyptian Gazette* of 17 November 1995 relates that a certain *sheikh* Ahmed Ibrahim Attia of Helwan (suburb of Cairo) claims to be married to nine *jinniyas* (Egyptian Arabic for female *jinn*), by whom he has a large number of children, who of course are visible only to him and his *jinniyya* wives. According to the healers the *jinn* takes the form of a man or a woman and enters into a relationship with a human; there is a clear, intimate and strong sexual relationship between *jinn* and human, but the human cannot see the face of the *jinn*. The healers are of the opinion that in all cases marriage with a *jinn* is extremely damaging to the human, making it impossible for an unmarried person to enter into a marriage and making a married person experience a strong aversion to his spouse (wife), making the marriage end in divorce. People who have to contend with such a difficult *jinn* must live in strict accordance with the Koran.

GLOSSARY (MSA/COLLOQUIAL)

abu gheet	*zar* music group, whose members originally come from a village to the north of Cairo
adhara/ azara	excuse, forgive
adat	customs
afandi/ effendi	civil servant
aib/ eeb	bad, shameful
aish/ eesh baladi	local flat bread
ajnabiyya/ agnabiyya	foreigner
alam al-ghaib	the transcendental world
amal bil-hubb	love magic
amal bil-karahiyya	hate magic
amal bil-marad	black magic
amal bis-samak	fish magic
amal bish-shagara	tree magic
amir	prince, leader
ammiya	vernacular
amr Allah	God's will
amrad aqliyya	mental illnesses
anashid	sufi songs
aqd	contract
aql	intellect, reason, understanding
armut	a sort of wolf-fish
arusa	bride
arwah	spirits, winds
asabiyya	nervousness
asyad	demons, "masters"
athar/ atar	personal item used in magic
a'uzu bi-llah mil-khubs 'wil-khabayis	God protect me from impurity
awlad taht al-ard	underground brothers, sisters
awlad al-balad	children of the land
awliya'	Islamic saints
aya	sign, Koran verse
aza'im	exorcism
bahrawi	person from the Delta
bahraya	place next to the bathroom or toilet
baht ijtima'i/ igtima'i	sociological research
baid/ beeda	egg, swelling
bait/ beet	house, tribe, clan
bait/ beet ma'din	metal casing for amulet
baladi	of the people, popular
baladiyya	"popular" woman
baraka	blessing
bas	evil power, contrariness
basar	mind's eye
basira	mental insight, mental perspicacity situated at the level of the heart
bawwab	porter, odd-job man
bid'a	innovation, heresy
bi-idhn/ izn-Allah	God willing

bikriyya	firstborn child
bint al-balad	daughter of the land
bismillah ar-rahman ar-rahim	in the name of the Merciful One
bismillah	in the name of God
biywishwish	whisper
biyitsaffar fi-wdani	he whispers in my ears
bukhur	incense
buzi	Buddhist
sharif pl. shurafa'	healer belonging to religious order (Mar.)
dabh	sacrifice, offering
dajjal/ daggal	charlatan
damm fasad	corrupt blood
damm khafif	light blood, sense of humour
damm tahara	purifying blood
daqqa	drums, drum music
dastur	apology
dawra	menstruation
dhanb/ zanb Allah	punishment by God
dhikr/ zikr harim	sufi ritual, women's ritual
dhur'/ tar'a	sudden shock, frightening experience
diniyya w-la dunyawiyya	proverbial phrase: "faithful and not worldly"
du'a	petitionary prayer
duff	round drum
fallah pl. fallahin	countryfolk/peasants
faqih	healer who works with Koran texts (Mar.)
faqqar	rhythmic dance movements
farah ma'a al-asyad	wedding party with the "masters"
fasiq	sinful
fatrit an-nafasa	period of impurity (after childbirth)
fatwa	formal legal decree
fez, tarbush	originally Turkish headcovering
firasa	intuition
firqa	music group
fujr	immorality
furn baladi	stone and earthenware oven
fus'ha	classical Arabic
fustan	dress
gallabiyya	long loose shirt, tunic (m)
gallabiyya samra	black "over-"dress (f)
jam'iyya/ gam'iyya	informal savings club
ghaib	hidden things, the occult
ghalat	mistake
ghalban, ghalbana	poor, needy m/f
ghina'	sufi song
ghul, ghula	demon of the desert m/f
jilbab/ gilbab	ankle-length dress
hadith	traditions, customs of the Prophet
hadra	meeting, small *zar*
haffit malayka	touching by an angel
hafiz pl. hafizin	someone who memorizes the Koran
hafla	party
hajat/ hagat tawila	something long, long skirts
hal	ecstasy
halal	permitted

halat nafsiyya	psychological problems
hall	solution
al-hamdu-lillah	praise be to God
hammam	bathroom, toilet
hana	sort of tambourine
haqq	law, right
haram	forbidden
harim masri	music group consisting of women
hasad	jealousy
hijab/higab	amulet, separation
hummus	chickpeas
hush	house in the nekropolis
ibada li-l-wali	saint veneration
ibtida'i	elementary (primary) school
idda	legally prescribed waiting period after divorce
ifranji/afrangi	western, European
ifrit pl. afarit	demon
ijaza	diploma
al-ikhwan al-muslimin	Muslim Brotherhood
ilag ad-da' bid-da'	healing of sorcery (illness) with sorcery (another illness)
ilaj/ilag bil-qur'an	Koran healing
ilm	knowledge
ilm al-ghaib	occult knowledge
imam	leader at the mosque
imma, imama	turban
al-infitah al-iqtisadi	economic liberalization
in-sha'-Allah	if God wills
al-islam huwa al-hall	slogan: "Islam is the solution"
isnad	"chain of tradents" of a tradition (saying or deed) ascribed to the Prophet
jahiliyya	Arabic paganism
jalsa	session, séance
al-jama'a al-islamiyya	militant Islamic group
jami'a khayriyya	Islamic wellfare organization
jinn/ginn/gann	demon
jinsiyya/harakat ginsiyya	sexy movements
jism/gism	the trunk
junun	*jinn*, demon (Mar.)
kafir pl. kafirun	unbeliever
kalam an-nas	gossip
kanisa	church
karama	hospitality
karamat	miracles of a saint
khadda	shock, fright
khalas	over, finished
khatib	preacher
khiliww	deposit (on the rent)
khimara	long, hanging headscarf
khul'	unilateral divorce
khurafa	superstition
kitaba	the opening of scripture at random in order to perform magic
kudya	*zar* leader

kufr	unbelief, godlessness
kursi	chair, sacrificial table
kushk	kiosk
kuttab	Koran school
la ilaha illa llaah	"there is no God but God"
labs	demonic "clothing"
lams	demonic "touching"
magzu'	separated, uncoupled
mahr	dowry
majnun/ magnun min al-jinn	possessed by a *jinn*
makhlu'	empty
makruh	reprehensible, abhorrent
malak/ mala'ik/ malayka	angel(s)
malayka ardiyya	good demons
malbusa	be clothed, possessed
mandal	divination
mangur	dance leader at the *zar*
mangur al-hawafir	belt made of goats' nails worn by the dance leader
marad gusmani	natural illness
marad ruhani	supernatural, spiritual illness
marbut	be bound, impotent
marid pl. marda	sickness
ma'rifa	mystical intuition, experience
marjas	two-sided drum
masakin sha'biyya	social subsidized housing
masarif	household expenses
mazhar	hand drum
ma'zun	civil servant
ma'zura	be possessed
milammisa	be touched, possessed
milaya laff	black cloth that is wrapped around the body (f)
mit'awwida	be accustomed (f)
mizaj/ mizag	physical disposition, state of mind, temperament
mu'akhkhar al-sadaq	postponed dowry
mu'alij/ mu'alig bil-qur'an	Koran healer
mu'azzim	exorcist
muhaggaba	veiled woman
al-mujtama' al-islami	Islamic brotherhood
mulid	folk-festival in honour of saints
mulid an-nabi	birthday of the prophet Mohammed
mu'min, mish mu'min	believing, non-believing
munaqqaba	completely veiled woman
murattal, mujawwad	devout, musical style of Koran recitations
muridun	members of a sufi order
mushahara, kabsa	sorcery connected with the phase of the moon
mushrik	polytheist
muslim pl. muslimin	Muslim
mut'a	alimony
muwazzafa	female civil servant
nafs, ruh	soul
nagis	impure
nasrani, misihi	Christian
nay	flute
nazra, al-ain	evil look, evil eye

nazra ardiyya,	supernatural staring
nazra insaniyya	human staring
niqaba	trade union
qa'ima/ ayma/ lista	list
qarin(a)/ 'arina pl. qurana'	a peron's *Doppelgänger*
qira'a, tajwid	recitation of the Koran according to fixed rules of pronunciation and intonation
qisma/ 'isma, talaq	divorce
al-qur'an shifa'	proverbial saying: "the Koran is healing"
rabt	impotence
radwa	"liberation"
ra'is, ra'isa	leader (male/female)
rajul/ ragil pl. riggala	man
raqs	dance
rihit hammam	toilet smell
riqq/ ri"	tambourine
rumi	Greek orthodox
ruqya	recitation/incantation
ruqya w-ta'awizat	Koran recitation and calling upon God
ruzz bi-laban	rice pudding
saghat	round metal clappers
sahir	magician, sorcerer
sahra diniyya	religious memorial service
salat al-juma'a	Friday prayers
sama'	sufi music
sanjak	leader of Sudanese *zar*
sara'	epilepsy
sha'bi, sha'biyya	popular m/f
shabqa	engagement gift
shafa'a	intercession, mediation
shaghghala	domestic help, cleaner (f)
shamm an-nisim	spring festival
sharb	scarf
shari'a	Islamic legislation
shaytan pl. shayatin	devil
sheikh, sheikha	elderly person/respectful form of address m/f
shifa'	healing
ash-shifa' burhan	proverbial saying: "the healing is proven"
shirk	polytheism
shisha	water-pipe
sheikh pl. shuyukh bil-baraka	sufi healer
sidi, sayyida	saint m/f
sihr al-ishq	sorcery (causing passionate love)
sihr al-mahabba	sorcery (love magic)
sihr al-marad	sorcery (causing illness)
sihr at-tafriq	sorcery (causing divorce)
sihr ta'til al-jawaz	sorcery (hindering a marriage)
si'idi	person from Upper Egypt
simsimiyya	stringed instrument
sirr	secret
sudani	Sudanese
sufli pl. sufliyyin	low, mean spirits
sukkan taht al-ard	underground inhabitants
sulha	reconciliation amulet

sultan, pasha, basha, malik	here: demon king
sunna	customs, traditions of the Prophet
sura	chapter of the Koran
ta'bana	tired (f)
tabikh	cooked food with meat or chicken
tabla	funnel-shaped drum
tabla nuss, darabuqqa	cylindrical drum
tabla tambura	drum beaten with a stick
tafsir	Koran interpretation, exegesis
tahara	female circumcision
tahqiq gharad maddi	magic for material gain
tahqiq gharad ma'nawi	magic for gaining prestige
tahsinat	pious sayings
tahtaniyin	underground beings
takhyil	hallucination, delusions
taksi bi-n-nafar	taxi with fixed route
tambura	stringed instrument, *zar* music group
tanwim maghnatisi	hypnosis
taqlid pl. taqalid	tradition, custom
taraf min al-junun	"a screw loose"
tarha	transparent veil
tariqa pl. turuq	sufi order
at-tariqa al-madhmuma	not-permitted way
at-tariqa al-mahmuda	permitted way
tasalluh bil-wudu'	ritual purification
tasawwuf	sufism
tathbit mulk al-hakim	magic for gaining power
tawhid	unity (of God), balance
ta'wizat	petitionary prayers
thawab, ajr	reward for good deeds
tibb al-mizaj/mizag	humoral medicine
tibb an-nabi, tibb nabawi	prophetic medicine
tibb islami	Islamitic medicine
ukhruj/ukhrug	go away!
ukht, akh	sister, brother
ulama	Islamitische scholars
umm	mother
urfi	unregistered marriage contract, temporary marriage
uzr	demon possession
wa'iz	preacher
wajh/wish(een)	(two) face(s)
wajib/wagib	compulsory
waqf	religious donation
widani bi-tsaffar	whisper in my ears
wiqaya	protection against jealousy
wird	recommended but not compulsory prayers
yifukk	"undoing" of magic
yiktib	"writing" in the sense of performing magic
yilbis	clothe, demonic clothing
zaffa	ceremonial procession
zakat	alms (Islamic)
zar	healing ritual
zayy islami, zayy shari'a	Islamic clothing
zina	adultery
ziyara	visit to sacred place

BIBLIOGRAPHY

Abdul-Aziz, Kamal
    1992   The qur'an is a healing. In: Abdul-Jawwad M. As-Saw (ed.) *Proposed medical research projects, derived from the Qur'an and sunna*. Mecca: Muslim World League.

Abdus Sattar S.M.
    1980   Moslims en gezondheidszorg. *Qiblah* 4 (4):4-7
    1982   *De genezende adem*. Roermond: Al-Misbah Publications.

Abu-Lughod, J.
    1971   *Cairo: 1001 years of the city victorious*. Princeton: Princeton University Press.

Ahmed, L.
    1992   *Women and gender in islam. Historical roots of a modern debate*. Cairo: The American University.

Alexander, B.C.
    1991   *Victor Turner revisited*. Atlanta: The American Academy of Religion series, 74. Atlanta, Georgia: Scholars Press.

Amin, Q.
    1992   *The liberation of women. A document in the history of Egyptian feminism*. (translation of: *Tahrir al-mar'a*, 1899). Cairo: The American University.
    1995   *The new woman. A document in the early debate on Egyptian feminism* (translation of: *al-mar'a al-jadida*, 1890). Cairo: The American University.

Ammar, H.
    1954   *Growing up in an Egyptian village, Siwa, province of Aswan*. London: Routledge & Kegan Ltd.

Assad, T.
    1980   The idea of an anthropology of Islam. *Poznan studies in the philosophy of the sciences and the humanities*. vol. 48:381-403.

el-Aswad, el-Sayed
    1987   Death rituals in rural Egyptian society: A symbolic study. *Urban anthropology and studies of cultural systems and world economic development*, Vol. 16: 205-241.

Baal, van J.
    1971   *Symbols for communication. An introduction to the anthropological study of religion*. Assen: Van Gorcum & Comp.N.V.

Badran, M.
    1996   *Feminists, Islam, and Nation. Gender and the making of modern Egypt*. Cairo: The American University.

Bakker, J.
    1993   *The lasting virtue of traditional healing. An ethnography of healing and prestige in the Middle Atlas of Morocco*. Amsterdam: Vrije Universiteit.

Beattie, J. & J. Middleton (eds.)
    1969   *Spirit mediumship and society in Africa*. London: Routledge & Kegan Ltd.

Beaulieu, J.
    1987   *Music and sound in the healing arts. An energy approach*. New York: Station Hill Press.

Becker, A.E.
    1995   *Body, self and society. The view from Fiji*. Philadelphia: University of Pennsylvania.

Behnstedt P. & M. Woidich
    1987   *Die ägyptisch-arabischen Dialekte.* Band 3, Texte I: Delta-Dialekte (1988), Band 3, Texte II: Niltaldialekte, III Oasendialekte. Wiesbaden: Ludwig Reichert Verlag.

Bell R.& W.M. Watt
    1970   *Introduction to the qur'an.* Edinburgh: Edinburgh University Press.

Binsbergen, W. M.J. van
    1980   Popular and formal Islam, and supralocal relations. The highlands of North-Western Tunisia, 1800-1970. *Middle Eastern Studies,* 20:71-91.
    1981   *Religious change in Zambia. Exploratory studies.* London: Routledge & Kegan Ltd.
    1985   The cult of saints in North-Western Tunisia. An analysis of contemporary pilgrimage structures. In: E. Gellner (ed.), *Islamic dilemmas: reformers, nationalists and industrializations: The southern shore of the Mediterranean,*199-239. Berlin: Mouton.
    1999   (a) *Culturen bestaan niet.* Inaugural lecture, Erasmus Universiteit te Rotterdam. Leiden: Centre for African Studies.
    1999   (b)'*We are in this for the money'. The sangoma mediumistic cult of Southern Africa: limitations and potential of an interpretation in terms of commodification.* Amterdam: paper presented at the international conference: Commodifications and identities: Social Life of Things revisited.

Binsbergen & W.M.J. van & F. Wiggermann
    1997   Magic in history. A theoretical perspective, and its application to ancient Mesopotamia, In: Abusch T. & K. van de Toorn (eds.), *Ancient Mesopotamian magic,* 1-43. Groningen

Blackman, W.S.
    1927   *The Fellahin of Upper Egypt: their religious and industrial life with special reference to survivals from ancient times.* (1968) London: Frank Cass & Co. Ltd.

Boddy, J.
    1988   Spirits and selves in Northern Sudan: the cultural therapeutics of possession and trance. *American Ethnologist,* 5: 4-27
    1989   *Wombs and alien Spirits. Women, men and the zar cult in Northern Sudan.* Madison: University of Wisconsin.

Böhringer-Thärigen, G.
    1996   *Besessene Frauen. Der zâr-Kult von Omdurman.* Wuppertal: Peter Hammer Verlag.

Bourguignon, E.
    1973   *Religion, altered states of consciousness, and social change.* Columbus: Ohio State University.

Brandt, E.
    1994   Pelgrimsoorden in Caïro: De islam van schrijnbezoekers. *Sharqiyyat* 1994:99-113.

Budge, E.A.W.
    1961   *Amulets and talismans.* New York: University Books.

Buitelaar, M.
    1985   De koran in het dagelijks leven in Marokko. In: Buitelaar, M. & H. Motzki (ed.), *De koran; ontstaan, interpretatie en praktijk,* 111-125. Muiderberg, Coutinho.
    1993   *Fasting and feasting in Morocco.* Nijmegen: Dissertation.

Burgess, R.G.
    1991   *In the field. An introduction to field research.* London/New York: Routledge.

Canaan, T.
1914   *Aberglaube und Volksmedizin im Lande der Bibel.* Hamburg: Friederichsen
1929   *Dämonenglaube im Lande der Bibel.* Leipzig: Hinrichs.
Caquot, A.
1971   Anges et démons en Israel. In: Sources Orientales VIII:115-151 *Génies, Anges et Démons.* Paris: Éditions du Seuil.
Catherine, L.
1997   *Islam voor ongelovigen.* Amsterdam: Baylon & De Geus.
Chelhod, J.
1964   *Les structures du sacré chez lez Arabes.* Paris: G.P. Maisonneuve et Larose.
Cloudsley, A.
1983   *Women of Omdurman. Life, love and the cult of virginity.* London: Ethnographica.
Colin, G.S.
1960   Baraka. In: *Encyclopaedia of Islam,* Vol.I, 1032. Leiden: Brill.
Crapanzano V.
1973   *The Hamadsha. A study in Moroccan ethnopsychiatry.* Los Angeles: University of California.
Creyghton, M.L.
1981   *Bad milk: perceptions and healing of a children's illness in a North African Society.* Leiden: Dissertation.

Desjarlais, R.R.
1992   *Body and emotion. The aesthetics of illness and healing in the Nepal Himalayas.* Philadelphia: University of Pennsylvania.
Devisch, R.
1985   Perspectives on divination in contemporary sub-Saharan Africa. In: van Binsbergen & W.M.J. & M. Schoffeleers (eds.) *Theoretical explorations in African religion,*50 -83. London: KPI Limited.
1993   *Weaving the threads of life. The Khita gyn-eco-logical healing cult among the Yaka.* Chicago: The University of Chicago.
Dols, M.W.
1984   *Medieval islamic medicine: Ibn Ridwan's treatise on the prevention of bodily ills in Egypt.* Berkeley: University of California.
1992   *Majnun: The madman in medieval islamic society.* (Edited by D.E. Immisch). Oxford: Clarendon Press.
Donaldson, B.A.
1938   *The wild rue. A study of muhammadan magic and folklore in Iran.* London: Luzac & Co.
Doutté, E.
1908   *Magie & religion dans L'Afrique du Nord.* Paris: Maisonneuve J. en P. Geuthner S.A. (1984)

Early, E.A.
1985   Fatima: A life history of an Egyptian woman from Bulaq. In: E.W. Fernea (ed.) *Women and the family in the Middle East,* 77-83. Austin: University of Texas.
1993   *Baladi women of Cairo: Playing with an egg and a stone.* Cairo: The American University.
Eichler, P.A.
1928   *Die Dschinn, Teufel und Engel im Koran.* Thur: Drud' von Reinhold Berger.

Eickelman, D.F.
1989   *The Middle East. An anthropological approach.* Second edition. Englewood
        Cliffs, N.Y: Prentice Hall.
Elgood, C.
1962   Tibb an-nabi or medicine of the prophet. In: *Osiris* 14: 33-192.
        Commentationes de scientiarum et ruditionis historia ratinoneque.
Fabian, J.
1985   Religious pluralism: An ethnographic approach. In: van Binsbergen
        W.M.J. & M. Schoffeleers (eds.) *Theoretical explorations in African
        religion,*138-163 London: KPI Limited.
Fahd, T.
1971   Anges, démons et djinns en islam. In: Sources Orientales VIII:153-
        215, *Génies, Anges et Démons.* Paris: Éditions du Seuil.
1994/5 Sada'. In: *Encyclopaedia of Islam,*Vol.VIII, 706. Leiden: Brill.
1995/6 The Karin. In: *Encyclopaedia of Islam,*Vol.IX, 406-408. Leiden: Brill.
Fakhouri, H.
1968   The zar cult in an Egyptian village. *Anthropological Quarterly* 1964-66.
        Washington.
1972   *Kafr el-Elow. An Egyptian village in transition.* New York/Chicago: Hold,
        Rinehart and Winston Inc.
Fergany, N.
1993   *Characteristics of women-headed households in Egypt.* Research Notes. Cairo:
        ALMISHKAT.
1994   *Urban women, work and poverty alleviation in Egypt.* Final report on a pilot
        study in a district of Cairo (Algawaber). Cairo: ALMISHKAT.
Fernea, R. & E.W. Fernea
1972   Variation in religious observance among islamic women. In: N.R.
        Keddie (ed.) *Scholars, saints and sufis,* 385-401. Los Angeles: University
        of California.
Fernea, E.W. & B.Q. Bezirgan (eds.)
1977   *Middle Eastern muslim women speak.* Austin: University of Texas.
Finkler, K
1986   The social consequences of wellness: a view of healing outcomes from
        micro and macro perspectives. In: *International Journal of health services,*
        vol.16 (4): 627-642.
Fouad, D.M.
1994   *Features of women present status in Egypt and their impact on development.*
        Cairo: Cairo Demographic Center.

Gaffney, P.D.
1994   *The Prophet's pulpit. Islamic preaching in contemporary Egypt.* Berkeley:
        University of California.
Gallagher, N.E.
1993   *Egypt's other wars. Epidemics and the politics of public health.* Cairo: the
        American University.
Gass, R. and Kathleen Brehony
1999   *Chanting. Discovering spirit in sound.* New York: Broadway Books.
Garrison, V. & C.M. Arensberg
1976   The evil eye: Envy or risk of seizure? Paranoia or patronal
        dependency? In: C. Maloney (ed.), *The Evil Eye,* 287-327. New York:
        Columbia University Press.
Geest van der, S. & G. Nijhof (red.)
1989   *Ziekte, gezondheidszorg en cultuur. Verkenningen in de medische antropologie en
        sociologie.* Amsterdam: Het Spinhuis.

Gellner, E.
    1972   Doctor and saint. In: Keddy N.R. (ed.), *Scholars, saints and sufis*, 25-28.
            Berkeley: University of California.
Gennep van G.
    1909   *The rites of passage: A classic study of cultural celebrations.* Chicago: The
            University of Chicago. (1960)
Gibb, H. A.R. & J.H. Kramers
    1953   *Shorter Encyclopaedia of Islam.* Leiden: Brill.
Gillin, J
    1948   Magical fright. *Psychiatry*, vol.11, nov. 1948, 4: 387-401.
Gilsenan, M.
    1973   *Saint and sufi in modern Egypt.* Oxford: Clarendon Press.
Giordano, O.
    1983   *Religiosidad popular en la alta edad media.* Madrid: Editorial Gredos, S.A.
Glaser, B.G. & A.L. Strauss
    1991   *De ontwikkeling van gefundeerde theorie.* Alphen aan de Rijn/Brussel:
            Samson.
Gluckman, M.
    1952   *Rituals of rebellion in South-East Africa.* The Frazer Lecture. Manchester:
            Manchester University Press.
Gray, R.F.
    1969   The Shetani cult among the segeju of Tanzania. In: J. Beattie & J.
            Middleton (eds.), *Spirit mediumship and society in Africa*, 171-187. London:
            Routledge & Kegan Paul.
Guenena, N.A.
    1986   *The 'Jihad'. An 'islamic alternative' in Egypt.* Cairo papers in social science
            (9)2. Cairo: The American University.
    1996   *Islamic activism in Egypt 1974-1996.* Cairo: Paper presented to islam in
            a changing world-Europe and the Middle East.

Haeri, F. Sheikh
    1990   *The elements of sufism.* Shaftesbury, Dorset: Element.
Haldeman, D.
    1990   *Models and mirrors: towards an anthropology of public events.* Cambridge,
            Cambridge University Press.
El Hamamsy, L. S.
    1994   *Early marriage and reproduction in two Egyptian villages.* Cairo: The
            Population Council/UNFPA.
Hammersley M. & P. Atkinson
    1983   *Ethnography. Principles in practice.* London: Routledge.
Hassan, R.
    1995   *Women's rights and Islam.* From the I.C.D.P. to Beijing. Cairo.
Helman, C.G.
    1984   *Culture, health and illness.* Oxford: Butterworth-Heinemann Ltd.
Haider, R.
    1996   *Gender and development.* Cairo: The American University.
Henein, N.H.
    1988   *Mari Girgis. Village de Haute-Égypte.* Cairo: Institut Français
            d'Archéologie Orientale.
Hiro, D.
    1988   *Islamic fundamentalism.* London: Paladin.
Hoffer, C.
    1994   *Islamitische genezers en hun patiënten. Gezondheidszorg, religie en zingeving.*
            Amsterdam: Het Spinhuis.

1995 Islam, volksgeloof en geneeswijzen in Nederland. *Sharqiyyat* 7/2; 1995,
   79-103

Hoodfar, H.
 1996a Egyptian male migration and urban families left behind.
   "Feminization of the Egyptian family" or a reaffirmation of traditional
   gender roles? In: Singerman D & H. Hoodfar (eds.), *Development,*
   change, and gender in Cairo. A view from the household, 51-79.
   Bloomington/Indianapolis: Indiana University.
 1996b Survival strategies and the political economy of low-income
   households in Cairo. In: Singerman D. & H. Hoodfar (eds.),
   Development, change, and gender in Cairo. A View from the Household, 1-26.
   Bloomington/Indianapolis: Indiana University.

Husein, Taha.
 1929 *Al-Ayyam, I & II*. Cairo: Dar al- Ma'arif.

Ibn Khaldun
 1967 *The Muqaddimah*. Translated from the Arabic by F. Rosenthal.
   Abridged and edited by N.J. Dawood. London: Routledge and Kegan
   Paul in association with Secker and Warburg.

Ibrahim, S.E.
 1980 Anatomy of Egypt's militant islamic groups. Methodological note and
   preliminary findings. *International Journal of Middle East Studies*, 12: 423-
   453.

Inhorn, M.C.
 1994 *Quest for conception. Gender, infertility, and Egyptian medical traditions*.
   Philadelphia: University of Pennsylvania.
 1996 *Infertility and patriarchy.The cultural politics of gender and family life in Egypt*.
   Philadelphia: University of Pennsylvania.

Ismael J & T.Y. Ismael
 1995 *Social policy in the Arab world*. Cairo papers in social science, vol.18,1.
   Cairo: The American University.

Jansen, W.
 1981 *Als gazellen uit de woestijn.Machtsverhoudingen tussen sexen in een Algerijns dorp*.
   Amsterdam: Universiteit van Amsterdam.
 1985 (ed.) *Lokale islam. Geloof en ritueel in Noord Afrika en Iran*. Muiderberg:
   Coutinho.
 1987 *Women without men. Gender and marginality in an Algerian town*. Leiden:
   Brill.

Jenkins, J. & Poal Rovsing Olsen
 1976 *Music and musical instruments in the world of Islam*. London: World of
   Islam Festival Publishing Company Ltd.

Jilek, W.G.
 1989 Therapeutic use of altered states of consciousness in contemporary
   North American Indian dance ceremonials. In: C.A. Ward (ed.),
   Altered States of Consciousness and Mental Health. A cross-cultural perspective,
   167-185. London: Sage Publications.

Joffé, G.
 1995 The islamist threat to Egypt. In: *The Middle East and North Africa*, 1996
   (42): 3-10. London: Europa Publications Ltd.

Jong, F. de
 1984 Die Mystischen Bruderschaften und der Volksislam. 3. Magie und
   Verwandtes. In: Ende W. & U. Steinbach (eds.), *Der Islam in der*
   Gegenwart, 492-5. MÜnchen: Verlag C.H. Beck

Kamphoefner, K.R.
    1996   What's the use? The household, low-income women, and literacy. In:
             Singerman D. & H. Hoodfar, *Development, change, and gender in Cairo. A
             view from the household*, 80-109. Bloomington/Indianapolis: Indiana
             University.
Kapferer, B.
    1979   Mind, self, and other in demonic illness: the negation and
             reconstruction of self. In: *American Ethnologist*, vol.6:1, 110-133.
    1983   *A celebration of demons. Exorcism and the aesthetics of healing in Sri Lanka.*
             Bloomington: Indiana University.
Kemp, S.
    1989   Ravished of a Fiend. Demonology and medieval madness. In: C.A.
             Ward (ed.), *Altered states of consciousness and mental health. A cross-cultural
             perspective*, 67-78. London: Sage Publications.
Kennedy, J.G.
    1967   Nubian zar ceremonies as psychotherapy. *Current Anthropology*, 26:4,
             185-194.
    1978   *Nubian ceremonial life. Studies in islamic syncretism and cultural change.* Los
             Angeles/Cairo: The University of California & The American
             University in Cairo.
Khan, I.
    1923   *The mysticism of sound.* Republished 1972: London/Southhampton, The
             Camelot Press Ltd.
Khattab, H.A.S.
    1983   *The daya. Knowledge and practice in maternal child health care.* Cairo:
             Newborn Care Project: El Galaa.
    1991   *Perceptions, knowledge, attitudes and practices of pregnant women.* Cairo: The
             Ford Foundation.
    1992   *The silent endurance. Social conditions of women's reproductive health in rural
             Egypt.* Cairo: UNICEF, Nour Arab Publishing House.
El-Khuly, H.
    1996   *A discourse of resistance. Spirit possession among women in low-income Cairo.*
             Paper presented at the panel discussion on: Gender and the
             indigenization of knowledge, Mafrak, Jordan.
Kleinman, A.
    1980   *Patients and healers in the context of culture.* Berkeley: University of
             California.
Koningsveld, P.S. van
    1988   *De islam. Een eerste kennismaking met geloofsleer, wet en geschiedenis.* Utrecht:
             De Ploeg.
Korayem, K.
    1996   *Structural adjustment. Stabilization policies, and the poor in Egypt.* Cairo
             papers in social science, vol.18,4. Cairo: The American University.
Kovalenko, A.
    1981   *Magie et islam. Les concepts de magie (sihr) et de sciences occultes ('ilm al ghayb)
             en Islam.* Geneve: (n.p.).
Kramer, F.W.
    1993   In the Grip of another Culture. In: *The Red Fez. Art en Spirit Possession
             in Africa*, 71-137. London/New York: Verso.
Kriss, R. & H. Kriss-Heinrich
    1960:   *Volksglaube im Bereich des Islams*, Vol.I Wiesbaden: Harrassowitz.
    1962:   *Volksglaube im Bereich des Islams*, Vol.II Wiesbaden: Harrassowitz.
Lambek, M.
    1981   *Human Sprits. A cultural account of trance in Mayotte.* London/New York:
             Cambridge University Press.

1989   'From disease to discourse'. Remarks on the conceptualization of trance and spirit possession. In: Ward, C.A. (ed.), *Altered states of consciousness and mental health. A cross-cultural perspective*, 36-61. London: Sage Publications Ltd.

1993   *Knowledge and practice in Mayotte. Local discourses of Islam, and spirit possession.* Toronto: University of Toronto.

Lane, E.W.
1895   *An account of the manners and customs of the modern Egyptians.*London: Alexander Gardner.

Langness L.L.
1965   *The life history in anthropological research.* New York: Holt.

Langness LL. & G. Frank
1985   *Lives. An anthropological approach to biography.* Novato: Chandler & Sharp Publishers, Inc.

Laoust, H.
1971   Ibn Qayyim. In: *Encyclopaedia of Islam*, Vol. III, 821-2. Leiden-London: Brill.

Leeder, S.H.
1973   *Modern sons of the pharaohs.* London/New York: Arno Press Inc. (1918)

Leemhuis, F.
1987   Trouwen met een djinni. In: *Midden-Oosten en Islam publicaties*, Witte reeks, nr. 14:18-27. Nijmegen: Nederlandse vereniging voor de studie van het Midden-Oosten en de Islam (Dutch society for the study of the Middle East and Islam).

1993   Épouser un Djinn? Passé et présent. In: *Quaderni di Studi Arabi* 11, 180-192, Venezia

Leibovici, M.
1971   "Génies et démons en Babylonie". In: *Sources Orientales* VIII: *Génies, Anges et Démons*, 85-113. Paris: Éditions du Seuil.

Lévi-Strauss, C.
1963   The effectiveness of symbols. In: *Structural Anthropology*, 181-201. New York: John Wiley and Sons.

Lewis, I.M.
1966   Spirit possession and deprivation cults. *MAN*, September 1966, 305-329

1969   Spirit possession in Northern Somaliland. In: Beattie J. & J. Middleton (eds.), *Spirit mediumship and society in Africa* , 188-219. London: Routledge & Kegan.

1971   *Estatic religion. A study of shamanism and spirit possession.* London/New York: Routledge.

1986   *Religion in context. Cults and charisma.* Cambridge: Cambridge University Press.

Littmann, E.
1950   *Arabische Geisterbeschwörungen aus Ägypten.* Leipzig: Harrassowitz.

Luck, G.
1985   *Arcana Mundi: Magic and the occult in the Greek and Roman worlds.* Baltimore: The Johns Hopkins University.

Macdonald, D.B.
1934   Sihr. *Enzyklopaedie des Islam*. Vol. IV, 438-47. Leiden: Brill/Leipzig: Harrassowitz.

1941   Sihr. *Handwörterbuch des Islam*, 697-699. A.J. Wensink & J.H. Kramers (eds.) Leiden: Brill.

1965   *The religious attitude and life in Islam.* Haskell lectures on comparative religion, Chicago university 1906. Beirut: Khayats.
1971   The Ghul. *Encyclopaedia of Islam,* Vol. II, 1078-9. Leiden: Brill.
1978   The Karin. *Encyclopaedia of Islam,* Vol. IV, 643-644. Leiden: Brill.
MacLeod, A.E.
1991   *Accommodating protest. Working women, the new veiling, and change in Cairo.* Cairo: The American University.
1996   Transforming women's identity: The intersection of household and workplace in Cairo. In: Singerman, D.& H. Hoodfar (eds.), *Development, Change, and Gender in Cairo. A view from the household,* 27-50. Bloomington/Indianapolis: Indiana University Press.
Masquelier, A.
1995   'Consumption, prostitution, and reproduction'. The poetics of sweetness in Bori. *The American Ethnologist* 22 (4): 883-906.
Masse, H.
1938   *Croyances et coutumes Persanes.* Paris: Librairie Orientale et Américaine.
McGuire, M.
1990   Religion and the body. Rematerializing the human body in the social sciences of religion. *Journal for the scientific study of religion,* 29 (3), 283-296
Meeks, D.
1971   "Génies, anges, démons en Égypte". In: *Sources Orientales* VIII: *Génies, Anges et Démons,* 17-85. Paris: Éditions du Seuil.
Mernissi, F.
1975   *Beyond the veil. Male-female dynamics in a modern muslim society.* Cambridge, Schenkman Publishing Company Inc.
1977   Women, saints, and sanctuaries. *SIGNS, Journal of women in culture and society,* vol. 3: 1, 101-112. The University of Chicago.
Mershen, B.
1982   *Untersuchungen zum Schriftamulett und seinem Gebrauch in Jordanien.* Koblenz: Dietmar Fölbach.
Messing, S.D.
1959   Group therapy and social status in the zar cult of Ethiopia". In: M.K. Opler (ed.), *Culture and mental health,* 319-332. New York: The Macmillan Company.
El-Messiri, S.
1978   Self-images of traditional urban women in Cairo. In: Beck, L. & N. Keddie (eds.) *Women in the muslim world.* Cambridge: Harvard University Press.
Mohsen, S.K.
1985   New images, old reflections. Working middle-class women in Egypt. In: E.W. Fernea (ed). *Women and the family in the Middle East. New voices of change,* 56-71. Austin: University of Texas.
Mommersteeg, G.
1996   *Het domein van de marabout. Koranleraren en magisch-religieuze specialisten in Djenné, Mali.* Amsterdam: Thesis Publishers
Morris, B.
1987   *Anthropological studies of religion.* Cambridge: Cambridge University Press.
Morsy, S.A
1978 (a) *Gender, power, and illness in an Egyptian village.* Michigan State University, PhD dissertation.
1978 (b) Sex differences and folk illness in an Egyptian village. In: Beck L. & N. Keddie, 599-615, *Women in the muslim world.* Cambridge: Harvard University Press.

1993   *Gender, sickness, and healing in rural Egypt. Ethnography in Historical Context.* Boulder: Westview.

Most van Spijk, M van der, H. Youssef Fahmy & S. Zimmermann
    1982 (a) *Remember to be firm. Life histories of three Egyptian women.* Cairo/Leiden: University of Leiden.
    1982 (b) *Who cares for her health? An anthropological study of women's health care in a village in Upper-Egypt.* Cairo-Leiden: Women and development series, Egypt.

Naguib N.G. & C.B. Lloyd
    1994   *Gender inequalities and demographic behavior — Egypt.* New York: The Population Council.

Nelson, C.
    1971   Self, spirit possession and world view. An illustration from Egypt. *The International Journal of Social Psychiatry*, Vol. XVII no. 3, 194-209.

Nelson, K.
    1985   *The art of reciting the Qur'an.* Austin: University of Texas.

Nicholson, R.A.
    1976   *A literary history of the Arabs.* Cambridge: Cambridge University Press.

Nieuwkerk, C.
    1991   *"A Trade like any other". Female singers and dancers in Egypt. An anthropological study of the relation between gender and respectability in the entertainment trade.* Dissertation.

Obeyesekere, G.
    1977   Psychocultural exegesis of a case of spirit possession in Shri Lanka'. In: Crapanzano V. & V. Garrison (eds.), *Case studies in spirit possession*, 235- 264. New York: John Wiley & Sons.

Ohtsuka, K.
    1990   How is islamic knowledge acquired in modern Egypt? *Senri Ethnological Studies*, 28.

Okasha, A.
    1966   A cultural psychiatric study of el-zar cult in U.A.R.. *British Journal of Psychiatry*, 112: 1217-1221.

Otto, R.
    1923   *The idea of the Holy.* English translation by J.W. Harvey, 1949. London: Oxford University Press.

Padwick, C.E.
    1923   Notes on the jinn and ghoul in the peasant mind of Lower Egypt. *BSOAS* III, 421–446.

Paret, R.
    1958   *Symbolik des Islam.* Published as: Symbolik der Religionen, II. Stuttgart: ed. Ferdinand Herrmann.

Pattison, E.M.
    1977   Psychosocial interpretations of exorcism. *Journal of Operational Psychiatry*, Vol. 8:2:264-277.

Peacock, J..L.
    1986   *The anthropological lens. Harsh light, soft focus.* Cambridge: Cambridge University Press.

Rabinow P.
    1977   *Reflections on fieldwork in Morocco.* London: University of California.

Rasmussen, S.J.
    1995   *Spirit possession among the Kelewey Tuareg.* New York: Cambridge
            University Press.
Raven, W.
    1995   *Leidraad voor het leven. De Tradities van de Profeet Mohammed.*
            Amsterdam/Leuven: Bulaaq/ Kritak.
Reeves, E.B.
    1990   *The hidden government. Ritual, clientelism, and legitimation in Northern Egypt.*
            Salt Lake City, University of Utah.
Rippin, A.
    1995/6 Shaytan.*Encyclopaedia of Islam*, Vol. IX, 1406-408. Leiden: Brill.
Robson, J.
    1971   Hadith. *Encyclopaedia of Islam*, Vol. I, 1129. Leiden/London: Brill.
Rouget, G.
    1985   *Music and Trance. A theory of the relations between music and possession.*
            Chicago/London: The University of Chicago Press
Rugh, A.B.
    1984   *Family in contemporary Egypt.* Cairo: The American University.
    1985   Women and work. Strategies and choices in a lower-class quarter. In:
            E.W. Fernea (ed.), *Women and the family in the Middle East. New voices of
            change.* Austin: University of Texas.
    1986   *Reveal and conceal. Dress in contemporary Egypt.* Cairo: The American
            University.

al-Saadawi, N.
    1979   *The hidden face of Eve. Women in the Arab world.* London: Zed Press.
Sabbah, F.A.
    1984   *Women in the muslim unconscious.* New York: Pergamon Press.
Sargant, W.
    1974   *The mind possessed. A physiology of possession mysticism and faith healing.*
            Philadelphia /New York: J.B.Lippincott Company.
Saunders, L.W.
    1977   Variants in zar experience in an Egyptian village. In: Crapanzano V.
            & V. Garrison (eds.), *Case studies in spirit possession*, 177-191. New York:
            John Wiley.
Schieffelin, E.
    1969   On failure and performance.Throwing the medium out of the seance.
            In: Laderman C. & M. Roseman (eds.), *The performance of healing*, 59-
            89. New York/ London: Routledge.
Schimmel, A.
    1995/6 Shafa'a. In: *Encyclopaedia of Islam*, Vol.IX, 177-179
Scott, J.C.
    1990   *Domination and the arts of resistance. Hidden transcripts.* New Haven: Yale
            University Press.
El-Sendiony, M.F.
    1974 (a) The problem of cultural specificity of mental illness: The Egyptian
            mental disease and the *zar* ceremony. *Australian and New Zealand Journal
            of Psychiatry* (1974) 8: 103-107.
    (n.d.) The problem of cultural specificity of mental illness. A survey of
            comparative psychiatry. *International journal of social Psychiatry*, Vol. 23,
            no.3
    1974 (b) Traditional therapies and therapists in the Arab world today. In:
            Pichot, P. &P. Berner, R. Wolf, K. Thau (eds.), *Psychiatry.* The state of
            the art, 667-672. (n.p.).

Sengers, G.C.
  1994   *Geboorterituelen en gebruiken in Egypte*. Dissertation, Universiteit van
          Amsterdam
  1995   Opvattingen van Egyptische vrouwen over de rol van boven-
          natuurlijke krachten bij zwangerschap en geboorte. *Medische Antroplogie*,
          Jaargang 7: 2.
Shadid, W.A.R. & P.S. van Koningsveld
  1983   *Minderheden, hulpverlening en gezondheidszorg. Achtergrondinformatie ten behoeve
          van de zorg voor moslim migranten*. Assen: Van Gorcum.
Shekar, C.R.
  1989   Possession syndrome in India. In:Ward, C.A. (ed.) *Altered states of conscious-
          ness and mental health. A Cross-cultural perspective*. London: Sage Publications.
Shiloah, A.
  1995   *Music in the world of islam: a socio-cultural study*. Aldershot (GB): Scholar
          Press.
Singerman, D.
  1996   The family and community as politics. The popular sector in Cairo.
          In: Singerman D. & H. Hoodfar (eds.), *Development, change, and gender in
          Cairo. A view from the household*, 145-189. Bloomington/Indianapolis:
          Indiana University Press.
Spooner, B
  1970   The evil eye in the Middle East. In: C. Maloney (ed), *The evil eye*, 77-
          83. New York: Columbia University.
Stephen, H.J.M.
  1990   *Winti en psychiatrie. Geneeswijze als spiegel van een kultuur*. Amsterdam:
          Karnak.
Steward, C.
  1991   *Demons and the devil. Moral imagination in modern Greek culture*. Princeton:
          Princeton University Press.
Stoller, P.
  1989   Stressing social change and Songhay possession. In: Ward, C.A. (ed.),
          Altered states of consciousness and mental health. A cross-cultural perspective,
          267-284. London: Sage Publications Ltd.
Sullivan, E.L.
  1986   *Women in Egyptian public life*. Cairo: The American University.
Sullivan, D.J. & Sana Abed-Kotob
  1999   *Islam in contemporary Egypt. Civil society vs. the state*. Colorado: Lynne
          Rienner Publishers, Inc.

Tadros, M.
  1998   *Rightless women, heartless men. Egyptian women and domestic violence*. Cairo:
          The Legal research and resource center for human rights.
Tennekes, J.
  1982   *Symbolen en hun boodschap. Een inleiding in de symbolische antropologie*. Assen:
          Van Gorcum & Comp. B.V.
Trachtenberg, J.
  1939   *Jewish magic and superstition. A study in folk religion*. New York: Behrman's
          Jewish Book House.
Tritton, A.S.
          1934   Shaytan. In: *Enzyclopaedie des Islams*, vol. IV, 307-308. Leiden:
          Brill/Leipzig: Harrassowitz.
Turner, V.W.
  1967   *The forest of symbols. Aspects of Ndembu ritual*. Ithaca/New York: Cornell
          University Press.

1969   *The ritual process. Structure and anti-structure.* Ithaca/New York: Cornell
          University Press.
1974   *Dramas, fields, and metaphors. Symbolic action in human society.* Ithaca/New
          York: Cornell University Press.
1975a   'Introduction', in: Victor Turner, *Revelation and divination in Ndembu
          ritual*, 15-33 Ithaca/New York: Cornell University Press.

Verrips, J.
1992   Over vampiers en virussen. Enige reflecties over de
          anthropomorfisering van kwaad. *Etnofoor*, V (1/2), 21-43.
Viaud, P.G.
1978   *Magie et coutumes populaires chez les Coptes d'Egypte.* Saint Vicent sur
          Jabron (France): Éditions Présence.

Waardenburg J.
1979   Official and popular religion as a problem in islamic studies. In: P.H.
          Vrijhof & J. Waardenburg (eds.), *Official and popular Religion*, 340-86.
          The Hague/Paris: Mouton.
Walker, J.
1934   *Folk medicine in modern Egypt*: translation of: 'Abd al-Rahman Efendi
          Isma'il, Tibb al-Rukka, Cairo 1892. London: Luzac & Co.
Ward, C.A.
1989 (a) The cross-cultural study of altered states of consciousness and mental
          health. In: *Altered states of consciousness and mental health. A cross-cultural
          perspective*, 15-35.London: Sage Publications.
1989 (b) Possession and exorcism. Psychopathology and psychotherapy in a
          magico-religious context. In: *Altered states of consciousness and mental health.
          A cross-cultural perspective*, 125-141. London: Sage Publications.
Wellhausen, J.
1995   *Reste Arabischen Heidentums* (second edition). Berlin/Leipzig: De
          Gruyter & Co.
Wester, F.
1987   *Strategieën voor kwalitatief onderzoek.* Muiderberg: Coutinho.
Westermarck, E.
1926   *Ritual and belief in Morocco.* Vol I & II. London: Macmillan & Co,
          Ltd.
Wikan, U.
1980   *Life among the poor in Cairo.* London: Tavistock Publications Ltd.
1996   *Tomorrow, God willing. Self-made destinies in Cairo.* London: The
          University of Chicago.
Winkler, H.A.
1930   *Siegel und Charaktere in der Muhammedanischen Zauberei.* Berlin: De Gruyter
          & Co.
1931   *Salomo und die Karina. Eine orientalische Legende von der Bezwingung einer
          Kindbettdämonin durch einen heiligen Helden.* Stuttgart: Verlag von W.
          Kohlhammer.
Wissa Wassef, C.
1971   *Pratiques rituelles et alimentaires des Coptes*, Cairo: (n.p.).
Wooding, C.J.
1984   *Geesten genezen. Ethnopsychiatrie als nieuwe richting binnen de Nederlandse
          antropologie.* Groningen: Konstapel.

Zbinden. E.
1953   *Die Djinn des Islam und der Altorientalische Geisterglaube.* Bern: Paul Haupt.

Zurayk, H.
    1994   *Women's reproductive health in the Arab world*. Cairo: The Population
            Council, no.39.
    1984   *al-Qur'an al-Karim*, Tafsir al-Jalalain, Beirut
Shakir, M.H. (translator)
    1999   *The Qur'an Translation*. (English translation). 12th edition. New York:
            Tahrike Tarsile Qur'an, Inc.

English-language papers, newspapers and pamphlets

The central agency for public mobilization & statistics (CAPMAS) and The
United Nations Children's Fund (UNICEF),
    1992   *The state of Egyptian children & women*. Cairo. Pp. 15-107.
The Central agency for publicantion mobilization & statistics, CAPMAS.
    1996   *The Middle East and North Africa (Egypt). Statistical survey*. Cairo. Pp. 398-
            415
The communication group for the enhancement of the status of women in Egypt.
    1992   *Legal rights of Egyptian women in theory and practice*. Cairo. Pp. 19-76.
Egyptian medical women association (EMWA)
    1995   *Profile of the girl-child in Egypt*. Cairo. Pp. 28-165.
Egyptian national committee for NGO preparation for Beijing, in collaboration
with UNICEF Egypt
    1995   *The situation of women in Egypt*. Cairo.
The legal research and resource center for human rights.
    1996   *People's rights — women's rights*. Cairo.
The legal research and resource center for human rights.
    (n.d.). *The dawn of the religious state in Egypt. The State: vulnerable to infiltrations or
            peaceful coups?* Cairo.
El-Nadim center for the management of victims of violence & New women
research and study center.
    1995   *Violence against women*. Results of a field study. Paper prepared for the
            Beijing conference 1995. Cairo.
The population council.
    1994   *Arab women. A profile of diversity & change*. Cairo.
The population council regional office for West Asia and North Africa.
    (n.d.). *Field methodology for entry into the community*. The policy series in
            reproductive health (3). Cairo.
UNICEF Egypt & The population council of West Asia and North Africa
    1995   *The Egyptian family*. Facts about the Egyptian family. Cairo.
    1996   The Egyptian Gazette
Uneducated women easily fall prey to husband's deception. Cairo. 15th October.
    1996   *The Egyptian Gazette*
Teachers complain they are forced to give private lessons. Cairo. 15th October.
    1996   Egyptian Mail
Crime outrages sacredness of Al-Hussein mosque.
    1995   Middle East Times Egypt.
A spiritual visitation. Cairo. 26th October.
    1996   Middle East Times Egypt
Slum housing campaign has failed, report concludes. Cairo. 15th — 21st October.
    1996   Middle East Times and al-Ahram
Mass wedding targets marriage crisis. Cairo. 15th — 21st September.

Arabic books on religion and magic

Abd-Allah, Mohammad Mahmoud
  (n.d.) *I'jaz al-Qur'an fi 'ilaj al-sihr, wa al-hasad, wa mass al-shaitan.* Cairo:
    Maktabat Zahuran.
Abu -Aziz, Saad Yusuf Mahmud
  1994 *Al-badil al-islami l-fukk al-sihr w-tard al-mass al-shaytani.* Cairo: (n.p.).
Amin, Ahmad
  1953 *Qamus al-'adat wa al-taqalid wa al-ta'abir al misriyya.* Cairo: (n.p.).
al-Arabi, (pseudo) Muhy al-Din Ibn
  (n.d.) *Al-kibrit al-ahmar.* Cairo: Maktabat Jumhuriyya Misr.
al-Azhar
  1989 *Bayan lil-nas, min al-Azhar al-sharif* (II). Cairo: Matba'a al-Azhar.
al- Buni, Ahmad ibn Ali
  (n.d.) *Shams al-ma'arif al-kubra wa lata'if al-'awarif* (photocopy of Indian
    original). (n.p.).
al-Hanafi, Al-sheikh Mahmud Abi al-Mawahib al-Khalwati
  (n.d.) *Kitab mafa'tih al-kunuz fi hall al-talasim wa al-rumuz.* Cairo: Maktaba al-
    jumhuriyya al-'arabiyya, al-Azhar.
Ibn al-Qayyim al-Jawziyya, Shams ad-Din Muhammed Abi Bakr Ibn Ayub Al-
    Zarghi Al-Dimasqi
  1926 *At-tibb an-nabawi.* Republished in Cairo, probably by the al-Azhar.
  1927 *Kitab at-tibb an-nabawi.* Aleppo: 1334, Cairo 1927, (n.p.).
Nomeir A.
  1995 *Al-mass wa al-sihr wa al-hasad: al-asbab, al-a'rad, al-wiqaya, al-'ilaj.* Cairo:
    (n.p.).
Sama'ha, Rahad Mohammad
  (n.d.). *Dalil al-mu'aligin bil-Qur'an al-karim.* Cairo: Dar Akhbar al-Yaum.
Sayyid Ali, Khalid
  1994 *At-tibb al-mujarrab; wasfat tibbiyya-sha'biyya-ghida'iyya mujarabba.* Kuwait:
    Maktaba Dar al-Islam.
Shawkat, Sabir
  1995 *Al-jann wa al-jamilat.* Cairo: Dar al-Jentil.
al-Suyuti, Jalal al-din abd al-rahman
  1989 *Laqt al-marjan fi ahkam al-jann.* Shibl, Khalid 'Abd al-Fattah (ed.).
    Cairo: Maktaba al-turath al-Islami. This book is a concise edition of:
    Kitab akam al-marjan fi ahkam al-gann, van Badr al-Din al-Sibli. (died
    1367).Cairo: 1908
  (n.d.) *al-Rahma fi al-tibb wa al-hikma.* Republication. Cairo. (According to
    Brockelman, GAL S II 252, this book is wrongly ascribed to *Suyuti*
    and is by the hand of *Sanawbari* (died 1412)).
al-Tukhi, Abd al-fattah al-sayyid
  (n.d.) *Ighathat al-mazlum fi kashf asrar al-'ulum.* Beirut: Maktaba al-thaqafiyya.
  (n.d.) *Al-sihr al-'ajib fi jalb al-habib.* Beirut: Dar al-kutub al-sha'biyya.
al-Ughanistani, Yusuf Muhammad
  (n.d.) *Al-jawhar al-ghali fi khawass al-muthallath li-l-ghazali.* Cairo: Maktabat wa-
    matba'at Muhammad 'Ali Subayh wa-awladihi.

INDEX OF AUTHORS

Egyptian daily and weekly newspapers that have published articles on demons, Koran healing and *zar* (1994:4,236): *Al-Akhbar, al-Ahram, Al-Arabi, Al-Liwa' al-Islami, Al-Ahali, Akhbar al-Hawadith, Al-Musawwar, Ruz al-Yussuf, Akhir Sa'a, Al-Muslimun, 'Aqidati en Al-Kawakib.*

INDEX OF SUBJECTS